CW01500078

War over Words

Censorship has been a universal phenomenon through history. However, its rationale and implementation have varied, and public reaction to it has differed across societies and times. *War over Words* recovers, narrates, and interrogates the history of censorship of publications in India over three crucial decades—encompassing the Gandhian anti-colonial movement, the Second World War, Partition, and the early years of independent India. In doing so, it examines state policy and practice, as also its subversion, in a tumultuous period of transition from colonial to self-rule in India. Populated with an array of powerful and powerless individuals, the story of Indians grappling with free speech and (in)tolerance is a fascinating one, and deserves to be widely known.

Drawing upon a range of sources as diverse as the banned material itself, legal judgments, legislative debates, memoirs and biographies, contemporary newspaper reports and letters to editors, government papers and reports, first-person accounts, and empirical and theoretical works by scholars of censorship across the world, *War over Words* focuses attention both on censors and the censored. It explores the diverse mechanisms and motivations for censorship and its role in the shaping of the modern Indian republic.

This book will help readers engage with contemporary debates over free speech and hate speech, illustrate historical trends that change—and those that do not—and enable them to appreciate how the past inevitably informs the present.

Devika Sethi teaches Modern Indian History at the Indian Institute of Technology Mandi, Himachal Pradesh.

War over Words
Censorship in India, 1930–1960

Devika Sethi

CAMBRIDGE
UNIVERSITY PRESS

University Printing House, Cambridge CB2 8BS, United Kingdom

One Liberty Plaza, 20th Floor, New York, NY 10006, USA

477 Williamstown Road, Port Melbourne, vic 3207, Australia

314 to 321, 3rd Floor, Plot No.3, Splendor Forum, Jasola District Centre, New Delhi 110025, India

79 Anson Road, #06–04/06, Singapore 079906

Cambridge University Press is part of the University of Cambridge.

It furthers the University's mission by disseminating knowledge in the pursuit of education, learning and research at the highest international levels of excellence.

www.cambridge.org
Information on this title: www.cambridge.org/9781108484244

First published 2019

Printed in India by Nutech Print Services, New Delhi 110020

A catalogue record for this publication is available from the British Library

ISBN 978-1-108-48424-4 Hardback

For
Professor Indivar Kamtekar

Contents

Part IV
The Censored Turn Censors: Freedom and Free Speech

Acknowledgements

I embarked on this research project with the hope that I would get to read all sorts of banned material under the guise of research. In the several years that it took for this research project to become a book, my hope was confirmed, and expectations exceeded. As I began to unearth the stories and rationale behind particular acts of censorship, and accommodation and resistance to them, I learnt that the content of banned material, fascinating as it was, was less important to the story than the context of the ban. In the narrative that follows, I have tried to present a coherent picture of both.

A book such as this draws on all my previous experience as a student and teacher of history, and I must therefore acknowledge several direct and indirect contributions to its making. My teachers at St Stephen's College, Delhi, set an example that I try to follow: I thank Dr Rohit Wanchoo, Dr Amrita Tulika, Dr Pankaj Jha, Dr Aditya Pratap Deo, Dr Upinder Singh and Dr Sangeeta Luthra Sharma. Faculty at the Centre for Historical Studies at Jawaharlal Nehru University (JNU), where I spent nine fulfilling and stimulating years, were erudite and patient in equal measure. I thank Dr Neeladri Bhattacharya, Dr Radhika Singha, Dr Sucheta Mahajan, Dr Bhagwan Josh and Dr Kumkum Roy. Dr Indivar Kamtekar supervised both my research theses, and I am immensely grateful for his wit and wisdom alike. As a research supervisor myself now, I realize what a difficult balancing act it is to offer cogent critique without eroding confidence. His scholarship and his ability to express complex ideas in formulations as elegant as they are interesting continue to be an inspiration to me. Academics like him make academia an idyll: may his tribe increase. Dr Charu Gupta, Dr A.R. Venkatachalapathy and Dr Sunil Khilnani's comments on my research and writing have both encouraged and helped me immensely.

Research fellowships of the University Grants Commission, Government of India, funded my MPhil and PhD research, and made it possible for me to function as a full-time 'scholar'. I am thankful to the Charles Wallace India Trust, and to

Mr Richard Alford, for supporting my trip to the British Library in 2010. I spent a semester at the Centre for Modern Indian Studies (CeMIS), Georg August University, Göttingen, Germany, in 2011, thanks to a grant from the DAAD under the Passage to India programme. This allowed me not only to draw upon the wonderful resources of German libraries in Berlin, Heidelberg and Göttingen, but also helped me exchange ideas with an international community of scholars, for which experience I am grateful. Dr Ravi Ahuja, Director of CeMIS, was kind enough to read and comment on part of my work, and his suggestion that I focus on the role of Patel is something that helped me immensely. I am grateful to Dr Ramachandra Guha for having the grace and kindness to talk to an unknown researcher about her in work in the foyer of the Nehru Memorial Museum and Library (NMML) in New Delhi.

Scholars would not exist if libraries and archives did not. I offer my thanks to the staff of the National Archives of India, the NMML, the Central Secretariat Library, the Department of Delhi Archives, the JNU libraries (all at New Delhi), the library of the South Asia Institute (Heidelberg), the Leibniz-Zentrum Moderner Orient library and the Staatbibliothek zu Berlin (both at Berlin), the India Office Records at the British Library (London), the US Library of Congress (Washington, DC) and the National Archives at College Park (Maryland). Reading (erstwhile) banned books in the cocoon of safety is just one of the many privileges these libraries have allowed me. At Cambridge University Press I would like to thank Ms Sohini Ghosh, Ms Qudsiya Ahmed, Mr Aniruddha De and their entire team for helping me translate the raw material of history into a narrative. The suggestions of three anonymous reviewers helped me revise and clarify many things. I bear full responsibility for all errors of fact and interpretation that remain.

Summer Schools at the University of Bologna, the National Institute of Advanced Studies, Bangalore, and the Indira Gandhi Institute of Development Research (IGIDR), Mumbai, helped me interact with practitioners of other disciplines, and taught me to present my research in an intelligible form to them. Attending the month-long 8th Annual Decolonization Seminar organized by the American Historical Association and the Library of Congress, Washington, DC (2013), opened my eyes to new ways of looking at the histories of different parts of the world. I am grateful to Dr Wm. Roger Louis, Dr Dane Kennedy, Dr Phillipa Levine, and Dr Pillarisetti Sudhir for their patient mentorship. I have had the privilege of presenting my research at conferences/lectures organized at/ by the Law and Social Sciences Network (LASSNET), New Delhi (2009), the Young South Asia Scholars Meet, Berlin (2011), the NMML (2014), the Indian Council for Historical Research (2015), the Japanese Association for South Asian Studies (JASAS), Kobe (2016), the Graduate School of Asian and African Area Studies, Kyoto University (2016), the American University of Paris (2018), the

Centre d'Études de l'Inde et de l'Asie du Sud, Paris (2018), and at Harvard Divinity School (2018). I am grateful to Dr Mahesh Rangarajan, Dr Rohan D'Souza, Dr Arudra Burra and to all organizers and participants at each venue for giving me a patient hearing, and for their approbation and criticism alike.

It is just as well that historians need day jobs to keep them grounded in reality and firmly bound to the present. Stints of teaching at St Stephen's College, Lady Shri Ram College, and Gargi College (all affiliated to Delhi University) have taught me more, I am sure, than anything that I could have possibly taught my students there. I am grateful for the friendship and advice of former colleagues Dr Meenakshi Jain and Ms Deeksha Bharadwaj. For the last three years, Indian Institute of Technology (IIT) Mandi has been home and holiday home combined; I am grateful for the encouragement of Professor Timothy A. Gonsalves and Dr Priscilla Gonsalves, and for generous Institute funding for research of all hues. Working alongside science and engineering faculty and teaching engineering students has taught me to evaluate, but never question, the relevance of historical research. My colleagues in the School of Humanities and Social Sciences here have together created, in a sea of equations and diagrams, an island of 'qualitative research' where I feel very much at home.

I thank my friends at and from JNU: Andrew, Anjali, Amita, Anish, Anu, Deepasri, Gaganpreet, Malavika, Maria, Mehrdad, Roopal, and Vikhar. At Kamand, members of the Friday film and food club—Deepak, Astrid, and Shyamasree—have livened up the idyllic river valley where we all live and work. Migratory birds Enakshi and Bringi have done much to raise our spirits. Rijul, on the other side of the world, has been no less a constant and very welcome presence. Bikram, writer of epistles, receiver of dispatches, has witnessed the evolution of this book, and much else. The Ramezannia and Kochhar families have been bulwarks in times good and bad. I thank Kailash, Neelu, Kanika, Sanjay, Veera, Anika, Aloke, and Mandakini for their interest in my work, and for their presence in my life. Josie appeared at a crucial time in the evolution of this book and could not have cared less about its progress. I thank you all.

Abbreviations

AICC	All-India Congress Committee
AINEC	All India Newspaper Editors' Conference
AIR	All India Radio
BJP	Bharatiya Janata Party
BVB	Bhartiya Vidya Bhawan
CID	Central Intelligence Department
Comintern	Communist International
CP	Central Provinces
CPA	Chief Press Adviser
CrPC	Code of Criminal Procedure
CWC	Congress Working Committee
CWSP	*The Collected Works of Sardar Vallabhbhai Patel*
DG	Director General
DIB	Director of the Intelligence Bureau
DIR	Defence of India Act and Rules
FA	First Amendment
GOI	Government of India
GSB	General Staff Branch
HD	Home Department
HSRA	Hindustan Socialist Republican Association
I&B	Information and Broadcasting
IB	Intelligence Bureau
ICS	Indian Civil Service
IPA	Indian Press Act
IPC	Indian Penal Code
LA	Legislative Assembly
LCM	*Nehru: Letters to Chief Ministers, 1947–1964*
LS	Lok Sabha

MLA	Member of Legislative Assembly
MP	Member of Parliament
NAI	National Archives of India
NMML OHP	Nehru Memorial Museum and Library Oral History Project
NWFP	North West Frontier Province
PA	Press Adviser
PAC	Press Advisory Committee
PDA	Preventive Detention Act
PIO	Principal Information Officer
PLEC	Press Laws Enquiry Committee
PPA	Provincial Press Advisor
PSV	Private Secretary to Viceroy
RSS	Rashtriya Swayamsevak Sangh
SCA	Sea Customs Act
SEAC	South East Asia Command
SLMU	*Sardar's Letters—Mostly Unknown*
SPC	*Sardar Patel's Correspondence, 1945–50*
SPA	Special Press Adviser
SPSC	*Sardar Patel, Select Correspondence*
SWJN1/2	*Selected Works of Jawaharlal Nehru, Series 1/2*
UP	United Provinces

Introduction

Debates over freedom of expression and censorship are all-pervasive in our world today. Even as changing technologies of communication have democratized the expression of opinion, and given a platform for all its conceivable shades, the fundamental issues and questions regarding regulation of expression remain unchanged. Most people would answer in the affirmative to the question 'Is freedom of expression desirable?' or 'Is freedom of expression the hallmark of a democracy?' Answers to the question 'Should freedom of expression be restricted on any grounds?' would probably draw less certain answers. 'Should a book or film be banned if it causes violence and deaths due to demonstrations against it?' would perhaps cause perplexity. There is also the question of intent. Does the government need to establish an author's intent to hurt community sentiment before banning her book? Or is intent irrelevant? What about 'truth' as a defence? If a statement made in a historian's study is verifiable but still causes offence, can that study still be banned? What does banning do, in any case? Does it remove the material from circulation, or does it increase public interest in it, or does the very process of seeking a ban publicize the material that is sought to be suppressed? Are people moved to action by what they read? Is there a direct connection between words and violence? These are some of the complex questions surrounding free speech. These issues are strewn in the historical record as well; historical reconstruction of free speech controversies and censorship has, therefore, much to tell us about our own times, and how things have come to be as they are.

Although the midnight of 14–15 August 1947 is the most famous in Indian history, it was another midnight—that of 31 December 1929 and 1 January 1930—that profoundly altered the very basis of the anti-colonial movement in India. In 1929 the British Viceroy, Lord Irwin, promised India Dominion status. The Indian National Congress (founded in 1885) sponsored the hoisting of a 'national' flag and the reading of an 'Independence Pledge' at Lahore on this midnight. This was followed, on 26 January 1930, by the declaration that henceforth complete independence—Purna Swaraj—was their aim. In the dramatic and chaotic years that it took for Purna Swaraj to become reality, the contest between the British-run Government of India (GOI) and its Indian nationalist opponents took many forms and required the use of many weapons, one of which was the printed word.

Historians—as much as the colonial state and participants in the national movement—are in agreement over the enormous power wielded by print.[1] If print has functioned historically as a means of propagating ideas and creating templates for various identities (including but not limited to national ones),[2] then it is also a realm where these very ideas and identities have been contested, with the added advantage that these contests are also recorded in print. That is to say that print is simultaneously the battlefield and the chronicler of the battle. In India, the contest over ideas and identities did not end in 1947; neither did the use of print as a means of disseminating views of various hues. Censorship, as a form of state intervention in the free propagation of news and views, also did not cease in 1947, and this book explores censorship of the printed word in India in the 15 years before, and after, independence from British rule. A historian of censorship in the United States has argued for the 'embedding' of its history within the larger social and cultural history of the period under study, so that 'the battle lines [become] more blurred, the villains less villainous, and the heroes a tad less heroic'.[3] This is especially required when studying the operation of, debates around, and reactions to state censorship in India in the transition from colonial to national rule, when we find historical actors behaving in unpredictable ways, as this book will demonstrate.

---

[1] It is Gyanendra Pandey's opinion, based on his study of Uttar Pradesh politics between 1920 and 1940, that a large-scale political movement is caused neither by poverty nor by political naiveté; as he puts it, 'It has taken stirring ideas and persistent propaganda to draw discontented men into open and extended political action.' According to Pandey, Congress propaganda played an important role in turning grievances into agitation. Gyanendra Pandey, *The Ascendancy of the Congress in Uttar Pradesh: Class, Community and Nation in Northern India, 1920–40* (London: Anthem, 2002), 61–64.

[2] Benedict Anderson, *Imagined Communities: Reflections on the Origins and Spread of Nationalism* (London: Verso Books, 1983).

[3] Paul S. Boyer, *Purity in Print: Book Censorship in America from the Gilded Age to the Computer Age*, 2nd ed. (Madison: University of Wisconsin Press, 2002), xii.

Defining the Terrain

Freedom of expression is a terrain over which the law, and research grounded in law, lays claims. However, a study of censorship in any historical context that restricts itself to the rarefied level of law, policy making and implementation alone tells only half the story. It is vital to examine the issue from the viewpoint not of the state alone but of that abstract yet vitally important constituency, the public. State censorship is often conducted by invoking public interest, although this invocation takes different forms: on occasion it is to protect from 'bringing into hatred' a particular community (religious, racial or other); during wartime it is to prevent the lowering of morale or leaking of military secrets that would jeopardize the safety of the defence forces or the country as a whole. What the public thinks of the censorship conducted in its name comes to us mainly through newspaper articles (where journalists claim to represent the voice of the public),[4] legislative debates (where the public's representatives speak, or ought to speak, for them) and memoirs of individuals. Partial as these sources of gauging public opinion are, they provide a necessary counterbalance to official sources. The issue of colonial continuity (between India before and after independence from colonial rule in 1947) is also seen in a fresh light when one considers the opinions—in this case, pertaining to the theme of censorship—of people who lived through this time of transition and therefore experienced for themselves censorship both colonial and national, in times of peace and of war. Using a varied palette of official and non-official sources, this book hopes to provide a three-dimensional model of how censorship of publications was envisaged, implemented and received in India over three crucial decades in her history.

The term 'censorship' derives from the Latin 'censure', to estimate or reckon, from which the term 'census' also derives. Since censorship, like the census, is a form of surveillance, in ancient Rome census takers and censors

---

[4] The value of newspapers as a source is well illustrated in this statement by the journalist N.S. Jagannathan: 'The contrast between the historian's tunnel vision of a frozen past and the shifting, multi-focused perspective of contemporary newspapers is striking.' N.S. Jagannathan, *Independence and the Indian Press: Heirs to a Great Tradition* (New Delhi: Konark, 1999), 129. Through a close reading of newspapers in his several books and in an ode to newspapers as a rich archive for historians, Ramachandra Guha makes a similar point. Ramachandra Guha, 'Silent Archivists: Historians and Newspapers', *The Telegraph*, 28 December 2013, available at https://www.telegraphindia.com/opinion/silent-archivists-historians-and-newspapers/cid/235603 (accessed 19 January 2019).

had closely aligned responsibilities.[5] Broadly defined, censorship occurs when there is 'authoritarian intervention by a third party in the act of sending message between author and reader', after which the message cannot reach the public.[6] Any history of censorship is multi- and inter-disciplinary: it is located at the intersection of political, legal, social and book histories.[7] It involves assumptions about human autonomy, political consent, power, knowledge and authority.[8] Censorship of the regulative variety, whether imposed by the state (through official bans and legal proceedings), the market (by proprietors of media houses or by consumers themselves) or the mob (by the public, through pressure, or violence, or threats thereof) is an act of attempted exclusion and/ or excision. Censorship enjoys a paradoxical relationship with modernity too: even as modernity bolsters state power by providing enhanced technologies of surveillance, yet other technologies facilitate subversion of censorship as proscribed material is circulated through new channels.

This book locates itself within the traditional model of censorship studies[9], and its focus is on direct forms of institutionalized and regulatory

---

[5] Sue Curry Jansen, *Censorship: The Knot That Binds Power and Knowledge* (New York: Oxford University Press, 1988), 14.

[6] Beate Muller's definition in 'Censorship and Cultural Regulation: Mapping the Territory', in *Censorship and Cultural Regulation in the Modern Age*, ed. Beate Muller, 1–31. (Amsterdam: Rodopi, 2004), 11.

[7] The growing field of book history defines the term 'book' very widely, to include 'virtually any piece of written or printed text that has been multiplied, distributed, or in some way made public'. See 'Introduction' in *A Companion to the History of the Book*, ed. Simon Eliot and Jonathan Rose, 1–6. (London: Blackwell, 2007), 2.

[8] Jansen, *Censorship*, 3.

[9] According to the proponents of 'new censorship' (who derive their inspiration from the theories of Michel Foucault and Pierre Bourdieu), censorship is not merely regulatory but structural or constitutive in nature. Judith Butler, for instance, refers to the kind of censorship that operates prior to speech, and which distinguishes, even before utterance, the speakable from the unspeakable. Another proponent is Sue Curry Jansen, who believes that constitutive censorship ('the power to name') exists even in those societies that have a free press. She states that constitutive censorship is a fundamental form of censorship that provides the precedent and anchor for all regulative censorship. She further suggests: 'No revolutionary compact in human history ... has ever abolished constitutive censorship. And, no proclamation or amendment has ever severed the knot that binds power and knowledge.' See Jansen, *Censorship*, 8. Beate Muller provides a convincing critique of this new model when she suggests that widening the ambit of what constitutes censorship to such an extent means equating censorship with any and all kinds of social control. Muller finds this

censorship. It describes censorial institutions, practices, policies, and debates over censorship in the late colonial and early post-colonial periods. Although its primary concern is with state-directed control of publications, it examines censorship demands originating outside the state via public pressure groups. It also examines state personnels' assertions (in the 1950s) that market censorship (by way of proprietorial control) was injuring press freedom more than state laws. Therefore, although the primary concern of this book is with state censorship, issues of the market and the mob do intrude.[10] It attempts to document the actual operation of state censorship through various agencies and laws, and concurs with Beate Muller's suggestion that censorship is 'an unstable process of actions and reactions in the struggle for power, publicity, and the privilege to speak out, rather than merely as a repressive tool with predictable results'.[11] Since most global academic scholarship on censorship concentrates on its operation in authoritarian states, by studying censorship in late colonial and early democratic India, this book bolsters the view that censorship is not the prerogative of totalitarian states alone.[12]

This book relies on but also tries to transcend a chronologically organized discussion of censorship. While some academic work has been done on *either* the colonial or the post-colonial censorship of publications in India, there has been no systematic or detailed attempt to compare censorship policies and practices across these periods. Numerous histories of the press in India, most written by

---

new model 'misleading' because it equates very different forms of control by confusing censorship with social norms that affect communication. In Muller's words: 'Analysis of censorship does not become simpler if censorship is identified everywhere.' She finds that overuse of the term obscures rather than reveals its history, and therefore finds it more useful to work with, and appreciate the differences between, four examples of discourse regulation—censorship, self-regulation, canon formation and social control—rather than to level them. J. Butler, 'Ruled Out: Vocabularies of the Censor', cited by Muller, and Muller's own views in 'Censorship and Cultural Regulation', 1–12. For a brief account of Foucauldian approaches to censorship, as well as its critics, see Deana Heath, 'Obscenity, Censorship, and Modernity', in *A Companion to the History of the Book*, ed. Eliot and Rose, 508–519, 510–512.

[10] For a theoretical discussion of market censorship (which Julian Petley calls a 'peculiarly insidious systemic form of modern media censorship which denies citizens their full communicative rights'), see Julian Petley, *Censorship: A Beginner's Guide* (Oxford: Oneworld, 2009), 5 and 172–178.

[11] Muller, 'Censorship and Cultural Regulation', 25.

[12] Tsarist and communist Russia, East Germany and South Africa during apartheid are the subjects of numerous studies of censorship.

journalists, refer to censorship, but the focus is mainly on the colonial period, and on 'seditious' publications alone, which fit neatly into the narrative of the Indian press fighting a heroic battle against the dark forces of imperialism. This perspective needs correction, and expansion.[13] This book examines state censorship beyond the conventional boundaries that circumscribe it in the existing literature. There are two directions in which this has been attempted. First, the boundary of race is complicated in a colonial context by focusing on works by non-Indian authors. Second, Indian independence is treated not as a dead end but as an open door that permits comparison of both policies and people's reactions to them.

Censorship is still the subject of much debate in India today, and the lack of scholarly research into the formative decade of the 1950s is therefore particularly puzzling. In the context of industrial planning in India, Vivek Chibber has shown convincingly that historians' focus on statements made by historical actors in the late colonial period to the exclusion of what actually happened in the early post-colonial period has led to a view that can be termed partial at best and distorted at worst.[14] This is as true of state policy towards free speech as it is of industrial policy, and this book aims to supply a corrective to this distorted view.

It is important to discern and illustrate changes in the intensity (or degree), the focus (or the targets) and the means (legal and extra-legal) of state censorship in India during the transition from colonial rule to independence. In order to do so, this book attempts to answer the following questions regarding the colonial and the national state and society: What hold did print have over the public? How did the colonial state react to the press and publications when they propagated anti-colonial ideas (of the violent and the non-violent variety) in the context of mass movements against colonialism? How did Indian nationalists, who tasted state power for the first time between 1937 and 1939, react to free speech issues? Did the Indian public have a role

---

[13] The two standard and oft-cited histories of the Indian press are J. Natarajan, *History of Indian Journalism* (Part II of the Report of the Press Commission) (New Delhi: Publication Division, Ministry of Information and Broadcasting, 1955), and S. Natarajan, *A History of the Press in India* (Bombay: Asia Publishing House, 1962). G.S. Bhargava's *The Press in India: An Overview* (New Delhi: National Book Trust, 2005) includes a discussion of press censorship during the Emergency as well, but lacks the rigour of the other two volumes. All three writers were journalists.

[14] Vivek Chibber, *Locked in Place: State–Building and Late Industrialization in India* (Princeton: Princeton University Press, 2006 [2003]), 225.

in acting as censors (or as instigators of censors) in certain contexts? How did the Second World War and attendant military preoccupations of the colonial state in India affect censorship policies? Did India continue or reject colonial censorship policies after Independence? Did Indians react differently to censorship by an alien and an indigenous state? And finally, a question of contemporary relevance: was censorship in the colonial and the early post-colonial period in India successful in meeting its own professed aims? Can censorship ever be successfully conducted, or is failure inscribed within every act of censorship itself?

Mapping This Book

Identifying and interrogating key moments in Indians' engagement with the operation of free speech over three seminal decades in modern Indian history is the task this book has set itself. In the context of the growth of the anti-colonial movement in India from the early 20th century onwards, freedom of expression became essentially the freedom to dissent, and words and ideas were persuasive weapons in swaying the undecided masses in favour of nationalists of various hues. The chapters in Part I of this book examine free speech issues from the perspectives of both readers and the state. Policies did not always translate to practice at ground level, and when they did, it was not always in the manner intended by policymakers, who, by the 1930s, included Indians as well. While making and amending censorship laws, British and Indian legislators and officials, before and after Independence—as censors everywhere—premised their discussion on the causal relationship between words read and actions committed. They then identified certain texts as dangerous.

The focus of Part I is on two distinct moments and developments in the 1930s. Chapter 1 narrates and analyses oral and written testimonies of participants in India's anti-colonial movement who were moved to action by the power of print. Which publications moved them, how they obtained these publications and how they resisted or subverted colonial censorship (in jail and outside it)—these are the three strands that are woven into the chapter. Chapter 2 critically examines the period of provincial autonomy (1937–1939) and the rhetoric as well as record of Congress governments in protecting or prosecuting free speech. The GOI's changing position on the 'Congress Pledge', traced over several years, is mined to illustrate the relative importance of content and context in determining censorship policies by a state.

While ideas that lead to proscription are contained in official correspondence, decisions, and legislative debates and acts, ideas that are outlawed can only be traced by reading the publication in question. Were writings only by Indians subject to proscription in the 1930s? Part II of this book discusses, with examples and extracts, various publications by non-Indians that were banned between the 1920s and 1940s, and the controversy they generated. While some were banned because of demands by Indians, others were banned by the colonial state without reference to Indian opinion; yet others were *not* banned even though the Indian press and public carried out sustained campaigns against them. By comparing publications that were banned by the state with those which were considered for banning but ultimately not banned, this chapter attempts to isolate the criteria used by the state to ban a publication, and also identifies context (at the time of publication) as the most important one. Close examination of the content of these works—and the debates surrounding their proscription—also illustrates how the aims of state censorship in India were never clearly defined, and often contradictory. To take one example, whereas the GOI banned Reverend Jabez T. Sunderland's *India in Bondage* (in 1928) because he urged the granting of self-government to India (at a time when to do so was not acceptable), it banned Katherine Mayo's *The Face of Mother India* (in 1936) because she opposed it in strong terms (at a time when to do so was not acceptable).

Given Charu Gupta and Deana Heath's demonstration of the complicity of Indians in demanding the censorship of publications deemed 'obscene', it is of some interest to contrast this with their attitude to censorship in another direction, that of publications by non-Indians, and especially those critical of Indian society and religions. We will see in the two chapters in this part of the book how the demand for the ban on several of the publications under discussion emanated not from the colonial state but from the Indian community. In his discussion of factors shaping industrial policy in India in the early post-colonial years, Vivek Chibber points to the importance of examining the policy process as it unfolded within the government so as to 'establish a causal chain, if there is one, between the political pressure exercised by the group and the ultimate shift in policy'.[15] He also points to the difficulty of such a project for the post-colonial years due to the paucity of archival material pertaining to GOI policymaking. For the colonial period, fortunately, archival material is aplenty, and the two chapters that follow juxtapose information about public campaigns against particular books with official correspondence reacting to

---

[15] Chibber, *Locked in Place*, x.

public pressure, so as to establish whether or not there existed a 'causal chain' between public pressure and GOI policy.

Chapter 3 discusses critiques of Indian society that were either banned or demanded to be banned: three books by Katherine Mayo on India (*Slaves of the Gods*, published in 1929; *Volume Two*, published in 1931; and *Face of Mother India*, banned in 1936) and two books by R.J. Minney (*Shiva, or the Future of India*, banned in 1929; and his *India Marches Past*, banned in 1933). It also explores the controversy surrounding the publication of Colonel E. Alexander Powell's *Last Home of Mystery* (published in 1929). The discussion also covers the bans on Arthur Miles' *Land of the Lingam* (banned in 1937), and the proposed bans on D.H. Southgate's *As a Man's Hand* (published in 1937) and Frank Harrison Beckmann's *Dust of India* (published in 1938). Chapter 4 analyses various books and magazines published in the 1920s–1940s that were banned—or demanded to be banned—because they caused offence to Indian Muslims.

Part III shifts our attention to an exceptional context, that of the Second World War. Although there is a revival of interest in India's role during the war, as evidenced by the recent publication of two excellent monographs on this theme by Yasmin Khan and Srinath Raghavan, censorship is of marginal interest to both works.[16] Given that for people living through a war—and for historians writing about it decades later—the spotlight is on the armed forces, much of existing literature on the impact of the Second World War on India has focused on the propaganda strategies employed by the GOI to keep the Indian armed forces loyal.[17] This book focuses attention elsewhere. In doing so, it is inspired by the research of pioneering historians such as Johannes Voigt[18] and Indivar Kamtekar[19], and new research by Yasmin Khan and Srinath Raghavan, all of whom have explored the implications of the Second World

---

[16] Yasmin Khan, *The Raj at War: A People's History of India's Second World War* (Gurgaon: Penguin Random House, 2016), and Srinath Raghavan, *India's War: The Making of Modern South Asia, 1939–45* (Gurgaon: Allen Lane, 2016).

[17] For an account of military morale, see Kaushik Roy, 'Discipline and Morale of the African, British, and Indian Army Units in Burma and India during World War II: July 1943 to August 1945', *Modern Asian Studies* 44, no. 6 (2010): 1255–1282. For propaganda strategies employed in Bengal, see Srimanjari, *Through War and Famine: Bengal 1939–45* (New Delhi: Orient BlackSwan, 2009), 40–41.

[18] Johannes Voigt, *India in the Second World War* (Michigan: Arnold Heinemann, 1988).

[19] For an account of anxiety surrounding the feared Japanese invasion of India in 1942, see Indivar Kamtekar, 'The Shiver of 1942', *Studies in History* 18 (2002): 81–102.

War for the larger Indian public, and the changes wrought by it in Indian (and South Asian) state and society in the following decades. This part explores how, during wartime, censorship was directed at gauging and manipulating Indian opinion by preventing the dissemination of news that could lower morale in India, or that which could be useful to the enemy abroad.

Chapter 5 explains the mechanics of official censorship over news reports, and the difficulty of separating political news from military news. Its focus is on what was not allowed to appear in the Indian press during the Second World War. Chapter 6 unveils an experiment in 'voluntary censorship' by the Indian press during the war, in cooperation with the GOI, and the strains to which this was subject during the Quit India movement (1942) and the Bengal Famine (1943). It also casts a glance at censorship in Great Britain, and how it was similar to and different from wartime censorship in India. It examines the changing strategies of the state in terms of co-opting rather than antagonizing the press by terming censorship 'press advice'. The acceptability of censorship in wartime is much more than at any other time, and it is interesting to explore how this happens and is rationalized by the state. The viewpoints of censors, war correspondents, and the general public are all mined in order to reveal a rounded picture of censorship in an exceptional—and therefore unusually illuminating—context.

Part IV concerns itself with India on the verge of attaining political independence, and with what happened in the years following Independence and Partition. The subject of Chapter 7 is press censorship during the Partition riots. It is argued that the horrors accompanying Partition coloured the state's—and its key personnels'—perception of not only the validity but also the necessity of censorship in certain contexts. This, as is demonstrated in this book, was to have significant ramifications for the future of free speech in early independent India. Communal publications—as well as publications that were not communal but contained factual reports that were nevertheless inflammatory—were closely monitored by the state immediately before and during Partition. This chapter begins with the period of the Interim Government (2 September 1946–15 August 1947), when the Congress controlled all except three (out of eleven) provincial legislatures, and when Indian journalists were already imagining a future golden age of free speech. It traces the history of an—ultimately unsuccessful—experiment in voluntary press censorship under the aegis of the state. This period has clear links with India's Second World War experience, in terms not only of continuity of assumptions about the power of the printed word but also of steps taken to curb its publication or circulation.

The Indian Constitution adopted in 1950 granted freedom of expression to Indian citizens, although this freedom was, like other fundamental rights, not absolute. The state could, therefore, make laws curbing the publication of material constituting 'libel, slander, defamation, contempt of court, or any matter which offends against decency or morality, or which undermines the security of the state or tends to its overthrow'. These, thus, were the original constitutional limitations imposed on the freedom of speech available to Indians. In 1951, the First Amendment (FA) to the Indian Constitution enlarged the scope of state censorship by adding three new grounds for the passage of restrictive laws in future: 'public order', 'incitement to offence' and 'friendly relations with foreign states'.[20] Nehru was initially not in favour of making the restrictions 'reasonable' (that is, justiciable, so that courts could intervene and comment on the constitutionality on any act so made) but later gave in to pressure from within and outside Parliament. Why this change was made, how it was justified and how it was received by the public: these are the questions that will be answered in Chapter 8.

This chapter analyses political censorship of the press in 1950s India, studies the making of the Press (Objectionable Matters) Act of 1951, and asks questions that clarify the nature of transitional polities, as well as of censorship itself. The continuation of censorship in post-colonial India was justified as being essential to the creation of a liberal, secular democracy. A fledgling state needed all the protection it could get. Although state censorship continued to attract criticism, 'national security' as a justification was certainly more palatable than the accusation of 'sedition'. 1950s India provides an example of the censored turned censor and this chapter traces the contours of this unusual situation, from the points of view of both.

Chapter 9 focuses attention on a specific case of a controversial publication. In September 1956, the re-printing in India of a book (*Living Biographies of Religious Leaders*) first published in 1942 in the United States aroused considerable controversy in both India and Pakistan. In addition to riots in many Indian towns, deaths, arrests and demonstrations, there was considerable activity and debate in Indian official circles and political circles, with Prime

---

[20] The Foreign Relations Act of 1932 penalized those who published or circulated statements that could promote unfriendly relations between the GOI and a foreign government. The maximum punishment for this offence was two years, with or without fine. For a survey of all these restrictions, see Lawrence Liang, 'Reasonable Restrictions and Unreasonable Speech', *Sarai Reader 04: Crisis/Media*, 434–440 (Delhi: Sarai, 2004).

Minister Nehru at the helm of affairs. An investigation into the circumstances surrounding the publication as well as banning of this long-forgotten book has much to tell us about the roots of present-day censorship debates and demands in India. This chapter recovers and presents the history of this long-forgotten case, and analyses its meaning and impact on contemporary India's relationship with controversial publications. How the Indian state tackled a free speech crisis, and what it tells us about the state: these are the concerns of this chapter.

Exploring the Backdrop

The demand of conducting a sharply focused and temporally balanced investigation restricts the period under survey in this book to three decades. The need for clarity necessitates a brief discussion of the period preceding the 1930s in order to historically contextualize the present discusson. In colonial India, the state monitored and banned or prosecuted publications falling in three main categories: those that transgressed norms of loyalty laid down by the state ('seditious' publications); those that transgressed moral norms as interpreted by the state and pressure groups within society ('obscene' publications); and, finally, those that incited communal or social disharmony ('hate' literature) or violence by members of one group against another. Although 'seditious' and 'obscene' are terms and categories frequently used in colonial discourse, their meaning was not fixed but subject to changes in time, place and political circumstances. These terms are used in this book not as objective definitions, but as source-dictated shorthand terms. The very lack of an objective definition of these terms, in fact, illustrates the difficulties inherent in conducting any kind of censorship, and the debates that are sure to arise even among the censors.

Censorship over newspapers, publications and even pictorial representations in colonial India was exercised through the operation of a diverse range of laws: Press Acts (which dealt directly with what newspapers could, and could not, publish), Customs Acts (to prevent the import of selected publications into India), and Postal Acts (to prevent the transmission of selected published material by post), in addition to provisions of the Indian Penal Code (IPC) and the Code of Criminal Procedure (CrPC). For example, section 99A of the CrPC was used to ban the circulation in India of publications that offended against sections 124A (pertaining to matter deemed 'seditious'), 153A (matter inciting hatred between classes of people) or 295A of the IPC ('matter which is deliberately or maliciously intended to outrage the religious feelings of a class of His Majesty's subjects by insulting or attempting to insult the religion or the religious beliefs of that class'). Because of the variety of sources from which publications emanated, and on account of the various means through which they entered India, a number of agencies were involved in their interception, examination, and in deciding their fate. This created some confusion even in the minds of officials entrusted with exercising surveillance over publications.[21] During periods of renewed nationalist agitation (the 1930s) and wartime (the 1940s), special legislation was enacted to prevent the publication of subversive views detrimental to the state and military news detrimental to the security of defence forces.

If the printed word was to be subjected to state control, how was this control to be exercised? To control the circulation of publications, the GOI first needed to have information about them, and this was achieved by mandatory registration. The early history of print regulation in India by the state was marked by a change from licensing (the refusal to grant which could be construed as censorship or preventive control) to registration, made mandatory in 1867. The controversial passage (1878) and subsequent repeal (1882) of the Vernacular Press Act represents in this context a failure of the government to re-impose licensing on Indian language publications.[22]

Another way by which the state could control the content of publications was to enlarge the scope of laws under which publications attracted penalties. The law of sedition (section 124A of the IPC) was formulated in 1870 and amended in 1898. The 1870 section only mentioned 'disaffection' and not the terms 'hatred' and 'contempt'. As amended in 1898, it covered words (spoken and written), signs and visible representation, though the addition of the term 'or otherwise' after this listing made its application much broader. The punishment prescribed for exciting 'hatred', 'contempt', or 'disaffection' against the government ranged from transportation for life, imprisonment

---

[21] For instance, in 1930, the Intelligence Bureau (IB) asked the Central Board of Revenue (CBR) if the Sea Customs Act (SCA) empowered police officials to detain or seize packages suspected to contain seditious matter, or any matter banned under the SCA. They received the answer that the act empowered the Chief Customs authority or the local government to depute any 'other officer' to detain or seize packages, and the phrase presumably could include a police officer. Query in note by M.F. Cleary of the IB, 29 September 1930. Answer in note by S.N. Roy of the Home Department (HD), 23 April 1931. CBR, Customs Duties, D.Dis f. 205-Cus-II-31, 1931, National Archives of India (NAI). This illustrates that even IB officials were unclear as to where the responsibility for censorship rested.

[22] Regulations in 1799, 1823 and 1827 required a licence to be obtained from the Governor-General in Council prior to publication of any book or newspaper. Act XI of 1835 repealed these regulations, and the Press and Registration of Books Act of 1867 provided for registration of the printer.

for three years or the payment of a fine. The original section 124A of 1870 as well as its amended version in 1898 made it clear that comments on or criticism ('disapprobation') of any action of the government, or the attempt to get government to change its policy ('with a view to obtain their alteration by lawful means') was *not in itself* an offence.[23]

The year 1898 was also significant as two new categories of offence were added to the IPC: those of 'promoting enmity between classes' (section 153A), and of articulating 'statements conducive to public mischief'. If the amplitude of punishment is a yardstick for the magnitude of a crime, then the first of these was clearly a less serious charge than sedition, the maximum punishment for it being two years' imprisonment with or without fine. As with section 124A, a description of the objectionable was accompanied by a description of what was *not* objectionable: if done without 'malicious intention and with an honest view of their removal', it was not an offence to point out matters which were producing enmity between classes. In other words, both intent and content would be taken into account while deciding cases that contravened this provision of the law. Section 295A was added to the IPC in 1927 as a direct response to the controversy over the pamphlet *Rangila Rasul*.[24] It was held by courts that the existing section 154A did not cover insults to religious leaders, and hence a new, specific provision was required. It applied to those who '... with deliberate and malicious intention of outraging the religious feelings of any class of His Majesty's subjects ... insults or attempts to insult the religion or religious belief of that class....' The consequences of its passage are discussed in Part II this book, with reference to books on Islam published by non-Indian authors and in foreign journals.

In the aftermath of the Swadeshi movement (1905; the first of the anti-colonial upsurges of the 20th century to protest the partition of Bengal) the GOI passed the Newspaper (Incitement to Offences) Act in 1908. This was followed by the Indian Press Act (IPA) of 1910, which made provision for the demand of a security deposit between 500 and 1,000 rupees from a newspaper or press at the discretion of a magistrate. This could then be forfeited; it was only forfeiture alone and not the demand itself that was subject to appeal. Both

---

[23] Section 124A was inserted in the IPC under Act 27 of 1870, and amended by Act IV of 1898.

[24] The making of this legislation is detailed and skilfully analysed in Neeti Nair, 'Beyond the "Communal" 1920s: The Problem of Intention, Legislative Pragmatism, and the Making of Section 295A of the Indian Penal Code', *The Indian Economic and Social History Review* 50, no. 3 (2013): 317–340.

these acts placed the Indian press under direct executive control.[25]

In 1930, the year in which this account of censorship in India begins, there was no press act in operation. This is because the 1910 Press Act was repealed in 1922. In 1915, an Indian lawyer returned to India from South Africa, and by 1920, Mohandas Karamchand Gandhi had spearheaded a mass movement against British rule. In another 10 years, he had launched an even larger movement, the Civil Disobedience movement. Between April and July 1930, the government promulgated as many as seven special ordinances to deal with the Civil Disobedience movement; some imposed restrictions on the press, while others dealt with intimidation and 'unlawful instigation'. It had been less than a decade after the repeal of the 1910 Press Act, and the GOI made a case for greater control of the press by stressing that the tone of the press had 'deteriorated' since 1922. Eventually, the GOI passed Indian Press Act of 1931, which was to provide the central framework for action against the press for more than two decades.[26]

Surveying the Surveyors

Censorship in India has been studied in the context of the Vernacular Press Act of 1878,[27] of the radio,[28] of individual newspapers,[29] of publications by

---

[25] For a brief summary of these acts, see Durga Das Basu, *Law of the Press in India* (4th ed., Nagpur: Wadhwa and Company, 2002 [1980]), 262–263. Robert Darnton has skilfully described the functioning of the 1867 registration of books and newspapers act, and the operation of the 1908 act in colonial courtrooms, in his 'Literary Surveillance in the British Raj: The Contradictions of Liberal Imperialism', *Book History* 4 (2001): 133–176.

[26] For a detailed analysis of the IPA 1931, see Devika Sethi, 'Proscribing Ideas: Censorship in India, 1930–60', PhD thesis submitted to Jawaharlal Nehru University, New Delhi, in 2012.

[27] For instance, Partha Chatterjee discusses the Vernacular Press Act as an example of the operation of colonial difference in his *The Nation and Its Fragments: Colonial and Postcolonial Histories* (Delhi: Oxford University Press, 1994), 24–26.

[28] For a discussion of colonial policy towards radio broadcasting, see Biswajit Das, 'Mediating Modernity: Colonial Discourse and Radio Broadcasting, c. 1924–1947' in *Communication Processes Vol. 1: Media and Mediation*, ed. Bernard Bel et al. (New Delhi: Sage, 2005), 229–254. Das emphasizes that the issue of censorship over radio broadcasts was one on which there was no unanimity among colonial officials.

[29] Milton Israel, *Communications and Power: Propaganda and the Press in the Indian Nationalist Struggle, 1920–1947* (Cambridge: Cambridge University Press, 1994),

prominent Indian nationalists of various hues, notably Bal Gangadhar Tilak (1856–1920),[30] Mohandas Karamchand Gandhi (1869–1948)[31] and Subhash Chandra Bose (1897–1945).[32] Books have been written on press laws and free speech in India from a legal and Constitutional history perspective (including by a Supreme Court judge) and eminent lawyers.[33] Post-colonial legal cases

216–245. Israel discusses the career of the *Bombay Chronicle* from the early 1920s up to the mid-1930s, its support of the Congress cause and conflict with the British government. Another example is Paul R. Greenhough's in-depth study of *Biplabi*, a weekly publication in Bengal that appeared for two years. Greenhough also discusses official anxiety about underground publications. Paul R. Greenhough, 'Political Mobilization and the Underground Literature of the Quit India movement, 1942–44', *Modern Asian Studies* 17, no. 3 (1983): 353–386, 361.

[30] For an account of the trial of Bal Gangadhar Tilak in 1879 and 1908 on charges of sedition, as well as a brief history of the struggle of the Indian press against the colonial state in the 19th century, see Bipan Chandra, et al., *India's Struggle for Independence, 1857–1947* (New Delhi: Penguin, 1989 [1988]), chapter titled 'The Fight to Secure Press Freedom', 102–112.

[31] For an account, with copies of original documents, of Gandhi's trial in 1922 on the charge of sedition for publishing four articles in *Young India*, see Mulk Raj Anand (ed.), *The Historic Trial of Mahatma Gandhi* (New Delhi: National Council of Educational Research and Training, 1987). Gandhi was sentenced to six years' simple imprisonment.

[32] The ban on Bose's *The Indian Struggle* (1935) is discussed in Sugata Bose, *His Majesty's Opponent: Subhas Chandra Bose and India's Struggle Against Empire* (New Delhi: Penguin/Allen Lane, 2011), 100–102, and Mihir Bose, *The Lost Hero: A Biography of Subhas Bose* (London: Quartet, 1982), 102.

[33] Justice V.R. Krishna Iyer and Vinod Sethi, *Essays on Press Freedom* (New Delhi: Capital Foundation Society, 1996). See also Das Basu, *Law of the Press*, and K.S. Padhy, *Battle for Freedom of Press in India* (Delhi: Academic Foundation, 1991), 32–42, for brief histories of press legislation in the colonial and post-Independence period. Rajeev Dhavan's *Publish and Be Damned: Censorship and Intolerance in India* (New Delhi: Tulika, 2008) and his *Only the Good News: On the Law of the Press in India* (New Delhi: Manohar, 1987) are valuable as they examine both state and social censorship, but the author's concern is more with the Emergency and events after it than with the 1950s. Two recent valuable additions to the legal history of free speech legislation in independent India are Gautam Bhatia, *Offend, Shock, or Disturb: Free Speech under the Indian Constitution* (New Delhi: Oxford University Press, 2016), and Abhinav Chandrachud, *Republic of Rhetoric: Free Speech and the Constitution of India* (New Delhi: Penguin Random House India, 2017). Lawrence Liang has discussed Articles 19(1)(a) and 19(2) and provisions pertaining to hate speech, obscenity and sedition in 'Free Speech and Expression' in *The Oxford Handbook of the Indian Constitution*,

pertaining to freedom of expression have also found their chroniclers.[34] Other accounts of censorship have tended to focus on the Emergency (1975–77), for instance, Soli Sorabjee's *The Emergency, Censorship and the Press in India*, written as a response to it.[35] The essays in *Gender and Censorship*, a volume edited by Brinda Bose, map post-colonial and contemporary media censorship through the important but limited prism of gender, and do not account for continuity in censorship policies with the colonial period.[36] Girja Kumar's *Censorship in India: With Special Reference to the Satanic Verses and Lady Chatterley's Lover* confines itself to censorship of fiction.[37] Censorship of visual media (films, posters, and so on) has received, and continues to receive, immense attention.[38] Moral regulation and censorship of 'obscene' publications in the colonial period has also received some attention. G.D. Khosla's *Pornography and Censorship in India* is an early work containing numerous extracts from ancient Indian literature.[39] More recent interventions included a comparative survey of 'moral regulation' (across India, Australia

ed. Sujit Choudhury, Madhav Khosla and Pratap Bhanu Mehta (New Delhi: Oxford University Press, 2016), 814–833.

[34] For instance, A.G. Noorani discusses various judicial pronouncements on free speech in the 1950s and 1960s in his 'Freedom of the Press and the Constitution', in *Freedom of the Press in India*, ed. A.G. Noorani, 24–35 (Bombay: Nachiketa Publications, 1971). See also Joseph Minattur, *Freedom of the Press in India: Constitutional Provisions and Their Application* (The Hague: Martinus Nijhoff, 1961), for a discussion of legal judgments on free speech in the 1950s.

[35] Soli J. Sorabjee, *The Emergency, Censorship and the Press in India, 1975–77* (New Delhi: Central News Agency, 1977). See also his *Law of Press Censorship in India* (Bombay: N.M. Tripathi Pvt. Ltd., 1976).

[36] Brinda Bose (ed.), *Gender and Censorship* (New Delhi: Women Unlimited, 2006).

[37] Girja Kumar, *Censorship in India: With Special Reference to the Satanic Verses and Lady Chatterley's Lover* (New Delhi: Har-Anand, 1990). Kumar discusses other famous cases of literary censorship in India in his *Censorship in India: Studies in Fundamentalism, Obscenity and Law* (New Delhi: Har-Anand, 2009).

[38] For instance, a majority of the articles in Raminder Kaur and William Mazzarella (eds), *Censorship in South Asia: Cultural Regulation from Sedition to Seduction* (Bloomington: Indiana University Press, 2009), deal with the censorship of film, advertisements and posters; see, for instance, William Mazzarella, 'Making Sense of Cinema in Late Colonial India' in this volume, 63–86.

[39] G.D. Khosla, *Pornography and Censorship in India* (New Delhi: India Book Company, 1976). Khosla was a member of the judiciary between 1926 and 1947, and retired as Chief Justice of the Punjab High Court. He also headed a film censorship inquiry committee in independent India.

and Great Britain) by Deana Heath,[40] and a study of Hindi publications in colonial north India by Charu Gupta.[41]

Mini Chandran has recently attempted to recover a pre-colonial history of censorship in India. She contends that the 'baffling lack of overt regulation of literature in pre-modern India' was on account of internalization of norms governing aesthetic representation. Chandran herself refers to 'an admittedly nebulous continuity in the literary practices of India from antiquity to medieval to contemporary times',[42] and it is questionable whether present-day censors (very often judges asked to pronounce on the validity of bans) see themselves as links in the chain of historical continuity with the ancient Indian past. Her discussion of censorship in medieval India also points to a paucity of concrete examples of state regulation of literature in the pre-modern, pre-colonial period.

Given the continuing presence and applications of censorship laws in India (and these are, of course, supplemented by various forms of mob and market censorship), it is surprising that the last major, full-length historical work on colonial censorship of publications in India appeared in 1974. This was N. Gerald Barrier's *Banned: Controversial Literature and Political Control in British India, 1907–1947*, which remains the classic historical work on colonial state censorship in India. Barrier's study (supplemented by a valuable, and till date the most comprehensive, bibliography of publications banned in colonial India) is concerned more with the political forces operating behind every major censorship legislation between 1907 and 1947, than with the content of what was deemed objectionable at various times. Barrier has shown how the GOI used various strategies including legislation, warnings, official news releases and subsidies to control the content of the press. His study is concerned with the question of how the colonial government dealt with controversial literature, and to this end he discusses the mechanics of policy formulation and implementation at the central and provincial levels of government. To

---

[40] Deana Heath, *Purifying Empire: Obscenity and the Politics of Moral Regulation in Britain, India and Australia* (Cambridge: Cambridge University Press, 2010).

[41] Charu Gupta, *Sexuality, Obscenity, Community: Women, Muslims, and the Hindu Public in Colonial India* (New Delhi: Permanent Black, 2001).

[42] Mini Chandran, *The Writer, the Reader and the State: Literary Censorship in India* (New Delhi: Sage, 2017), xxix. Chandran terms the two traditions (with regard to the normative principles governing the relationship between artists and the state): the 'Kautilyan' and the 'Bharatan'. She defines the 'Kautilyan' attitude as one of haughty indifference to the arts and the 'Bharatan' as a sympathetic one.

make his discussion more relevant, he divides the period into three phases: the period just before the First World War being that of emergence of controls, the period between 1914 and 1929 being one of coercion as well as conciliation, and the period till Independence largely being one of confrontation. Focusing on this last phase and extending it to the period after the departure of the British from India, this book has relied on a wider source base that includes public reactions to various censorship measures in India, so that the picture that emerges is fuller, and the spotlight is not on state measures of censorship alone, but also on public reactions and resistance to them.

Contrary to Barrier, who argues that 'official action tended to be responses to immediate crises rather than products of careful planning',[43] this book suggests that the GOI did indeed have a blueprint for censorship, particularly that of seditious publications, and more so during the Second World War. It is less of a comment on colonialism and more one on censorship itself that the 'products of careful planning' had to keep changing with time. In other words, although it is in the nature of censorship (as an activity dealing with subjective reality) that it has to evolve constantly in order to appear effective, this is not to say that colonial censorship in India was carried out arbitrarily.

Milton Israel's book on the role of the press in the nationalist movement in India between 1920 and 1947 demonstrates the immense support the Indian National Congress received from a large section of the press in India. Israel acknowledges the power of print in the first half of the 20th century by stating that it played the role of an opposition party in a colonial context.[44] While Israel's analysis of the press does not take into account the specificity, or legacy, of wartime measures, a richly detailed account of propaganda and censorship in India during the Second World War is provided by Sanjoy Bhattacharya. Bhattacharya's focus in on the formulation and implementation of official propaganda strategies (including but not limited to print) at the central and provincial levels, as well as that of the locality. He highlights the failures of these strategies, and the disagreements among officials about their implementation as a comment on cracks within the state. Bhattacharya's discussion of censorship during the war emphasizes its surveillance—as opposed to proscriptive—dimension, and he provides ample evidence that censorship was more rigorously implemented at the district level than at higher levels. Ultimately, in the sense

---

[43] N. Gerald Barrier, *Banned: Controversial Literature and Political Control in British India 1907–1947* (Columbia: University of Missouri Press, 1974), 17.

[44] Israel, *Communications and Power*, 21.

of preventing criticism of the colonial state, he argues that censorship failed in achieving its objective.[45]

※

The American historian Arthur Schlesinger Jr. has commented on a great shift in the moral balance between expression and authority: whereas earlier only heretics and blasphemers dared challenge traditional claims of authority over expression, in the last five centuries expression has established powerful claims against authority.[46] In other words, it is only relatively recently in human history that censorship has lost some of its legitimacy. The impulse to censor, and the necessity to legitimize censorship, are themes addressed by this book in the context of colonial and post-colonial India. An illustrious commentator predicted (in 2005) a 'bright future' for censorship in India,[47] and his prediction seems to be coming true. For this reason, it becomes all the more important to delve into the historical operation of—and debates over—censorship of the printed word in India, and this book is an attempt in that direction.

---

[45] Sanjoy Bhattacharya, *Propaganda and Information in Eastern India, 1939–45: A Necessary Weapon of War* (Richmond: Curzon, 2001), passim, 122 and 134–138.

[46] 'Preface' by Arthur M. Schlesinger Jr. to *Censorship: 500 Years of Conflict* (New York: Oxford University Press, 1984), 7.

[47] Ashis Nandy, 'Manufacturing Consent: How Thought Police States Are Created', *Times of India*, 15 January 2005, available at https://timesofindia.indiatimes.com/edit-page/THE-LEADER-ARTICLE-Manufacturing-Consent-How-Thought-Police-States-Are-Created/articleshow/990705.cms (accessed 19 January 2019).

PART I

Guarding the State, Protecting the Public
Censorship Policies and Practices in the 1930s

Laying the foundation stone of a new building for *The Pioneer* newspaper in Lucknow in 1936, the British Viceroy, Lord Linlithgow, reminded his audience, likely comprising many journalists, of the power the press wielded over public institutions and public opinion. The proprietors and editors of newspapers have a 'grave responsibility', he said, 'towards the State and towards the public'.[1] In a sense, censorship of publications was acknowledgment—howsoever perverse—of the power wielded by the printed word. An Indian journalist has described the 1930s as the decade of the 'adulthood of the Indian Press, not to say middle age!'[2] At the beginning of that decade, *The Hindu* had already been around for 50 years; the *Times of India* for almost a century. At the same time, according to the 1931 census, fewer than 10 out of every 100 Indians could read.[3] In fact, colonial authorities termed this low level of literacy a 'very serious obstacle' to attaining 'full self-sufficing

---

[1] *Speeches by the Marquess of Linlithgow*, vol. 1, 17 April 1936 to 23 April 1938 (Simla: Government of India Press, 1940), 137.

[2] N.S. Jagannathan, *Independence and the Indian Press: Heirs to a Great Tradition* (New Delhi: Konark, 1999), 90.

[3] In 1931 the literacy rate was 9.5 per cent. *Census of India 1931* (Delhi: Manager of Publications, 1933), vol. 1, part 1, 325.

nationhood on modern democratic lines'.[4] However, they also recognized
that it was precisely this low level of literacy that accorded educated Indians
disproportionate influence and gave rumour peculiar force. In 1930 the Simon
Commission report commented:

> In a country where the number of literates is very small, the formation of
> opinion depends far more on the spoken than on the written word. Rumour
> counts for more than reading; but the most exaggerated rumour finds its
> way into a certain class of Indian newspaper, and the influence of the man
> who can read is necessarily very great. We have pointed out ... how gravely
> the interests of good government are undermined, and confidence in the
> administration is shaken, by the distortion and misrepresentation practiced
> with impunity by some Indian newspapers, and by the absence of adequate
> means of counteracting it.... Except for an occasional address by the Viceroy,
> or by a Governor, and except for speeches made by officials in the legislatures,
> political advocacy is left to the critics.... The danger [to organized authority]
> is all the greater because India is a place where hearsay, however improbable,
> seems to gain widespread credence and to be capable of rousing fierce passion.[5]

The impact of newspapers was thus magnified because their content was
shared by the literate with the illiterate, and their impact therefore far exceeded
their circulation figures. In 1933, the chief editor of *The Hindu*, A. Rangaswami
Iyengar, estimated that readers of a newspaper in India represented 'at least
ten times as much as the number of copies actually printed'.[6]

The idea that the Indian press—and not the state—exercised 'tyranny' and
hampered free expression of many shades of opinion by giving vent only to anti-
government views was current in official circles India long before the Simon
Commission. Colonial officials who wanted neither to denounce free speech
as a principle nor apply it fully in practice in India reconciled this dilemma by
a sleight of hand. In 1908, for instance, the Chief Secretary of Bengal wrote
to the Home Secretary, Government of India (GOI):

---

[4] *Moral and Material Progress and Condition of India during the Year 1930–31* (London:
India Office, 1932), 625.

[5] *Report of the Indian Statutory Commission*, vol. 1: *Survey, 1930* (London: His Majesty's
Stationery Office, 1930), part 8: Public Opinion in India, 406-407. This report is
better known as the Simon Commission report, named after Sir John Simon, chairman
of the seven-member committee of British Members of Parliament that prepared it.

[6] A.R. Iyengar, *The Newspaper Press in India* (Bangalore: The Bangalore Press, 1933), 7.

There is certainly in the press very much that might lead to grave doubts as to the applicability of the doctrine of the freedom of the press to India…. There is also a tyranny exercised by the press which has interfered again and again with the free expression of opinion. It requires no moral courage whatsoever in India to criticize government measures or even to write in terms of violent abuse about Europeans in general and the British government in particular; for those who write in this manner know perfectly well that, however violent their language, and however inaccurate their statement of fact, no harm can, in the vast majority of cases, accrue to them. But of recent years it has often required moral courage to support the government, to express goodwill to Europeans, or to advocate any measure that is repugnant to the press; and again and again men even of high status and of much influence have been kept silent by its tyranny…. All the same, the advantages of a free press cannot be gainsaid. It is most desirable to obtain a free expression of opinion, and to permit grievances to be fully ventilated. On the other hand, the natural complement of a free press must be the firm administration of a clear and severe law against libel and a clear and severe law against sedition….[7]

Here, in the self-image of the state, the government was the victim; the press was a barrier to free expression, not its facilitator; laws circumscribing the press were a 'natural complement' to a truly free press, and not antithetical to it.

The colonial state in India was deeply concerned with public opinion. Resigned to the fact that there were some Indians beyond the scope of influence, official discourse displayed maximum concern for those people who could easily be swayed by articles in the press criticizing the government and even advocating violence against its personnel. Additionally, franchise was extremely limited at the beginning of the 1930s. In 1929–1930, only 1 out of 32 Indians could vote (that is, 7.4 million Indians out of 239.6 million were enfranchised).[8] If few Indians could read, even fewer from among these literate Indians could vote. For this reason it was necessary for the GOI to control, in some measure, publications at the disposal of educated Indians who had a say, however limited, in government. In an era of anti-colonial nationalism, it became necessary for the state to police print. It is in this context that historian Peter Robb's assertion that while the 19th century was for the British in India

---

[7] Letter no. 2186, 17 July 1908, from Chief Secretary Bengal, F.W. Duke, to Home Secretary, GOI. GOI Home Political A, nos. 124–125 (Confidential), July 1909, NAI.

[8] *Moral and Material Progress Report*, 1929–30, 78, Diagram 'The Voters of British India'.

a period of collecting information about the country, the 20th century was one in which they realized the need to 'direct the information which was available to others—to monopolise it at source if possible and otherwise to influence its flow'—makes sense.[9]

---

[9] Peter Robb, *The Evolution of British Policy towards Indian Politics, 1880–1920: Essays on Colonial Attitudes, Imperial Strategies, and Bihar* (New Delhi: Manohar, 1992), 293 and 301.

1

The Power of Print

Debates about freedom of expression and censorship in official files and in the legislative realm had very tangible—and traceable—consequences on the lives of people both ordinary and extraordinary. This chapter recovers and narrates the experiences of Indians from various walks of life: school and college students, journalists and revolutionaries, politicians (and their families) and Indian Civil Service (ICS) officers, future prime ministers and at least one future president of the Indian republic. Indians who grew up in colonial India and continued their lives and careers in independent India have written or spoken about the role played by print in shaping their life choices. For many participants in and observers of India's anti-colonial movement, reading banned or controversial literature was a rite of passage. Some have recalled the thrill of reading a banned book; others have recounted the lengths to which they had to go to procure their choice of newspaper. There are accounts aplenty of the means used to send banned literature to India, and also of the experience of reading—and writing—in jail. Their testimonies, in print and in interviews recorded decades after the events in question, convey a flavour of lived experience that our other official sources—crucial as they are—lack. How did Indians consume ideas in print, and how did they resist state censorship? These are the questions this chapter seeks to answer.

Although words do inspire action, measuring their impact is not an exact science. Censorship is guesswork: its basis is speculation as to what words will inspire whom and to what effect.[1] To the official mind in India, the causal connection between words inciting violence against the state, or other

---

[1] According to J.E. Daily, all censorship is irrational 'to the degree that conclusions about the effects of the message are drawn without basis in fact or science'. Jay E. Daily, *The Anatomy of Censorship* (New York: Marcel Dekker, 1973), 6.

communities or classes, and the actual incidence of such violence was clear. According to the GOI, 19 crimes of a 'terrorist nature' were committed in India in 1929; in 1930 these nearly quadrupled to 74.[2] In 1930 alone, 15 government employees were killed and 31 injured in bomb blasts and armed attacks. Additionally, 9 'innocent victims' were killed and 62 injured in these attacks.[3] An official statement of terrorist crime in 1929 and 1930 included a list of seven 'confessing accused' (two of whom were named) who stated that they had 'imbibed revolutionary ideas from the reading of newspapers'. One credited *Kirti* (a monthly Urdu and Gurmukhi newspaper with left-wing sympathies, published by the Ghadr Party) with providing him an account of a revolutionary's life, such that 'the fire of freedom increased in him'. Another confessed to reading newspapers containing the poems of the young revolutionary Ram Prasad Bismil at the Arya Samaj Library in Kanpur. Reading about the Kakori case (1925) and the Lahore Conspiracy case (1915) judgments in newspapers inspired two others to become revolutionaries. Yet another was motivated by reading newspaper accounts of the Jallianwala Bagh incident (1919) as well as Lala Lajpat Rai's death (1928). Still another, who had already prepared explosives, contacted the staff of the newspaper *Swadhinta* (a Bengali weekly organ of the revolutionary Jugantar party), and offered his services after reading about revolutionaries' plans in it.[4]

The power of ideas in print was as apparent to revolutionaries as it was to the colonial state. In the typed leaflet that accompanied the bombs thrown by young revolutionaries Bhagat Singh and Batukeshwar Dutt in the Central Legislative Assembly in Delhi on 8 April 1929, the authors referred to the long life of ideas, and their tendency to outlive empires.[5] The leaflet was

---

[2] Tabular statement of the number of 'Crimes of a Terrorist nature committed in India during the years 1929 and 1930', in 'Statement of Terrorist Crime compiled from January 1929 up to 31 August 1931', 7. This statement accompanied the Indian Press (Emergency Powers) Bill. GOI Home Political, f. 4/36 & K.W., 1931, NAI.

[3] 'Statement of Terrorist Crime compiled from January 1929 up to 31 August 1931', 18, GOI Home Political, f. 4/36 & K.W., 1931, NAI.

[4] Ibid., 8, GOI Home Political, f. 4/36 & K.W., 1931, NAI.

[5] The bombs were thrown by them in their capacity as Central Committee members of the Hindustan Socialist Republican Association, to protest against the Public Safety Bill and the Trade Disputes Bill. A scholar was able to trace 153 proscribed publications relating to Bhagat Singh alone, not only in Urdu and Punjabi but also in Gujarati, Tamil, Sindhi, Tamil and Kanarese, indicating not only his pan-Indian popularity, but also the challenge before a state seeking to suppress material in so

published in a special evening edition of the *Hindustan Times* the same evening. It referred to the 'Press Sedition Bill' as a repressive measure the government was reserving for the next session.[6] Legendary revolutionary Bhagat Singh had, after all, some experience of journalism: he began writing for the newspaper *Pratap* (using the pen name Balwant) after moving to Kanpur in 1923, and also wrote for *Kirti*. According to Chaman Lal, the compiler and editor of Singh's *Jail Notebook*, Singh's access to the Dwarka Dass Library of Lahore and its collection of Marxist literature was an important influence in shaping his thinking.[7] Indeed, the notebook (written in English) contains extracts and notes from a wide range of books, from Omar Khayyam to Lenin.[8] While in jail, Singh not only read Marx, Engels and Trotsky but also novels, including Victor Hugo's *Les Miserables* and Fyodor Dostoevsky's *Crime and Punishment*, and non-fiction, including Valentine Chirol's *Indian Unrest*.[9] It is only fitting that the execution of Bhagat Singh and his comrades generated an immense volume of 'eulogy literature' (most recently analysed by historian Kama Maclean), which in turn served as a source of inspiration to many other revolutionaries, and as a source of concern (and impetus for legislation) for the colonial state.[10] As a *Times of India* headline put it in 1935: 'Terrorists Not Born but Made by Section of Indian Press'.[11]

History and Allegory in the Classroom

Colossus of Indian journalism, Durga Das, who attended an Arya Samaj–run high school in Jalandhar in the second decade of the 20th century, recalled

---

many languages but sharing a common theme. See Gurdev Singh Sidhu (ed.), *The Hanging of Bhagat Singh, Volume IV – The Banned Literature* (Chandigarh: Unistar Books, 2007).

[6] Chaman Lal (ed.), *Bhagat Singh: The Jail Notebook and Other Writings* (New Delhi: LeftWord, 2007), 137–138.

[7] Ibid., 22–23.

[8] Ibid., 14.

[9] S. Irfan Habib, *To Make the Deaf Hear: Ideology and Programme of Bhagat Singh and His Comrades* (Gurgaon: Three Essays Collective, 2007), 143–144.

[10] Kama Maclean, *A Revolutionary History of Interwar India: Violence, Image, Voice and Text* (New Delhi: Penguin, 2016), 36–37 and ch. 8, 'Controlling Political Violence', 169–184. Maclean discusses the 1931 Press Ordinance in this context.

[11] Ironically the headline quoted an Indian member of the Legislative Assembly, and a journalist himself, R.S. Sarma, as saying this on the floor of the house. *Times of India*, 10 September 1935.

being caught by the superintendent of his boarding house reading a banned book (Bhai Parmanand's *Tarikh-i-Hind* or *History of India*). He was warned that if the British got to know that a boarder was reading the book they would arrest the superintendent and shut down the school.[12] The reach—and success—of colonial censorship was, of course, vastly exaggerated by the superintendent. Seditious ideas, or ideas inspiring revolution, were to be found not only in proscribed books but also in school and college syllabi, especially when interpreted by teachers with a nationalist bent of mind. Journalist N.S. Jagannathan's teacher at Presidency College, Madras, Professor K. Swaminathan (who later edited the *Collected Works of Gandhi*) would 'deconstruct' Shelley's *Prometheus Unbound* as an allegory of Gandhi's struggle against the British; the work lent itself to such an interpretation as it told the tale of a chained man defying a tyrant, and being liberated by the spirit of the people. It also helped that the name of the man's beloved was Asia.[13] P.D. Tandon, a journalist affiliated with the Congress who served as Uttar Pradesh's Minister for Information, Higher Education and Culture after Independence, recalled that in his school days 'terrorists and revolutionaries were heroes. Their brave deeds thrilled us.'[14] Future ICS officer Y.D. Gundevia's Indian history syllabus at Wilson College in Bombay in the mid-1920s included Mughal history, but also some European history, 'including the French revolution and the storming of the Bastille, with the focus on the guillotine and the lovely head of Marie Antoinette, bemoaned by great orators in the British Parliament'.[15] Whereas historical tracts pertaining to bloody revolutions were often banned in colonial India (the rationale being that these would inspire Indians to do likewise), stories and histories of revolutions were being taught to Indian students in the 1920s—the heyday of anti-colonial nationalism—in educational institutes. It was permissible to study the French Revolution in school but not through pamphlets.

---

[12] Durga Das, *India from Curzon to Nehru and After* (London: Collins, 1969), 33–34. *Tarikh-i-Hind* was first published around 1918 and reprinted many times. It was banned for vilifying the British, for its account of 1857 and for its account of Sikh revivalism.

[13] N.S. Jagannathan, *Independence and the Indian Press* (New Delhi: Konark Publishers, 1999), 2.

[14] P.D. Tandon, *Flames from the Ashes: Memoirs of a Lone Traveller* (Allahabad: St. Paul's Society, 1981), 21.

[15] Y.D. Gundevia, *In the Districts of the Raj* (Bombay: Disha Books, 1992), 10.

University students were especially fond of reading banned books. Durga Das Khanna (a revolutionary who was jailed in December 1930 for participating in a conspiracy to shoot the Punjab Governor and again during the Quit India movement in 1942) used to read revolutionary literature at the Dwarka Dass library in Lahore, from where he borrowed and read Bukharin's *ABC of Communism* and John Reed's *Ten Days That Shook the World* (about the Russian Revolution). An active member of the Hindustan Socialist Republican Association (HSRA), he was introduced to Bhagat Singh and Sukhdev via two books that were lent to him by a friend, who had in turn borrowed them from the two soon-to-be-famous revolutionaries. The books were *Great Thoughts of Lala Har Dayal M.A.* and *Selections from Bande Matram* by Aurobindo Ghose. Khanna recalled that he found the books so 'inspiring' that he read them cover to cover in the course of one night. The two also asked him to read Don Breen's *My Fight for Irish Freedom* and the *Life of Barrister Savarkar*. Khanna, in turn, in his capacity as acting president of the Lahore Students' Union before he was jailed, bought books with his own money to lend to students individually as well as collectively.[16] As a B.Sc. student in Lucknow University during the Quit India movement, P.K. Tandon read banned communist literature, including a cyclostyled copy of the *History of Communist Party of the Soviet Union* by Stalin, which a friend had given him. He also read R.P. Dutt's *India Today*. When the ban on the Communist Party was removed in 1942, he began reading *People's War*, a newspaper published by the Communist Party of India.[17]

The famous author Yashpal imbibed not only revolutionary ideas but also recipes for bombs from books. As a student at National College, Lahore, along with his classmates Bhagat Singh and Rajguru, and his senior Bhagvaticharan

---

[16] Khanna, interviewed by S.L. Manchanda, 19 May 1976, 5–8, Nehru Memorial Museum and Library Oral History Project (NMML OHP). Khanna practised law from 1933 onwards; after Independence, he served on various municipal boards, and was elected to the Punjab Legislative Council in 1960 and 1966.

[17] Tandon, interviewed by S.L. Manchanda, 27 July 1988, 5–6, NMML OHP. Pratap K. Tandon (b. 1924) participated in a students' demonstration at Lucknow during the Quit India movement, joined the Communist Party while he was studying at Benaras Hindu University, and was active in the All India Students' Federation from 1944 onwards, serving as state secretary in 1949 at the time of his arrest. He was arrested and jailed between February 1949 and May 1950 for communist activities, at a time when there was a general round-up of communists in the United Provinces (UP). After his release, he worked with peasants in eastern UP. He served as the general secretary of the UP Kisan Sabha.

Vohra, he read about armed revolutionaries in Bengal, the Rowlatt report (with its description of terrorist activities), and books including *My Fight for Irish Freedom* and R.P. Dutt's *India Today* and *Modern India*.[18] He learnt bomb-making with the aid of a library chemistry book, borrowed from a friend studying for a master's degree in chemistry at Lahore Government College. Bombs made this way were placed under the Viceroy's train. Yashpal went on to co-author the tract *Philosophy of the Bomb*. In an interview conducted four decades later, Yashpal emphasized that revolutionaries in his day not only concerned themselves with guns and bullets but also with books.[19]

Acquiring and Smuggling Print

The pleasure of reading banned books was matched by the thrill of acquiring and reading newspapers with nationalist sympathies. Inam Aziz, who migrated to Pakistan in 1947 and became one of its most prominent journalists, recalled that as a child in pre-Independence India, he was able to read newspapers because his father worked for the railways. After reading the *Zamindar*, *Pratap*, *Milap*, and *Vir Bharat*, which arrived from Lahore on the morning train, he would return them to the local newsagent.[20] Journalist M.V. Kamath read nationalist papers such as *Bombay Chronicle* and *Free Press Journal* for 'every statement our leaders made and every counter-measure that the British rulers took'.[21] Rangaswami Parthasarathy, who began his career with the *Madras Mail* in 1936 and ended it with *The Hindu*, would wait for hours to get a chance to read the paper in the local reading room; by common consent its pages were split and distributed, the front page being most in demand. Indeed, nationalist leaders' speeches and activities as reported in the newspapers were 'more

---

[18] Yashpal, interviewed by S.L. Manchanda, 10 February 1972, 3, NMML OHP. Yashpal (1903–1976) studied at National College, Lahore, and participated in the Non-Cooperation movement. In 1920 he stood first in Ferozpur district in the matriculation examination and was awarded a scholarship, which he declined as he became a Congress volunteer. He was declared an offender in the Saunders murder case as well as the Assembly bomb case. He was sentenced to 14 years' imprisonment in 1932, but released in 1938. He published the journal *Viplav* and was arrested in 1941. *Dada Kamred* (1941) and *Jhutha Sach* (1958–1960) are his most famous novels.

[19] Ibid., 11–16.

[20] Inam Aziz, *Stop Press: A Life in Journalism*, translated from Urdu by Khalid Hasan (Karachi: Oxford University Press, 2008), 11.

[21] M.V. Kamath, *Behind the By-Line: A Journalist's Memoir* (New Delhi: Vision Books, 1985), 5.

important ... than our daily lessons in the classroom'. As he put it, 'Our mind and heart were electrified by their fiery orations and call for resistance to the alien rulers.' To his father, a Congressman and a devoted reader of *The Hindu*, that paper was '... literature, source book, and party Bible all combined into one.... There was no questioning what it said and wrote'. Of press censorship during the Salt Satyagraha (1930), Parthasarathy recalled:

> There was strict press censorship then and the newspapers were prohibited from publishing any news of the Civil Disobedience Movement. The Hindu was a law abiding paper and although it could not publish all the news about the Salt Satyagraha it managed to carry enough to give us an idea of the ferment and the turmoil in the country. Wanting to know more and not satisfied with what The Hindu had to offer, I would dash to a shop across the street where the Bombay Chronicle was being sold. The Bombay Chronicle splashed the Satyagraha news on page one in banner headlines.... Patriotic tears streamed from my eyes as I read of the arrests ... and of the police beatings of defiant volunteers.... The Bombay Chronicle did not survive for long and the British saw to it that it did not 'poison' the minds of young people like me. And so I had to fall back on The Hindu as the only source to feed my fiery soul.[22]

Indians based abroad experienced the additional thrill of smuggling publications into the country. Litterateur and public intellectual Sajjad Zaheer too attributed his foray into politics to his love of reading. As a student in Lucknow in 1920 at the time of the Non-Cooperation movement, he went through a two-year phase when he gave up wearing foreign cloth, and took to spinning. In this change in lifestyle, he recalled, he was influenced by the *Independent*, Motilal Nehru's paper edited by Syed Hossain from Allahabad, as well as a speech of Gandhi's he heard in Lucknow. As a student at Oxford, Zaheer became a member of the first Indian communist students' group formed in England. This group tried to make contact with groups in Bombay and Delhi, and smuggled communist literature into India. Zaheer explained the procedure of smuggling proscribed publications from England to India: 'Sometimes eminent Indians would come to England, eminent in the sense that they were not suspected by the British government.... We would give them a parcel of books or a little handbag consisting of Marxist literature and ask them to deliver it to so and so in India.' One such Indian was Professor S.

---

[22] Rangaswami Parthasarathy, *Memoirs of a News Editor: 30 Years with the Hindu* (Calcutta: Naya Prakash, 1980), 66–68.

Radhakrishnan, who carried a League of Nations passport at the time. Zaheer and his friends requested him to carry some books and told him they were of Lenin and Marx. He agreed, but when he saw the 'very big bundle, almost a suitcase', he said he could carry only some and not all. At any rate, the first President of India (who had been knighted by the British in 1931) was complicit in the bringing of proscribed literature to the country.[23]

The World of Politics

For people who made politics their career, an interest in national and local events was often sparked by the written word. Inder Kumar Gujral, who served as Minister of Information and Broadcasting (1975) as well as Prime Minister (1997–1998) in independent India, used to read books by Premchand and Lajpat Rai as well as biographies of 19th-century Italian nationalists Guiseppe Mazzini and Guiseppe Garibaldi. His father subscribed to Gandhi's English weekly, *Harijan*, and to other daily papers in Urdu and English. Every night, from when Inder Kumar was six or so, his father read books to him. Among others, he read James Tod's *Annals and Antiquities of Rajasthan*, containing stories of Rajput valour. 'That was how we imbibed nationalism in our minds and he did all this without lecturing', Gujral was to recall several decades later.[24] As a student at Lahore's Forman Christian

---

[23] Zaheer, interviewed by Dr Hari Dev Sharma, 4 December 1969, 32, NMML OHP. Zaheer was born in Lucknow in 1905, and studied at the Universities of Lucknow and Oxford. In 1927 he went to Oxford for a BA degree and then again in 1932 to study law. In 1930 he joined the Communist Party. Upon his return to India he served on the executive committee of the Congress Socialist Party in 1938 and was elected general secretary of the All India Progressive Writers' Association in 1936. He published the first Marxist journal in Urdu called *Chingari*, and went to Pakistan in 1948. In 1951 he was arrested there in the Rawalpindi conspiracy case, and he returned to India in 1956.

[24] Gujral, interviewed by Usha Prasad, 3 June 2002, 34, NMML OHP. Gujral was born in 1919; participated in the Quit India movement and served as president of Lahore Students' Union and general secretary of Punjab Students' Federation between 1935 and 1943. His first detention, for a few hours, was when he was 11, and shouted slogans such as 'Zindabad' near a police station. In 1942 he was jailed again for communist activities. He served as Union Minister of State for Information and Broadcasting during 1969–1971 and 1972–1975, as Ambassador to USSR between 1976 and 1980, and as Minister for External Affairs between 1989 and 1990, in addition to serving as member of both houses of Parliament.

College, he remembered storing proscribed literature in his hostel room; the English principal prevented the police from raiding his room, and as Gujral remembers it, 'Since he was a British, the police were scared of him. So they would not raid my room.'[25] Achyut Patwardhan, founder of the Socialist Party of India, confessed to being drawn into the nationalist movement as the result of Gandhi's Dandi March (1930), and after being influenced by his speeches during the march, 'which were daily reported in the press'.[26] He was also influenced by Bertrand Russell's *Roads to Freedom* and *Principles of Social Reconstruction*.[27] Similarly, prominent nationalist J.B. Kripalani traced his awakening to national causes to a specific event involving a publication. While he was studying for a BA degree at Wilson College (Bombay) in 1906, he chanced upon the B.C. Pal edited weekly *New India*, and confessed that this awoke him from the 'dreamland' he had been inhabiting. Sixty years later, he recollected that it was reading the lucid and persuasive arguments in this journal that convinced him that Indians were enslaved and prompted him to do something about it. Reading journals involved both sacrifice and effort: in 1907, as a student at Fergusson College, he subscribed to the daily *Bande Mataram* by economizing on his other expenses, and recalled going half a mile to fetch a copy from the postman.[28]

---

[25] Ibid., 36–40.

[26] Patwardhan, interviewed by Dr Hari Dev Sharma, 6 December 1989, 1, NMML OHP. Patwardhan (1905–1992) taught economics at Central Hindu College of Banaras Hindu University until 1932, when he participated in the Civil Disobedience movement and was jailed. He was a founder member of the Congress Socialist Party in 1934, was jailed between October 1940 and April 1942 for certain speeches, and participated in the Quit India movement. He also edited the *Janata*, and again taught at the same college between 1950 and 1966.

[27] Ibid., 4.

[28] Kripalani, interviewed by Dr Hari Dev Sharma and K.P. Rungachary, 15 November 1966, 5–6, NMML OHP. Kripalani (1888–1982) applied for a teacher's post at Karachi High School after graduating in 1908, but resigned when the Risley circular required all teachers in government schools to sign an oath of loyalty. He taught at the Green Bhumihar Brahman College in Muzaffarpur between 1912 and 1917, joined Gandhi in the Champaran struggle in 1917, and later taught at Kashi Vidyapith and Gujarat Vidyapith. He served as Congress president in 1946–1947, and was a member of the Constituent Assembly, and the Provisional Parliament (1950–52). He left the Congress to form the Kisan Mazdoor Praja Party in 1951, and served four terms as member of the Lok Sabha.

Ideas in Incarceration

The accounts of yet other Indians who were jailed for anti-colonial activism point not only to the impossibility but also to the absurdity of censorship. Sher Jung, an Indian revolutionary who spent 14 years of his life in jail on charges of sedition, recalled the words that had inspired him in his youth, seven decades earlier:

> I had just crossed my teens and was living on the crumbs of sentiments left behind by the Russian nihilists, Irish Sinnfeins and Bengal martyrs—a galaxy of heroes whose deeds were applauded and sung by great writers and poets like Pushkin and Turgenev in Russia, and Tagore and Nazrul Islam in India.[29]

Of the four authors that Sher Jung listed as having inspired him (and, presumably, many others in his generation) to revolutionary acts, only one was ever banned. One other was, in fact, honoured by the British with a knighthood. This is as damning an indictment of the success of colonial censorship as any other.

Far from complaining about censorship in the colonial jails in which he was incarcerated, Sher Jung was grateful for the jail officials' ignorance. In return for praising the poems of the Assistant Jailor, Sher Jung could have 'all the books sent by friends or libraries, without delay or censor'. There was only one condition: the word 'revolution' was not to appear in the title. The consequence: the jailor-cum-censor passed all classical works on philosophy, history, economics and political science; he allowed his prisoner to read the founding texts of Anarchism, but did not permit any book on the Industrial Revolution.[30] In Sher Jung's own words:

> He [the Assistant Jailor] had no objection to giving me the works of Marx, Engels, Lenin and for the matter of that, even of Sorel (on Violence), Schmidt, Proudhon, Kropotkin, and Bakunin (on Anarchism), but he would withhold any book, even fiction, by HG Wells because, according to his information,

---

[29] Sher Jung was born in 1906, incarcerated for the period between 1929 and 1938 and then again between 1940 and 1945, and wrote his memoirs in 1991. At other places in his memoir he named or quoted other authors who had inspired him: Tolstoy, the poems of Christina Rossetti, Hafez, Oscar Wilde, Nietzsche, as also Kazantzakis' commentaries on him. Sher Jung, *Prison Days: Recollections and Reflections* (New Delhi: BR Publishing, 1991), 45.

[30] Ibid., 129–130.

Wells had written something derogatory (what and where, he did not know) about the Prophet Mohammad. The other writers he did not like were Laski and Freud—yes! His writings, as he was told on authority by someone he knew, consisted of nothing but stark pornography. The other most hated author was Havelock Ellis. His 'Studies' according to him (though he never read them) were another version of *Kamasutra*, an illustrated edition in translation of which he had in possession.

As Jung recalled, '… the more formidable looking and dry a book, the easier it was to get it through him.' At times, the content of the book was irrelevant even to the prisoner. Library books carried messages about the collection of arms and explosives. These were successfully transmitted when the book was, in due course, returned to the library. [31]

The ignorance of colonial jail authorities is attested to in another account by a prisoner. A veteran of colonial and post-colonial jails, P.K. Tandon (who was jailed for over a year in 1949 for helping organize a railway workers' strike in the United Provinces [UP]) recalled that clashes in Benaras jail with the authorities were often on the issue of non-supply of newspapers. According to jail rules, one paper for every six people was allowed, and these were not supplied. He recalled that books from outside the jail faced severe restrictions. N.G. Ranga's *Revolutionary Peasants* was not allowed as it contained the term 'revolution'; neither was Lenin's *Collected Works* allowed. According to Tandon, jail authorities had a list of papers and books not permitted. After all, as they readily admitted to him, '… we cannot check them [books to be allowed to prisoners from outside]; we are not the people who are supposed to know about Lenin or what he has written. We do not know which book was objectionable, which was not.' [32] At the same time, Tandon recollected that even in jail, communist detainees managed to 'somehow' get party resolutions and some pamphlets, and were able to have discussions with each other on the basis of communist literature, including the *Communist Manifesto*.[33]

Chandralekha Mehta, Jawaharlal Nehru's niece, who was imprisoned for seven months for participating in the Quit India movement in 1942,

---

[31] Ibid., 123.

[32] Tandon was first detained under the Maintenance of Public Order Act, and then under the Preventive Detention Act. The Communist Party had been banned by the GOI in March 1948. Tandon, interviewed by S.L. Manchanda, 27 July 1988, 29–33, NMML OHP.

[33] Ibid., 35.

remembered reading Bankim Chandra's patriotic novel *Anandmath* in Naini jail. Of the books that prisoners were allowed to read (after inspection by the jail superintendent), she recalls that Sholokhov's *Virgin Soil Upturned* (about Soviet communes) was released only after some delay as the superintendent 'Mr. Gardener may have expected something racy and kept it to read!'[34] P.D. Tandon, jailed in Naini in 1942, recalled that a copy of the *Leader* (an English daily run by prominent nationalist leaders) was smuggled in daily by a sweeper, 'concealed inside the thick bamboo on both ends of which he hung the shit cans'. Prisoners had to pay a rupee per copy, which was then shared by 500 of them. The sweeper was thrashed by the jailor once when he was caught, but smuggling resumed in a week's time.[35] Nehru himself recounted in his *Autobiography* that while in jail he could not obtain all the books he wanted. Incompetent censors held up, for example, Spengler's *Decline of the West* as the title appeared to them 'dangerous and seditious'. Nehru recalled that despite censorship, he was able to get a good variety of books, although the only ones that British officials enthusiastically recommended were religious books and novels.[36]

The Limits of Censorship

Let alone prisoners, even serving ICS officers were not immune to the temptations of different ideologies in print. Michael Carritt, an Oxford educated ICS officer in Bengal in the 1930s, began reading the work of socialist theoreticians in the early 1930s. He knew he was breaking the law: books by Marx and Lenin, Harold Laski and G.D.H. Cole, which he read, were all banned under the General Communist Notification of 1932. Furthermore, he knew that there was 'vigilant censorship of all incoming mail from Europe in order to exclude such seditious stuff'; even as, later in his career, he signed police orders for the interception of such parcels, as a young officer he thought it was a 'safe bet that parcels addressed to a District Officer would slip through the fishing net of a suspicious police'.[37] In 1934–1935, while on

---

[34] Chandralekha Mehta, *Freedom's Child: Growing Up during Satyagraha* (New Delhi: Puffin Books/Penguin, 2008), 165–166.

[35] Tandon, *Flames from the Ashes*, 73.

[36] Jawaharlal Nehru, *An Autobiography* (New Delhi: J.N. Memorial Fund/Oxford University Press, 1989 [London: John Lane, 1936]), 350.

[37] Michael Carritt, *A Mole in the Crown: Memoirs of a British Official in India Who Worked with the Communist Underground in the 1930s* (Calcutta: Rupa, 1986), 126. Carritt

home leave in England, his ideas were further refined after 'political study and conversations with a number of left-wing politicians'.[38] After making contact with Ben Bradley (convicted in the Meerut conspiracy case against communist leaders), he received instructions and money to make contact with the banned Communist Party of India, to publish an illegal news-sheet, and to carry Communist International (Comintern) literature to India. During the course of his activities, he was 'surprised by the outstanding inefficiency of the methods and detective work of the Police Intelligence Bureau in Bengal'.[39] As an Under Secretary in the Political Department in Calcutta, he had access to weekly reports from the districts regarding the activities of Indian nationalists, workers and peasants, and claimed, in his memoirs, that the warnings he gave about impending detentions helped agitators to escape the police net.[40]

These examples are very revealing: censorship by the state was demonstrably ineffective in several ways: policymakers at the upper echelons of the state, who obsessed over the content of books and labelled them offensive or otherwise, were acting in vain. More often than not, the 'man on the spot' (the jailor, for instance), lived and operated in a completely different context. At other times, even the incarcerated revolutionary was not interested so much in the content of a book as in its use as a carrier of coded messages (library books, for example). For this purpose, one book was as good as another. In any case, if prisoners of colonial jails with a censorship regime in place could read some of the most revolutionary literature produced in the world, then by definition 'free' people outside jail could—and would—surely read all that and much more.

Official records provide evidence of the success of colonial censorship but Indians' recollections, as available in their memoirs, are somewhat different, emphasizing successful resistance. The truth lies somewhere in between. Nehru's niece Chandralekha Mehta recalled that in August 1942, during the Quit India movement and after the arrest of Congress leaders, Lal Bahadur Shastri (later to follow Jawaharlal Nehru as India's Prime Minister) hid in the

---

resigned in 1938, aged 33, when he thought the authorities were on to him. His pension was cancelled in 1940; in 1980 he saw the file the government had maintained on him. The GOI and the Secretary of State had found out the truth about his activities, but each wanted the other to take discreet action as news of a communist mole within the ICS would dampen European morale at a time of nationalist fervour. Afterwards he taught at the Universities of Oxford and Sussex.

[38] Ibid., 128.

[39] Ibid., 129–130.

[40] Ibid., 142.

Nehru family home at Allahabad. He used a cyclostyle machine to produce copies of Congress instructions asking people to obstruct the government. When he heard that the police were on their way to search the house, he flushed the papers down the toilet and left his hostess (Nehru's sister Vijaya Lakshmi Pandit) worrying about the possibility of a blocked toilet in a crowded house. A few days later, Nehru's sister and Chandralekha's mother, Vijaya Lakshmi Pandit (who went on to serve as independent India's ambassador to the United Kingdom, the United States and the Soviet Union) hid the pamphlets under her sleeping daughters' mattress, telling the police when they arrived that they had all been distributed.[41]

Journalists could, on occasion, censor official opinion as well. Durga Das recalled in an interview that after the Non-Cooperation movement was called off following the Chauri Chaura incident, some British officials felt that Gandhi had cheated them by terminating the movement when he realized that the government was going to come down strongly on it. On the other hand, Das recalled that journalists who were convinced of the principled reasons for calling off the movement '… dramatised this [Gandhi's decision] to such an extent, by interviewing people, by reporting comments, that the bureaucrats' reaction did not get a chance of being recorded in the Press. It remained within private conversation'.[42] It is ironical that M.K. Gandhi—unarguably the best-known anti-colonial figure India has produced, who used the power to print to such potent effect—claimed in his famous autobiography that he had never read a newspaper till he went to London at the age of 18.[43] In this, as in many other respects, he was exceptional.

Testimonies of individuals who played important public roles in postcolonial India are crucial in order for us to understand the centrality of debates over freedom of expression after Independence. This was a generation of Indians which took great risks to read material of their choice, which made sacrifices of time and money to acquire this material, and which was aware of numerous individuals who were jailed for their writings in colonial India. Scholars

---

[41] Mehta, *Freedom's Child*, 152. These events are also recounted in Mehta's sister's memoir. See Nayantara Sahgal, *Prison and Chocolate Cake* (New Delhi: Harper Perennial, 2007 [1954]), 22 and 108.

[42] Durga Das, interviewed by B.R. Nanda, 26 February 1969, 25–26, NMML OHP.

[43] M.K. Gandhi, *An Autobiography or My Experiments with Truth*, trans. Mahadev Desai (Ahmedabad: Navajivan Publishing House, 1927; repr. 1969), 35. 'In India I had never read a newspaper. But here [in Great Britain] I succeeded in cultivating a liking for them by regular reading.'

including Christopher Pinney and Sukeshi Kamra have argued that the colonial state perceived nationalist texts as mere seditious propaganda and refused to take their political content (and Indians' aspirations) seriously.[44] However, even as colonial officials undermined or underplayed the ideological content of the works they banned, by banning them, however unsuccessfully, they surely paid tribute to the power of print.

---

[44] Christopher Pinney, 'Iatrogenic Religion and Politics', in *Censorship in South Asia: Cultural Regulation from Sedition to Seduction*, ed. Raminder Kaur and William Mazzarella (Bloomington: Indiana University Press, 2009), 57; Sukeshi Kamra, 'The "Vox Populi," or the Infernal Propaganda Machine, and Juridical Force in Colonial India', *Cultural Critique* 72, Spring (2009), 189.

2

Provincial Autonomy (1937–1939) and Free Speech Controversies

Issues of free speech continued to be important after the grant of provincial autonomy (in keeping with the Government of India Act of 1935) and the formation of elected Congress ministries in seven out of eleven provinces of British India in 1937.[1] In the words of historian Sunil Chander, Congress ministries had to perform a 'delicate manoeuvre': 'to combat the [political] militants, they required the support of the authorities and to challenge the Raj, they required the support of the militants'. While performing this balancing act they also had to be 'seen as being uncompromisingly nationalist'.[2]

In late December 1937, the (now Congress-run) UP government issued a statement warning political activists not to use 'irresponsible language'. A newspaper that supported this decision commented that it could 'understand the embarrassment of a Government which in the interests of law and order feels compelled to enforce a law which it has been all along the pride of its members to violate and disobey'.[3] Noting the growing indiscipline among party members, and the increasing 'spirit of license' manifesting itself in violent speech and action, the article continued:

---

[1] The Congress emerged victorious in all provinces of British India except Assam, Bengal, Punjab and Sind.

[2] Sunil Chander, 'Congress, the Raj and Conflict in Provincial Autonomy, 1937–39' in *Oxford University Papers on India*, vol. 1, part 2, ed. N.J. Allen et al., 74–96 (New Delhi: Oxford University Press, 1987), 83.

[3] *National Call*, 30 December 1937, *Towards Freedom 1937–47*, vol. 1: *Experiment with Provincial Autonomy 1 January–31 December 1937*, ed. P.N. Chopra (New Delhi: Indian Council for Historical Research, 1985), 1310–1312.

A person who talks in terms of fiery extremism at one time may be a hero but at another time he may be worse than a traitor to his party, and a dangerous associate. We do not wish to suggest that just because Congress ministries govern seven provinces, we should cease to think progressively or even in radical terms.... But just because our nominees are in power, we must not say or do things which impair discipline, and militate against peace, law and order. If we do so we betray our utter incompetence to govern ourselves.... We may criticise them [Congress ministries]. We may guide and advise them. We may at times even oppose them. But at no time and on no account must we embarrass them.[4]

Reading this newspaper's comment against the grain, it is clear that tendencies that were tolerated or encouraged by the Congress-as-opposition returned to haunt the Congress-as-government. In a mirror image of the protagonist of George Orwell's story 'Shooting an Elephant' (whose actions were forced by what he thought the 'natives' expected of a white man) Congress ministries were constrained on the one hand by what the white man they had replaced thought of their administrative abilities, and on the other by negative comparisons with repressive actions of those they had just replaced. Seditious speech was an important arena where these tensions became apparent; this chapter will excavate these fault lines.

According to Gerald Barrier, the difference between Congress ministries and their British predecessors with regard to control of the press during the period of provincial autonomy was one of degree rather than of kind. He argues that Indian ministries were somewhat more tolerant of criticism, but 'when necessary, political pressure and inherited British assumptions on maintaining peace and order overrode theoretical commitment to freedom of the press'. Barrier has also highlighted that Congress ministries were as intolerant to communal propaganda as their British predecessors.[5] On occasion, British officials found it ironic when demand for bans emanated from Congress ministries, which had—before assuming power—railed against all kinds of bans.[6]

---

[4] Ibid.

[5] Barrier, *Banned*, 140–142.

[6] In 1937, after the Madras government asked the GOI to ban the import of a nudist journal titled *Health and Efficiency*, not only did the GOI not ban it (as they judged it not legally obscene), but a HD official found it 'interesting' that a Congress

The lead up to, as well as the operation of, provincial autonomy brought several free speech dilemmas and paradoxes to the fore. The assumption of state power, however partial, by an opponent of the colonial state, but under the overaching framework of colonial rule, was a unique situation, and provides the historian distinctive insights into the challenges of free speech. This was a trial run with significant implications for the future of free speech in independent India. This chapter delves into the history of two distinct episodes: the chequered history of the Congress Pledge between 1937 and 1943, and the dilemmas of Congress leaders while dealing with issues of free speech during the period of the Congress ministries (1937–1939), including the 'Parmanand case'.

'Seditious Formula' as 'Solemn Creed': Banning the Congress Pledge

A close reading of official correspondence reveals both uncertainty and difference of opinion among colonial administrators (within and among different provinces) and the dilemmas behind what may otherwise appear as, and has certainly been interpreted as, 'colonial repression', without room for debate and doubt. The case discussed in this section is a vivid illustration of the ambiguities of colonial repression.

Less than a week before the planned commemoration of 'Independence Day' by the Congress on 26 January 1937, the GOI telegrammed a note to all provincial governments suggesting that the words of the Congress Independence Pledge of 1930 were 'definitely seditious', and asking them (if they believed the pledge was likely to be read in their province) to ban it. Provincial governments were urged to consider the impact of this ban on the forthcoming elections, and reminded that Nehru's action was 'a challenge to Government which should be met'. The GOI also thought it desirable that the notification banning the pledge be accompanied by an explanation of why it was banned, and a statement of the government's intention to take firm action, as this would act as a deterrent. On the other hand, explained the GOI, 'mere academic advocacy of Independence need not be regarded as seditious'. The GOI note cited in particular the following extract from the pledge as an

---

government wanted to use the SCA 'to prohibit the importation of literature which admittedly does not offend against the law'. Note by J.A. Thorne, 21 December 1937, GOI Home Judicial, f. 372/37, 1937, NAI.

example of why it needed to be banned: 'The British Government in India has not only deprived the Indian people of their freedom but has based itself on the exploitation of the masses and has ruined India economically, politically, culturally and spiritually.'[7]

As far as the GOI was concerned, similar sentiments when uttered in speeches by Nehru and others could have—and had—been ignored, but the pledge needed to be banned because '... there is an essential difference between the use of isolated expressions by an individual in the course of an electioneering speech and the public recitation of a seditious formula as a solemn creed, accompanied by a pledge, as the central function of a formal Congress ceremony'.[8]

The same words uttered in different contexts or by different numbers of people attracted different penalties. The Home Member, Sir Reginald Maxwell,[9] was of the opinion that since few attempts had been made by the Congress to give publicity to the pledge after 1930, Nehru had chosen to challenge the GOI via the pledge in 1937 so as to 'enhance the prestige of the Congress on the eve of the elections'.[10] As in the case of censorship of 'obscene' publications, in the case of seditious publications and speeches too, it was the context—and not content alone—that determined whether or not they invited proscription.

There was lack of communication among provinces over the question of banning the pledge; in any case, all provinces did not think alike. The pledge was banned first by the Bombay government, which referred to it by its first few words: 'We believe that it is the inalienable right of the Indian people'.[11] Within a few days, the governments of UP, Central Provinces (CP), North

---

[7] It was to be banned under the IPA of 1931, and action against persons who publicized it was to be taken under section 124A of the IPC or section 5 of the Criminal Law Amendment Act of 1932. HD's 'Instructions with Regard to Celebration of Independence Day', 20 January 1937, Extracts from GOI Home Political, f. 4/1, 1937, *Towards Freedom 1937–47*, vol. 1, 52–53. See the full text of the 1930 Congress pledge in Chandra et al., *India's Struggle for Independence, 1857–1947*, 268–269.

[8] Note from R.M. Maxwell to R.T. Peel, 26 January 1937, *Towards Freedom 1937–47*, vol. 1, 74–76.

[9] Sir Reginald Maxwell joined the ICS in 1906 and served the Bombay government. He was appointed Private Secretary to the Governor of Bombay in 1929, and also served as the Home Secretary in the Bombay government.

[10] Note from R.M. Maxwell to R.T. Peel, 26 January 1937, *Towards Freedom 1937–47*, vol. 1, 74–76.

[11] Bombay government notification, 22 January 1937, *Towards Freedom 1937–47*, vol. 1, 60. The pledge had been published in the *Bombay Chronicle* on 18 January 1930.

West Frontier Province (NWFP), Orissa, Delhi, Madras and Bengal too had banned the pledge. In its notification, the Orissa government gave the following reason for the ban: '... the reading of the pledge would be a direct challenge to the Government which could not be ignored.' The notifications were accompanied by action, as offices and homes of a few provincial Congress committee leaders were searched.[12] At this stage, the Governor of Madras, Lord Erskine, communicated to the Viceroy, Lord Linlithgow, some of the ideological and practical problems attendant in banning the pledge in that province. Lord Erskine's Executive Council had initially decided that it was unwise to ban the pledge for various reasons: one, because it would give 'prominence to a document that would otherwise pass unnoticed'; two, because banning it would be termed a repressive measure and the Congress would gain political capital from this during the elections; and three, since Nehru as Congress president had been saying similar things without any interference from the authorities, it therefore seemed unfair to 'prosecute the minor fry'. Erskine informed the Viceroy that although Madras had initially decided not to ban the pledge for these reasons, it was forced to do so when Bombay banned it, so as to display uniformity on this issue. The episode prompted the Governor to suggest to the Viceroy that it would have been better if this important decision, a 'reversal of policy', had either been taken centrally or by all provinces at the same time. Erskine's complaint against the Home Department (HD) was that its orders were too vague, and that news of the ban in other provinces only reached Madras via newspapers.[13] This correspondence bears eloquent testimony to the challenges of implementing bans at an all-India level.

The Governor of UP, Sir Harry Haig, also revealed in a letter to the Viceroy that his Executive Council too had felt that banning the pledge would go in the Congress' favour during elections, and that it was an action better avoided. It was, therefore, only to conform to the other local governments' decision that UP had decided to ban the pledge. Haig admitted that he personally had changed his view regarding Congress propaganda: he had earlier considered it 'vigorous' but not dangerous, and now considered dangerous enough to deserve being banned. The change was caused by reports reaching him of the success of Congress propaganda in UP; apparently, Congress volunteers there were preaching the end of the British government within two months, and

---

[12] *The Pioneer*, 26 January 1937, *Towards Freedom 1937–47*, vol. 1, 71–74.

[13] Letter from Erskine to Linlithgow, 24 January 1937, Erskine Papers, *Towards Freedom 1937–47*, vol. 1, 67–69.

impressing villagers by promising (and giving in writing) starkly reduced rent demands in the event of a Congress victory in the elections.[14]

Nehru's reaction to the banning of the pledge was almost triumphant. The sudden banning, by provincial governments, of a pledge that had been in circulation for seven years signified to him that the growing mass enthusiasm about the Congress had 'upset the nerves of these governments'. Attracting a ban was, therefore, an index of the powerful appeal of the Congress. He suggested that the ban be respected, the pledge in question not be used, but that during Independence Day meetings 'a brief pledge reiterating the old pledge should be taken'. Nehru urged people to respect the ban as 'for the present, it is not our policy or desire to commit breaches of such orders....' [15] For people familiar with the general drift—if not the exact words—of a pledge in circulation since many years, a commitment even to mere 'reiteration' could evoke powerful sentiments against the British without falling afoul of censorship laws. What may be interpreted today as a subtle strategy of resistance was interpreted then by the GOI as an admission of weakness on Nehru's part. According to an HD official, '... the Congress do not at present feel strong enough to defy the Government, or at any rate it does not suit their plans to provoke a conflict at the present moment.' [16]

While Nehru accused the GOI of using accusations of 'sedition' to express its hostility towards the Congress, particularly in UP, the GOI considered the election campaign there as 'a pretext for preaching sedition on a wide scale'.[17] After the elections of 1937 and the formation of Congress ministries in seven provinces of British India in July 1937, Nehru wrote to the Chief

---

[14] 'This, I fear', wrote Haig, 'is how the ideas of democracy are presented to the ordinary voter.' Letter from Haig to Linlithgow, 26 January 1937, Linlithgow Papers, *Towards Freedom 1937–47*, vol. 1, 76–78. Sir Harry Haig joined the ICS in 1905, and before he was appointed Governor of UP in December 1934, he had served as Private Secretary to the Viceroy (1925), Home Secretary, GOI (1926–1930), and Home Member, GOI (1930–1934).

[15] Nehru's instructions regarding Independence Day Pledge issued at Kanpur on 24 January 1937, and reported in the *Hindustan Times*, 25 January 1937, *Towards Freedom 1937–47*, vol. 1, 69.

[16] Letter from R.M. Maxwell to R.T. Peel of the India Office, 26 January 1937, *Towards Freedom 1937–47*, vol. 1, 74–76.

[17] The GOI's views on this matter come through clearly in extracts from 'Confidential Appreciation of the Political Situation in India', issued on the authority of the Secretary of State for India, 17 February 1937, Cabinet Papers 24/268, *Towards Freedom 1937–47*, vol. 1, 141–142.

Commissioner of Delhi (where the pledge had recently been banned) pointing out the ironic situation: while seven provincial governments had accepted office on the basis of the pledge, and were committed to the sentiments it expressed, the same pledge was banned in Delhi. In other words, when what was once considered 'seditious' became 'official', at least in the majority of British India, did it cease to be seditious? Another related problem, in Nehru's opinion, was that books that contained the pledge had also been seized by the police. As he put it:

> This Independence pledge appears in various books which give a historical record of recent political events in India. I do not know how far these books also come within the ban, but I am informed that some of these books have also been seized by the Police. This suppression of historical and current literature seems to be extraordinary. History, if it is to teach anything, must deal with the facts as they are and not with distorted versions of it. As some of our official Congress publications give this Independence pledge, I shall be grateful to you if you will let me know what your present policy is in regard to them.[18]

The story of the pledge did not end in 1937. The outbreak of the Second World War in 1939 complicated matters further; among other things, the Congress ministries resigned in protest against India's participation in the war. In January 1941 an official Press Adviser of the GOI passed an item in the *Hindustan Times* containing the Congress pledge as well as Gandhi's instructions as to how Independence Day was to be celebrated.[19] At the same time, the Press Adviser had blocked the publication of Gandhi's instructions regarding the non-payment of fines, as this was considered a 'prejudicial report', which could be blocked under the Defence of India Rules. This, to the HD, illustrated the dilemma of 'treating anti-war campaign as distinct from political movement for Independence for which Congress stands'. In any case, in 1941, caught up in a World War, the Viceroy was keen to avoid a

---

[18] Extract from letter from Nehru to Chief Commissioner Delhi, 1 October 1937, *Towards Freedom 1937–47*, vol. 1, 993–994.

[19] The article reproduced the text of the pledge, including a line accusing the British government of being based on exploitation, and of ruining India 'economically, politically, culturally and spiritually'. Gandhi added the instruction that there was to be no civil disobedience on Independence Day, so as not to invite disturbance of the meetings. *Hindustan Times*, 13 January 1941. See also GOI Home Political, f. 41/20, 1941, NAI.

showdown with the Congress.[20] Accordingly, the GOI instructed provincial governments that the pledge's publication had been allowed because it had been published before, and because it did not contain any incitement to an anti-war campaign, *even though* it contained seditious passages. During wartime, the offence of sedition has slipped down the hierarchy of offences, making place for the crime of fomenting 'anti-war' opinions and activities. The GOI instructed local governments not to take action against recitation of the pledge so as to avoid a confrontation with Congress, unless there was disruption of peace or eruption of anti-war demonstrations.[21]

In January 1943, the Intelligence Bureau (IB) received information that the All-India Congress Committee (AICC) had issued 'Independence Day Instructions' to all Congress organizations asking them, among other things, to recite a new Independence Day Pledge. This revised pledge asked people to pledge themselves to

> … the early and final overthrow of the usurper authority whose insecure continuance is based on bribe and murder. Until we have rid our country of this shame and horror and until we have created out of our Declaration of Freedom made at the beginning of this Revolution the Republic of India, we shall not rest but suffer and strive and struggle.

The pledge concluded with Gandhi's message of 'Do or Die'. By 15 January, another document purporting to be issued by the AICC had been found in Bihar, carrying a much longer pledge. This pledge blamed the British government for exploiting Indians, reiterated faith in non-violent means, and mentioned that since August 1942 thousands had died, and over a lakh people had been jailed. The Bihar version was similar to the 1942 version of the pledge. The pledge issued in Bombay and Madras was the same as the Bihar version. [22]

As we have seen, a version of the pledge had been banned by the GOI in 1937 under the IPA 1931. In 1943, in changed circumstances, Additional

---

[20] Telegram R. no. 100-Sc from the Private Secretary to Viceroy (PSV) to HD, 15 January 1941. The telegram ended, 'It would in his [the Viceroy's] opinion be a great mistake to make an issue such as the present [the Congress pledge] the occasion for a show-down with Congress.' GOI Home Political (I), f. 3/7, 1941, NAI.

[21] Express letter no. 3/7/41-Political (I) from HD to Chief Secretaries of all provincial governments, 17 January 1941, GOI Home Political (I), f. 3/7, 1941, NAI.

[22] IB note, 12 January 1943, GOI Home Political, f. 3/3, 1943, NAI.

Secretary Richard Tottenham (who favoured prohibition of the reading of the pledge) was not in favour of banning the pledge itself for two reasons: because the GOI did not have definite information about the form of the pledge and because 'it would be undesirable to give it any kind of unnecessary publicity'. The Home Member, Sir Reginald Maxwell, on the other hand, was emphatic that publication and propagation of the pledge was punishable.[23] The Madras government, on its part, wrote to all editors that since the pledge declared 'open rebellion', it was objectionable and actionable under the Defence of India Rules, and requested them not to publish it.[24] However, the pledge was not formally banned by the GOI.

In its chequered history, the Congress pledge was not banned when it was first adopted and publicized in 1930, then banned in many provinces in 1937; the ban was removed in 1938 when Congress ministries were in office, and nothing done against it in 1938 and 1939 either.[25] In 1943 the GOI attempted to stop the circulation of the pledge without formally banning it. The history of the pledge reveals the tension between the urge to ban and the sure knowledge that a ban would bring the Congress more popularity. Although there were several versions of the pledge, the sentiments expressed in all were anti-colonial; yet it was the context—and not the content—of the pledge that determined the chances of it being banned in any given year.

Ideology versus 'Law and Order': Congress Ministries' Dilemmas

During their period in office (1937–1939), Congress ministries were dogged by the tension between administrative exigencies and ideological commitments. The arena of free speech was one where these tensions were dramatically apparent. Even as Congress governments assumed power, its senior personnel were not very sure of how censorship would operate in this changed context. In September 1937, Hridaynath Kunzru, a member of the Council of State

---

[23] Note by Tottenham, 3 January 1943. Note by Maxwell, 13 January 1943, GOI Home Political, f. 3/3, 1943, NAI. Sir Richard Tottenham joined the ICS in 1914 and began his career as Assistant Collector with the Government of Madras. In 1936, he served as Secretary, Army Department, GOI.

[24] Government of Madras Public (Press) Department (Deptt) communication no. S/85-3/43, 19 May 1943, GOI Home Political, f. 3/3, 1943, NAI.

[25] Position summarized in telegram R no. 164 from HD to PSV, 13 January 1941, GOI Home Political (I), f. 3/7, 1941, NAI.

wanted to know, for instance, if 'proscriptions of books in the provinces [would] depend in future on the Government of India or on the Provincial Governments'. The Home Member, Sir H.D. Craik,[26] explained that the power of banning was shared: the GOI could ban imported books under the SCA, while provincial governments could use either the IPA 1931 or section 99 CrPC to ban publications. This meant that publications from abroad could be banned by the GOI in India even if they were not banned by provincial governments. When discussing the General Communist Notification of 1932 (banning all publications emanating from or affiliated in any way to the Comintern), P.N. Sapru wanted to know what would be done if there were communist governments in the provinces; the president of the Council of States disallowed the question as it was 'hypothetical'.[27]

There were variations within Congress ministries with regard to repressive measures to be used against radicals. Sunil Chander has indicated that with regard to political militancy the Premiers of Madras and Bombay (C. Rajagopalachari and B.G. Kher respectively) favoured repressive action administered promptly, while those of UP and Orissa (G.B. Pant and Biswanath Das respectively) were more cautious. This difference of attitude was visible to leftists, who considered Madras and Bombay the 'hardest' Congress provinces, while the British found them the 'safest'.[28] The Madras government under C. Rajagopalachari, for instance, prosecuted two Congress Socialists (S.S. Batliwala and Y. Meherally) for seditious speeches in 1937. The latter was let off, and the former sentenced to six months' imprisonment.

Although Nehru in his capacity as Congress president occasionally found attitudes in his own party erring on the repressive side, men on the ground— both British officials in an earlier period and Congressmen in the phase of provincial autonomy—exercised their own discretionary powers when it came to banning, and unbanning, publications.[29] A vivid illustration of this comes from Bombay: during a visit to Bombay, Nehru asked K.M. Munshi, the

---

[26] Sir H.D. Craik was an ICS officer who served as Chief Secretary, Punjab (1922–1927), Home Member (1934–1938) and Punjab Governor (1938–1941).

[27] Council of State debate, 14 September 1937, extracts in GOI Home Political, f. 27/18, 1937, NAI.

[28] Chander, 'Congress, the Raj and Conflict in Provincial Autonomy', 91.

[29] K.M. Munshi, interviewer not mentioned, 18 October 1966, 3–6, NMML OHP. Speaking of a later period, Munshi (1887–1971) commented that Nehru erred in that he wanted a full-fledged democracy in addition to fundamental rights, as well as supremacy of Parliament; Munshi opined that the three could not exist together.

Home Minister of Bombay, why he had not removed the ban on communists, and why he had not cancelled proscription orders of books. When Munshi replied that there were hundreds of files on proscribed books, and he had to go through all of them, Nehru lost his temper and commented: 'You have already become a police officer!' On the other hand, the Governor of Bombay, Lord Brabourne, told Munshi that communists leaders would be released only 'over his dead body'. Such were the competing pulls and pressures operating on the Congressmen on the spot.

In the self-assessment of Congress leaders immediately after assumption of power, the victory of the Congress had also been the victory of civil liberties in India. In October 1937, for instance, Nehru contrasted the situation with regard to civil liberties before and after the elections. In his opinion, 'It seemed that a heavy burden had been taken away, and people in towns and villages breathed more freely': organizations that were earlier banned were now no longer so, many political prisoners were released, newspaper securities returned, and the 'continuous shadowing of and spying on the people engaged in public work became less obvious'. On the other hand, in his opinion, non-Congress governments in Punjab and Bengal continued suppressing the press: the press was 'terrorized' by demand for heavy securities in both these provinces, and by a strict censorship in Bengal. However, Nehru admitted that even Congress ministries were in some respects helpless on account of the interference of the central government; one such matter concerned the banning of books (or refusal of entry) under the SCA, which provincial governments could not control. As he put it: 'This banning and stoppage of books has been the public scandal in India. The scandal continues.'[30]

Committed to policies enunciated and promised when they were not in power, Congress ministries did in fact remove restrictions on newspapers and associations, and committed themselves to the release of political prisoners. The Secretary of State noted in December 1937:

> Everywhere in Congress provinces, almost complete liberty of speech has been allowed to agitators and, in some cases, restrictions have even been placed on the reporting of their speeches by the police. Where, as in one case in Madras, a speaker has been prosecuted for sedition, the Ministry has been severely criticised. The Ministries thus find their hands tied in using measures to

---

[30] Nehru's statement published in the *Bombay Chronicle*, 17 October 1937, *Towards Freedom 1937–47*, vol. 1, 1041–1042.

suppress disorder while, on the other hand, the Left wing Socialists … have been emboldened to conduct open agitation, threatening peace and stability.[31]

The Madras case was a reference to an event in October 1937 when C. Rajagopalachari, the Congress Premier of Madras, sanctioned the prosecution of a member of the Congress Socialist Party (S.S. Batliwala) for 'violent speech'. At the same time, he released two political prisoners held by the government to deflect attention from this prosecution. This created a 'furore' in the Congress, and it was only on account of the support he received from Gandhi and Nehru that this action escaped condemnation.[32]

What Nehru considered the liberty of the press, the colonial state deemed irresponsible license. The Secretary of State noted that after the assumption of office by Congress ministries in 1937 in UP, for example, an anti-police day was held in Kanpur on 24 October, in which speeches were made including 'incitements to murder the police'. In his opinion, these sentiments were not approved of by Nehru or the Congress ministry; at the same time they were either unwilling or afraid to use their powers to curb such activities.[33]

In October 1937, the AICC directed Congress ministries to lift the ban on political literature, which was a reference mostly to communist publications, of which the GOI had been wary, afraid that communist ideas combined with nationalist ones could prove to be a potent and dangerous mix. Soon after, however, the process of backtracking began. Nehru conceded in late October 1937 that although it would be 'perfectly absurd' for the Congress—members of which bore the tag 'seditious' as a badge of pride—to take action against supposedly seditious activities, he could also imagine cases (he listed 'violence against the state' and 'communal violence' as examples) when doing so became inevitable. He hoped that the Congress would take a 'nonviolent approach' in such cases, but also left the door open for state action, 'for fear of a higher wrong'.[34] Writing in the *Harijan* the same month, even Gandhi clarified that

---

[31] Secretary of State's 'Appreciation of Political Situation in India', 21 December 1937, Cabinet Papers 24/273, *Towards Freedom 1937–47*, vol. 1, 1287–1289.

[32] Sunil Chander, 'The Congress Ministries and the British Authorities in the Working of Provincial Autonomy, 1936–39: Aspects of Conflict between the Congress and the Raj', unpublished M.Litt. dissertation submitted to Trinity College, Oxford, 1983 (copy in NMML, New Delhi), 28–29.

[33] Secretary of State's 'Appreciation of Political Situation in India', Cabinet Papers 24/273, 26 November 1937, *Towards Freedom 1937–47*, vol. 1, 1195–1198.

[34] 'On the Congress Attitude to Sedition', *Selected Works of Jawaharlal Nehru, Series 1 (SWJN1)*, ed. S. Gopal (New Delhi: Jawaharlal Nehru Memorial Fund), vol. 8,

'Civil Liberty is not criminal Liberty', as he considered the issue of Congress governments inflicting punishments for activities that interfered with the maintenance of law and order. He sought to make his commitment to non-violence compatible with the state's need to protect itself. In his opinion, civil liberty was the right to say and do what one liked 'within the ordinary law of the land'. He urged that those provisions of the IPC, the CrPC and the Special Powers Legislation enacted by the British for their own protection be 'ruled out of operation' by Congress ministries, but the latter were nevertheless to retain powers to exercise against those who 'in the name of civil liberty, preach lawlessness in the popular sense of the term'. Gandhi continued that although some argued that Congress ministries pledged to non-violence could not 'resort to legal processes involving punishments', 'I have, personally, not found a way out of punishments and punitive restrictions in all conceivable cases'. There was no doubt in his mind that Congress ministers, while exploring the possibilities of 'non-violent punishments', 'cannot ignore incitements to violence and manifestly violent speech, even though they themselves run the risk of being styled violent'.[35] Assumption of state power came with its own set of responsibilities and constraints, and demanded the reconciliation—however uncomfortable—of oft-stated principles with harsher ground realities.

In January 1938, the Congress Working Committee (CWC) passed a resolution outlining broad policies for its ministries to follow when faced with law and order problems. Although the principles of civil liberty and democracy were to guide the ministries, and persuasion was to be the first weapon of choice, 'but in spite of every desire to avoid it, coercive action may become necessary and in such cases Ministries will inevitably have to undertake it. Such coercive action should only be undertaken where there has been violence or incitement to violence or communal strife'.[36]

---

343. This was a speech made at the AICC session in Calcutta on 30 October 1937 during a discussion on the policy of Congress ministries to tackling sedition and violence. Nehru stated: 'We cannot say straightaway that even when the question of violence in involved, even when the whole policy of the Congress should be to avoid prosecution, even though a person has offended against the law, the right approach to this problem for the Congress Ministry should be a nonviolent approach.'

[35] *Harijan*, 23 October 1937, *Towards Freedom 1937–47*, vol. 1, 1065–1066.

[36] CWC resolution passed on 4 January 1938, quoted in letter from the Secretary of State, Marquess of Zetland, to the Viceroy, Lord Linlithgow, 17 January 1938, Linlithgow papers, *Towards Freedom: Documents on the Movement for Independence in India 1938*, ed. Basudev Chatterji (New Delhi: Indian Council for Historical Research/Oxford

Later the same year, in September 1938, a resolution drafted by Gandhi was passed at the AICC session. This stated that the Congress would support measures by its ministries 'for the defence of life and property', in a context where many people, including Congressmen, were 'found in the name of civil liberty to advocate murder, arson, looting and class war by violent means' and when 'several newspapers are carrying on a campaign of falsehood and violence calculated to incite the readers to violence and to lead to communal conflicts'. The resolution therefore warned the public that 'civil liberty does not cover acts of or incitement to violence or promulgation of palpable falsehoods'.[37] In protest, Congress Socialists walked out of the meeting. At times, the voice of nationalists in power did not sound very different from that of the colonial state.

Functionaries of Congress ministries were animated by their desire to not be compared to colonial officials in their functioning. Writing to the Premier of Bombay, B.G. Kher, in April 1939, Congress leader Vallabhbhai Patel suggested that a ban on the Communist Party could only be imposed on the basis of evidence in the form of confidential surveillance reports linking them with violent activities. But the problem, wrote Patel, was: 'We cannot quote such report as evidence against our own people; when we have ourselves in the past condemned such a process when it was so used against us.' Ever the pragmatist, Patel did not think the ban was a good idea in any case, as '…would [it] not be better to let that organization function openly instead of a nominal ban which is not at all effective and which puts you in an embarrassing position'.[38]

Not only the GOI, but even newspapers made (unfavourable) comparisons between Congress ministries and their colonial predecessor. In August 1939, the Bombay government forbade five newspapers (three Muslim-owned and two Parsi-owned) from reporting riots that marked the onset of Prohibition

---

University Press, 1999), part 1, document no. 1.i.5A., 14. The Secretary of State found this attitude 'unexpectedly reassuring', although he was surprised that the CWC had passed such a resolution. The Secretary of State for India, the Marquess of Zetland, was appointed to that position in June 1935. He had served as Aide-de-camp to the Viceroy between 1900 and 1907 and as the Governor of Bengal between 1917 and 1922. He had authored a number of travelogues on Asia and also Curzon's authorized biography in 1928.

[37] Gandhi's draft resolution on civil liberty, passed on 26 September 1938, *Towards Freedom 1938*, part I, document no.1.ii.10, 102–103.

[38] Letter from Patel to B.G. Kher, 10 April 1939, in *Nehru–Patel: Agreement Within Differences, Select Documents and Correspondences, 1933–50*, ed. Neerja Singh (New Delhi: National Book Trust, 2010), 48–49.

in Bombay. This was pre-censorship, as the papers were forbidden (under section 144 of the CrPC) from carrying any news, articles, or comments on the riots for a period of two months, as well as on any other riots within the two month period, unless the matter was approved by the Public Relations Officer. Additionally, these papers were also restricted from covering protests against the new Urban Immovable Property Tax. A *Times of India* editorial supported the government's first measure (as it was seen as a much-needed effort to dampen communal feeling) but bitterly criticized the second as being an attack on the rights of the press as well as the public to hold up government decisions to scrutiny. The newspaper accused the government of being 'unduly squeamish', the censorship 'unwarranted', and a Congress ministry attacking the liberty of the press most ironic.[39]

It is not surprising that the GOI took a keen interest in the successes—and, more importantly, the failures—of their erstwhile opponents, who became their partners in government in 1937. In this context, what came to be known as the 'Parmanand case' was illustrative not only of the difficulties arising during the operation of provincial autonomy but also of the difficulties regarding practically implementing an abstract principle. What was essentially a conflict over freedom of speech assumed such serious proportions that the UP Governor confided to the Viceroy that he thought there was a 'very definite possibility' that the Congress government would resign.[40] Pandit Parmanand had been sentenced to death by the British in 1915 for participating in an anti-colonial conspiracy, although the sentence was reduced to transportation for life. All other 42 prisoners sentenced with him were released in 1928 except him, as he had 'persistently shown a complete absence of any sign of having reformed'. He was released only in August 1937 after the Congress assumed power in UP. Along with other released prisoners, Parmanand began a tour of UP where he gave speeches that were deemed to be 'progressively more violent'.[41] While the

---

[39] *Times of India*, 'Bombay Press Ban', editorial, 3 August 1939. For the situation prevailing in Bombay, and B.G. Kher's rule, see Margarita Barns, *The Indian Press: A History of the Growth of Public Opinion in India* (London: George Allen & Unwin, 1940), 428–431.

[40] Letter from UP Governor, Sir Harry Haig, to the Viceroy, 13 December 1937, Haig Papers, *Towards Freedom 1937–47*, vol. 1, 1259–1262. In fact, Haig wrote to Linlithgow detailing the action to be taken if and when the ministry resigned. See letter from Haig to Linlithgow, 14 December 1937, Haig Papers, *Towards Freedom 1937–47*, vol. 1, 1263–1265.

[41] Memorandum from the Secretary of State to the British Cabinet, Cabinet Papers 24/273, *Towards Freedom 1937–47*, vol. 1, 1277–1282. Pandit Parmananda (of Jhansi)

British Governor of UP, Sir Harry Haig, thought his prosecution a necessity, both the UP Cabinet as well as the Congress Premier of UP, G.B. Pant, were in favour of a warning being given instead, as they feared that public opinion would turn against them.[42] Pant assured the Governor that once a warning was given, 'he would not shrink from prosecution, and considered that he would have no difficulty in justifying his position to his followers'.[43] He also told the Governor that he feared that his followers would pass a vote of 'no-confidence' against him if he agreed to the prosecution. He did not want, he said, to be 'drawn gradually into a policy of prosecution for seditious speeches'.[44] In other words, the Congress Premier had to keep his core constituency—the Indian public, as well as Congress workers—in mind when proceeding with penal action. Although even the Governor of UP credited Pant with being committed to the idea of freedom of expression,[45] it is clear from the negotiations over

---

is not to be confused with Bhai Parmananda, a prominent leader of the Hindu Mahasabha. For his biographical profile, see Anil Nauria, 'Some Did Not Seek Clemency: Pandit Parmanand of Jhansi', *Indian Express*, 1 March 2001, available at https://www.scribd.com/doc/93896220/Pandit-Parmanand-of-Jhansi (accessed 19 January 2019).

[42] Telegram from Haig to Linlithgow, 27 November 1937, Haig Papers, *Towards Freedom 1937–47*, vol. 1, 1199. G.B. Pant wrote to the Governor regretting that the two sides (the Governor and the Cabinet) were not able to reach a mutually acceptable decision on the case, and mentioning that the Congress government was not prepared to take responsibility for the decision taken (to prosecute). Letter from Pant to Haig, 28 November 1937, Haig Papers, *Towards Freedom 1937–47*, vol. 1, 1203.

[43] Letter from Pant to Haig, 13 December 1937, Haig Papers, *Towards Freedom 1937–47*, vol. 1, 1259–1262. The policy of the Congress ministry in UP was 'not to institute prosecutions for seditious speeches without a personal warning having been previously given'. Memorandum from the Secretary of State to the British Cabinet, Cabinet Papers 24/273, *Towards Freedom 1937–47*, vol. 1, 1277–1282.

[44] According to the Secretary of State, Pant emphasized 'his objection in principle to prosecution without individual warning, but declared that where such warning had been given, he would prosecute'. Memorandum from the Secretary of State to the British Cabinet, Cabinet Papers 24/273, *Towards Freedom 1937–47*, vol. 1, 1277–1282.

[45] Haig wrote to the Viceroy that '… he [Pant] has exceedingly strong personal convictions about democratic principles, and actions which circumstances force upon him which are in conflict with his general ideas of the liberty of the subject are extremely repugnant to him. His reluctance [to prosecute Parmanand] should not be attributed merely to fear of criticism; it represents in large part his convictions'.

the Parmanand case that for the Congress ministries it was simply not enough only to be tolerant of expression of opinion, but to be seen to be so.

In the event, even as Haig and Pant were working out a compromise solution, Parmanand was arrested in Delhi for a different offence. After consultation with the Congress high command, the UP government decided not to agree to Parmanand's prosecution on charges of sedition, suggesting instead that he be imprisoned on the basis of the Delhi case. The UP Premier would then issue a warning against violent speeches, but would not be directly blamed for Parmanand's prosecution for another charge, a prosecution that would in any case have the effect of removing him from circulation for a few months at least.[46] Lord Linlithgow could barely conceal his glee at the dilemma caused by violent speeches to his political opponents, who very publicly espoused non-violence:

> I have some reason to believe that Congress themselves feel that this particular case is a bad one from their point of view, that they find themselves (though entirely as a result of their own action) on bad ground, and that they would be not unwilling to compromise, though the position is complicated by Pant's somewhat doctrinaire outlook.... In this particular instance our ground is very good, given the objectionable nature of the speech made by Parmanand which is, I would judge, of such a character as to offend grievously against the Mahatma's non-violent theories, and equally of such a character that the public, whether here or at Home, could not well blame us for taking drastic action.[47]

Even as the Parmanand issue was being resolved, the Congress ministry in UP supported the Kanpur District Magistrate when he prohibited 14 people from making speeches or issuing statements for two months during a period of labour unrest in November 1937. As the UP Governor put it:

> ... he [Pant] has an exceedingly vigorous and troublesome left wing opposition. He is prepared, *when in his judgment conditions require it*, to face this opposition, and at present he can, when he faces it, beat it. This was shown in the attack

Letter from Haig to Linlithgow, 24 December 1937. Linlithgow Papers, *Towards Freedom 1937–47*, vol. 1, 1292–1296.

[46] Memorandum from the Secretary of State to the British Cabinet, Cabinet Papers 24/273, *Towards Freedom 1937–47*, vol. 1, 1277–1282.

[47] Letter from Linlithgow to Governor Punjab, Sir H.W. Emerson, 22 December 1937, Linlithgow Papers, *Towards Freedom 1937–47*, vol. 1, 1290–1291.

made on him over his action taken at Cawnpore. But I think he had to exert all his authority on that occasion.[48]

Freedom of expression, then, was a principle to be trotted out on some occasions, and held in abeyance in yet others. It was an argument summoned by the Congress ministry when the emotive issue of sedition came up, and when public opinion was in favour of the transgression (as in the Parmanand case), but forgotten when its other was required to tackle left-wing ideas (as in Kanpur).[49] At any rate, as the subsequent years were to prove, it was easier for Indian nationalists to uphold the ideal of fully free speech when they were in opposition to the colonial state than when they themselves assumed state power.

---

[48] Letter from Haig to Linlithgow, 24 December 1937, Linlithgow Papers, *Towards Freedom 1937–47*, vol. 1, 1292–1296, emphasis added.

[49] My interpretation of this episode, though based on the same primary sources as those used by Gyanesh Kudaisya, differs since he takes a much more sympathetic view of Pant's actions. Kudaisya, *Region, Nation, 'Heartland': Uttar Pradesh in India's Body Politic* (New Delhi: Sage, 2006), 236–239.

PART II

Protests and Publicity
Banning Non-Indian Authors

In official circles in 20th-century colonial India, to ban or not to ban, that was the question. In a colonial context, and against the backdrop of an anti-colonial movement, it is all too easy to see censorship of publications operating along racial lines, and to assume that only publications by Indian authors were subject to censorship. However, non-Indian authors—former colonial officials and soldiers, journalists, missionaries and travellers—writing in English on matters concerning India commanded audiences in their home countries in addition to being read by an influential section of the Indian population. Precisely because they escaped colonial stereotyping about 'seditious natives', non-Indian authors' words carried a greater illusion of neutrality, and sometimes more weight. It was one thing to ban books written by leaders and ideologues of anti-colonial movements and quite another to ban those written by well-known Western writers. The former could be justified as an administrative decision made in the interest of preserving law and order; the latter smacked of a cover-up. By reconstructing the question of—and the controversy over—the possible banning of such books by the colonial state in the 1920s–1930s, it becomes possible to question commonly held assumptions about the conduct of the censorship of publications in late colonial India.

Newspaper articles in contemporary India routinely dredge up lists of books banned by the colonial state, including many by foreign authors, but these lists are reproduced from official gazette notifications without any comment on—or understanding of—how they came to be banned in the first place.[1] By examining debates within the state and in the public sphere about some of these banned books, Part II of this book seeks to complicate the easy association of censorship with race and nationality in a colonial context. What criteria did the colonial state use to decide if a book by a non-Indian author was worth banning? Was it the content of the book? Was it the political context in which it was published? Or did factors like the potential size of readership and range of circulation, popularity of the author, price of the book, or protests against it by the public also play a role? In other words, was there a combination of criteria that we may term and identify as the 'ban formula'? Can such a formula give us insights into the rationale for state censorship of publication—then, and now? In order to recover and recount the histories of some of these banned books, the two chapters that follow juxtapose accounts of public campaigns against particular books with official correspondence, often reacting to public pressure.

Publications from abroad were banned by the GOI—and not by provincial governments—under the provisions of the SCA. Decisions on bans were made by officials of the HD, in consultation with the IB and in cooperation with the India Office in London. Publications that were sent to India from abroad could be detained by either customs or postal authorities. Officials who were doubtful about the status of a publication consulted either the police or the IB, upon whose advice they released or confiscated the item in question. If the publications were not returned, then confiscation was presumed, else the book was passed along to the recipient.[2] Once the HD of the GOI decided to ban a particular title, a notification was issued by the Finance Department and published in the *Gazette of India*.

---

[1] For example, see Hasan Suroor, 'You Can't Read This Book', *The Hindu*, 4 March 2012; Rajeev Dhavan, 'Book Bans Are Not New', *Times of India*, 28 October 1988. In the chapter titled 'Censorship and Intolerance in India' in his *Publish and Be Damned*, Rajeev Dhavan lists books banned under the SCA without mentioning any details other than those that accompanied the notifications published in the *Gazette of India*. See Dhavan, *Publish*, 148. These books are also listed, but not discussed, in two (non-comprehensive) bibliographies of literature banned in colonial India: N. Gerald Barrier, 'A Guide to Banned Literature', which forms Part Two of his *Banned*, 163–297, and Graham Shaw and Mary Lloyd (eds), *Publications Proscribed by the Government of India* (London: The British Library, 1985).

[2] Note by I.H. Stephenson, 4 November 1937, GOI Home Political, f 41/17, 1937, NAI.

The historian Diana Heath estimates that by 1911 India was importing 12 million packages of books and newspapers annually from Britain.[3] Given this figure, the number of individual titles banned under the SCA (excluding those banned under the General Communist Notification of 1932)[4] was never very large. Between 1909 and 1945, the SCA had been invoked 132 times to ban specific books, issues of newspapers or even all publications emanating from a single source. For instance, all publications issued by the Hindustan Ghadr Party in San Francisco were banned in 1920.[5] However, the significance of these publications as case studies for providing insights into the rationale for censorship cannot be overstated. Records of centralized decision making about them convey considerable insight into the rationale for—and disagreements over—banning the circulation of specific titles in India. In the case of books published in Britain that were banned in India, the India Office and the GOI worked together to address publishers' complaints; even as they presented a united front in public, they occasionally failed to agree on whether, and how, to ban.

---

[3] Deana Heath has shown how British booksellers expanded book exports to India and Australia since the 1870s, facilitating a more culturally interconnected empire. Deana Heath, 'Purity, Obscenity and the Making of an Imperial Censorship System', in *Media and the British Empire*, ed. Chandrika Kaul (Basingstoke and New York: Palgrave Macmillan, 2006), 162–163.

[4] In 1932, the import of publications emanating from the Communist International (Comintern) or affiliated organizations was banned under the SCA, and this blanket ban was referred to subsequently as the 'General Communist Notification'. Finance Department (Customs) notification 61, 10 September 1932. CBR, Customs Duties, f. R. Dis.453-Cus-II-32, 1932, NAI.

[5] Data compiled from 'Revised Statement of Newspapers, etc. prohibited from entering India under Section 19 of the Sea Customs Act (Act VIII of 1878), Completed to 14 June 1941', prepared by the IB. GOI Home Political, f. 41/4, 1946, NAI. This list contains addenda till 1945.

3

Critiques of Indian Society
Katherine Mayo's Long Shadow

Ironically, almost all books by foreign authors that were considered worthy of being banned in India were measured against an extremely controversial book that was *not* itself banned: American journalist Katherine Mayo's extremely critical account of India, titled *Mother India*, published in 1927.[1] In fact, of the four books that Mayo wrote on India over the course of almost a decade, only the last one (*The Face of Mother India*) was banned (in 1936). *Mother India*, a polemic against Indians' suitability for self-rule, was considered 'a must-read for many in British colonial circles in the 1920s', and had 20 printings between 1928 and 1930.[2] At the time of its publication in 1927, the allegation was frequently made in India that the GOI had assisted in its production financially and otherwise, that the India Office had been complicit in ensuring that it was widely distributed and read, and that the book itself was intended to slow

---

[1] Mayo's *Mother India* has received considerable attention from scholars. In 1971, Manoranjan Jha established that social reform in India was not Mayo's primary concern; he also outlined the official patronage given to Mayo. Jha argued that ever since American Independence, public authorities in Great Britain were wary of 'the possibility of American attitude towards British rule in India turning hostile'. Manoranjan Jha, *Katherine Mayo and India* (New Delhi: People's Publishing House, 1971), 1. Mrinalini Sinha refers only in passing to the banning of *The Face of Mother India*. See Mrinalini Sinha, *Specters of Mother India: The Global Restructuring of an Empire* (Durham, NC: Duke University Press, 2006), 150. Kumari Jayawardena has also examined the controversy over *Mother India* in *The White Woman's Other Burden: Western Women and South Asia during British Colonial Rule* (New York: Routledge, 1995), 95–98.

[2] Andrew Muldoon, *Empire, Politics, and the Creation of the 1935 India Act: Last Act of the Raj* (Farnham: Ashgate, 2009), 21.

down constitutional reform (by indicting Indians as unsuitable for it). All these allegations were denied repeatedly by the GOI and the India Office.[3] In her full-length work on this book and its legacy, Mrinalini Sinha has conclusively established that the India Office had in fact asked the GOI to assist Mayo, and that Mayo's central thesis (about Hindu promiscuity) was suggested to her by an India Office official.[4]

The controversy over the GOI's failure to ban Mayo's *Mother India* was revived, or referred to, in the case of Mayo's other books as well as in other cases of negative assessments of Indian society by foreign authors. However, scholars have focused their attention exclusively on the controversial *Mother India*, to the exclusion of Mayo's other books.[5] This chapter will begin by examining three of Mayo's lesser-known books on India, including the banned one, in order to isolate the factors that led to the banning of some books and not others. Subsequently, it will discuss banned books by other non-Indian authors.

Katherine Mayo's *Slaves of the Gods* (1929)

In March 1929, the GOI informed the India Office in London about the forthcoming publication of Mayo's *Slaves of the Gods*, which was described in an intercepted press telegram as 'a collection of stories of Hindu India, prominence

---

[3] In 1927, the Home Member, Sir James Crerar, 'emphatically' repudiated the suggestion made in the Legislative Assembly (LA) that the GOI had assisted Mayo financially and otherwise in the writing of *Mother India*. Crerar's answer in response to questions asked by M.S. Aney on 20 September 1927, GOI Home Political, f. 10/62, 1927, NAI. The same year in the British Parliament the Under Secretary of State for India asserted that Mayo had received no assistance either from the India Office or the GOI 'beyond the supply of official information on matters of fact which is afforded to any member of the public who asks for it'. The question was asked by Ronnie Smith on 14 November 1927. When the Allahabad based *Leader* alleged, quoting 'a distinguished Indian who returned from Europe this morning', that the India Office had purchased and distributed to the public 5,000 copies of Mayo's book, a question about this was asked in the LA, and the allegation denied by Crerar in March 1928. The *Leader* article was published on 9 November 1927 and answer in the LA was given to a question asked by R.K. Shanmukham Chetty on 2 March 1928. GOI Home Political, f. 20/II, 1928, NAI.

[4] Sinha, *Specters*, 78–79.

[5] Although Manoranjan Jha briefly discusses official debates over the question of banning Mayo's books *Slaves of the Gods* and *Volume Two*, he does not discuss the actual ban on *The Face of Mother India*. Jha, *Katherine Mayo*, 99–101.

being given to child-wife, temple prostitute, etc., and to contain twelve records carefully verified from real life which illustrate evils from which India suffers'. According to Mayo herself, the book was fact-based fiction. Each story was preceded by a statement to the effect that 'This narrative is taken from real life.… The names assigned to the characters in the narrative are substitutes for those actually borne by the persons concerned.' Each story was followed by a section called 'Sidelights from India', where Mayo quoted Legislative Assembly (LA) debates, memoirs, official reports and newspapers to substantiate the charges made in the stories. The arrival of the Simon Commission to India (in February 1928, to examine questions of constitutional reform) with no Indian members, and the attendant protests by Indian nationalists against the Commission had foregrounded issues of Indians' political rights in a colonial context. The GOI took the view that the publication of the book could have 'very unfortunate political consequences', and suggested that either pressure be brought to bear upon its London based publishers (Jonathan Cape) or the book be banned entry into India. The GOI asked the India Office for an advance copy of the book, and for advice regarding a possible ban on it. The India Office did not think it 'advisable to approach either the author or publishers with a request for suppression as this is certain to be of no use'. They admitted that they had no means of suppression unless the police took action on grounds of indecency, which again was unlikely.[6] Even as this trans-continental discussion was going on, the GOI had to face a question in the LA in India asking if they were planning to ban it, and to this they gave a non-committal answer.[7]

Given Mayo's reputation and the controversy *Mother India* had caused only two years prior, the GOI swung promptly into action. After receiving and examining an advance copy of the book, the India Office summarized its contents in a long telegram to the GOI. The stated purpose of the author was to cite concrete examples of the points she had made in *Mother India*, and she dealt with 12 subjects, each said to be based on facts, and supplemented by quotations from Indian speeches and writings testifying to the existence of these ills. The themes addressed included a child widow's sati, the conversion

---

[6] Telegram P. no. 1037-S, 9 March 1929 from the Viceroy to the Secretary of State; Telegram P. no. 929, 14 March 1929 from the Secretary of State to the Viceroy, GOI Home Political, f. 93, 1929, NAI.

[7] Question asked by Gaya Prasad Singh in the LA on 18 March 1929. The Home Member, Sir James Crerar, replied that the government had read about the book in the press, but as it had not been published, they could not comment on a possible ban. GOI Home Political, f. 93, 1929, NAI.

to Islam of a Hindu girl about to be forced into marriage with an old man, the death of a child bride in Bengal, a description of the life of *devadasis* (temple dancers), and the problems faced by an Indian doctor treating outcastes. Other stories dealt with the reformation and heroism of sweepers attached to a regiment in Mesopotamia, an account of palace intrigue in an Indian state and child sacrifice, the suicide of a Bengali widow after her refusal to give up her only garment (a Manchester sari), female infanticide in Punjab, the refusal of Hindus to kill useless and harmful animals, and the fate of a child patient in a women's hospital. The India Office commented that some chapters compared Hinduism unfavourably with Islam, and were likely to be controversial. At the same time, they urged that it would be a 'great mistake' to ban the book, as it was likely to be ineffective, and would expose the GOI to the charge that they were shielding Hindus from the unpleasant truth.[8]

In the meantime, the book had caused a sensation in both the British and Indian press. All through March 1929 several Indian-owned newspapers commented adversely on it. One headline screamed 'Gutter Inspectress at Her Dirty Game!' and commented that the GOI's refusal to ban *Mother India* had encouraged Mayo further.[9] In the last week of March, newspapers all across India—including *Hindu Herald* (Lahore), *The Tribune* (Lahore), *Bombay Chronicle* (Bombay), *Justice* (Madras), *Hindustan Times* (Delhi), *Basumati* (Calcutta), *Princely India* (Delhi) and *Mahratta* (Poona)—railed against the book in strong terms, the last one even stating that if the book was not banned people would conclude that it had been sponsored by the government.[10] Even British-owned newspapers published in India did not spare the book. *The Pioneer* commented that the book was 'a series of hazardous generalizations', and predicted that it would exacerbate Hindu feeling; the *Civil and Military Gazette* did not approve of her general body of work, terming it 'a prostitution of the art for the sake of the sensational'.[11] Even the *Muslim Outlook* (Lahore), which appeared to support some of the charges made in the book (it reported

---

[8] Each of the 12 stories was summarized succinctly by the India Office in their telegram to the GOI. Telegram P. no. 1017, 21 March 1929 from the Secretary of State to the Viceroy, GOI Home Political, f. 93, 1929, NAI.

[9] *Indian National Herald* (Bombay), 4 March 1929.

[10] *Hindu Herald*, 27 March 1929; *The Tribune*, 28 March 1929; *Bombay Chronicle*, 28 March 1929; *Justice*, 28 March 1929; *Hindustan Times*, 30 March 1929; *Basumati*, 31 March 1929; *Princely India*, 5 April 1929; and *Mahratta*, 31 March 1929.

[11] *The Pioneer*, 28 March 1929; *Civil and Military Gazette*, 29 March 1929. *The Englishman* (Calcutta) repeated reviews from the British press without taking an independent stand on the matter. *The Englishman*, 8 April 1929.

an interview of Mayo with the *Daily Mail* of London, but headlined the piece 'Hindus a Decadent Race', and the tone of the report seemed to support the charge), nevertheless termed the author vindictive, and felt that she was 'determined' to be at war with Hindus.[12]

However, somewhat lost in the clamour of demands for a ban, there were also segments of Indian society that did *not* want the book banned. For instance, the Audi (Depressed Classes) Sabha of Ferozepore (Ferozpur) Cantonment petitioned the GOI urging them not to make up their minds about the book without taking their views into account. Calling Mayo 'a merciful humanitarian of the West', this organization claimed that *Mother India* had been a great help to them. The Congress—whom they accused of monopolizing the Indian press and platform and controlling 'thousands of newspapers and their editors'—was not, they urged, to be allowed to 'gag the voice of truth' by demanding a ban on the book.[13] Here is a revealing fragment of the divisions within Indians, come to the fore in the context of banning a book.

Slaves of the Gods received mixed reviews in the British press: *The Spectator* termed the work a 'hideous travesty', while the *Manchester Guardian* wrote that although Mayo had helped the cause of Indian women, sati and infanticide were no more characteristic of the Indian than lynching was of the American civilization.[14] It was against this backdrop that the GOI and the India Office discussed banning the book. Before he had read the book himself, the Home Secretary GOI, Sir Harry Haig, had suggested that banning *Slaves* 'would not be without definite political advantage', as it would remove the suspicion that Mayo was working under the direct patronage of the GOI.[15] However, a month later, he changed his mind after reading the book. In his view, *Slaves* was

> ... simply 'Mother India' presented in the form of sensational fiction. As such it does not carry nearly as much conviction as 'Mother India', for the ordinary reader distinguishes pretty clearly between sensational fiction and fact. Moreover there is nothing new in it, and everyone is getting a little tired of 'Mother India'. It seems to me that unless the Indian press behaves with a

---

[12] *Muslim Outlook*, 28 March 1929 and 31 March 1929.

[13] Petition issued along with a resolution passed by the Audi Sabha at Ferozepore Cantonment on 28 March 1929. Printed pamphlet in GOI Home Political, f. 93, 1929, NAI.

[14] Reported in *The Pioneer*, 8 April 1929, and the *Daily Chronicle*, 10 April 1929, respectively.

[15] Note by Haig, 15 March 1929, GOI Home Political, f. 93, 1929, NAI.

great lack of intelligence (unfortunately we cannot discount this contingency) the book should not attract very much notice either outside or inside India. My conclusion, therefore, is that we should leave it alone.[16]

The Viceroy, Lord Irwin, agreed with this course of action[17] and the India Office was duly informed that the book was not going to be banned.[18] Despite having attracted considerable attention—and excited public outrage—in India and Britain, it was still not banned. Because it was packaged as fiction (albeit based on fact), and because it was perceived to be unoriginal, it was deemed to be safe for consumption in India. Originality and genre: these were the two yardsticks employed in this case.

Katherine Mayo's *Volume Two* (1931)

Mayo's books on India were published with alarming regularity; news about the forthcoming publication of *Volume Two* in London by Jonathan Cape in 1931 received wide publicity in India. *Volume Two* dealt with the subject of child marriage, and was a summary, with comments, of the Age of Consent Committee's report and evidence. The committee consisted of nine Indians and a British woman doctor. The evidence collected by the committee filled nine volumes and over 4,500 pages. Its report resulted in the raising of the legal marriage age of Indian girls to 14 years. Mayo emphasized that even if there was child marriage among non-Hindus in India, this was a result of Hindu influence, and the concept was a Hindu 'concept', 'concern' and 'responsibility'.[19] The book was dedicated 'To Those Persons in India Who Strive to End Hindu Child Marriage'. She termed the Child Marriage Act an 'April Fool joke', and a smokescreen that did not address the main issues.[20]

In May 1931, the Secretary of State for India, William Wedgwood Benn, based in London, wrote to the Viceroy, Lord Willingdon, to consider the possibility of banning the book under the SCA as 'a gesture to appease possible

---

[16] Note by Haig, 15 April 1929, GOI Home Political, f. 93, 1929, NAI.

[17] Note by Haig, 1 May 1929, GOI Home Political, f. 93, 1929, NAI.

[18] Telegram P. no. 1577-S, 3 May 1929 from the Viceroy to the Secretary of State, GOI Home Political, f. 93, 1929, NAI.

[19] Katherine Mayo, *Volume Two* (London: Jonathan Cape, 1931), 8.

[20] Reported in the *Amrita Bazar Patrika*, 17 February 1931, in a news item titled 'The Incorrigible Miss Mayo'. The book was also discussed in *Justice*, 21 February 1931, and *The Pioneer*, 3 May 1931.

Hindu resentment'.[21] (This was, we must remember, just after the political truce between mainstream Indian nationalists and the colonial state, as embodied in the Gandhi–Irwin pact signed on 5 March 1931.) After receiving this communication, as many as three senior HD officials read the book in order to decide its fate. Joint Secretary, HD, C.W. Gwynne, commented that it was 'written solely from the point of view that child marriage is a Hindu custom'. He suggested that as the report as well as evidence had already been published in India, there was no point in taking action against the work under consideration, as 'such action would not appease Hindu sentiment and would give undue publicity to the present work'. In any case, once the book was published in England and America, extracts were bound to appear in Indian newspapers. He agreed with Mayo's contention (expressed in *Volume Two*) that *Mother India* had caused opposition among Indian Hindus not because it had appeared in India, but because it had appeared in the United States. The Home Secretary, H.W. Emerson,[22] and Deputy Secretary HD, S.N. Roy (an Indian), too were not in favour of banning the book, even though the latter conceded that it was biased against Hindus.[23] The Viceroy—who incidentally asked Emerson to leave him the book as he wanted to read it—did not think any action was necessary either, and none was taken. This time, Mayo's book was saved from a ban because it repeated material that was already in the public domain. Additionally, the GOI realized that if the purpose of a ban was to stop circulation of certain material, then this was likely to be unsuccessful in any case on account of press interest in the publication, and the publication of extensive extracts in newspapers. Ironically, the Indian press had given immense publicity to the very material that it wanted to be kept out of the public domain. Publicity and the likely success of prosecution were thus two factors that determined the fate of this book. A notable feature of this, and other, cases is that state personnel on the ground in India were able to exercise their judgement and take decisions on the fate of a book even when it was contrary to the advice of the Secretary of State for India.

---

[21] Telegram R. no. 1413, 1 May 1931 from the Secretary of State to the Viceroy, GOI Home Political, f. 29/6, 1931, NAI.

[22] Sir Herbert William Emerson, appointed the Governor of Punjab in 1933, joined the ICS in 1905, served as Chief Secretary to the Punjab government between 1927 and 1928, and as Home Secretary, GOI, between 1930 and 1932.

[23] Note by Gwynne, 9 June 1931; by Emerson 10 June 1931; and by Roy, 13 June 1931, GOI Home Political, f. 29/6, 1931, NAI.

Katherine Mayo's *The Face of Mother India* (1935)

Although all her books on India were controversial, and the GOI and the India Office debated the merits of banning them, Mayo's only book that finally claimed the dubious distinction was, ironically, one that contained more photographs than words. This was her fourth book on the country, titled *The Face of Mother India* and published in December 1935 in London by Hamish Hamilton. Two-thirds of the book consisted of 406 photographs; the introductory part covered only 41 pages; the subject matter was Hindu–Muslim conflict.[24] In late December 1935 the book was reviewed in the British-owned *The Statesman*, which described it as 'a picture book of India with a running commentary and it is preceded by forty pages of "story"'. It also cited the following lines to indicate the author's bias against Hinduism: 'The Muslim is the purest of monotheists.... The Hindu ... worships millions of gods, some by acts that are cardinal offences against any moral code of civilized humanity.'[25] At another place in the book, Mayo suggested:

> To all this gathering blackness there are two, in India, who remain struck blind—the Hindu, political, so wound in his own cocoon of words and arguments that he cannot discern the reality that holds a knife at his throat ... and the Terrorist, Moscow trained, who believes that when the crash for which he is working actually comes, he himself will emerge as ruler of a new world. But there is in India a third—a man as simple as the Hindu is involved, as law abiding as the terrorist is anarchic, a fanatic, if you will, but one of enormous moral courage and resistance ... he cedes nothing to the idolater, nothing to the revolutionary, and each day, gun loose in holster, he kneels before the one God, the Lord God of Israel, in the reconsecration of believing prayer.[26]

The Statesman found Mayo's argument a 'powerfully inflammatory one', and regretted that her arguments would only antagonize reformers within Hinduism. The book caused a storm of protest inside and outside India. The executive committee of the Indian National Congress of Great Britain asked

---

[24] *Star of India*, 17 December 1935.

[25] *The Statesman*, 29 December 1935.

[26] Extract from *The Face of Mother India* cited in *The Statesman*, 29 December 1935. The Home Secretary, GOI, M.G. Hallett, too cited this passage in his review of the book. GOI Home Political & K.W., f. 41/1, 1936, NAI.

the Secretary of State to ban the book throughout the empire.[27] The secretary of the Indian Journalists' Association Abroad termed the book 'the dirtiest and filthiest book of the year', and asked the British Prime Minister to ban the book in the entire empire.[28] Sir Stanley Reed, erstwhile editor of the *Times of India*, reviewed the book for the British publication *The Spectator.* While he appreciated the photographs, he thought the introduction was biased and inaccurate.[29] Another old India hand, Sir Alfred H. Watson, former editor of *The Statesman*, thought the book lacked a sense of proportion and did not qualify as impartial history.[30]

Negative press reports started appearing in India from December 1935 about the book. The *Daily Herald* (Lahore) announced its publication under the headline: 'Katherine Mayo's Latest: Another Filthy Book on India', while the *Star of India* (Calcutta) carried the news under the title 'Some More Mischief for India'. *The Tribune* (Lahore) criticized the publication of the book in an article titled 'Another Filthy Book'. The Home Member, Sir H.D. Craik,[31] urged the HD to get a copy as soon as possible.[32] The Home Secretary, M.G. Hallett,[33] himself read a copy (which was on sale in Delhi), and wrote a long review, running into 12 typed pages. He did not think that a ban on the

---

[27] Reported in the British paper *Daily Herald*, 17 December 1935. The same organization also complained to the Lord Chamberlain against a play titled *Vicky* running at the Garrick Theater in which the page boy was called 'Gandhi'.

[28] B.B. Ray Chaudhuri wrote a letter to the British Prime Minister as well as to C.R. Attlee, then leader of the Labour Party in the House of Commons and later to become the British Prime Minister. Reported in the *Amrita Bazar Patrika*, 27 December 1935. Chaudhuri was also the joint secretary of the Indian National Congress of Great Britain. GOI Home Political & K.W., f. 41/1, 1936, NAI.

[29] Review in the British newspaper *The Spectator* quoted at length in the *Amrita Bazar Patrika*, 27 December 1935.

[30] Review by Sir Alfred H. Watson in the *Sunday Times* quoted in the *Amrita Bazar Patrika*, 27 December 1935. Watson also mentioned that Mayo described Calcutta's weather incorrectly.

[31] Sir H.D. Craik was appointed to the ICS in 1899, and served as Chief Secretary to the Punjab government (1922–1927), Home Member GOI (1934–1938) and as Punjab Governor (1938–41).

[32] Note by Craik, 20 December 1935, GOI Home Political & K.W., f. 41/1, 1936, NAI.

[33] Sir Maurice Hallet was appointed to the ICS in 1907, and served the Bihar and Orissa government as Chief Secretary between 1930 and 1932. He also served as Home Secretary, GOI (1932–1936), Bihar Governor (1937–1939) and UP Governor (1939–1945).

book was legally justified. Although he discerned in the book an attempt to 'discredit the Hindus and to extol the Muslims' (by giving example of the latter's military victories, by Mayo suggesting that 'suttee has troubled the Hindus [*sic*] conscience hardly at all', and by her assertion that terrorism was 'essentially a Hindu movement') he himself agreed with some of the charges, especially the last one.[34] Hallett thought the photographs (including scenes from Benaras, the Moplah rising, communal riots at Kanpur, and a 'lurid' picture of Chauri Chaura, in addition to village scenes) 'excellent', although he admitted that some captions too discredited Hindus, such as the reference to untouchable women being exploited by upper caste men in the village. All in all, in Hallett's opinion these photographs were 'good propaganda against civil disobedience'. At the same time, Hallett also termed as incorrect various statements in the book to the effect that Hindu *sadhu*s had murdered Muslim refugees outside Kanpur, and that in 1934 there had been four attempts to wreck the Viceroy's train in the course of a single journey. Overall, his assessment was:

> The writer no doubt throughout the book uses grossly exaggerated language and makes some incorrect statements. But, as I have already said, it can hardly be denied that there is a very considerable substratum of truth. Indians of all classes will no doubt and rightly so resent being represented in this unfavourable manner in foreign countries. But we have no control over publications elsewhere than in India.... Many of the illustrations are, as I have said, useful in showing the dangers of civil disobedience and similar subversive movements, and I do not think, on the whole, that a book of this kind can be held to be likely to increase the tension between the two communities. In normal times it would certainly not be desirable to take action against it and though feelings are at present more strained than before, I consider that action is not desirable.[35]

Hallett commended the book for its stand against Civil Disobedience. The Home Member, however, disagreed with Hallett's assessment. Craik admitted the excellence of the photographs, and considered it 'cleverly written', but thought that the book was also 'vitiated by a prejudiced outlook and disfigured by certain fairly serious inaccuracies of fact'. He predicted that the book would be offensive to Hindus as well as to Hindu nationalists, and felt that it would

---

[34] *The Face of Mother India*, 39, cited by Hallett in his review, 4 January 1936, GOI Home Political & K.W., f. 41/1, 1936, NAI.

[35] Hallett's review, 4 January 1936, GOI Home Political & K.W., f. 41/1, 1936, NAI.

also exacerbate communal hatred, especially the photographs of the Kanpur riots, and on this ground suggested that its import be banned.[36] As there was a difference of opinion about the book in the highest echelons of the GOI, two other 'referees'—significantly, both Indians—were sought out. Hallett sent a copy of the book to Sir Girija Shankar Bajpai, an ICS officer (then the Member for Education, Health and Lands Department)[37] for his opinion.[38] Bajpai termed the book 'thoroughly vicious'; in his opinion, Mayo had more or less suggested that Hindus should have been exterminated en masse by Mahmud Ghazni and Ahmad Shah Abdali. According to him, the book deserved to be banned for two reasons: it caused offence and was likely to stir a political storm. In his words:

> I am sure this will give deep offence and pain to every Hindu who reads the book, to say nothing of the communal capital that will be made out of the book by the anti-British Hindu politician who will eagerly misrepresent the omission of Government to keep the book out of the country as a fresh proof of its hostility to the Hindus and its desire to encourage the glorification of Indian Muslims.[39]

The other referee was Sir Nripendra Nath Sircar (then the Law Member of the Viceroy's Executive Council)[40] who was in no doubt that Hindus would be outraged by the book, and especially by the references to Kali. He found references in the work to Hindu holy men with their 'eyes inflamed with

---

[36] Note by Craik, 7 January 1936. He was certain that a question about the book would be raised in the LA. GOI Home Political & K.W., f. 41/1, 1936, NAI.

[37] Sir Girija Shankar Bajpai was appointed to the ICS in 1915, and began his career as Assistant Magistrate and Collector in UP between 1915 and 1919.

[38] D.O. no. D 8189/35-Poll., 7 January 1936, from Hallett to Bajpai. Hallett also sent the book to the Finance Member, Sir James Grigg, asking him to return it once he and his wife had both read it. D.O. no. D.69/36-Poll., 9 January 1936 from Hallett to Grigg. Sir C.P. Ramaswami Aiyar (the *dewan* [Prime Minister] of Travancore state) was also keen to the read the book. Note by Hallett, 22 January 1936, GOI Home Political & K.W., f. 41/1, 1936, NAI.

[39] Letter from Bajpai to Hallett, 8 January 1936, GOI Home Political & K.W., f. 41/1, 1936, NAI.

[40] Sir Nripendra Nath Sircar was appointed the Law Member of the Viceroy's Executive Council in 1934, prior to which he had served as Advocate General of Bengal between 1929 and 1934. He started his career as a pleader in Bhagalpur in 1897, and served in the Subordinate Judicial Service between 1902 and 1905.

drugs' offensive, and was certain that it would increase communal tension. Sircar thought proscription could be justified on the ground of hurting Hindu religious feelings alone, and did not think that the argument (initially made by Hallett) that banning the book would increase its sales abroad was a good one: demonstrations against the book were likely, in his opinion, to have the same effect.[41] After soliciting all these opinions, the GOI asked the Viceroy, Lord Willingdon, for his approval; the Viceroy, even though he had not read the book, agreed with the opinions of his Indian colleagues, agreed for the book to be banned, and asked for a spare copy to read.[42] Bans were, evidently, for readers other than Viceroys. The book was banned under the SCA by the GOI, as well as under the Press Act by the Bombay, Bengal and Assam governments. The former ban prohibited fresh imports; the latter covered copies already in circulation in India. However, there were no powers or law under which action could be taken against the book in Britain and an empire-wide ban was impossible. In fact, by February 1936, British publishers had started advertising the book as 'banned in India'.[43] The colonial state was caught in a double bind: banning a book gave it publicity, but so did public demonstrations against a book.

After the book was banned, the Director of Public Information, I.M. Stephens, who admired the book, confessed that although nationalist papers had passed favourable comments about the ban, the 'Indian public seem to have taken less interest than one might have expected'.[44] However, the GOI and the India Office were not answerable only to the Indian public. In February 1936 a British Member of Parliament (MP) wanted to know why the book had been banned; when told that it was banned as it increased communal tension, Major General Sir Alfred Knox wanted to know how an expensive book, and one which was 'published in the most artistic manner', could increase

[41] One picture bore the caption, 'Priests chop off heads of goats before the face of the goddess, in order that she may exult in their shrieks, terror and their blood'. Cited by N.N. Sircar in note, 10 January 1936, GOI Home Political & K.W., f. 41/1, 1936, NAI.

[42] Telegram R. no. 114, 14 January 1936 from HD to Sir Eric Mieville, PSV and Telegram R. no. 45-C, 14 January 1936 from PSV to the HD, GOI Home Political & K.W., f. 41/1, 1936, NAI.

[43] Telegram R. no. 457, 5 February 1936 and Telegram R. no. 508, 10 February 1936, both from the Secretary of State to the Viceroy, GOI Home Political & K.W., f. 41/1, 1936, NAI.

[44] D.O. no. 98, 27 January 1936 from Stephens to H. MacGregor, Information Officer, India Office, GOI Home Political & K.W., f. 41/1, 1936, NAI.

communal tension.[45] On the other hand, an Indian Member of the Legislative Assembly (MLA), S. Satyamurti,[46] wanted to know if the GOI had done anything to prevent its circulation abroad.[47] At any rate, the GOI could not keep all constituencies happy.

This survey of three books by Mayo, all controversial, but only one of which was banned, illuminates a simple fact of censorship of publications in India: in determining whether or not a book was banned by the GOI, its content was secondary to the political context in which it was published. All of Mayo's books had deeply offended one or the other section of Indian society, and all had attracted sustained negative attention in the Indian press. However, the only book to be banned was one in the banning of which the Indian public had taken (as the Director of Public Information admitted) the least interest. This also happened to be a book over which the Home Secretary and the Home Member could not agree, the former not favouring a ban, and the latter strongly urging it. Why then, was *The Face of Mother India* banned when three other equally or more controversial books by the same author were not? An answer to this question is not to be found in the pages of the book, but in the timing of its appearance. Its publication after, and not before, the constitutional reforms of 1935 was central and not coincidental to it being banned. At a time when the GOI solicited Indian cooperation to ensure the continuation of the Raj, banning this book was compensation for not banning the other three. Context, not content, was the ultimate determinant of a ban. We now move on to lesser known, but no less fascinating and revealing, authors, their books, their histories and fates.

R.J. Minney's *Shiva, or the Future of India* (1929)

Rubeigh James Minney's *Shiva, or the Future of India* was published in London in 1929, and the blurb hailed the author as an 'experienced observer', who had

---

[45] Reported by the Secretary of State for India to the Viceroy in Telegram R. no. 508, 10 February 1936, GOI Home Political & K.W., f. 41/1, 1936, NAI.

[46] S. Satyamurti was trained as a lawyer in Madras and an active member of the Congress who was elected to the LA as a Congress candidate from Madras city in December 1934. He was an active participant in the Civil Disobedience movement, in the course of which he was arrested and imprisoned.

[47] Satyamurti was told that although the GOI had requested the Secretary of State to prevent its circulation in England and other countries, there were no powers that provided for this. Reply given by Craik on 6 March 1936 in the LA. GOI Home Political & K.W., f. 41/1, 1936, NAI.

taken up the task of summing up the prospects of the Indian people.[48] Minney, born in Calcutta, had studied history at King's College London. In the course of a varied career he worked as a journalist in India (on the editorial staff of *The Pioneer* at Allahabad and *The Englishman* at Calcutta) and as a novelist, playwright and film producer in Britain, and later in the US. Much later, he ran for Parliament in the United Kingdom's general election in 1955 as a Labour candidate, and was defeated by Edward Heath (who later went on to become the British Prime Minister in 1970).[49]

At first glance (and if one were to read *Shiva* without knowing it had been banned) the book appears more likely to have been distributed free by the GOI as publicity material rather than having been banned. Minney made a case for India's British connection to continue in perpetuity; in fact, if there was any criticism of the government, it was directed towards the government in Britain, for fettering the GOI. Minney argued that the 'unlettered hordes of Hindustan' were unworthy of participating in democratic government. He made a strong case for colonial officials to be answerable to their own conscience; in other words, he advocated that they assert greater autonomy from the directives of the British Parliament.[50]

With its repeated and strongly worded assertions of the very many blessings of colonial rule, Minney's book could well have been written by a colonial administrator of the old school. At one point in the book he scoffed, 'Political advancement! A suburban half-wit might just as well climb a tree in his back garden to snatch at the moon.'[51] He found it deeply ironic that 'unification, effected by Britain, should fructify in a unified demand for the removal of the benefactor'. In fact, *Shiva* began with the pronouncement that India's future (but only under British rule) appeared brighter than China's, and that she could aspire to be 'the greatest and most prosperous country in the world' within the next hundred years. If, on the other hand, the British left India, it would become a 'second China'. In 1929, this was not the compliment that it may be considered by some today. His verdict was as dismal as it was uncompromising:

---

[48] R.J. Minney, *Shiva, or the Future of India* (London: Kegan Paul, 1929). The book was published as part of the 'Today and Tomorrow' series, which also included S. Radhakrishnan's *Kalki, or the Future of Civilization*.

[49] Minney was the author of many books relating to India, among them *The Road to Delhi* (1923) and *Clive* (1931).

[50] Minney, *Shiva*, 35.

[51] Ibid., 44–45.

'… left to herself India can accomplish nothing.'[52] Minney's only criticism of British rule in India was expressed in *Shiva* in his distaste for racism and for the contempt shown by the British in India towards Indians.[53]

However, Minney's praise for British rule was accompanied by pronouncements on the three obstacles faced by all schemes of progress in India: 'caste, religion, and sex'. A critique of all three as manifested in Indian life formed the rest of the book. Caste divided the people, and religion, according to him, sanctified sexual indulgence. Minney claimed that during his tour of the brothels of Calcutta, he found not only 'Babu clerks, lawyers, judges', but also much married Indian Members of Council.[54] In Minney's opinion, these indulgences were present in the West as well, with the difference being that while Westerners spread them out during the course of a lifetime, Indians enjoined to embrace asceticism later on in life tried to 'crowd these delights into his more vigorous youth'. Like Gandhi, Minney advocated sexual self-restraint; unlike Gandhi, he did so for reasons more economic than moral. In his view, '… in so far as civilization succeeds in conserving energy sexually and expending it, often just as recklessly, to industrial advantage, every nation that has to contend in world markets for prosperity must do likewise or perish.'[55] Not content with diagnosing present ills in India, Minney also provided simple, if stern, remedies: 'Religion will have to be purged of its impurities. Caste distinctions will have to be jettisoned … Material ambitions must be infused into the peoples.'[56] Minney's agenda was stated clearly in his book: he wanted to focus attention on the social ills that plagued India so as to emphasize that political development ought to be a secondary concern. As he put it, Indians were simply not ready to handle their political affairs until they had reformed their society. Given Minney's support of the colonial state in India, the question arises: why then was his book banned by the colonial state?

As this book was being published on the eve of the Simon Commission report, it was certain to be in the public eye even as the British Parliament was considering reform proposals. Upon *Shiva's* publication the Home Member, Sir James Crerar, termed it 'crude, offensive, superficial and stupid'. The GOI thought the book, though not a very serious work, was likely to raise protests

---

[52] Ibid., 5–12.

[53] As he put it, '… those who do not like associating on terms of absolute equality with the blacks have no right in their country at all.' Ibid., 67–70.

[54] Ibid., 17–18.

[55] Ibid., 24–25.

[56] Ibid., 15.

and offend public opinion in India. Consequently the book was banned entry into India under the SCA in February 1929.[57] In the British House of Commons, when an MP asked the Under Secretary of State for India why Minney's book had been banned, he was informed that the book was offensive to the Indian people, and its contents so coarse that it would be improper for the book to be read there.[58] A review in the *Times of India* suggested that while the book could cause annoyance, it did not merit serious engagement.[59] The British Marxist journal *Labour Monthly* speculated the *Shiva* had been banned because it was so frivolous that it would bring the British into contempt in India![60]

Despite being critical of Indian political aspirations and *not* of colonial rule per se, *Shiva* was banned by a colonial state resisting precisely those Indian political aspirations in 1929. It appears as if the ban on *Shiva* was the compensation the colonial state paid to the Indian public for choosing not to ban Katherine Mayo's *Mother India*. While *Mother India* was viewed by many colonial officials as 'serious' and well-researched, Minney's was seen as frivolous, and therefore its claims not worthy of being defended, even when in large part they echoed the dominant view in the colonial state. Banning such a book was a small gesture to placate Indian public opinion.

Colonel E. Alexander Powell's *The Last Home of Mystery* (1929)

Powell was an American author and traveller who had worked as special correspondent for various publications since 1905. He served in Military Intelligence during the First World War, and attained the rank of Lieutenant Colonel. He wrote this book in 1929 after visiting India, Afghanistan and Nepal the previous year.[61] After the publication of this book, the Indian-owned English newspaper the *Hindustan Times* ran a vocal campaign against it, calling it 'filth for filth's sake', and describing it as a book that had surpassed books

---

[57] Position with respect to Minney's *Shiva*, summarized by HD official while giving his comments on another book by Minney titled *India Marches Past*. GOI Home Political, f. 35/13, 1933, NAI.

[58] *The Times*, 12 March 1929.

[59] Review published in *Times of India*, 12 February 1929.

[60] Clemens Dutt, 'The Outsider's India', *Labour Monthly* 11, no. 5 (May 1929): 313–316, available at Marxists Internet Archive, https://www.marxists.org/archive/dutt-clemens/1929/05/x01.htm (accessed 19 January 2019).

[61] *Who's Who of America*, 1694, extract in GOI Home Political, f. 21/61, 1929, NAI.

by Mayo and Minney.[62] In a subsequent editorial against the book and others in the same genre, the paper thundered that books like this one and that of Mayo were written with disregard for truth, and only as a means of giving Americans a chance of 'further wallowing in the slime of sexuality'. This did not, however, prevent the paper from reprinting sizeable extracts from the work in its own columns over a period of two days.

In his book Powell attributed all the ills of the Hindus to their religion, and stated that Hinduism consisted of degraded cults and phallic worship. He commented adversely on the personal hygiene of Hindus, their caste marks and ascetics, and condemned the sacred writings of Hinduism as indecent in the extreme. The *Hindustan Times* also found it significant that although the book had been published in the United States in March 1929, copies had not arrived in India even after two months. They attributed this to the author and the publisher desisting from sending the book 'where, if it passed governmental barriers, its absurdities would be exposed'. By railing against and publishing detailed extracts from a book not yet available in India, the *Hindustan Times* succeeded only in raising public awareness about it.

After this newspaper's campaign, the matter reached the LA, where an Indian member wanted to know not only if the GOI were aware of the book, but also if they—as alleged by the author—helped him during his visit.[63] In the preface to his book, Powell had thanked two officials by name, in addition to the Bengal Political Department, and had clearly stated that he had been recommended to the Viceroy by the India Office. Official enquiries revealed that although an India Office official had written a letter of introduction for the author and arranged a meeting of the author with the Prime Minister of Nepal, no other assistance had been given.[64] The Bengal government stated that neither the Governor nor the officers of the Political Department knew

---

[62] It also lambasted the book as 'perhaps the last word in sexual nonsense'. *Hindustan Times*, 11 July 1929. The paper urged that it was time America halted 'this mean exploitation of its baser instincts by its publishers'. Editorial titled 'Pornographic Literature: Sex Perversion of the Yankee' in the *Hindustan Times*, 13 July 1929. Extracts were published in the *Hindustan Times* on 11 and 12 July 1929.

[63] Question asked by Gaya Prasad Singh on 2 September 1929, GOI Home Political, f. 21/61, 1929, NAI.

[64] Telegram no. 2600 from the Secretary of State to the Viceroy, 21 August 1929, GOI Home Political, f. 21/61, 1929, NAI.

about either the author or his book.[65] Consequently the Home Member, Sir James Crerar, stated in the LA that they were aware that the book had been published but had not examined it, and were not aware of any official help extended to the author. It emerged in the course of time that the Bengal government had in fact helped the author with accommodation.[66]

The publicity the book attracted led the GOI to set about examining the book, which was at this time available neither with the IB nor with the booksellers contacted by the GOI. The Director of Public Information, J. Coatman, who reviewed the book, commented that the author had referred to 'filthy-looking natives'. Powell's descriptions of the Hindu gods and religious customs were deemed 'as unfortunate as they are offensive', and an entire chapter was devoted to 'unclean Gods'. Coatman did not, however, recommend action against the book, for three reasons: one, it was 'nothing more than the production of an adventurous journalist'; two, banning it would 'invest it with greater importance than it deserves'; and three, the book had not attracted notice in what the GOI considered important newspapers, and banning it would act as an advertisement.[67] A few days later, the Home Secretary, Sir Harry Haig, offered two other reasons for not banning the book: 'We got little gratitude', he wrote, 'from Indian opinion for prohibiting "Shiva", and feelings on this subject are now a good deal calmer.'[68] The Home Member, Sir James Crerar, termed it 'an unpleasant book' but agreed that it should not be banned.[69] Ultimately the book was not banned, and the *Hindustan Times*'s campaign against the book was to no avail. The campaign against the book by one newspaper alone could be safely ignored by the state.

---

[65] Telegram R. no. 10029-P. from Bengal government to HD, 28 August 1929, GOI Home Political, f. 21/61, 1929, NAI.

[66] H. Wilkinson of the British Legation in Nepal, after hearing about the LA question, wrote to the Foreign Secretary, Sir Denys Bray, that the author had stayed for a day and two nights in Kathmandu in February 1928, and on the basis of a few photographs and gossip he had 'raised a structure which for vulgarity tactlessness and inaccuracy it would be hard to beat. It is a mass of impudent fabrications…. He describes in full detail places he has not visited and conversations which did not take place'. Powell was, however, given place to stay at the legation, and Wilkinson thought that the Bengal government had probably assisted him with accommodation too. D.O. no. 118-C., 7 September 1929 from Wilkinson to Bray, Home Political. f. 21/61, 1929.

[67] Note by Coatman, 30 October 1929, GOI Home Political, f. 21/61, 1929, NAI.

[68] Note by Haig, 6 November 1929, GOI Home Political, f. 21/61, 1929, NAI.

[69] Note by Crerar, 7 November 1929, GOI Home Political, f. 21/61, 1929, NAI.

R.J. Minney's *India Marches Past* (1933)

Minney was to enjoy the dubious distinction of having not one, but two, books banned by the GOI within five years. In January 1933 the India Office in London informed the HD in New Delhi that Minney's latest book, *India Marches Past*, was due to be published in Britain, as well as in the United States, and was expected to contain objectionable matter. When the book was finally published in July 1933, the India Office neglected to send the GOI a copy. It only came to the GOI's attention when the Director of the IB (DIB), Sir Horace Williamson,[70] noticed a review in the *New York Times* that suggested that the book was likely to give 'deep and justifiable offence to public opinion in India'.[71] The India Office then sent the GOI a copy of the book, which was read by at least four officials.

The first part of the book outlined the history of India from 2500 BC onwards, and implied as well as suggested explicitly that many benefits had accrued to India through British rule. The book contained incidents from Mughal history, an account of the Mutiny of 1857, and of revolutionary activities in Bengal and Poona. However, it was not this section, but a chapter titled 'Sex' in a section titled 'Fetters' that caused most consternation in official circles. It began with the statement that the East regarded it as 'spiritual and ennobling', and that in India, due to the absence of other diversions, 'sex is the one joy'. He commented that 'both religion and tradition have thrown the reins to passion, which, given its head, is carrying the race to destruction'. Minney outlined the 'lewd practices of the gods' in some detail, despite finding them 'too abundant even to catalogue'. Minney stated that Hindu sacred books encouraged sexual license. In this wide-ranging chapter he also discussed female infanticide, mentioned Gandhi's remorse at not practicing celibacy after his marriage, cited Katherine Mayo's description of a child bride in hospital, commented on the prevalence of venereal disease, referred to the sufferings of widows, listed the types of prostitutes in India, summarized the *Kamasutra* and described polyandry.[72]

Senior HD officials of the GOI who read the book gave conflicting opinions: One found the 'Fetters' section 'frankly disgusting', and suggested that the best course of action would be for the GOI to ban entry of the book into India, and then instruct provincial governments to ban the circulation of existing copies

---

[70] Williamson was an Indian Police officer who served as the DIB between 1931 and 1936.

[71] *New York Times*, 9 July 1933, cited in note by HD official (signature illegible), 10 November 1933, GOI Home Political, f. 35/13, 1933, NAI.

[72] R.J. Minney, *India Marches Past* (London: Jarrolds, 1933), 201–224.

within the country. Another disagreed; he argued that book did not deserve to be banned as it tended to 'direct attention to wrongs and customs rather than to deliberately give offence'.[73] C.M. Trivedi, an Indian ICS officer, thought some passages in this section of the book would offend Hindus; one derogatory reference to the Prophet could also give offence to Muslims. However, in his opinion there were two factors in favour of not taking action: the book had attracted little attention since its publication in July 1933, and its price (16 shillings) was high enough to limit its circulation. As Trivedi put it, there was a case for taking action against the book 'on merits', but not on practical grounds.[74] The yardsticks of price (high price indicating limited circulation) and popularity (or lack thereof) were thus the criteria involved in this case.

Another factor to be considered was that the author thanked India Office officials for their 'patience and guidance'.[75] The DIB, Sir Horace Williamson, who was the next person to read the book, recommended that it be banned on the grounds that the author's acknowledgment meant that official patronage had been given to a book that 'libels Indians'. This was no longer acceptable in the 1930s, and especially after the furore that *Mother India* had caused in 1927 on the same grounds. He also termed the book 'pornographically offensive', even if 'a great deal of what is said may be true'. In other words, when it came to taking a decision about banning a book, its capacity to cause offence, and the magnitude of offence caused (and to whom) were factors that were considered important; its truth claims were not relevant to the decision. Taking all this into account, he recommended that the book be banned under the SCA.[76] Although opinion was divided among officials who had read the book, it was banned in December 1933.[77] Minney had to pay for the mistake

---

[73] Note by HD officials EW (signature illegible), 29 November 1933, and H (signature illegible), 4 December 1933, GOI Home Political, f. 35/13, 1933, NAI.

[74] Note by Trivedi, 30 November 1933, GOI Home Political, f. 35/13, 1933, NAI.

[75] Minney acknowledged various texts, including books by V.A. Smith, R.C. Dutt, Abbe Dubois, Katherine Mayo, H.G. Wells, E. Alexander Powell, Gandhi's autobiography, and so on, and in the end thanked 'India Office officials for their patience and guidance'. Minney, *India*, 283–284. Note by Trivedi, 30 November 1933, GOI Home Political, f. 35/13, 1933, NAI.

[76] Note by Williamson, 30 November 1933. Trivedi came to agree with this view as he modified his own after reading Williamson's comments. Note by Trivedi, 4 December 1933, GOI Home Political, f. 35/13, 1933, NAI.

[77] Finance Deptt (Customs) notification no. 58, 16 December 1933, GOI Home Political, f. 35/13, 1933, NAI. In February 1934, Travancore state banned *India Marches Past*. *Times of India*, 27 February 1934.

of making the India Office a co-defendant (by acknowledging its help) against critics of the book.

Arthur Miles' *Land of the Lingam* and D.H. Southgate's *As a Man's Hand* (1937)

In September 1937 Congress MLA S. Satyamurti wrote to Home Secretary J.A. Thorne informing him about two books which 'ought not to be allowed to be circulated and read in any civilized country and certainly not in India'. The two books to which he referred were *Land of the Lingam* (non-fiction) by Arthur Miles (the pseudonym of Gervee Baronte) and *As a Man's Hand* (fiction) by Dora Hilda Southgate.[78] *Land of the Lingam* contained chapters titled 'Blood Sacrifice', 'Tortures', 'Superstitions' and 'Dancing Girls', in additions to chapters on the various castes of India. The introduction itself stated:

> India can never be a nation until Hinduism, with its superstitions and beastly rites, is wiped out. India will remain as she is to-day, until her castes, with the corrupt intelligentsia of the Brahmin cast [*sic*] ... be recognized for just what they are, trade unions. Until the people are divided, if any division is needed at all, simply by their trades and not by any social and 'religious' barriers existing only in the minds of the degenerate Brahmans.[79]

The *Times Literary Supplement* (London) was not impressed with the book, stating that 'it must inevitably be resented in India and English readers will find in its pages of prejudice and abuse little that can help them to form a just appreciation either of the caste system or of Hinduism'.[80]

Home Secretary Thorne read *Land of the Lingam*, first published in 1933 (four years before the protest against it), as did the Home Member, Sir H.D. Craik. The latter described it in the following terms:

> I am surprised that this book has not aroused protest before: but apparently the first cheap edition was only published in Jan. 1937, and few copies may

---

[78] *Land of the Lingam* was published by Hurst and Blackett in their Paternoster Library series. *As a Man's Hand* was published by Malthuens Publishers. Satyamurti planned to take up the matter in the LA, and wanted to know in advance what the GOI's views were on the matter. Letter from Satyamurti to Thorne, 9 September 1937. Later, Satyamurti sent a copy of *Land of the Lingam* to Thorne. Letter from Satyamurti to Thorne, 25 September 1937, GOI Home Political, f. 22/65, 1937, NAI.

[79] Arthur Miles, *Land of the Lingam* (London: Hurst & Blackett, 1933), 7–8.

[80] *Times Literary Supplement*, 21 September 1933, 635.

have been in circulation till recently. This would be a reason justifying action now although the 1st edn. was published some time ago.... I think any Hindu would have cause to resent the book strongly. The author seems to wallow in filth and goes out of his way to represent Hindu customs in the worst possible light. A book like this, which has apparently had a large circulation at home, is an offensive libel in India and the Indian government would I think be justified in retaliating in any way open to it. There are not many such ways, but prohibition of import is one of them and whether it is much use or not I think this should be done.[81]

Even as the GOI was mulling over the question of the two books, Satyamurti raised the issue in the LA, quoting a statement on the cover of *Land of the Lingam* to the effect that the work was aimed at exposing the 'insanity and filth that is corrupting two-thirds of India's population today'. The quotation (adapted from a review of the book in a London journal) continued to the effect that 'until Hinduism is broken down nothing can be accomplished'.

On the same day, another member of the LA, Seth Govind Das, asked about *As a Man's Hand*.[82] The LA was informed that the GOI had tried but failed to find the book in all the bookshops of Simla and elsewhere, and that the GOI would not prevent the circulation of the book in India without first reading it. *As a Man's Hand* was a novel which narrated the life of an Indian woman between 1876 and 1936, who had been 'brought up under the influence of Hindu tradition and priest-ridden society'. It narrated the story of a girl from an orthodox Brahmin family who married young and had a miserable life, and whose son grew up to be an emancipated Christian doctor, and who married a modern woman.[83]

Less than a month after hearing from Satyamurti, Thorne was able to reply to him that *Land of the Lingam* had been banned under the SCA.[84] On the other hand, *As a Man's Hand* had been read by three HD officials (including Thorne himself), and their unanimous opinion was that the book did not deserve to be banned. When a question was again asked in the LA in November about

---

[81] Note by Craik, 29 September 1937, GOI Home Political, f. 22/65, 1937, NAI.

[82] Question asked in the LA by S. Satyamurti on 22 September 1937, GOI Home Political, f. 22/65, 1937, NAI.

[83] D.H. Southgate, *As a Man's Hand* (London: Methuen & Company, 1937).

[84] Letter from Thorne to Satyamurti, 6 October 1937. The book was banned by Finance Deptt (Customs) notification no. 84, 2 October 1937, GOI Home Political, f. 22/65, 1937, NAI.

As a Man's Hand, Thorne replied that the GOI had examined the book and decided that it did not call for action.[85]

Why was one book banned and the other spared? HD officials who read *As a Man's Hand* felt that the book was an honest and serious critique of Hindu society, and any offence taken by Hindus was unintentional on the part of the author. The book was favourably reviewed in the *Times of India* in early October 1937. The review was informed by the controversy over the book, and began with the comment that indignation over critical accounts of India was 'often artificially aroused'. The newspaper took the view that the account of three generations of a family had, like all fiction, good as well as bad characters, and that the book in fact was an affectionate treatment of India and its women.[86] An HD official felt that the book had tried to reveal the 'degradation which results from tradition and priestcraft, with special reference to the evil of child marriage'. The book was, in his opinion, 'aimed at serious social evils and could hardly be described as written for sensation'. The official cited Mayo's *Mother India*, which had not been banned despite arousing controversy.[87] I.H. Stephenson, who also read the book, opined that it 'makes no attempt to detail squalor and ignorance for the sake of it but tries to show the evolution of a new generation which at the same time is quite beyond the comprehension of the old'.[88] The next person on the proscription assembly line to read the book was Thorne himself. He thought the blurb somewhat sensational, but also incorrect, and conceded that the book could be distasteful to Brahmins. Overall, however, he felt that the work was 'honest and informed', and 'so far as it shows hostility towards a system the motive by compassion for the victims rather than dislike for those who exploit it'. Thorne did not favour a ban on the work.[89] The author's intention, therefore, was a factor more potent in deciding the fate of the book than any offence that readers may take after reading it. Indeed, the book was not banned, and its American edition appeared in 1938 with an altered titled (*Root in the Rock: An Indian Saga, 1876–1936*), the cover bearing an illustration of a woman in a

---

[85] Question asked by Raja Yuveraj Dutta Singh on 15 November 1937, GOI Home Political, f. 22/65, 1937, NAI.

[86] Review titled 'Three Decades: Sympathetic study of Indian Life' in *Times of India*, 2 October 1937.

[87] Note by H.R.H. (signature illegible), 6 October 1937, GOI Home Political, f. 22/65, 1937, NAI.

[88] Note by Stephenson, 11 October 1937, GOI Home Political, f. 22/65, 1937, NAI.

[89] Note by Thorne, 20 October 1937, GOI Home Political, f. 22/65, 1937, NAI.

sari standing against the silhouette of a building with domes and a minaret, and caparisoned elephants.[90]

On the other hand, *Land of the Lingam* was banned after circulating in India for four years (since 1933) only after a cheap edition of the book was published in 1937, and after there was a demand made in the LA for it to be banned.[91] Its author, G. Baronte/Arthur Miles, an admirer of Hitler's *Mein Kampf*, had in any case continued her literary career, publishing a handbook of reincarnation (*You Have Lived Before!*) in 1936. This belated ban of her earlier book incensed Baronte, who wrote to the India Office in January 1938, asking if she was 'simply condemned without the chance of defending myself'.[92] She was informed that the law did not require the GOI to state the reasons for the ban, and that the GOI was entitled to ban matter that they thought gravely offended Indian feeling.[93] The author then complained directly to the GOI, but to no avail. She averred that although the book had received some severe reviews, 'not one critic' had been able to refute her statements, and drawing the conclusion that 'truth was not acceptable in the land'. She also included an extract from a Sunday newspaper (unnamed and undated) of Britain reporting a human sacrifice in Nahan (India) to appease the rain god. Then she asked, 'As such accidents continue to occur in India am I still to be banned for calling attention to them?'[94] The GOI maintained that they were the 'best judges of what is likely to cause grave offence to Indian feeling'.[95] In these two cases, it was not so much the timing of the book as their genre (non-fiction and fiction) that condemned one and saved the other. In the case of *Land of the Lingam*, the price of the book also played a role, and explains the timing of the ban (just as a cheaper, and therefore accessible to a wider readership, edition was published).

---

[90] D.H. Southgate, *Root in the Rock: An Indian Saga, 1876–1936* (New York: A.A. Knopf, 1938).

[91] D.O. no. 41/6/38-Poll, 17 February 1938, from F.H. Puckle (now in the HD) to Peel, GOI Home Political, f. 41/6, 1938, NAI.

[92] She asked for the names of the people who had complained against the book. Letter from Baronte to Under Secretary of State for India, 17 October 1937, GOI Home Political, f. 41/6, 1938, NAI.

[93] Letter no. P & J (S) 987/37 from Peel to Baronte, 21 October 1937, GOI Home Political, f. 41/6, 1938, NAI.

[94] Baronte wrote directly to the 'Governor-General's Department' at New Delhi. Letter from Baronte, 13 January 1938, GOI Home Political, f. 41/6, 1938, NAI.

[95] D.O. no. 41/6/38-Poll. from Puckle to Peel, 17 February 1938, GOI Home Political, f. 41/6, 1938, NAI.

Frank Harrison Beckmann's *Dust of India* (1938)

In August 1938, S. Satyamurti again wrote to wrote to J.A. Thorne complaining about a book, this time American travel writer Frank Harrison Beckmann's *Dust of India*. He also enclosed a cutting from the *Kaiser-i-Hind Illustrated Weekly* about the book, adding that although he 'did not want to seem to be repressive', the book ought not to be allowed to circulate in India.[96] The enclosed article—titled 'Male Miss Mayo Slanders India: Is it All a Part of Govt. Plan Here and Everywhere to Bring India into Contempt? A New Book Which Should Not Have Been Allowed Into India'—referred to Beckmann's book as 'even more outrageous and more libellous' than Mayo's. The writer of the article suggested that the GOI had permitted the circulation of the book so as to bring the Congress into contempt and ridicule outside India. In his book—which was in the form of a dialogue between an American and an Indian—Beckmann had made statements to the effect that India was a place of insanitary conditions ('the distinction of being the dirtiest nation on the face of the earth'; 'Sanitation, as Americans understand it, is almost wholly lacking'). He dismissed Indian temples for being dirty as compared to American churches, and suggested that far from exaggerating, Mayo had in fact economized on the truth. He also derided Indians for lack of honesty, and stated that 'a great percentage of them ... are not only untruthful but tricky'. Other statements in the book generalized that Indians were lazy, and their faiths based on myth and consisted of 'silly ridiculous customs' based on 'superstition and habit'. Beckmann stated that India was not ready for self-government, and would not be for the next 25 to 50 years.[97]

Upon enquiry the IB confirmed that the book was on sale in India, and officials who read it termed it 'an elementary sort of mixture of a Baedeker and a Socratic dialogue in childish style', and thought it 'harmless' and also not comparable to Mayo.[98] After a fortnight, Thorne wrote back saying that he had read the book and felt that the review in the *Kaiser-i-Hind Illustrated Weekly* had torn statements out of context. Thorne did not favour banning the

---

[96] The book was published in the United States by The Stratford Company, Boston. Letter from Satyamurti to Thorne, 21 August 1938, GOI Home Political, f. 41/49, 1938, NAI.

[97] Extracts from the book in *Kaiser-i-Hind Illustrated Weekly* 2, no. 33 (14 August 1938), GOI Home Political, f. 41/49, 1938, NAI.

[98] Note by V.T. Bayley of the IB, 29 August 1938, and note by R.B. Elwin, 31 August 1938, GOI Home Political, f. 41/49, 1938, NAI.

book, and consequently the book was not banned.[99] In this case, as in the case of *The Last Home of Mystery* discussed earlier in this chapter, one newspaper's campaign alone was not enough for the state to take action against it.

Identifying the Ban Formula

Manoranjan Jha has attributed the GOI's failure to ban a controversial book like Katherine Mayo's *Mother India* to British authorities' 'desire to divide the Hindus and the Muslims'.[100] In light of the case studies discussed in this chapter, this seems too simplistic a conclusion. Although Mayo was critical of the religious and social practices of the Hindus, then three-fourths of the Indian population, her larger agenda was to prove Indians as a whole unfit for self-government. This was a sentiment with which the GOI was in agreement at the time of the book's publication. Had a policy of 'divide and rule' been the criterion, or even a motivation, for the GOI to ban books, Mayo's *The Face of Mother India* would not have been banned in 1936, since it was aimed precisely at creating conflict between the main religious communities of India. Yet it was banned. Viewing publications through the prism of articles of faith or received wisdom—including 'divide and rule'—obscures the history of banned publications instead of bringing their individual histories and fates into sharper focus. We must look elsewhere for the explanation for why certain books were banned and certain others escaped banning.

As the case studies discussed in this chapter indicate, colonial officials, while considering a publication's suitability for circulation, had to weigh the exemplary effect obtained from banning it against the advertisement a ban lent a publication. In the case of R.J. Minney's two books, which were critical of Indian society and religions, some gratitude could be expected from the public if the books were banned. In the case of Powell's book, the author's claim of getting official help was likely to enrage public opinion much more than any gratitude they felt that the book was out of circulation.

By identifying, with the help of these case studies, certain criteria used by colonial officials to decide on book bans, this chapter in no way suggests that

---

[99] Letter from Thorne to Satyamurti, 5 September 1938, GOI Home Political, f. 41/49, 1938, NAI. Documents from this file have been reproduced in Basudev Chatterji edited *Towards Freedom 1938*, part I, 1012–1015. However, Chatterji's contention that the book was banned upon Satyamurti's request is incorrect. See *Towards Freedom 1938*, part I, editorial note, 1012.

[100] Jha, *Katherine Mayo*, 98.

the ban formula was written in stone or that one formula applied to every case. As the Indian context and GOI policy changed, so did the formula. However, certain factors almost always played a role, quite apart from and often independently of, the actual content of the book in question. The precise configuration of rationale invoked for censorship kept changing, but the rationale were all drawn from a common pool, which we here term the 'ban formula'.

On the basis of the cases discussed in this chapter, it is possible to compile a 'checklist' of criteria, a formula as it were, invoked by colonial officials when deciding whether to ban or not to ban. It must be added that in each case factors in favour of and against banning were totalled up, then weighed against each other to arrive at a final decision. Banning was *not* considered a good option if it was likely to be ineffective; if the book was 'dull' rather than lively; if the work in question was fiction rather than fact-based; if it repeated allegations already made frequently in the past; if no gratitude for banning could be expected from the Indian public; if its price was prohibitively expensive so as to limit its circulation to a small group; if the period of circulation had been long (without attracting any attention); and if the demand for a particular book was not likely to be high. On the other hand, banning was considered a viable option if it could remove doubts that the GOI had patronized or sponsored its publication; if 'communal capital' could be made of a book; and if a book (and not banning it) could be used as evidence of the GOI's hostility to any community. If a book was deemed to be a less-than-serious work two things could happen: in some cases it was thought that banning a frivolous book would not be a loss to academia and humanity, and it was banned. In other cases, it was spared, as it was not thought to be worth the trouble of banning. Most importantly, a book was most likely to be banned if vociferous protests led to, or threatened to lead to, violence.

The price of a book (if high) was considered as rendering it somewhat 'safer', as it was assumed that it would be read by fewer people. This is clear from statements of colonial officials in the case of Minney's *India Marches Past*. However, while price was a factor that was taken into consideration, it was one of many, and the interaction of this factor with others produced the complex formula of a ban. The likely size of readership, and the ease of access (in terms of price and also ease of comprehension) were important factors that determined whether or not a particular book was banned at a particular time. This has been true in other historical contexts as well. To cast an eye outside India for a moment, in 1872 a translation of a German book was allowed in

Tsarist Russia (where between 1866 and 1904, the import of more than 12,000 titles were banned) on the grounds that it was a 'difficult, inaccessible, strictly scientific work' and that it was too obscure to have any impact. As it happened, this book arguably changed the course of Russian history. The book was Karl Marx's *Das Capital*. Similarly, in a Russian censorship decree of 1865, lengthy books were exempted from censorship and only short ones subjected to it; in Russia and Austria, censors had the option of designating a book to be available only to certain designated professions; some books were not allowed to be sold as single volume, but as part of a set, an example of which is Tolstoy's *The Kreutzer Sonata*, which was allowed to be published only as volume 13 of his collected works in 1891.[101]

Finally, context—much more than content—determined the likelihood of a publication being banned. Powell's *The Last Home of Mystery* (1929) and Minney's *India Marches Past* (1933) both contained similar allegations. The former was not banned, but the latter, published after the Civil Disobedience movement and the Gandhi–Irwin Pact, was banned. Debates among colonial officials—Indians and British, by the 1930s—over the success or otherwise of instituting a prosecution against an author, and the repercussions of a failed prosecution, lay bare to us an anxious colonial state, not an authoritarian one. For anti-colonial nationalists in India, books banned by the colonial state acquired a virtuous halo, a fact which was known to the colonial state, and which also explains its reluctance to ban certain books. Indeed, the causal relationship between banning, on the one hand, and publicity and increased sales (or, in contemporary times, instant availability on the internet), on the other, is not only a universal one, but one which exercises—and has, historically, exercised—some measure of restraint on censors as well.

---

[101] Examples in Robert Justin Goldstein, *Political Censorship of the Arts and the Press in Nineteenth-Century Europe* (London: Palgrave MacMillan, 1989), 42–44.

4

'Hurt' or 'Hatred'?
Publications by Non-Indians Offensive to Indian Muslims

On 30 September 2005, a dozen caricatures of Prophet Muhammad appeared in the Danish newspaper *Jyllands-Posten*. They were captioned 'The Face of Muhammad', and the accompanying editorial criticized the 'sickly oversensitivity' of Muslims. Whereas the Western media interpreted the adverse reaction to the cartoons as emanating from the Islamic ban on images (variously interpreted as all images, or images of Muhammad, or religious images), Jamal J. Elias has argued that Muslims were in fact protesting against the '*intention* to cause offence to the prophet and their religion'.[1] Questions of religious sentiment and intention in the context of colonial India have been skilfully analysed by Neeti Nair, who has studied events and debates surrounding the addition of a new section (295A) to the IPC in 1927 penalizing 'outraging the religious feelings' of others. Nair has suggested that British intervention in the *Rangila Rasul* case (involving derogatory references to Prophet Muhammad in a pamphlet produced in 1924 by a Hindu publicist in Lahore) 'stoked' the fury of the already enraged Muslim public. In her words, 'It was the intervention of the British government at this juncture [after the acquittal of the publisher, M. Rajpal by the Punjab High Court in 1927] that reinforced the sense of wrong felt by the Muslim community at large.'[2] Nair has also demonstrated that far from being an abstract, rarefied entity, the law,

---

[1] Jamal J. Elias, *Aisha's Cushion: Religious Art, Perception, and Practice in Islam* (Cambridge, Mass: Harvard University Press, 2012), 8–9, emphasis in original.

[2] Nair, 'Beyond the "Communal"', 320. This famous case has been discussed at length in Kumar, *Censorship in India*, in the chapter 'Jehad for the Rasul in Lahore', 163–181.

lawmakers and lawmaking were all subject to negotiation by pressure groups from within society.[3] These two keywords—intention and offence—are at the heart of the biographies of publications narrated in this chapter.

The case studies (books and articles in popular journals published in Great Britain or the United States between the 1920s and 1940s) discussed in this chapter all have two things in common: one, they were all concerned with representations of Islam and Prophet Muhammad; two, all were written by non-Indian authors and published outside India. During this period there were several publications emanating from Britain that offended a vocal section of Muslims there as well as in India. There were vociferous demands from pressure groups for a ban on these books and popular journals. A survey of cases where the demand for a ban was met, as well as those where it was rejected, helps clarify the criteria used by the GOI and the India Office. It also illustrates the politics of public protests, in this case on a trans-national scale. It also helps us understand the creation of what David Gilmartin has termed a 'distinctly Muslim public' in late colonial India.[4] His argument is that colonial rule rested on the 'recognition and protection' of communities (based on caste, tribe or religion). This book argues on the basis of evidence presented in this chapter that such communities had an interest in presenting a united and coherent face in order to lobby the colonial state. Controversies over publications provided them with a good opportunity, and today provide the historian with a rich source to study the process of community consolidation. These little-known cases, hitherto consigned to the ash heap of history, also help us better understand the controversy over similar cases closer to our times: the Rushdie case (1988 onwards), the *Jyllands-Posten* case (2010) and the *Charlie Hebdo* case (2015 onwards). 'Truth', in recreating the life of a 7th-century figure, 'intention' (to mock or to reconstruct?) and 'violence': these are the three themes that are in focus in the case studies that appear in this chapter, all of which pertain to a period decades before the Rushdie affair startled the world.

Commentators and authorities on present-day hate speech issues—including Bhikhu Parekh—have commented that Salman Rushdie's controversial book *The Satanic Verses* (publication of which precipitated a death sentence on Rushdie by the Iranian theological leader Ayatollah Khomeini) does not qualify as hate speech because it

---

[3] Ibid., 329.

[4] David Gilmartin. 'Democracy, Nationalism and the Public: A Speculation on Colonial Muslim Politics' in *The Decolonization Reader*, ed. James D. Le Sueur, 191–203 (New York: Routledge, 2003), 191.

... neither ascribes undesirable qualities to Muslims nor impugns their ability to share a common life. It mocks Prophet Muhammad and casts doubt on the authenticity of some of the Qur'anic verses but does not advocate hostility to Muslims, and is not a case of hate speech.[5]

A related question is: What is 'hate literature'? Can any and all critical depictions of the Prophet be termed 'hate literature' or 'hate speech'? Deepak Mehta has defined hate literature as 'an archive of ideas about particular groups of people', and described its 'multiplication effect', as printed words metamorphose into rumour, incendiary speeches and riots. Mehta believes that hate literature was 'entangled with the state, through the laws that dealt with the incitement of religious hatred'.[6] In order to clarify our understanding of the concept, and of the period under survey, we begin with a biography of the Prophet—R.F. Dibble's *Mohammed: A Biography of the Prophet and the Man*, published in New York in 1926—that exemplifies many of the issues that were to recur repeatedly in the context of other publications, down till the end of colonial rule in India, and beyond.[7]

---

[5] Bhikhu Parekh, 'Is There a Case for Banning Hate Speech?' in *The Content and Context of Hate Speech: Rethinking Regulation and Responses*, ed. Michael Herz and Peter Molnar, 37–56 (Cambridge: Cambridge University Press, 2012), 42. In this view, he is in agreement with the judgment of the European Commission of Human Rights in 1991. Kenan Malik and Bhikhu Parekh epitomize two contradictory positions on the regulation of hate speech. Parekh holds that hate speech ought to be proscribed on the basis of its content, and not its effect (public disorder). As he puts it, 'What matters is its content—what it says about an individual or a group—and its long term effect on the group and the wide society, rather than its immediate consequences in terms of public disorder.' Parekh, 'Is There a Case for Banning Hate Speech?' 41. On the other hand, Malik believes in 'effects-based' and not 'content-based' regulation. In his view, prohibition of only that speech should be allowed 'that creates imminent danger'. For Kenan Malik's views, see 'Interview with Kenan Malik', in *The Content and Context of Hate Speech*, ed. Herz and Molnar, 81–91, 83–84.

[6] Deepak Mehta. 'Words That Wound: Archiving Hate in the Making of Hindu-Indian and Muslim-Pakistani Publics in Bombay', in *Beyond Crisis: Re-evaluating Pakistan*, ed. Naveeda Khan, 315–343 (New Delhi: Routledge, 2010), 333. Mehta's article has extracts from and analysis of hate literature and hate speech produced in India, by Indians, against other Indians, in the 1920s.

[7] See Chapter 9, 'The *Living Biographies of Religious Leaders* Controversy (1956)' in this book.

R.F. Dibble's *Mohammed: A Biography of the Prophet and the Man* (1926)

Roy Floyd Dibble, an American author of historical biographies, was well aware of the difficulty of the task he had undertaken. The Prophet was, Dibble wrote, a figure caught between two antagonistic forces of opinion: while Christian commentators had dwelt on the worst elements of his life and teachings, his followers had 'been guilty of the most fanatical panegyrics'.[8] The author's self-proclaimed task was to establish whether the Prophet was an 'unabashed fakir', 'dishonest from the start', 'a coward', 'utterly unscrupulous' or 'wholly sincere'. As he put it, 'In short, was he a vicious paranoiac who developed into a maniacal monster, or an unrivaled genius who was all that his worshipers claimed—or both?'[9] Dibble showed awareness that the prevailing Western discourse about Islam was very critical, and at times appeared anxious not to be seen to be part of this camp. Although he attempted to steer clear of both extremes, his obvious scepticism of the divine role of the Prophet caused him to fall foul of colonial authorities who were eager, in a period of anti-colonial nationalism, not to antagonize Muslim opinion in India. The book bears detailed scrutiny as many of the themes it discussed were to recur repeatedly in other publications that offended Muslim opinion.

Dibble began his account by describing Arabs as people who were 'at once independent and servile, patriotic and anarchistic, friendly and hostile, thievish and chivalric' and who 'frequently plunged with limitless enthusiasm into the gratifying job of slitting fraternal throats'.[10] That Dibble did not give much credence to the Prophet's account of his own life is obvious from Dibble's statement that although he claimed to be an 'orphan, poor and astray … one can hardly refrain from noting that most boys who attain a position of unrivaled eminence in later life are prone to give a suspicious amount of emphasis to the hardships of their youth'.[11] Dibble's portrayal of the Prophet's wife, Khadija, was also less than flattering.[12] Although Dibble acknowledged

---

[8] R.F. Dibble, *Mohammed: A Biography of the Prophet and the Man* (New York: The Viking Press, 1929), 25.

[9] Ibid., 44–45.

[10] Ibid., 10–12.

[11] Ibid., 25.

[12] Dibble claimed, without citing any sources, that Khadija wooed Muhammad, and that she got her father drunk so that he would allow her marriage. Ibid., 40–41.

that detractors of Islam had 'exaggerated its largely fictitious sensuality',[13] he himself made frequent allusion to the Prophet's alleged promiscuity.[14] In Dibble's long account of the Prophet's early skirmishes with other tribes, he was alleged to be a coward,[15] as also being excessively sensitive to criticism.[16] Like William Bolitho (whose book *Twelve Among the Gods* published three years later—and containing a chapter on the Prophet's life—was also banned by the GOI), Dibble emphasized the derivative nature of Muhammad's teachings; neither was he an admirer of the literary style of the Quran.[17] In common with many other critics of Islam, he ridiculed the vision of heaven outlined in its scripture.[18] Another common theme in many accounts of the Prophet's life, including Dibble's, is that of violent plunder. Dibble stated, for example, that 'Islam's inventor entertained no silly scruples about blood-letting'. He tempered his criticism of Islam, trenchant as it was, with an acknowledgment of at least some elements that it shared in common with Western historical events:

---

[13] Ibid., 106.

[14] Dibble also alleged that Muhammad's followers were encouraged by him to possess the wives and possessions of unbelievers. Ibid., 83. Also, he alleged, 'as was only natural' the Prophet 'allowed himself a wider latitude of encounters than was granted to his adherents'. Ibid., 185. Further, Dibble also suggested that the revelations were self-generated: he recounted the story of and the opposition to Muhammad's marriage with Zeinab, his adopted son Zeid's wife; at this point, 'it seems highly advisable for him to have recourse to Allah' and another revelation followed permitting such a marriage, after which criticism collapsed'. Ibid., 188–190.

[15] 'For Mohammed, no less than many other religiously-minded emperors and tsars, appears to have conducted himself in battle according to the wise principle that a head without a halo is infinitely more desirable than a halo without a head.' Ibid., 126–127.

[16] '... being wholly incapable of retorting in kind [to the puns and satires of the Jews], he was only too pleased when the Moslems showed a demoniacal readiness to avenge his wounded horror with sharper-pointed weapons than epigrams.' Other examples of intolerance were given, including the assassination of Asma, a Jewish poetess who composed verses against him, and who was allegedly assassinated by one of the Prophet's men. Ibid., 165–168.

[17] Dibble criticized the literary style of the Quran in the following terms: it abused 'the indefeasible privilege of all Holy Writ to be dull', there was absence of cohesion between chapters and sentences, it contained a 'hodge-podge of inchoate and irrelevant ideas' and, finally, was marked by a 'pervasive lack of charm'. Ibid., 60.

[18] He summarized what Muhammad offered in paradise: 'a haven bulging with sensuous delights of the most naïve and ephemeral sort'. Ibid., 74.

The Crusades, the French Revolution, and Cromwellian Puritanism were attended by an amount of sadism that may well make one pause before too severely condemning the blood mania and sex-obsession that mark every stage of Islam's triumphant progress.[19]

Although Dibble's book was critical of most aspects of the Prophet's life, the concluding pages attempted to convey a sense of the author's impartiality. Dibble appreciated the 'humanity and foresight' of the Prophet (as evident from his banning anything that caused torture to be inflicted on animals), his attempt to end blood feuds by emphasizing the brotherhood of Islam, his setting up of laws that enabled women to inherit and hold property, and his asking for slaves to be treated humanely.[20] In the balance-sheet of the self-professedly impartial biographer, the accounts were evenly settled. This enumeration of the Prophet's virtues did not prevent this biographer from deriding his descendants, who were revered by the Shias; he called Hasan and Husain 'scurvy fellows who excelled only in incompetence and cowardice'.[21]

Advance notice of the book had reached India before the arrival of actual copies, and the book, priced at 12 rupees, had already been advertised in the *Times of India* in July 1927.[22] Alarm bells rang in official circles in India even before the book had reached India: the HD took the view that banning the book under the SCA was desirable 'at once', as it 'may prevent the agitation that a book of the nature described would almost certainly cause even if proscribed'.[23] Home Secretary Sir Harry Haig agreed with the view that action should be taken under the SCA, but was worried about the timing, as neither the Secretary of State nor the GOI had seen copies of the book. He suggested that the copies of the book be intercepted while entering India (based on a warning by the DIB, Sir David Petrie, who later went on to head MI5, Great Britain's internal security agency) till the GOI had examined it and come to a decision regarding a possible ban.[24] The DIB asked the Bombay Commissioner of Police to detain all copies of the book, and warned maritime

---

[19] Ibid., 116.

[20] In fact, Dibble commented in the latter part of the book, even the 'luridly overemphasized harem system, Pagan though it may be, has some virtues that are perhaps absent from the Occidental system of prostitution'. Ibid., 242–243.

[21] Ibid., 247–248.

[22] *Times of India*, 11 July 1927.

[23] Note by Hodge of the HD, 4 September 1927, GOI Home Political, f. 65/IX, 1927, NAI.

[24] Noted by Haig, 22 September 1927, GOI Home Political, f. 65/IX, 1927, NAI.

Central Intelligence Department (CID) personnel as well. Petrie concluded that 'as the importation of the book would almost inevitably lead to riots and bloodshed', the Police Commissioner could get orders to ban the book from the Chief Presidency Magistrate under section 144 of the IPC.[25] In a parallel development, the Secretary of State, Lord Birkenhead, telegrammed the Viceroy, Lord Irwin, to the effect that he had information about this book, written in 'Babu English', which was 'very malicious in parts'. The Secretary of State suggested that importation of the book into India be watched with a view to proscribing it if necessary.[26] After the book went on sale in London in September 1927, a copy of it was sent by the India Office to the GOI so that they could form their own opinion of it.[27] The DIB, after reading passages marked in the book, thought:

> The author has approached his subject in a spirit of irreverence and levity. The book, as it stands, is bound to give deep offence to Mahomedans, and will probably be gloated over by many Hindus.... Perhaps in itself it is not so outrageously bad that there can be no two opinions on the question of prohibition.... And it may be productive of no small mischief by irritating the Mahomedans and providing the Hindus with fresh material for attacks on the prophet and his followers. The book is scarcely a serious production; it can do no good and can do only harm. There is nothing to be lost, therefore, by prohibiting.[28]

The DIB also gave an ingenious answer to the potential question as to why *Mother India* was not banned while this book was: *Mother India* was, in his opinion, unlike Dibble's book, 'a serious production and if it had possibilities for harm, it had also great possibilities for good'.[29] It was not the possibility of causing offence alone that was the criteria, but also the 'seriousness' of the work. After reading the book, he confessed, 'rapidly', Haig proffered the following opinion:

---

[25] Note by Petrie, 26 September 1927, GOI Home Political, f. 65/IX, 1927, NAI.

[26] Telegram P. no. 2617 from Secretary of State to Viceroy, 20 September 1927, GOI Home Political, f. 65/IX, 1927, NAI.

[27] Confidential letter P & J (S) 1432 from India Office to Haig, 22 September 1927, GOI Home Political, f. 65/IX, 1927, NAI.

[28] Note by Petrie, 4 October 1927, GOI Home Political, f. 65/IX, 1927, NAI.

[29] Ibid.

The book is an essay in cheap cynicism. It is written in a style of flippancy and irreverence, which applies just as much to Christian beliefs, where they happen to be touched upon by the author, as to Muhammad. It is also full of unpleasant innuendos of a sexual type. The book professes to treat the subject impartially and to represent the character of Muhammad as a strange enigma and combination of opposite qualities. But there is no doubt that the real object of the [unclear] is to exercise the author's talent for flippant [unclear] at the expense of the beliefs of others.

Haig felt that while the book could have been ignored in ordinary circumstances, in existing conditions some Hindus would be likely to reproduce extracts, and therefore it was advisable to keep the book out of India. This, then, was the reverberation of the *Rangila Rasul* controversy. In any case, 'no one could represent it as a serious historical enquiry'. Haig suggested action under the SCA, even though a ban under this could not touch copies that had already found their way to India.[30] As the Home Member, Sir James Crerar, too agreed with these views,[31] the book was banned by a notification on 8 October 1927.[32] After the GOI had established that the American and English editions of the book were identical except for page numbers, a supplement was added to the banning notification indicating that the English edition was prohibited as well.[33]

While this process was in progress, the Viceroy expressed a desire to read the book, and it was sent to him.[34] By 7 October 1927, a fortnight after receiving the original communication from the Secretary of State, the Viceroy telegrammed him indicating that while some copies of the book had come to India, others were held up by Customs as 'its circulation during present communal tension could be mischievous'. The Bombay government had been asked to establish if any appreciable number of copies had already reached India, in which case the GOI would also consider banning it under the (then new) section 295A

---

[30] Note by Haig, 5 October 1927, GOI Home Political, f. 65/IX, 1927, NAI.

[31] Note by Crerar, 5 October 1927, GOI Home Political, f. 65/IX, 1927, NAI.

[32] Finance Deptt (Customs) notification no. 100, 8 October 1927, prohibited the import of the book under the SCA, GOI Home Political, f. 65/IX, 1927, NAI.

[33] Note by Petrie, 10 October 1927. Finance Deptt (Customs) notification no. 101 specified that the importation of the book 'wherever printed' was banned. GOI Home Political, f. 65/IX, 1927, NAI.

[34] Letter from Haig to PSV, G. Cunningham, 5 October 1927, GOI Home Political, f. 65/IX, 1927, NAI.

of the IPC, which applied to case where there was 'deliberate and malicious intention of outraging religious feelings'.[35]

Although the initiative for banning Dibble's book was taken by the GOI, some pressure was put on the India Office by a representative of a Muslim pressure group in London. The head of the Ahmadiyya Muslim Mission in London, A.R. Dard, wrote to the India Office reminding them of the agitation that had been caused in India by the publication of *Rangila Rasul*, and bringing to their notice Dibble's book. He termed the publication of the book 'dangerous to Public Peace', and included detailed extracts that he deemed 'abominable and execrable'. In keeping with the general rule that what offends needs to be repeated to prove how offensive it is, demands for proscription usually—and ironically—quote copiously from the very publications they want to suppress. This representation too referred to and repeated the most outrageous portions of the book. The writer of the letter confessed that he had been unable to locate the author in London (his name was not found in the London directories, and the publishers had refused to give his address), and recorded his protest against the publication of 'this most ignominiously disgraceful book', which was 'bound to inflict a deep wound on the religious susceptibilities of the Moslems'. He requested that the book be banned, and action taken against the author. At the very least, the government was to make the author apologize publicly. The writer of the letter also cited the English law of blasphemy which laid down that 'profane scoffing' at Jesus Christ and the Holy Scripture or exposing them to 'contempt or ridicule' was punishable by the English courts with 'fines, imprisonment and corporeal punishment'. He suggested that if similar provisions were not applied to founders of other religions, the prestige of the British in the colonies would be damaged. The writer's larger agenda was, therefore, to urge amendment of the existing English law so that it would 'protect the religious susceptibilities of the followers of all other religions as well'.[36] This, according to the India Office, was an impossible request, and they decided to respond merely with a sympathetic and non-committal letter.[37] The Secretary of State 'entirely' approved of the action of the GOI in banning the import of the book, but also recognized that in Britain 'it is impossible to take

---

[35] Telegram P. no. 2040-S from Viceroy to Secretary of State, 7 October 1927, GOI Home Political, f. 65/IX, 1927, NAI.

[36] Letter from A.R. Dard to the India Office, 6 October 1927, GOI Home Political, f. 65/IX, 1927, NAI.

[37] Letter no. P & J (S) 1656 from the Secretary P & J to the Under Secretary of State, India Office, 2 November 1927, GOI Home Political, f. 65/IX, 1927, NAI.

action against a publication that is not technically blasphemous or obscene'. Mr Dard was to be informed that while the British government 'realise the pain that such a book must produce among Muslims', they were 'not prepared to undertake an alteration of the law'. Here, then, was admission that different rules applied to, and in, the colonies than in Britain.

What are some of the notable features of this case, visible in its historical reconstruction? Colonial officials were worried about the possible impact of the book even before it arrived in India. The Viceroy, the Home Secretary and the DIB certainly read the book; very possibly the Home Member and the Secretary of State did too. There was no question of banning it without reading it first. Their decision to scrutinize the book was, as the timing of the feverish correspondence indicates, not a response to public pressure, but preceded it. The reasons for banning the book were clearly enunciated: for one, it was deemed to be flippant and not a serious academic study. For another, given the state of communal tension in India prevailing in that period, the book was seen as ready-made ammunition for one group against another. We will see the recurrence of many of these features in other cases in the following decade.

'… a thousand times worse than Rangila Rasul': The *Britannia and Eve* Case (1930)

Britannia and Eve: A Monthly Journal for Men and Women was a London journal containing fiction, fashion and articles on housekeeping and general interest. In its January 1930 issue it published an article that was to become highly controversial at the time, and a reference point for officials as well as protesters in that and the subsequent decade. This long article (spread over four pages and ten columns) was part of a series, 'Famous Women of History', by Norman Hill and titled 'Ayesha: The Favourite Wife of the Prophet Mahomet'.[38] It was accompanied by three illustrations, two of which depicted a bearded man (purporting to be sketches of the Prophet) and all of which also contained drawings of a young woman referred to as Ayesha. One was a black and white

---

[38] The entire issue of *Britannia and Eve: A Monthly Journal for Men and Women* 2, no. 1 (January 1930) is available in GOI Home Political, f. 29/I, 1930, NAI. This article is on 34–37 and 130 of the journal. Previous articles in this series were devoted to Messalina, Sappho, Helen of Troy and Cleopatra, among others. The Italian illustrator F. Matania was famous in his own right, and specialized in portraits of historical figures. His name appeared right next to that of the author, Norman Hill.

illustration of a robed and bearded man sitting on the carpet holding the hand of a richly attired girl-child, and captioned 'Mahomet meets his future wife'. The other was a pencil sketch of a woman on horseback surrounded by men on camels and on foot with arrows, shields and spears, and was captioned thus: 'She became a warrior herself, led the Arabs to victory and succoured them in defeat. In battle she was always to the forefront.' The third, full-page, colour illustration depicted an old, bearded and robed man on a bed, covered by a blanket in a well-furnished room, with his head resting against the near-naked and richly jewelled body of a young girl with a fly whisk in her hand. This image was captioned 'Ayesha blew on his cheeks to keep them warm and repeated the Islamic prayers for the departing; she rubbed his hands, but he motioned her to desist. Then a few more incoherent prayers, and his head settled in death on his young wife's bosom.'

The text of the article was written like a play complete with dialogues. It described Ayesha as being betrothed at the age of seven, married at the age of nine, and widowed before the age of twenty. It dwelt in detail on the Prophet's relationship with his wives, and the references were mostly derogatory. The text of the article referred to the Prophet as a man of many wives, but 'emphatically not one of the World's Great Lovers'. It also referred to him as having 'as many concubines as Solomon, and almost as many wives' and described Ayesha as having 'a biting tongue and shrewish demeanour' that made men like and women loathe her. It described in great detail the episode of Ayesha's alleged infidelity, and the resolving of the issue by the Prophet. The rest of the article described the Prophet's encounters with all his wives, jealousy among them, and various events in the women's quarters. The article concluded with the statement that of all his wives, only Ayesha lived on in human memory.

When he was shown the issue in January 1930, Home Secretary Haig considered the pictures 'very offensive' to Muslim sentiment, and produced in 'complete ignorance' of them. However, he was doubtful if the *Britannia and Eve* could be banned legally unless it could be proved that there was a deliberate intention to promote enmity or outrage religious feelings.[39] Even as the GOI was deliberating on a suitable course of action, their attention was again drawn to the article by the Punjab Chief Secretary, H.W. Emerson, who in turn had received a complaint about it from Chaudhri Shahabuddin, President of the Punjab Legislative Council, who found the article 'a thousand times worse than the notorious book—Rangila Rasul', and likely to be translated into

---

[39] Note by Haig, 31 January 1930, GOI Home Political, f. 29/I, 1930, NAI.

vernacular languages and broadcast widely.[40] The Government of Punjab was of the view that the present article was 'very much worse' than the controversial book *Rangila Rasul*, and that if it was circulated it would 'greatly incite the feelings of Muhammadans'. Emerson was apprehensive that Hindu publicists would use the article to assert that comments in the *Rangila Rasul* were correct, and for this reason urged the GOI to immediately ban this issue from sale throughout India. Since booksellers were not at fault, he suggested that they be compensated for the copies seized. Additionally, Emerson wanted the Secretary of State to be informed, so that the publishers of the magazine could be persuaded to stop all further consignments to India. The reason that the Punjab government had not taken any action was because they wanted action to be taken all over India simultaneously.[41]

Events moved fast. On 1 February 1930 a protest meeting against the article was organized in London by about 25 Muslims.[42] The Imam of the London Mosque met an India Office official and agreed to temporarily suspend agitation pending steps taken by the India Office.[43] On its part, the India Office urged the Imam that 'your best course of action is not to give it further publicity than it would normally secure by independent action'.[44] In the meantime, the India Office wrote to the editor of *Britannia and Eve*, informing him that although the article was likely published in good faith, its matter and illustrations were causing offence to Muslims, as pictorial representations of the Prophet were 'intolerable to good Moslems', more so when they and the accompanying text were 'derogatory to his life and character'. The India Office requested the editor to publish a statement in the journal at the earliest so as to reassure Muslim opinion.[45] In response the editor stated that he had no intention to give offence, but as he was currently preparing the April issue, to refer to something published

---

[40] Letter from Chaudhri Shahabuddin to Finance Member, Punjab, Sir Alexander Stow, 4 February 1930, GOI Home Political, f. 29/I, 1930, NAI.

[41] D.O. no. 334-P.A. from Emerson to Haig, 4 February 1930, GOI Home Political, f. 29/I, 1930, NAI.

[42] Reported in letter no. P & J 451/30 from V. Dawson of the India Office to Haig, 6 February 1930, GOI Home Political, f. 29/I, 1930, NAI.

[43] Letter from Maulvi Farzand Ali, Imam of the London Mosque, to V. Dawson of the India Office, 9 February 1930, GOI Home Political, f. 29/I, 1930, NAI.

[44] Letter from V. Dawson of the India Office to Maulvi Farzand Ali, 10 February 1930, GOI Home Political, f. 29/I, 1930, NAI.

[45] Letter from Under Secretary of State, Sir A. Hitzel, to editor, *Britannia and Eve*, J. Heitner, 1 February 1930, GOI Home Political, f. 29/I, 1930, NAI.

in the January issue would, in his opinion, 'only draw more forcefully, attention to something which is better forgotten'.[46] The India Office impressed upon the editor the seriousness of the issue, informed him that the GOI was taking steps to suppress the article, and asked him to insert a slip in the March issue.[47] The India Office clearly wanted to be seen to be active in the case. On his part, the editor of *Britannia and Eve* reported to the India Office that he had met with the Imams of the London Mosque and the Woking Mosque, and offered them one whole page in the April issue of the journal so that they could 'correct any erroneous impressions' which the original article had created in the 'minds of Moslems here and in India'. He had also apologized to them for the 'pain and annoyance' caused by the original publication.[48]

Even as the India Office was engaging in this damage control exercise, the GOI was taking steps of its own that culminated in the ban on the import of this particular issue of the journal. Legal opinion received by the GOI had indicated that the issue could not be banned under section 99A of the CrPC, as this only applied to publications that were within the scope of sections 124A, 153A and 295A of the IPC. The article depicted Ayesha's life as a historical subject, was not seditious under any definition of that term, and it could not be argued that the intention was either 'deliberate and malicious intention of outraging religious feelings' (section 295A) or 'intention to promote feelings of enmity or hatred between different classes of people' (153A). The essence of the offence was 'malicious intention', and since this could not be proved, the GOI was advised not to take action under section 99A (to ban circulation of the book).[49] In any case, this section could only be used by local governments and not by the GOI.

In the meantime, sections of the press and public in India began their own campaign against the journal. On 6 February, a deputation of Muslims visited the Kotwal of Lahore city to ask him to take appropriate action.[50] Two days later, an article appeared in the *Muslim Outlook* demanding that the government

---

[46] Letter from Heitner to Hirtzel, 4 February 1930, GOI Home Political, f. 29/I, 1930, NAI.

[47] Letter to Heitner from Hirtzel, 7 February 1930, GOI Home Political, f. 29/I, 1930, NAI.

[48] Letter from Heitner to Hirtzel, 13 February 1930, GOI Home Political, f. 29/I, 1930, NAI.

[49] Note by GOI official (initials unclear), 6 February 1930, GOI Home Political, f. 29/I, 1930, NAI.

[50] D.O. no. 338-P.A. from Emerson to Haig, 6 February 1930, GOI Home Political, f. 29/I, 1930, NAI.

take action against the offending publication, while some Muslims met the Viceroy to communicate their views on the matter to him. The Government of Punjab, panicking by this time, banned the January issue under section 99A invoking section 153A. Although they were well aware that if this was challenged in court then intention could not be proved, they decided to go ahead nevertheless. As the Punjab Chief Secretary put it, 'This was clearly a case in which political considerations made it incumbent on Government to risk the legality of the order being challenged.'[51] On 8 February 1930, the GOI acted on the issue by banning import of the January issue of the magazine into India under the SCA.[52] Before they did this, however, the GOI wrote to all local governments that since the legality of a ban under section 99A was 'very doubtful', they were to 'as unobtrusively as possible … buy up all copies that may be available for sale (and detain, pending issue of notification under Sea Customs Act, any copies that may come in by sea)'.[53]

Although the GOI had taken steps to curb the publication, and these steps had been publicized in newspapers, pressure groups still did not cease their campaign. For instance, in mid-February 1930 some Muslims of Seohara (in Bijnore district of UP) wrote a petition to the Viceroy in Urdu demanding a ban on the January issue.[54] In late February the Viceory received a strongly worded complaint against the journal by the president of the Young Sunni Vohra Society, who thought that the magazine tried to pass off filthy matter 'under the sacred name of History', and that it had tried to rake hostile feelings between Islam and Christianity.[55] The Ahmadiyya Anjuman-i-Ishaat-i-Islam of Lahore wrote directly to the India Office on 12 February stating:

---

[51] D.O. no. 12538-S.B. from Emerson to Haig, 8 February 1930. The Punjab government banned the journal via notification no. 12538-S.B., 7 February 1930. The ban was also reported in the *Daily Chronicle* (Delhi) on 12 February 1930, GOI Home Political, f. 29/I, 1930, NAI.

[52] Finance Deptt (Customs) notification no. 5, 8 February 1930 banned import of the book, GOI Home Political, f. 29/I, 1930. This was also reported in the *Hindustan Times*, 9 February 1930, NAI.

[53] Telegram R. no. 395-S from HD New Delhi to all local governments, 7 February 1930, GOI Home Political, f. 29/I, 1930, NAI.

[54] Letter from Mohammad Hifzur Rahman, Member of the Jamiat-e-Ulema Hind, forwarded to the HD by the Foreign and Political Deptt, GOI Home Political, f. 29/I, 1930, NAI.

[55] Letter from the President of the Young Sunni Vohra Society to the PSV, date not mentioned, stamped 25 February 1930 by the Office of the Private Secretary to the Viceroy, GOI Home Political, f. 29/I, 1930, NAI.

The manner in which the writer has painted the character of the Holy Person who has 1/5 population of the world as his followers, smacks of the spirit of medieval crusaders. It is unfortunate that the British scholars after a long and close contact with the Muslims for the last two centuries have not been able to grasp the true sentiments of the Muslims and have ignored the esteem and respect which they have for their Holy Prophet. Disrespect towards their Holy Prophet and his wives is the last thing a Muslim can tolerate.... He [the layman] blames all the nation for the indiscretion of a writer or a padre, who attacks his Holy Prophet so outrageously.

The letter warned that as the article was bound to stir up feelings of Muslims in other Crown territories outside India, it could be used by enemies of the British empire to create ill-feeling in Muslim minds against the empire. The letter was accompanied by two pamphlets on Islam and a short biography of the Prophet so that the Secretary of State for India could form a 'correct idea about our religion and our sentiments'.[56] In response, the HD wrote to this organization apprising them of action taken by them, and assuring them that the GOI did indeed 'deeply sympathise' with Muslim sentiment regarding the article, and had done all that was possible to counteract it.[57]

The controversy reached the British Parliament as well as the Indian Council of State in March 1930, and questions were asked in both about the ban on the journal.[58] Here was a case of the India Office and the GOI working in tandem on many fronts: pressuring the editor to withdraw copies, debating the legality of a ban internally, justifying it in legislative fora in England and in India, and combining legal measures with extra-legal ones in order to remove

---

[56] Letter from Moh. A. Din Jan [sic], Honorary General Secretary Ahmadiyya Anjuman-i-Ishaat-i-Islam, Lahore, to the Secretary of State for India, 12 February 1930, GOI Home Political, f. 29/I, 1930, NAI.

[57] Draft of letter no. D 1441 from India Office to Ahmadiyya Anjuman-i-Ishaat-i-Islam of Lahore, 28 April 1930, GOI Home Political, f. 29/I, 1930, NAI.

[58] On 17 March a question was raised in the British Parliament asking on what grounds the journal was banned; the answer given was that the journal was banned as the article was 'grossly offensive to Moslem religious feeling'. Question asked by Wardlaw Milne, 17 March 1930. On 18 March a question about the journal was raised in the Council of State in India by Sir Ebrahim Jaffer, asking why it was banned, whether any attempt was made to buy up copies, and whether the possession of copies was prohibited. The reply given was that the ban was because it was thought the article would 'give just cause of offence to Muslims', that local governments were asked to buy up copies, and that the Punjab government had banned the issue. GOI Home Political, f. 29/I, 1930, NAI.

the publication from the public domain. Public pressure from groups in Britain and in India also played an important role in forcing the government's hand. The *Britannia and Eve* case was one of many in the 1930s involving British publications that became controversial in Britain and in India for causing offence to Muslim opinion, and the ban imposed on it was invoked by pressure groups subsequently as a precedent for demanding other bans. The pressure groups operated in Britain and in India, inside the legislature and outside it.

The *Everyman's Weekly* Case (1932–1933)

In November 1932, the India Office received a representation from a Muslim resident of Bombay complaining against two articles that had been published in Britain the previous month. One, titled 'A Prophet 1000 Years Ago', was published in *My Magazine* and the other, titled 'Smiling Gigolo Who Began a New Religion', in *Everyman's Weekly*. The writer of the complaint requested the Secretary of State to ensure that such articles 'should not be permitted in Journals or Magazines sent to India from Great Britain'. He also enclosed an article that he had written in response, and his letter contained the warning that the publication of such articles would convey the 'false impression' to millions of loyal subjects that British policy was antagonistic to Islam.[59]

After receiving this complaint the India Office first corresponded with the editor of the journal, R. J. Minney (whose book *Shiva* had already been banned in India in 1929). The objection 'from India by a Moslem resident' was communicated to Minney, and he was asked to view the article from the 'standpoint of a devout Moslem leader'. Minney was asked to 'guard against similar offence being given in the future', especially as it appeared that the journal was circulated in India as well.[60] Minney replied that he did not intend to give offence; indeed, 'there is no community which I hold in greater esteem'. However, he stood his ground regarding the content of the article. As he put it:

> The life of Mahomet is a matter of history. The facts for the article were obtained very largely from H.G. Wells' 'Outline of History', a book which must be enjoying a very large sale in India, as elsewhere. I trust I shall be

---

[59] Letter from Al-Haj Qassim Ali Jairazbhoy to Secretary of State, 28 November 1932, complaining against the 8 October 1932 issue of what he referred to as 'Everybody's Weekly'. GOI Home Political, f. 39/5, 1933, NAI.

[60] Letter P & J 40/33 from R. T. Peel on behalf of Secretary of State, Sir Samuel Hoare, to Minney, 12 January 1933, GOI Home Political, f. 39/5, 1933, NAI.

pardoned for wondering whether any protests have been received against that publication and any attempts made to prohibit its sale in India.[61]

The India Office was forced to acknowledge that in fact no protests had been received by the Secretary of State regarding Wells' book.[62] (As it happened, a complaint against Wells' book was made several years later in 1938, and is discussed later in this chapter.) After corresponding with Minney, the India Office wrote to Home Secretary Hallett regarding this case, informing him that there were not many copies of the periodical coming into India, and in any case it was too late to take action.[63] The HD agreed that they had no information about the circulation of the journal in India (neither did the DIB for that matter, as the journal had never come to their notice previously) and that it was too late to take action against it.[64] As for the complainant, the Bombay government wrote to him stating that appropriate action had been taken, and he in turn expressed his gratitude to the Secretary of State for acceding to his representation.[65] This matter ended here, but the issue was still alive, and flared up periodically. As compared to the case against *Britannia and Eve*, which had attracted the attention of various pressure groups in Britain and in India, the *Everyman's Weekly* case involved only a single complaint by an individual, which perhaps explains why the GOI did not think it fit to act on it by way of banning the import of the issue. The next year, however, an article on the Prophet in another journal called *Pearson's Weekly* was taken more seriously. Clearly, it was the quantum of offence, as gauged by the number of complaints and/or the prominence of the complainant, that determined the chances of a ban.

---

[61] Letter from Minney to Peel, 13 January 1933, GOI Home Political, f. 39/5, 1933.

[62] Letter P & J 163/33 from Peel to Minney, 18 January 1933, GOI Home Political, f. 39/5, 1933, NAI.

[63] Letter P & J 163/33 from Peel to Hallett, 26 January 1933. According to the India Office, Minney's attitude regarding this was 'not very satisfactory' although he had apologized. In this letter Peel also informed the GOI about the imminent publication of Minney's new book, *India Marches Past*. Although it was to be published in Britain and the United States, its high price was thought to limit the circulation of the book which was deemed 'likely to contain objectionable matter on religions and other subjects'. GOI Home Political, f. 39/5, 1933, NAI.

[64] Note by C.M. Trivedi, 15 February 1933 and by the DIB dated 20 February 1933, GOI Home Political, f. 39/5, 1933, NAI.

[65] Letter from Jairazbhoy to Maxwell, 20 March 1933. Maxwell's letter to Jairazbhoy is not on file, GOI Home Political, f. 39/5, 1933, NAI.

The *Pearson's Weekly* Case (1934)

Pearson's Weekly was a journal for light reading, containing jokes, advertisements for romance novels, puzzles, short stories and pen pal columns. An article titled 'Mahomed: Prophet of Allah' written by W.J. Makin appeared in its 10 February 1934 issue. It covered seven columns, and was illustrated with five black and white sketches, one of which depicted the Prophet, and another Ayesha. Yet others showed Muslims at prayer, a Muslim reading the Quran, and a Bedouin follower (complete with camel) at prayer. The largest illustration was captioned 'Mahomet preached from his cave while Bilal, the giant negro, called Islam to prayer', and showed a man in a flowing beard and robe with one arm raised, while a tall man with a spear stood behind him. Another illustration captioned '"If I confess," declared Ayesha, "God knoweth I am not guilty…"' showed a number of men surrounding a woman with long hair in revealing clothes.[66] The article began by describing how life in many parts of the world came to a standstill when 250 million men prayed visualizing what was described as: 'A piece of ground not as large as Trafalgar square, infinitely more dirty and dusty. An old house crumbing into rubble. A black stone which occasionally reflects red streaks. Nothing more.' The Kaaba was described as once having been used for human sacrifices. Muhammad was described as 'a shrewd, common-sense business man until he reached the dangerous age, the forties'. The article went on to describe the influence of Jewish traders on him, attributed his belief in one God to their influence, alleged that he was victim to epileptic attacks, described the Hejira in dramatic language, and stated that women were his 'great weakness' as he enlarged his harem. It also described his marriage 'at the age of fifty-two' to a 'girl of nine', carried an account of Ayesha's suspected infidelity, and so on. It contained the comment, 'If there was renunciation, it was not necessarily the renunciation of manly appetites', and described Muhammad's concept to paradise (in verse) as a place of gardens, vineyards, wine and women. The article concluded with the promise that the next week's journal would carry a piece on Buddha.[67]

In India, within two weeks of the article's publication in Great Britain, Sir Harry Haig's attention was drawn to the article in end-February 1934 by Sir Fazl-i-Husain, the Member for Education, Health and Lands.[68] Subsequently,

---

[66] An original copy of the journal is available in GOI Home Political, f. 37/III, 1934, NAI.

[67] *Pearson's Weekly*, 10 February 1934, 14–15 and 17.

[68] Letter from Sir Fazl-i-Husain to Sir Harry Haig, 28 February 1934. Enclosed was a clipping in English (name of publication not clear, dated 27 February 1934) that

the Home Secretary (who confessed that he had some difficulty in getting hold of the publication) suggested that its import be banned; even though it was much after publication, such a measure would 'show to Muslims that we have taken notice of the article and that the Government of India were prepared to prevent the dissemination of anything which offended their religious susceptibilities'. This was, clearly, censorship as a public relations exercise. Additionally, local governments were to be asked to buy up copies that were still available for sale.[69]

Various papers in India contained news about the article, and the GOI monitored the press for such news. While news of the publications of this article was reported in three English language papers (*Eastern Times*, *Star of India* and *National Call*), vernacular papers of north India took much more interest, and articles and editorials appeared in *Zamindar*, *Alaman*, *Siyasat*, *Aljamiat*, *Pratap*, *Inqilab* and *Medina*. In these papers, according to an official entrusted with scanning them for this news, 'indignation has been aroused not so much by the actual text of the article—though this of course was strongly objected to—but by the fact that it was illustrated'.[70]

The 10 February issue of *Pearson's Weekly* was banned by the Punjab government on 3 March 1934, as were all documents carrying translations, copies and extracts from the article, citing section 153A of the IPC.[71] Subsequently, the Viceroy asked the Secretary of State for India to bring this to the attention of the publishers of the journal in Britain, to tell them about how such articles were 'likely to cause serious mischief in India', and to ask them to publish a statement to reassure public opinion.[72] On 5 March, after

---

expressed objection to the article in strong terms, termed it 'totally false, indecent and misleading', and stated that the Muslim world was tired of repeated instances of such attacks, which 'may be a survival from the savage days of the Crusades'. It asked the British government to do something before Muslims 'take the law into their own hands'. GOI Home Political, f. 37/III, 1934, NAI.

[69] Note by Hallett, 8 March 1934. After the Home Secretary received news that the Punjab government had banned the journal, he added a post-script to this note to the effect that action under the SCA was not necessary. GOI Home Political, f. 37/III, 1934, NAI.

[70] Note by GOI official (initials unclear), 8 March 1934, GOI Home Political, f. 37/III, 1934, NAI.

[71] Punjab Government notification no. 1505 P.B., 3 March 1934, GOI Home Political, f. 37/III, 1934, NAI.

[72] Telegram R. no. 572 from Viceroy to Secretary of State, 9 March 1934, GOI Home Political, f. 37/III, 1934, NAI.

the Punjab ban, a group of Muslims in Lahore held a public meeting and demanded from all Muslim countries that they compel the British government to 'punish severely' those responsible for such attacks, and that the people responsible not be allowed to enter Muslim countries.[73] Later that month, a resolution was passed at a public meeting in Madras, at the other end of the country, condemning the publication, and warning that if the publication was not seized and those responsible for it punished, then Muslims would be forced to protect the honour of their Prophet 'regardless of consequences'. The meeting also thanked the Government of Punjab for banning the issue.[74] Much after the ban on the original issue, Anjumani Sufia in Madras wrote to the Viceroy demanding forfeiture of all copies, translations and extracts of the publication,[75] and Muslims from Fatèhpur in Barabanki district (UP) sent an urgent telegram to the Viceroy asking him to confiscate the magazine and punish the editor.[76]

As the publication emanated from London, the India Office informed its editor of the reaction in India to the publication, and the ban on it by the Punjab government, and asked him to publish a statement at the earliest.[77] The editor—like editors before him in the same predicament—wrote back stating that he was unaware of the offence the article would cause, and intended to publish 'another article on the Muslim movement which will be in the nature of an appreciation of the Muslim subjects of the Empire'.[78]

The *Every Woman's* Case (1935)

The publication of controversial articles about the Prophet, his wives, and Islam generally, in British journals had become an annual affair in the 1930s. In May

---

[73] Reported in the *National Call* (Delhi), 7 March 1934.

[74] Resolutions forwarded in letter from Kazi M. Habibullah Sahib to the Viceroy, 21 March 1934. GOI Home Political, f. 37/III, 1934, NAI.

[75] Letter from Anjuman Sufia, Madras, to the Viceroy, 24 March 1934, GOI Home Political, f. 37/III, 1934, NAI.

[76] Telegram from Mahudali, 'President Protesting Muslims', Fatehpur, Barabanki, 28 March 1934. Sometime in March, an individual from Jullunder wrote a petition in Urdu to the Viceroy protesting against the article. This [date unclear] was forwarded to the HD on 29 March 1934, GOI Home Political, f. 37/III, 1934, NAI.

[77] Letter P & J 848/34 from R.T. Peel to editor of *Pearson's Weekly*, 20 March 1934, GOI Home Political, f. 37/III, 1934, NAI.

[78] Letter from editor of *Pearson's Weekly* to the Under Secretary of State, 21 March 1934, GOI Home Political, f. 37/III, 1934, NAI.

1935, *Every Woman's*, a monthly fashion magazine (containing, for example, an article on London debutantes) published an article on the Prophet as part of a series called 'Other People's Gods'. This was titled 'Mohammed—Visionary—Warrior—Man of many wives', and written by A.L. Easterman. The text was spread over six columns, and accompanied by a full-page illustration captioned 'Mohammed, the warrior-prophet, carried on his crusade against unbelievers by the power of the sword'; the background depicted was that of Mecca, and superimposed on it was a sketched portrait of a man in a robe and plumed turban, with a flowing beard.[79] It began by describing an imaginary scene of the marriage of Muhammad's parents. He himself was described as 'divinity of three hundred million Moslems', as having a 'thoughtful turn of mind', and enjoying 'high repute for the honour and integrity' with which he conducted his business. It reported 'tradition' as saying that at the time of his first marriage his wife Khadija was 40 and he 25, but did not comment on the matter further. It also suggested that he was influenced by Judaism and Christianity. Commenting that 'Blood and Banditry now marked his way', it described the Prophet's soldiers' alleged plunder and capturing of women, and referred to him roaming 'the desert in search of blood and rapine'. There was also one reference to 'young Ayesha' and other wives. The article concluded that within 10 years he had laid the foundations of a religion that, 13 centuries later, bound together millions.

It was not until five months after this article appeared that the India Office first received a complaint about it. In November 1935, the Jamiat-e-Ahrar-ul-Muslemeen of Bombay wrote to the Secretary of State for India protesting against it. The Secretary of State though the article was 'well-intentioned' on the whole, and that the 'only really offensive feature' was the pictorial representation of Muhammad. On its part the India Office informed the editor of the magazine to the attention the article was receiving in India, but did not propose to take any further action.[80]

In the meantime, a campaign against the article began in the Indian press. The *Haqui* (an Urdu paper from Lucknow) appealed to the GOI in November 1935 to take action against the journal.[81] Articles against it also appeared in

---

[79] Clipping of article from *Every Woman's* monthly magazine, May 1935, in GOI Home Political, f. 37/10, 1935, NAI.

[80] Letter P & J 4510/35 from R. T. Peel to Home Secretary GOI, 5 December 1935, GOI Home Political, f. 37/10, 1935, NAI.

[81] Clipping of the paper, 10 November 1935, and gist in English in GOI Home Political, f. 37/10, 1935, NAI.

the *Bombay Chronicle*, some Urdu newspapers in Bombay, and the *Amrita Bazar Patrika* of Calcutta. In Bombay, 10 Muslim organizations stated at a meeting that as no picture of the Prophet had ever existed, any portrait of his could not be a true representation.[82] When the GOI tried to get hold of the journal to examine it, they found that the May issue was not available in India and had to be ordered.[83] The Home Secretary, referring to the *Britannia and Eve* and *Pearson's Weekly* cases, felt:

> ... we must do everything to prevent the dissemination of matter regarded as offensive by Muslims. We or local Governments have taken action previously ... and with Muslim temper being as it is at present, it is the more necessary to do so now.[84]

However, legal opinion sought by the Bombay government considered that the matter did not come within the purview of the Indian Press Act or section 99 of the CrPC.[85] Another HD official offered the following opinion:

> This is I think another example of exaggerated sensitivity on the part of some of the Muslim community. It can be understood that they might take exception to parts of this article, but I think the point is that it appeared in the issue of 'Everywoman' of May 1935, the paper is almost entirely devoted to women's fashions, and its circulation is probably confined for the most part to European women in India. Probably no one bothered to read the article, and certainly no one is likely now to buy a fashion paper seven months old, even after it has been advertised in the Muslim Press.[86]

Although Home Secretary Hallett as well as Home Member Craik agreed with this assessment, they both felt it was important to inform the India Office

---

[82] Newspaper reports were communicated by the Government of Bombay to the GOI in letter no. 2/27-Poll from H.F. Knight to Home Secretary GOI, 3 December 1935, GOI Home Political, f. 37/10, 1935, NAI. *Bombay Chronicle*, 20 November 1935, and *Amrita Bazar Patrika*, 24 November 1935, carried articles against this publication.

[83] Note by HD official (signature illegible), 26 November 1935, replying to the Home Secretary's request for a copy of the controversial issue. GOI Home Political, f. 37/10, 1935, NAI.

[84] Note by Hallett, 29 November 1935, GOI Home Political, f. 37/10, 1935, NAI.

[85] Note, 12 December 1935, reporting the view of the Remembrancer of Legal Affairs, Bombay, GOI Home Political, f. 37/10, 1935, NAI.

[86] Note by HD official (initials unclear), 13 December 1935, GOI Home Political, f. 37/10, 1935, NAI.

how sensitive Muslim opinion in India was 'at present', and make English publishers realize the position.[87] They did not, however, ban the issue of the journal. In March 1936 when a question was asked in the LA about articles offensive to Muslim sentiments, referring specifically to the *Every Woman's* case, Home Member Craik was able to reply that the Secretary of State had already written to the editor, and issued a circular to all British editors calling their attention to the matter.[88]

One of the consequences of repeated controversies on the issue of representing (in words as well as in illustrations) the Prophet, his life, his family and the religion founded by him—the *Every Woman's* case being the catalyst—was that in January 1936 the India Office wrote a general letter to British editors through their (three most important) professional associations 'warning them of the main dangers to be avoided when writing any article dealing with Islam'. The associations replied to the effect that they were conveying the warning to their members.[89] The guidelines began with the statement that although editors in Britain had responded helpfully in the past in cases where Muslim sentiments had been hurt, it was now desirable to *prevent* objectionable references, rather than merely take action post publication. Two reasons were given for this: one, it was stated, Muslim affairs were in sharp focus; two, the number of representations against such articles had increased in number. The guidelines were summarized thus:

> The all-important point is never to mention the Prophet's name except in terms of studied respect. This is the Muslims' attitude to Christ, and all that is needed is reciprocity. Objection is taken to
>
> Any direct ridicule of the Muslim religion;
> Any pictorial representation of the Prophet or of his wives;
> Derogatory references to the Prophet's private life and character, and to the age of Khadija or the youth of Ayesha as compared with Mohammed's own age, and;
> Over-emphasis on the martial character of Mohammedanism.[90]

---

[87] Notes by Hallett, 13 December 1935 and by Craik, 13 and 14 December 1935, GOI Home Political, f. 37/10, 1935, NAI.

[88] The question was asked by Sir Muhammad Yakub on 27 March 1936, GOI Home Political, f. 37/10, 1935, NAI.

[89] This was reported, and the letters enclosed, in letter no. P & J 4510/35 from R.T. Peel to Hallett, 26 February 1936, GOI Home Political, f. 37/10, 1935, NAI.

[90] Letter from H. MacGregor of the India Office to E.W. Davies of The Newspaper Society, Great Britain, 30 January 1936. The same letter was also sent to the secretaries

According to the letter, editors were *not* to regard this as interference, but 'as a form of help offered in dealing with a specialist subject'. More importantly, the letter continued:

> From our English and Christian point of view many of the Muslim representations may seem to be over-sensitive. But all are based on sincerity and there is the fact that Muslims constitute something like 90 millions of our fellow-subjects of the King. Therefore it would seem to be both a matter for toleration and policy to meet their point of view as possible.[91]

Despite this letter, publications continued to offend; censorship by diktat had its limits.

H.G. Wells' *Outline of History* (1938)

In 1938, the GOI received protests from Muslims in London and in India asking them to ban H.G. Wells' *Outline of History* (first published in 1920; hereafter *Outline*) and his *A Short History of the World* (an abridged version of the former, published in 1922, with many revised editions; hereafter *Short History*).[92] The Anjuman-i-Islamia at Simla passed a resolution asking that H.G. Wells' *The New and Revised Outline of History* be banned in India, and legal action taken against the author.[93] Protests were made in October 1938 by the Muslim Students' Union at Ahmedabad, which wanted both books to be banned.[94] In the same month, the Assam Arabic Students' Association at Calcutta made the same request.[95] Far flung parts of India were united in protest.

---

of the Newspaper Proprietors' Association and the Periodical, Trade, Press and Weekly Newspaper Proprietor's Association. GOI Home Political, f. 37/10, 1935, NAI.

[91] Ibid.

[92] Note by R.B. Elwin, 14 October 1938. All documents in GOI Home Political, f. 150, 1938, NAI.

[93] Resolution passed on 26 September 1938 was communicated to the Viceroy in letter, 3 October 1938, GOI Home Political, f. 150, 1938, NAI.

[94] Letter to the Viceroy from the Muslim Students' Union at Ahmedabad, 8 October 1938, GOI Home Political, f. 150, 1938, NAI.

[95] Writing to the GOI again in August 1941, the association reminded it of its earlier demand and expressed its 'sense of abhorrences [*sic*] at the vilest attack on the life of the Holy Prophet' made in *Short History*. It urged the government ensure that the objectionable portion of the book was 'expunged at once'. Letter from the Assam Arabic Students' Association, Calcutta, to the GOI, dated 20 August 1941. The

The DIB, Sir John Ewart, while reviewing a revised version of *Outline*, thought that it could not but offend religious sensibilities, and stated that no action had been taken as the books had been published some years ago.[96] Another official who had read the books thought that *Outline* consisted of much material to which 'Muslims may well object', and *Short History* too consisted of a summary of this material. However, the books were also 'standard works of an international reputation', and the time lag since publication had also to be considered.[97] R.B. Elwin, Under Secretary in the Home Department, thought it was worthwhile ignoring the resolutions until 'further protests are made'.[98] Consequently, the GOI took no action against the books. This did not, however, mean that the book could circulate in India freely. Local governments, responding to local pressures, could and did take their own initiatives. Thus, for instance, after receiving complaints from a London bookseller about the non-delivery of four copies to India (sent to a bookshop in Hyderabad, Sind), the GOI made enquiries, only to discover that the Sind government, on the advice of the local CID, had ordered the detention of all copies under section 26 of the Indian Post Office Act (which authorized confiscation of material in the post if it posed a risk to public tranquility). They had done so as there was agitation in some newspapers against the chapter 'Muhammad and Islam' in the book.[99]

If we compare the content of this book with other publications that were indeed banned (or put out of circulation due to the government's efforts), Wells' words appear to be no better. Wells wrote, for instance:

> He [Muhammad] was diplomatic, treacherous, ruthless, or compromising as the occasion required and as any other Arab king might have been in his place; and there was singularly little spirituality in his kingship. Nor was his domestic life power and freedom one of exceptional edification. Until the

---

earlier letter was probably not received by the GOI as they could not trace a copy. As 'similar resolutions from similar bodies' were ignored in 1938, the HD decided to ignore this letter as well. Note by SRN, 2 September 1941. GOI Home Political, f. 150, 1938, NAI.

[96] Note by HD official AH (signature illegible), 8 November 1938, citing the DIB's views, GOI Home Political, f. 150, 1938, NAI.

[97] Note by JSS (signature illegible), 12 November 1938, GOI Home Political, f. 150, 1938, NAI.

[98] Note by Elwin, 12 November 1938, GOI Home Political, f. 150, 1938, NAI.

[99] D.O. no. S.D.-3/59 from Chief Secretary Sind, I.H. Taunton, to C.J.W. Lillie, 15 March 1939, GOI Home Political, f. 70, 1939, NAI.

death of Kadija, when he was fifty, he seems to have been the honest husband of one wife; but then, as many men do in their declining years, he developed a disagreeably strong interest in women.... Because he, too, founded a great religion, there are those who write of this evidently lustful and rather shifty leader as though he were a man to put beside Jesus of Nazareth or Gautama or Mani. But it is surely manifest that he was a being of a commoner clay; he was vain egotistical, tyrannous, and a self-deceiver; and it would throw all our history out of proportion if, out of an insincere deference to the possible Moslem reader, we were to present him in any other light.[100]

Why, then, was this book not banned? Keeping aside the question of any individual official's preferences and literary inclinations, the reasons seem to have been the time that had lapsed since the book's publication, the reputation of the author as a 'serious' writer and the short-lived duration of the protests.

The *Parade* Case (1940)

In 1940, the September issue of *Parade* magazine was banned by the Punjab government for carrying an article titled 'He Put Islam on the Map' that also carried a picture of the Prophet. The Punjab government also suggested to the GOI that appropriate advice may be given to the press in Great Britain.[101] Another official thought that the text of the article (which had been condensed from a book) did not seem objectionable, and in fact was a 'great improvement' on *Britannia and Eve* and *Pearson's Weekly*, but the inclusion of the picture of the Prophet was 'a bad blunder'.[102] This was duly communicated to the India Office by the GOI, and the India Office in turn wrote to the editor of the magazine, stating:

> No editor can avoid offence to all susceptibilities in the world, however great his gift and exercise of discretion. But a special plea for even more than the usual watchfulness may be put in on behalf of the Muslims, especially at a time

---

[100] H.G. Wells, *Outline of History: Being a Plain History of Life and Mankind* (New York: Garden City Publishing, 1920).

[101] Letter no. 4499/7537 from Chief Secretary Punjab, J.D. Anderson, to Home Secretary GOI, 4 November 1940. The picture had not attracted much attention in any other province. Note by HD official (initials unclear), 13 December 1940, GOI Home Political, f. 37/122, 1940, NAI.

[102] Note by HD official (initials unclear), 14 December 1940, GOI Home Political, f. 37/122, 1940, NAI.

when it is particularly desirable to bear in mind their sensitiveness in matters of their belief. Numerous representations have been made to the India Office from time to time regarding references to Islam. Many of these representations may be unreasonable from an English and Christian point of view, but all are based on sincerity. It is, therefore, only fitting that every endeavour should be made to meet them as far as possible.

The India Office reassured the editor that they did not want to interfere with his editorial judgement, but merely draw his attention to a 'specialist point'.[103] On his part, the editor agreed to avoid pictorial representation of the Prophet and to avoid 'anything likely to give offence on religious grounds'.[104] In this case, it was the combination of concrete action (the ban by the Punjab government) as well as persuasion (the letter to the editor) that was used to prevent the appearance of a certain type of matter.

Britannia and Eve Revisited (1946)

This chapter has discussed, in some detail, the landmark *Britannia and Eve* case of 1930, cited frequently by petitioners who compared offensive material published later to that published in this journal, and who cited the GOI's ban on it as a precedent when seeking other bans. After discussing numerous cases in the 1930s and 1940s, we return, 16 years later, to *Britannia and Eve* again.

In its July 1946 issue, *Britannia and Eve* published an article on the Prophet's first wife, Khadija, titled 'Old Tales Re-told: Cadijah—The First and Devoted Wife of Mahomet', with pictorial representations of the Prophet.[105] The four-page article was written and illustrated by F. Matania, the same artist who had illustrated the controversial 1930 article. The text was overshadowed by four large illustrations: one depicted three women standing on the roof of a house, one of them being Khadija, waiting for the Prophet to return; another showed a man and a woman sitting in a cave (the man being the Prophet) and the caption referred to Khadija sacrificing all comforts to share his life in the cave with him, and referred to Muhammad being 'a helpless prey to fits of paroxysm, trances, and strange convulsions of the body'. The third illustration showed a

---

[103] Letter from A.N. Joyce of the India Office to editor *Parade*, L.J. Coulter, 19 February 1941, GOI Home Political, f. 37/122, 1940, NAI.

[104] Letter from Coulter to Joyce, 20 February 1941, GOI Home Political, f. 37/122, 1940, NAI.

[105] Clipping of article in GOI Home Political, f. 41/8, 1946, NAI.

group of angry men and women surrounding a couple, with the caption that in the streets Muhammad was pointed out as insane, and had rubbish thrown on him. The fourth illustration showed a man gazing at a near naked Adam and Eve, and was captioned to the effect that during his time in the hills of Safa Muhammad conjured up a vision of the first sinners.

In late August 1946 the GOI received a representation from the Majlis Ahrar Delhi expressing their distress at the publication of pictures of the Prophet's wife, and of Adam and Eve. They asked the British government to take action against the printer and publisher, 'or the British Government will be responsible for all the bad consequences arising out of it'.[106] This was followed by a representation by the president of the All India Jamiat ul Ulema to the Viceroy as well as to the Secretary of State, referring to the 'four fictitious, libellous and scoffing illustrations', to the number of Indians who followed Islam ('100 millions'), and to the reference in the text of the article to the Prophet having married Ayesha only a month after the death of Khadijah.[107] A Muslim employee of the HD, Assistant Secretary Abdullah Jan, wrote to the GOI about this article too, and sent them a copy, explaining that Muslim government servants were agitated about it. Abdullah urged the GOI not only to ban the article, but ask the India Office to warn the publishers 'sternly to lay off articles about any Muslim personality'. Jan did not find anything offensive in the content of the article, and could not say whether it was published with malicious intent. He commented that the magazine, in its 17 years of existence, was prone to publishing articles with almost pornographic illustrations. Because of this, he strongly condemned the magazine, recalling the 1930 controversy. In his words:

> To publish an article about the Prophet, even if it were not accompanied by any illustrations at all, would be tantamount to an insult of the Prophet.... That anybody should dare to draw pictures of the Prophet and of his wife, and should show in the same picture a semi-nude woman supposed to be Eve, is still more offensive. The Muslims respect Adam as the forefather of us all, and as a major Prophet. Eve, as his wife, must thus have her due share of respect.[108]

---

[106] Representation from Secretary Majlis Ahrar, Babu Abdul Latif, to the Viceroy, 23 August 1946, GOI Home Political, f. 41/8, 1946, NAI.

[107] Letter from the President of All India Jamiatul Ulema, Husain Ahmed, to the Viceroy, GOI Home Political, f. 41/8, 1946, NAI.

[108] Note by Abdullah Jan, 5 September 1946, GOI Home Political, f. 41/8, 1946, NAI.

Upon considering the matter, Home Secretary A.E. Porter was of the opinion that the issue be banned under the SCA.[109] The Home Member, Vallabhbhai Patel, agreed that this was the only action that needed to be taken, commenting that

> the Editor probably knows that the publication of such pictures does offend Muslim sentiment, but people in free countries have greater value for the liberty of press than for susceptibilities or prejudices of others.[110]

On the instructions of the HD, the July issue was banned under the SCA on 21 September, and the Finance Department also issued a press note about the ban.[111] On their part, the India Office wrote to the editor of the magazine, informing him of the ban, and reminding him of the 1930 case.[112] This editor, of course, needed no reminding, because he was the same editor who had been informed, in 1930, of a ban on his journal in India, and who had then earnestly stated that he had intended no offence. The illustrator of the 1930 article was the illustrator and the writer of the 1946 one too. The 1930 and 1946 versions of the *Britannia and Eve* case exemplify the stark limits of the ability of the GOI and the India Office in affecting, amending or censoring the content of British publications.

In the Dibble case (1926) the GOI and the India Office acted prior to and independent of pressure groups. In the *Britannia and Eve* Case (1930), discussion within government and activities of pressure groups were simultaneous. The conflation of an antagonistic or inflammatory article in one journal with the entire policy of the British state was a common thread in all the letters of complaint sent by various Muslim pressure groups discussed in the last section of this chapter. While the GOI, as we have seen, frequently took the view that frivolous publications did not deserve to be banned as this would invest them with undeserved importance, Muslim pressure groups demanded

---

[109] Note by A.E. Porter, 6 September 1946, GOI Home Political, f. 41/8, 1946, NAI.

[110] Note by Patel, 10 September 1946, GOI Home Political, f. 41/8, 1946, NAI.

[111] Press note, 19 September 1939, and Finance Deptt (Customs) notification no. 14, 21 September 1946, banned the issue, GOI Home Political, f. 41/8, 1946, NAI.

[112] Letter no. Pol (S) 1297/46 from India Office to the editor, *Britannia and Eve*, 16 December 1946. The editor stated that a correction would be carried in the January 1947 issue, and that there was no intention to offend. Letter from J. Heitner to the Under Secretary of State for India, 18 December 1946, GOI Home Political, f. 41/8, 1946, NAI.

bans on light-weight journals, the audience and circulation of which (primarily among European women in India) was extremely limited. On several occasions, complaints were made much after publication, and public agitation focused attention on long-forgotten issues of journals and obscure books. In the case of publications that outraged Muslim sentiments, every petition to the state and to the public opinion seeking ban necessarily gave enormous publicity to the offensive material.[113] Ironically, the demand that certain words be put out of circulation was accompanied by the determined, repeated and widely publicized circulation of those very words.

While the archive tends to reflect public opinion that demanded bans on publications (and this is only to be expected: after all, these demands were usually communicated in writing, some times accompanied by threats, and often successful), occasionally one gets a glimpse of arguments made by individuals *against* banning books that offended religious sentiment. These arguments are valuable: one letter-writer to *The Statesman* (in the aftermath of demands to ban H.A.L. Fisher's *History of Europe*) urged the GOI not to ban it for two reasons. One, because banning the book would 'only expose Indians to the obvious taunt that they are by nature too sentimental and capricious'. Two, because in his opinion, 'the Prophet during his life-time was assailed and criticised by his enemies, but he did his work unmindful of them. So should his followers, if they are true adherents of Islam and know its essence'.[114]

In May 1931, three 'Peshawaris' killed three men, including Bholanath Sen, the proprietor of Messrs. Sen bros., who had authored the Bengali book *Prachin Kahani*, some passages of which dealt with the life of Prophet Muhammad.[115] A few days later, the secretary of the Indian Journalists' Association expressed the view that the vernacular press could do a great deal 'to create the proper mentality for communal peace', something that no legislation or executive ordinance could accomplish.[116] It is clear from the case

---

[113] In his stirring defence of Salman Rushdie, Norman Mailer makes a similar point by arguing that had the *Satanic Verses* not met with such 'formal outrage', it would have 'suffered the fate of other serious books', that is, modest sales and a small group of serious readers. Instead, the campaign against the book gained it 'oceans of publicity'. Normal Mailer, 'The Folly Repeated' in *War of Words: The Censorship Debate*, ed. George Beahn, 63–66 (Kansas City: Andrews and McMeel, 1993), 65.

[114] Letter to the editor by 'Literary Critic' from New Delhi, *The Statesman*, 30 December 1935.

[115] *Hindustan Times*, 10 May 1931.

[116] *Hindustan Times*, 18 May 1931.

studies discussed in this chapter that the colonial state was most responsive to demands for censorship of publications when these took the form of lobbying by groups threatening violence. Rajnarayan Chandavarkar has argued that the colonial state was sensitive to the threat of violence because social conflict laid bare its weakness.[117] The case studies discussed in this chapter confirm the ingredients of the ban formula as identified in the previous chapter. The precise configuration of the formula in any given instance was, of course, determined by the context.

---

[117] Rajnarayan Chandavarkar, *Imperial Power and Popular Politics: Class, Resistance and the State in India, c. 1850–1950* (Cambridge: Cambridge University Press, 1998), 178.

PART III

Political or Military?
Censorship in India during the Second World War

On 1 September 1939, two days before Britain and France declared war on Germany, the GOI imposed censorship on telegrams going out from India, and also shut down wireless, telegram and telephone services till further notice.[1] On the same day, the government of New Zealand issued regulations regarding censorship and publicity, the Canadian government assumed special emergency powers over censorship and the German government instructed Germans over the wireless 'to make it their duty to ignore broadcasts from abroad ... designed to undermine the patriotism of the people'. Surveillance and censorship in India was 'substantially relaxed' only six years later, after formal Japanese surrender.[2] Conventional wisdom holds that with the coming of the Second World War, 'all powers assumed by the government were fully exercised and the civil and military censors ... freely suppressed events and views of political significance on the ground that such publication impeded the effective prosecution of the war.'[3] The two chapters in this part of the book question and complicate this neat picture of successful censorship during wartime.

---

[1] All news reports in *The Times*, 2 September 1939.
[2] *The Times*, 'Censorship in India Relaxed', 7 September 1945.
[3] J. Natarajan, *History*, 203.

5

Blue Pencils, Red Pencils
Censoring the News in Wartime

The colonial state needed Indian resources and the support of the Indian public during the Second World War. The concern with public opinion—and in wartime, morale—was also linked with the desire of the colonial government to pose as the 'sole spokesman', as it were, of the Indian people. In other words, if the government could gauge public opinion correctly and act accordingly, then there was no need for parties such as the Indian National Congress to voice nationalist demands. Concern with public opinion in India on the conduct of the war remained a constant hum in the background. During the course of the war, the colonial state in India varied both methods and degree of censorship, but was consistent about the central aim of surveillance: to prevent useful information from reaching the enemy, and to obtain useful information for itself. This was true of the aim of wartime censorship in the United States as well. According to Byron Price, the Director of the Office of Censorship of the US government, its use was defensive, offensive and limited. As Price put it, 'That which does not concern the war does not concern censorship.'[1] This of course, as we shall see, was easier said than done, especially in India in the context of anti-colonial agitation running in parallel to the war.

The Mechanics of Wartime Censorship

Wartime censorship had two legal pillars: the first consisted of provisions predating the war (the CrPC, the IPC, the SCA, the Press Act of 1931, and

---

[1] Statement made by Price to the United States Senate at a hearing titled 'Investigation concerning the disclosure of information obtained through censorship' held on 23 May 1944 at Washington D.C. Box 10, Office of Censorship, Record Group 216, National Archives and Records Administration, College Park, USA.

so on); the second (the Defence of India Act and Rules; hereafter DIR) were issued as wartime measures.[2] The DIR had provisions to pre-censor certain articles appearing in the press; violation could attract a penalty of up to five years' imprisonment. The Official Secrets Act was amended too, and its violation invited the death penalty or transportation for life.

The chief objectives of censorship of news reports—which the GOI preferred to call 'Control of Publicity'—were three in number: one, to 'prevent public opinion from being stirred to enthusiasm for the [anti-colonial] movement or to indignation against the Government'; two, 'to guard against the propagation of noxious rumours and mis-representations both in India and abroad'; and three, to deny publicity to individuals that would lead them to win 'a martyr's crown'.[3] Newspapers were expected to suppress 'plainly dangerous' news, to avoid sensationalism, and to not publicize 'the innumerable rumours, most of them of a sensational or alarming character, which are bound to be current throughout the course of the war'.[4] These amorphous rumours had tangible ramifications: as historian Indivar Kamtekar has demonstrated, they resulted in large-scale withdrawals of deposits from banks and post office savings accounts, indicating a loss of faith in the colonial government during crucial points in the war years.[5]

The GOI was also very clear on the point that censorship of press messages was more important than that of private messages (letters, for instance). This was because a press message was 'intended for publication and, if published, may reach a very large number of people. It may create general alarm and despondency and it may find its way, through wireless transmitters or by other channels, to the enemy'.[6] The potential audience size and range of dissemination of a piece of news or rumour was the foremost factor determining the state's decision to ignore or publicize it.

---

[2] For a discussion of wartime laws pertaining to the press, see Aurobindo Mazumdar, *Indian Press and Freedom Struggle, 1937–42* (New Delhi: Orient Longman, 1993), 159–170, and Barrier, *Banned*.

[3] Memorandum on Press Control including (1) control of Publicity and (2) control of Press messages, sent to all provincial governments by R. Tottenham, Additional Secretary GOI, with letter no. 3/13/40-Poll.(I), 2 August 1940, GOI Home Political (I), f. 3/13 and unprinted K.W., 1940, NAI.

[4] *Press Instructions for War*, 1–3, GOI Home Political, f. 122, 1941, NAI.

[5] Kamtekar, 'The Shiver of 1942'. A rich description of rumours floating in Calcutta during the war years is found in Srimanjari, *Through War and Famine*, 64–71.

[6] Note by R. Tottenham, 15 September 1941, GOI Home Political, f. 88/14 (I), 1941, NAI.

By August 1940, the GOI had decided how *not* to suppress news of the revolutionary movement in India: they would not carry out a total blackout of news. For one, the GOI did not want to antagonize the press and fight a new war on another front; for another, it was felt in official circles that suppression of news would lead to the spread of 'alarmist rumours', these then 'providing an obvious "gift" to German broadcasting authorities'.[7] Ironically, Germany played a major—albeit unintentional—role in preventing total blackout of news in India during the Second World War. The activities of German broadcasting authorities were, according to Home Secretary E. Conran Smith,

> ... a fatal objection to any complete black-out. The widest and most exaggerated stories will be broadcast by the German propaganda people and in the absence of any news in the Indian press such stories will stand a good chance of acceptance. In other words, German propaganda will have an almost unoccupied field for their atrocity stories.[8]

The official discourse on wartime censorship in India was characterized by a major contradiction, never easily resolved: suppression of news could lead to alarmist rumours; allowing all news to be freely published could lead to panic and loss of morale among the civilian population. This contradiction informed the *Press Instructions for War*, a 24-page document prepared for the guidance of staff engaged in censorship work. This document stated clearly that information of value to the enemy was not only that which related to the movement of troops and warships but also included 'information relating to such matters as food and other supplies, political relations with neutral and other States and internal political conditions'. At the same time, it also stressed that 'as much and as accurate news' as possible was to be published so as to keep the public informed about the course of the war as also to 'combat baseless and demoralizing conjectures'.[9]

What, then, was un-publishable during wartime? The list of don'ts for the press was long. According to subject-wise 'Press Notices' attached to the *Press Instructions for War*, the press was forbidden to disclose without official authorization, directly or indirectly, the absence from India of senior military

---

[7] Memorandum on Press Control including (1) control of Publicity, and (2) control of Press messages, sent to all provincial governments by Tottenham along with letter no. 3/13/40-Poll.(I), 2 August 1940. GOI Home Political (I), f. 3/13 and unprinted K.W., 1940, NAI.

[8] Note by E. Conran Smith, 16 May 1940, GOI Home Political, f. 3/2, 1940, NAI.

[9] *Press Instructions for War*, 1.

and civil officials. The Viceroy's movements within India could be given full publicity, but no prospective announcement was to be published unless first checked with the Principal Information Officer (PIO).[10] Without official sanction, the press was forbidden to publish news of the outbreak of an epidemic among the forces at home or abroad. They were also forbidden to publish anything that suggested that any naval, military or air action was the result of information received about the enemy's projects or intention.[11] Without prior permission from the Chief Censor (a military official), no articles regarding operations at the front could be published other than the ones by authorized correspondents; no summary of casualties by units or dates, no statements describing 'either the fire of the enemy or its result'; no description of the effects of gas on His Majesty's forces, or of the results of the use of any novel weapon of war, 'or of their moral effect on our men' was to be published either. As the censoring (deleting portions, not banning) of defence personnels' letters at the front authorized their delivery but not their publication, officers' and soldiers' letters to their families were not to be published either. No articles by a military expert or critic and no photographs of any incident related to the war were to be published without prior sanction from the Press Adviser (a civilian official; hereafter PA). Another forbidden item: advertisements inviting officers and men in the field to communicate with strangers. This was because, during the First World War, the GOI had discovered that enemy agents ('especially women') began corresponding with troops and collected all sorts of information.[12] The press could also not publish details about the escape of British or Allied prisoners, as this was 'certain to lead to greater vigilance by the enemy'. Accounts of prisoners commenting adversely on their captivity was not allowed either, since this would cause the enemy to treat prisoners still with them even worse.[13] Accounts of air raids were not to be published unless an official report had been issued or permission obtained to publish an unofficial account from the PA. Unless official figures had been released, no mention was to be made of the number of casualties, nor were photographs of the injured or the dead to be published.[14] Without the approval of the Chief Censor or the PA, no information (articles, letters or statistics) was to

---

[10] *Press Instructions for War*, part II, Press Notice no. II: The Viceroy, the Indian Legislature, the Government, etc., 5.

[11] Ibid., Press Notice no. III: Naval, Military and Air Force matters generally, 6.

[12] Ibid., Press Notice no. V: Military Matters, 9–11.

[13] Ibid., Press Notice no. VII: Prisoners of War, 13.

[14] Ibid., Press Notice no. IX: Air Raids, 15–16.

be published about the stocks of grain and flour, or their shipment to and from India.[15] Finally, circulation of this long list of banned subjects was itself banned: it was a confidential document, and was not to pass into the hands of persons who were not intended to know what it contained.[16]

The boundary demarcating publishable from un-publishable material was subjected to strains, resistance and amendment, and not only from journalists. In March 1942, the Chief Secretary of the United Provinces, Sir Francis Mudie, suggested to the GOI that newspapers be allowed to publish news of the arrival in India of British and Allied troops (prohibited under the *Press Instructions for War*). Why? Because this news was likely to 'hearten people and sustain their morale'.[17] The General Staff Branch (GSB) agreed with the suggestion. While exact information regarding number of troops and aircraft, and so on, could not be divulged, 'A certain amount of information will, however, be permitted to "leak out".'[18] Censorship in wartime was a delicate balancing act, and the state had to be sufficiently flexible to accommodate changing circumstances and juggle competing priorities.

The censorship organization was under the control of the military Commander-in-Chief, and the Chief Censor (also a military official) was enjoined to cooperate with civilian departments of the GOI, and to advise the HD on press control during the war. Additionally, the HD appointed a civilian Chief Press Censor, and F.D. Bartley of the Indian Police was the first to be designated as such. After Desmond Young (editor and managing director of *The Pioneer*) succeeded him, the Chief Press Censor came to be known as the Chief Press Adviser (CPA). Although the formal designation was Chief Press Censor and Adviser, he was referred to only as Chief Press Adviser in all official correspondence, in keeping with the GOI's—revealing—preference for the term 'advice' over 'censorship'.

Who served as press censors in India during the war? Not only civil servants and military officials but also journalists. Whether these people were formally designated 'censors' or 'advisers', they performed a similar function, that of deciding what could and could not be published. By co-opting journalists ('Poacher Turned Gamekeeper', as *The Times* referred to one in his obituary) to

---

[15] Ibid., Press Notice no. XIV: Supplies, 22.

[16] Ibid., Press Notice no. I: Censorship and Control generally, 4.

[17] D.O. no. 7/42-P.A. from F. Mudie to R. Tottenham, 28 March 1942, GOI Home Political (I), f. 33/11, 1942 NAI.

[18] Note by Brigadier W.J. Cawthorn, Director Military Intelligence (DMI), GSB, 7 April 1942, GOI Home Political (I), f. 33/11, 1942 NAI.

police other journalists, the GOI hoped to soften criticism against censorship. In 1940, for instance, the CPA's office consisted of two officers, both erstwhile journalists: Desmond Young of *The Pioneer* was assisted by E.V. Britter, the Assistant PA, who had worked for six years as assistant editor and news editor with *The Pioneer* and for five years as assistant editor with the *Times of India*. Young was succeeded as CPA in 1941 by Bernard Kirchner, who had previously served as managing editor of the Delhi edition of *The Statesman*.[19] Journalists monitoring the press were the perfect alibi for state censorship masquerading as self-regulation. Although neither official at the apex of the press advisory organization was Indian, Indians were appointed Provincial Press Advisers.[20] Of a total of 31 Press Advisers in India in 1940–1941, 15, or just about half, were Indian. At the provincial level, senior civil servants doubled as censors.[21] At the local level, District Magistrates or Deputy Magistrates tendered 'press advice' when required. In Britain too, journalists did serve as censors, but the pool from which censors were drawn was much more variegated, including 'retired officers, barristers, solicitors, publishers, journalists, teachers, art critics, and advertising agents'. [22]

GOI Attitude to Anti-War Propaganda

The first challenge faced by the GOI on the outbreak of war was to combat anti-war propaganda. The GOI was sceptical about the likely success of anti-war propaganda at the local level, but nevertheless desired to stem it. For example, in October 1940, an IB report quoted the Gandhian leader Vinoba Bhave as having told an audience of 300 in Paunar in Wardha district (Central Provinces) that

> the people of Germany are intelligent and that as they had chosen Hitler as their leader he could be as bad a man as he was painted; there was in fact nothing to choose between Hitler and the British and that it would therefore be a sin for Indians to join in a fight against people with whom they had no enmity.[23]

---

[19] Bernard Kirchner's obituary in *The Times*, 20 January 1982.
[20] GOI Home Political (I), f. 8/3, 1940, NAI.
[21] See Appendix I of Home Political (I), f. 33/32, 1941.
[22] Donald Thomas, *Freedom's Frontier: Censorship in Modern Britain* (London: John Murray, 2008), 131. See also Robert Mackay, *Half the Battle: Civilian Morale in Britain during the Second World War* (Manchester: Manchester University Press, 2003).
[23] DIB report, 17 October 1940, GOI Home Political(I), f. 3/16, 1940, NAI.

The GOI's reaction to this speech is revealing, since it focused not on its anti-war content, but its political dimensions. In the words of the Additional Secretary HD, Richard Tottenham:

> *The sort of utterances that are being made will probably have no effect on the conduct of the war, nor is that their object.* The object is to invite 'repression' by Government so as to stimulate popular indignation throughout the country. Each paper that reproduces speeches made by Vinoba Bhave or any other selected individual, is really indulging in civil disobedience itself.[24]

Thus, senior functionaries of the GOI did realize that censorship of an individual's opinion was only likely to win that individual more popularity. Tottenham went on to suggest that it would be justified to use rule 41 of the DIR to prohibit publicity to 'this anti-war propaganda stunt'. He suggested that if any newspaper (he named the *National Herald* and *Harijan* as potential transgressors) were to defy this prohibition, action should be taken to confiscate the press and close the paper. Tottenham continued:

> I feel very strongly that it is not the meetings and speeches themselves that we ought to stop at present. That is what Gandhi wants us to do. The local effect of the speeches, as the Provincial Government says, is negligible. The prevention of publicity is what we ought to go for....[25]

In this case the Home Member, Sir Reginald Maxwell, asked his department to arrange an 'informal talk' with press representatives asking them not to publish Bhave's speeches or accounts of his meeting; provincial governments were to do the same, that is, discuss the matter with 'editors of the more important papers'.[26] This incident prompted activity within the GOI. In November 1940, the CPA instructed all PPAs and Special Press Advisers (SPAs) about the GOI's policy towards the publication of news and views on anti-war movements and agitation. These instructions were to be conveyed to editors *verbally*; though editors were allowed to take notes, they were to be briefed that these were confidential, and 'must not be divulged'. In other words, censorship by these informal means was itself subject to censorship. The

---

[24] Note by Tottenham, 18 October 1940, emphasis added, GOI Home Political(I), f. 3/16, 1940, NAI.

[25] Note by Tottenhan, 19 October 1940, GOI Home Political(I), f. 3/16, 1940, NAI.

[26] Note by Tottenham, 22 October 1940 and 24 October 1940, GOI Home Political(I), f. 3/16, 1940, NAI.

rationale for this was explained thus: by withholding help from the GOI, the Congress anti-war movement amounted to helping the enemy; therefore the government was 'bound' to deny this movement any publicity. The press was *not* to publish—in full or in brief—a whole range of material that supported the anti-war movement: speeches, public announcements, press interviews, contributed articles, news of strikes and *hartals*, and news about the enlistment of Congress volunteers. Comments were allowed so long as they did not incite breaking the law, and did not contain 'news disguised as comment'. The press could publish, however, reports of meetings, arrests (including names), trials and convictions or acquittals related to anti-war agitation. However, this liberty was conditional on the news being presented 'factually and objectively', without emphasis (by the use of different types, for instance), and there being no comment in headlines. This meant that an anti-war meeting could be reported but not the speeches made in it; arrests could be reported but not strikes; convictions could be reported but not the enlistment of volunteers. The GOI envisioned that once the oxygen of publicity was denied to anti-war activities, they would pass unnoticed. The penalty for a first offence was to be a formal warning, while prosecution would be launched for subsequent offences.[27] Although PPAs were not told this, the GOI instructed provincial governments that these instructions would vary according to the situation, depending on the way the anti-war movement developed, and also on the reaction of the press. For instance, if the number of meetings increased, then there could be a bar on reporting them.[28]

At the same time as it was drawing up an array of censorship regulations, the GOI itself preferred to informalize censorship, so as to minimize open conflict with the press at a crucial juncture.The war years were marked by the use of such informal methods to censor news and views in print. Indeed, this was an enduring legacy, as we shall see in Part 4 of this book, for India in the decade after Independence.

Demands of a 'Total War'

Within the GOI as well as in the public sphere, there was debate over the relative importance of political and military considerations governing

---

[27] Express letter no. C.P.A.-301-B/40 from the CPA to all PPAs and SPAs, 2 November 1940, GOI Home Political(I), f. 3/18, 1940, NAI.
[28] Express letter no. 3/16/40-Political(I) to all provincial governments, 2 November 1940, GOI Home Political(I), f. 3/18, 1940, NAI.

censorship. In the GOI this debate took the form of establishing a working relationship between the CPA (civilian) and the Chief Censor (military). By September 1941, two years after the commencement of the war, the actual functioning of censorship was somewhat different from the prescribed rules. Significantly, the subordination of the political agenda to the military agenda (as envisaged in the original structure of censorship) had been overturned. Instead of the Chief Censor being the military adviser of the HD, the HD (through the CPA) had become the political adviser of the Chief Censor in matters affecting the press. In other words, two years into the war, military censorship was more influenced by political considerations than the other way round.[29] Military authorities were not comfortable with the HD becoming the final arbiter of what news on political and military affairs could be received into or sent out of India. They insisted that the censors' responsibilities were 'neither military nor political but general'. After all, they insisted, 'in war, matters normally purely political acquire direct military importance'.[30] Conflict between political and military priorities—and between the civilian and military branches of the GOI over the intensity and priorities of censorship—continued throughout the war.

At the same time, public opinion in India was prepared to accept a measure of military censorship but bristled the moment it perceived censorship to be politically motivated. In 1943 Hridaynath Kunzru tried (and failed to pass) a resolution in the Council of State urging the GOI to remove restrictions on publication of news not relating to the war, and especially from news pertaining to internal political and economic conditions. Kunzru also complained about the lack of coordination between the GOI and provincial governments with regard to imposing controls on the press. Although the resolution was rejected, the Home Secretary, E. Conran Smith, expressed sympathy with it, and reiterated that the GOI was keen to see freedom of the press preserved in India, so long as it was consistent with 'the overriding demands of security and the demands of a totalitarian war'. On the whole, Smith stated, the policy of voluntary control (more about which later), as opposed to statutory control, had worked, and the GOI only gave general guidance to provincial governments on the matter of press control, leaving them to 'adjust local control to local conditions'.[31] As Sanjoy Bhattacharya demonstrates in his examination of press

---

[29] Note by Tottenham, 15 September 1941, GOI Home Political, f. 88/14, 1941, NAI.
[30] Note by Brigadier Cawthorn, DMI, GSB, 6 October 1941, GOI Home Political, f. 88/14, 1941, NAI.
[31] *Times of India*, 25 November 1943.

control in eastern India during the war years, at the district level this local control was often very stringent.[32]

Regarding the tricky matter of political versus military censorship, in 1943 the GOI expressed the view to the All India Newspaper Editors' Conference (AINEC) that they were averse to censorship of political news and views in principle but 'matter that may be unpalatable to Government will, for that very reason, be highly palatable to enemy propaganda agencies and prima facie prejudicial to India's prosecution of the war'.[33] In an internally circulated note, the CPA admitted that the principles of censorship were prescribed by high authority, but the implementation was left to individual censors, 'and no human judgment is infallible'. To the CPA, evidence for the liberality of the GOI was to be found in the newspapers, which contained much that was critical of the government, yet had been allowed by the censors. In any case, the censoring of outgoing messages was not seen to affect the Indian press.[34]

In 1944, in response to a LA resolution to the effect that censorship of press telegrams in India should be solely on grounds on military security, and not on political grounds, the War Department prepared a note on the operation of censorship. They emphasized that there were no instructions to prohibit press messages on political grounds, and that censorship was governed only by considerations of military security (albeit, they admitted, using the term military 'in the broadest sense necessitated by total war').[35] In their opinion:

> Censorship in total war is inevitably affected by the fact that the war is total. Although political matters come within the purview of censorship, political censorship is a complete misnomer because those political aspects which require censorship are only censored if they can, either at a particular moment or from a longer view, in any way adversely affect the prosecution of war and the speedy

---

[32] Sanjoy Bhattacharya, *Propaganda and Information in Eastern India*, 134–138.

[33] Letter from GOI to AINEC sent in July 1943 quoted in brief prepared by the CPA for the Home Member to answer a resolution on censorship in the LA, undated, likely end-January or early February 1944 (hereafter cited as 'Brief for Home Member by CPA, January/February 1944'), Appendix II in GOI Home Political (I), f. 24/3, 1944, NAI.

[34] Ibid.

[35] In the resolution on 8 February 1944 Akhil Chandra Dutta had demanded that all cases of suppression and deletion of news items be placed before the Central PAC along with the reasons for the action. Note by DMI and Director Public Relations, undated, probably late January or early February 1944, prepared in response to the resolution, Appendix I in GOI Home Political (I), f. 24/3, 1944, NAI.

achievement of victory. Matters that affect this are inevitably governed by the state of affairs at a particular time; this is to say, by the course of operations in any particular part of the world, whether by land, sea or air; by anything which might affect economic, diplomatic or political pressure being brought against the enemy; by anything calculated, unnecessarily to assist enemy propaganda or to hearten the enemy in his resistance.... All the above may be regarded primarily as political or economic matters rather than military ones in the narrow sense but, as has been proved time and again in the present war (with the facilities offered by radio at the enemy's disposal) they can directly affect the efficiency of basic military operations.[36]

Another example given by the War Department of the inter-connectedness of political and military matters was this:

... information or violent opinions expressed on internal political disputes which are giving, or may give, rise to disturbances and may even force the commitment of military units to duties other than the direct prosecution of the war against the enemy, is of military definite value to our foes. It may easily, for that very reason, provoke action on the part of the enemy which would bring death and destruction to citizens of a country for the security of which a particular Government is responsible. *There is nothing more heartening to the enemy, or useful to his intelligence, than information which helps him to gauge the extent to which internal trouble, whether political or economic in origin, is locking up resources that would otherwise be directly used against them.*[37]

In other words, the political was military, and the GOI realized that it was impossible to separate 'military considerations' in a sealed compartment with no connection to other factors. Irrespective of the publicly stated claims of the GOI that censorship in India was being conducted on military (and not political) grounds, GOI personnel were under no illusion that purely military censorship was desirable—or even possible. Irrespective of the GOI's public proclamations to the contrary, in India political censorship and military censorship were allies so close as to be virtually indistinguishable from each other.

Censoring Outgoing Press Telegrams

There were two directions in which censorship over press telegrams was exercised. One was that of incoming telegrams (for publication of news

---

[36] Ibid.

[37] Ibid., emphasis added.

in India), which the GOI justified as being necessary so as not to impede prosecution of the war. The other was that of outgoing telegrams, which was justified as being necessary to deprive the enemy of matter that could be used for propaganda, and thereby for undermining public morale in India. As regards the censorship of press messages, the GOI made a clear distinction between those meant for circulation in India and those which were to be published abroad. 'Greater latitude' was to be allowed to the ones being sent out, the reason being that

> any attempt to prevent news about a revolutionary movement in India from reaching America, for instance, would be likely to result in the publication in that country of exaggerated stories of atrocities or repression, while in countries like Germany such stories will be invented anyhow, whether any news actually reaches them or not.[38]

However, three types of press messages still needed to be 'definitely withheld' from going out of the country: 'atrocity mongering' (with regard to police or military action), reports of inflammatory or seditious speeches, and comment 'deliberately designed to exhibit Government in an unfavourable light'. This information was to be supplied to PAs for their reference.[39] In end-March 1941, censors were asked not to permit references to communal disturbances in outgoing press messages.[40] Two months later, the HD clarified that they had 'no objection to messages being allowed to go out of India regarding internal disturbances *provided that such messages make it clear that the disturbances are communal and not anti-Government*'.[41] In other words, from the GOI point of view and during the war at least, bad news was arranged in a hierarchy in which news of communal disturbances was preferable to news of anti-colonial agitation. The anxiety of the GOI is clearly on display in this blacklist.

The GOI feared that press messages entering or leaving India (usually transmitted by beam wireless) could be 'overheard' by Axis powers, and this

---

[38] Memorandum on Press Control, sent to all provincial governments by Tottenham, along with letter no. 3/13/40-Poll.(I), 2 August 1940, GOI Home Political (I), f. 3/13 and unprinted K.W., 1940, NAI.

[39] Ibid.

[40] Reference to GSB order no. 47618/II/22 (Censors), 31 March 1941, in note by J.G. Simms, Under Secretary HD, GOI Home Political (I), f. 5/27, 1941, NAI.

[41] Note by Tottenham, 29 May 1941, emphasis added, GOI Home Political (I), f. 5/27, 1941, NAI.

necessitated censorship of even that matter which did not directly involve military security. To take one example, in July and August 1943, the CPA admitted that 'it was considered necessary to stop alarmist reports which might have constituted an invitation to the Japanese to bomb Calcutta'.[42] At the same time, HD officials admitted that they themselves were keen to have information about internal problems in Germany and Japan.[43]

Censoring Incoming Press Telegrams

Incoming press telegrams were censored at Bombay, Calcutta and Madras, and military Telegraph Censors (military personnel) as well as PAs (civilians) had to work in tandem; however, in practice, coordination proved to be difficult. Telegraph Censors were supposed to screen, amend or delete portions from telegraphs if they contained information of military value. They were to take the advice of PAs only when in doubt about non-military news and this led to considerable delays in handing over press telegrams to the press. An additional complication was that friction between the two sets of censors (military and civilian) was 'chronic and constant'. Most Telegraph Censors were civilians appointed as officers, and there was likely to be 'jealousy between civilians in mufti and those in khaki'.[44] Then there was the problem of excessive excisions: PAs were inclined to excise more than was necessary from press telegrams, and Telegraph Censors too went outside the purely military sphere while making deletions. Additional Secretary Tottenham suggested that Telegraph Censors could mark militarily objectionable passages in blue, and ask PAs to mark those objectionable from a civil or political point of view in red.[45] In 1944 Tottenham estimated that 'probably less than 2%' of incoming messages were subject to censorship by Indian authorities.[46] The problem, however, lay not

---

[42] Brief for Home Member by CPA, January/February 1944, Appendix II in GOI Home Political (I), f. 24/3, 1944, NAI.

[43] Draft prepared by Tottenham on behalf of the Home Member, who was to respond to a resolution in the LA passed by Akhil Chandra Dutta on 8 February 1944, Appendix IV in GOI Home Political (I), f. 24/3, 1944, NAI.

[44] Note by Brigadier Cawthorn, DMI, GSB, 6 October 1941, GOI Home Political, f. 88/14, 1941, NAI.

[45] Note by Tottenham, 15 September 1941, GOI Home Political, f. 88/14, 1941, NAI.

[46] See note 43. The typed draft initially stated 'probably less than a fraction of 1%', and Tottenham crossed this by hand and replaced it with '2%'. Appendix IV in GOI Home Political, (I) f. 24/3, 1944, NAI.

in the number of messages subjected to censorship, but in the amount excised from each message.

The problem of excessive censorship is exemplified by the censorship of a press telegram in June 1941, sent from London to *The Hindu* at Madras. The original text was amended thus by the Telegraph Censor and the SPA in India:

[~~Harsh~~] treatment of prisoners in India and [~~barbaric~~] punishments permitted parofficial jail codes were ~~strongly condemned~~*discussed at meeting in Holbornhall yesterday stop Englishman who had formerly been in charge of jails himself described ~~evils~~*drawbacks of Indian penal system stop [~~he said that jail staff were often corrupt ---(50)--- and cruel and sometimes used illegal punishments stop jails were overcrowded and insanitary and food was frequently verminous resulting in breakdown of prisoners health stop use of handcuffs and fetters and putting of prisoners to heavy labour was savage by any civilized standard stop jail officials made it point to ---(100)--- illtreat political prisoners fullstop~~] Miss Margeryfry of Howardleague for penal reform regretted rejection of hoshis motion in assembly last February and deplored statement then made by Maxwell stop [~~quote if we are driven to imprisonment of our fellow subjects on groundsof political differences tis surely strange commentary on our ---(150)--- fight against Nazism to denounce them as worse enemies than those who openly uphold nazi doctrines unquote missfry said that seven years ago Indian government claimed that they were following standard minimum rules framed by international penal and penitentiary commission and circulated by league nations stop this did not seem ---200--- to be case stop yet Government were scrupulously observing Geneva convention regarding Fascist prisoners~~] ~~fullstop~~ there should be ~~immediate~~ enquiry into conditions ~~in~~*under ~~indian jails~~*Penal system ---Matters.

Source: Secret CM/105 from Censor Station Madras dated 30 June 1941 to the Chief Censor India, GHQ Delhi. Original telegram from Matters London to *The Hindu* Madras dated 28 June 1941. GOI Home Political (I) f. 88/21 1941, NAI.[47]

---

[47] The text of the telegram has been reproduced exactly as it appears on file. The terms in brackets were deleted by the SPA, and the underlined terms were deleted by the Telegraph Censor, and substituted by words indicated by a star. I have changed the lines under the text to a line through the text to more starkly indicate the range of excisions. The term 'hoshis motion' has been reproduced as it appears in the original telegram on file.

The telegram—now drained of all life and blood—transmitted to *The Hindu* read:

> treatment of prisoners in India and punishments permitted par official jail codes were discussed at meeting in Holbornhall yesterday stop Englishman who had formerly been in charge of jails himself described drawbacks of Indian penal system stop Miss Margeryfry of Howardleague for penal reform regretted rejection of hoshis motion in assembly last February and deplored statement then made by Maxwell stop there should be enquiry into conditions under indian Penal system ---Matters.

This particular message did start a chain of discussion in the GOI in July 1941, when the CPA noticed the changes. He thought the motive 'laudable', but also felt it would have been better to 'kill' the whole message, as *The Hindu* was likely to lodge a strong protest.[48] Chief Censor Lieutenant Colonel S.W. Longhurst took the opposite view, stating that censors were entitled to stop, delay, amend or paraphrase any telegram, while the Director General (DG) Information F.W. Puckle thought that when a message required considerable amendment to make it acceptable, then it was 'better to put it into the waste paper basket'. According to Puckle, the general principle to be followed was: 'Either release news or suppress it; don't "cook" it.'[49]

The difference of opinion also highlighted inconsistency in the law: Rule 18 of the DIR gave the power to paraphrase (and not alter) telegrams only when they were suspected of carrying a hidden meaning.[50] On the other hand, postal censors could cut out portions from letters or destroy them. Even as HD officials were debating the finer points of the law, a Defence Department official pointed out that 'individual Censors, who are often new to their jobs and heavily over-worked' would not be expected to understand the distinction between 'paraphrase' and 'alter'.[51] Tottenham conceded (and the Legislative Department agreed) that Telegraph Censors had no powers to 'alter', 'amend' or 'tone down' a message, and from the legal point of view,

---

[48] Note by Kirchner, 10 July 1941, GOI Home Political (I), f. 88/21, 1941, NAI.

[49] Notes by Longhurst, 15 July 1941 and by Puckle, 17 and 19 July 1941. Kirchner was inclined to agree with Puckle rather than with Longhurst. GOI Home Political (I), f. 88/21, 1941, NAI.

[50] Note by J.W. Simms of the HD, 7 August 1941, GOI Home Political (I), f. 88/21, 1941, NAI.

[51] Note by RMS (signature illegible) of the Defence Department, 1 September 1941, GOI Home Political (I), f. 88/21, 1941, NAI.

could only paraphrase it, and that too if it carried a secret meaning.[52] Later, when the GOI realized that the DIR did not even give censors the powers to delete objectionable parts of a telegraphic message (only giving them the power to stop the whole message), this power was given to them in November 1941, by an amendment of the DIR rules.[53] The GOI was conscious that the amendment would draw attention to the fact that censors had been deleting material without legal sanction in the past, but thought that this could be countered by saying that the amendment removed a 'possible' legal doubt. The alternative, to do nothing and let censors delete at will, was considered by Tottenham 'rather dangerous' as 'some busy body [*sic*] may try to take the matter further and make things awkward for us'.[54]

Although the liaison between military and civil authorities was regular, it did not always proceed smoothly. However much the GOI wanted to present a united front to Indian and international audiences, attitudes to censorship of news were split along the civilian/military axis. There were, as examples taken up in this chapter indicate, issues over 'territory' between the civilian and military branches of the GOI in charge of censorship. Occasionally, newspapers escaped punitive action on account of internal wrangling within the government. For instance, Delhi's Urdu paper *Tej* published an article on 2 April 1942 titled (in translation) 'Postdated Cheque on a Bank on the Verge of Insolvency' (quoting Gandhi's assessment criticizing the British Cripps mission sent to negotiate with Indian leaders). Following this, the Delhi government, the GOI, the CPA and the Central Press Advisory Committee (PAC) all traded requests for action. A month passed by before the authorities decided on a course of action, and it was eventually decided to overlook the 'stale' article.[55] At other times, for instance during the Bengal famine of 1943, a press message on the food situation passed by the GOI was met with 'considerable protest' by the Government of Bengal.[56]

---

[52] Notes by Tottenham, 4 September 1941, and by R. Sundaram of the Legislative Department, 6 September 1941, GOI Home Political (I), f. 88/21, 1941, NAI. See also notes by Tottenham, 15 September 1941, and by Brigadier Cawthorne, DMI, GSB, 6 October 1941, GOI Home Political (I), f. 88/14, 1941, NAI.

[53] GOI Defence Coordination Department Notification no. 1129-OR/41, 29 November 1941, GOI Home Political (I), f. 88/14, 1941, NAI.

[54] Note by Tottenham, 29 October 1941, GOI Home Political (I), f. 88/14, 1941, NAI.

[55] The article and its translation, and this correspondence is in file GOI Home Political (I), f. 33/12, 1942, NAI.

[56] Note by Tottenham, 4 February 1944, GOI Home Political (I), f. 24/3, 1944, NAI.

The colonial state in India was well aware of the importance of censorship during war. Senior officials in charge of administering it were also aware of its perils. In 1944 the Director of Military Intelligence, Brigadier General W.J. Cawthorn, called censorship 'probably one of the most difficult and intricate responsibilities of war'. He also acknowledged that implementation of censorship was fraught with problems:

> ... no system which is dependent to a large extent on individual executive action by many hundreds of different persons can be made fool-proof or can claim perfection. There have often been slips by censors on the side of liberality which have given the enemy valuable information and to which can be directly traced, in not a few cases, the loss of Allied lives. Equally there have been cases of over-rigid censorship, applied very often at moments or great difficulty on the principle, well known in journalism, of 'when in doubt cut it out'. Censorship rules and stops, however, are subject to constant, and by constant we mean almost daily, review by those responsible for its operation, and to this end the liaison between the military and civil authorities is close and regular.[57]

As this section has shown, although it took a process of trial and error to achieve, the GOI was determined, even in wartime, that the legal basis of their action would indeed be unassailable.

The Rules of the Game: War Correspondents' Experience of Censorship in India

In order to grasp and convey the complex reality of wartime censorship, accounts of policy and official hand-wringing need to be supplemented with a narrative of the lived experience of censorship. The job of a press correspondent during wartime was not an easy one. They stayed and were briefed together when they were covering organized theaters of war, and this left little scope for individual scoops. In an already difficult situation, the operation of censorship added a further complication. Sending news out from the war front was no easy task either: it could be sent out on a plane or via army signaling equipment, in which case the word limit was severely restricted. Dinker Rao Mankekar, who served as Reuters' correspondent first in Colombo and then on the Burma front, recalled that as he was the only correspondent to stay with the British Second Division till the end (in the Burma front), they—not unmindful of the benefits

---

[57] Note by DMI, undated, Appendix I in GOI Home Political (I), f. 24/3, 1944, NAI.

of publicity—allowed him use of their wireless transmitter with a daily word limit of 600 words. This was transmitted to the closest signaling point, either Calcutta or Comilla. On the other hand, the American sector provided better facilities, and General Stilwell's headquarters in north Burma even carried a mobile wireless transmitter for the use of the press.[58] In his opinion, soldiers (via letters from family) received press cuttings featuring their activities, and this had a positive impact on their morale.[59]

And then there were the censors. Margaret Bourke-White, accredited as a war correspondent with the US Air Force in 1942 (and best known in India for her photographs of Partition refugees), described censors thus: 'Censors are a peculiar breed of mankind. They are born with red pencils in their mouths, and they simply have to use them....'[60] Mankekar's account of life as a war correspondent is replete with stories of dealing with military censors, and of the irrationality of censors and of censorship generally. In Mankekar's profile of the Nagas that referred to their poison-tipped spears, the censor deleted the term poison, on the grounds that international law forbade the use of poison in war. The report was passed only after the journalist assured the censor that the reference was not to the present war.[61]

Between 1942 and 1943, the army in Burma was a forgotten army, as British and Indian newspapers gave maximum coverage to the European and Pacific theatres of war. It was only in March 1944 that Burma became front-page news, and remained so for three months.[62] On the Burmese war front, censorship was imposed by two authorities: the GOI as well as South East Asia Command (SEAC) censors. Mankekar was in Burma when news reached him about the Japanese invasion of India via Manipur and Assam, and SEAC censors refused him permission to file the story citing GOI instructions. At Calcutta too he was told by Lieutenant Colonel Thompson that there was an order to the effect that no story about the Japanese invasion was to be passed. The taboo words, according to the order, were 'Japanese invasion of India'. Mankekar wrote the following cable, faithful to the letter of the law:

---

[58] D. R. Mankekar, *Leaves from a War Reporter's Dairy* (New Delhi: Vikas, 1977), 58–60, 93, and 129.

[59] Ibid., 99–100.

[60] Margaret Bourke-White, *Portrait of Myself* (New York: Simon and Schuster, 1963), 252.

[61] Ibid., 53.

[62] Ibid., 99–100.

DATELINE IMPHAL: FOR FIRST TIME IN 120 YEARS THERE IS
WAR ON INDIAN SOIL...

Lieutenant Colonel Thompson was puzzled, then re-read the rules.
Mankekar threatened to report the delay to the SEAC headquarters in Kandy.
Thompson picked up his rubber stamp and stamped the cable 'passed'. The
9.30 p.m. All India Radio (AIR) bulletin carried the news. This report gave
Mankekar an international by-line for the first time, and the next morning he
found himself on the front page of many newspapers.[63] The GOI was furious
and launched an investigation. As Mankekar put it:

> The rules of the game were fully accepted by the Government, under which the
> correspondent's duty is to get his story through and that of the Censors is to see
> that the wrong story did not escape their lynx-like eyes, and if any did, then it
> is the Censor and not the correspondent that is to blame. Col. Thompson, I
> can never forgive myself, became Major Thompson, as a sequel—which was
> far from my intention.[64]

This incident contains at least two important insights into the nature of
censorship. One, that even rigorously enforced censorship could not stand
between a determined journalist and his readers. Two, while in times of peace
journalists were the ones who were prosecuted, in times of war, when censors
took on enlarged powers, their responsibilities also increased. As this incident
shows, the journalist merely went to his next assignment, the censor was the
one who was penalized.

Mankekar's memoirs are full of examples of how censors' decisions were
often counter-productive. During the Japanese siege of Imphal, for example,
when newspapers were forbidden from calling it a siege, Mankekar took
recourse to an indirect strategy: in his report he described the topography of
the Imphal valley in great detail, as well as the fact that there were only three
land outlets from it. He then mentioned the distance of the Japanese from
Imphal on each of these outlets. Nowhere was the term 'siege' mentioned. In
his words, this roundabout method of reporting gave a 'much more alarming
picture of the ever-tightening ring on Imphal than the word "siege" could ever
have given. The story passed the Censor and that night it created a crash in
the Calcutta stock market'. Another scoop was his report about the lifting of

---

[63] Ibid., 46–47.
[64] Ibid., 46.

the siege of Imphal. Mankekar had exclusive access to this news as all other correspondents had left the town during the monsoon months, but he had stayed on with the 33 Corps.[65]

Another example of the counter-productive nature of censorship: war correspondents had been forbidden from reporting the fall of Kohima, even when almost all of Kohima was captured by the Japanese except for a tiny hill holding a British garrison. Consequently, when the British army began reclaiming the town, a problem arose:

> Having maintained that they had never lost Kohima, the military authorities had to explain what they were attacking in Kohima. Hence, they re-christened nine-tenths of Kohima which was in the hands of the Japanese as the 'Naga village,' and renamed the remaining one-tenth, comprising a small hill on the edge of Kohima town, as 'Kohima!'[66]

Mankekar himself had great difficulty while trying to 'explain to readers why British troops were attacking a British-held town!' In his opinion, this censorship was self-defeating: Japanese radio could easily be listened to in India and it broadcast exaggerated reports of their military successes in Indian territory. By censoring news, this propaganda could not be countered.[67] Furthermore, even when Kohima was re-captured by the British after two months, the British army was unable to make the most of this victory in terms of propaganda since

> far from going to town, with all fanfare, on the great and deserved Allied victory, the correspondents were set to the embarrassing task of having to explain to the world how the British forces performed the feat of recapturing what they had themselves been valiantly defending all that time!

What was worse for the colonial state was that in the meantime Japanese radio had been broadcasting news of the arrival of Subhas Chandra Bose's Indian National Army in Kohima, the ceremonial unfurling of the Indian flag on Indian soil, and the establishment of the Azad Hind government in that area. Here was a case where censorship left a vacuum easily filled by rumours.

---

[65] Ibid., 52–53.
[66] Ibid., 53–54.
[67] Ibid.

Some journalists (or at least the British ones) even had the luxury of seeing the lighter side of censorship. The GOI had asked newspapers not to carry information about the weather so as to deny this information to the Japanese. One day *The Pioneer* (then edited by its last British editor, H.E.B. Catley) carried a news item to the effect that there were leaves on the streets and the electricity supply was disturbed. The column asked if there was a storm, and concluded, 'Hush, the censor is listening.'[68] Although correspondents usually got the best of the censor, even Mankekar acknowledged that there were times when an intelligent censor was of great help in pointing out errors. The censor during wartime was thus also editor and proofreader. Occasionally—if unintentionally—the censors did get it right. Mankekar recounts an incident when he filed a story, based on a British military intelligence report, that the Rani of Jhansi regiment (a women's regiment of Bose's Indian National Army) had arrived in Kohima. The story was killed by the censors, and it later turned out that Sikh *jawan*s of the Indian National Army drying their hair, when seen from afar, had been mistaken for women.[69] The conflict between journalists and censors was, in his opinion, mainly over the terms 'security' and 'morale'. Censors applied rules mechanically, and war correspondents interpreted them more flexibly. The GOI, especially in the India–Burma theatre of war was inclined to be inflexible about allowing any information that they considered could dampen morale. The problem, in Mankekar's opinion, occurred because this covered 'almost everything in those tense days of external war cum internal-nationalist struggle'.[70] The line dividing the political from the military was not thin, but invisible. According to Mankekar, it was for reasons entirely political and not military that it was considered advisable by the powers in Delhi that the Indian public should not know about Kohima's capture, or about the Japanese invasion in the Manipur sector.[71] Corroboration of this statement is provided by examples cited by the journalist Kedar Ghosh in his memoirs. Ghosh's report on a strike in a steel factory engaged in war production was not passed by a press censor.[72] Irrespective of the colour of pencils used, the political was impossible to separate from the military.

---

[68] Joglekar, *Press Freedom*, 128.

[69] Mankekar, *Leaves*, 54–55.

[70] Ibid., 56–57.

[71] Ibid., 53.

[72] Kedar Ghosh, *No Apology* (New Delhi: Orient Longman, 1971), 29–32.

6

A Contradiction in Terms?
'Voluntary Censorship'

In 1940 and again in 1942, the organized press in India and the GOI arrived at two 'gentleman's agreements' with each other. According to the terms of the Delhi Agreement of 1940, the Indian press committed not to impede the war effort. In October 1942, with Japan at the border of India, the Bombay Agreement went further and committed the press to holding back any information that would benefit the enemy or incite readers to subversion. This chapter explores the operation of these agreements, the problems arising during their implementation, and the enduring imprint they left on press–government relations in India after the war, and even after Independence.

In November 1940, the GOI passed an order under the DIR, banning publication of 'matter calculated directly or indirectly to foment opposition to the successful prosecution of the war' and providing for pre-censorship of material intended for publication. The order caused consternation among journalists, and one editor publicly stated that the measures would reduce editors to the position of 'an inanimate automaton'.[1] However, after discussions with and assurances from representatives of leading newspapers, the order was withdrawn, and the matter was left to the discretion of editors, who were to act in consultation with PAs to ensure that nothing was printed that impeded India's war effort. Representatives of the Indian and Eastern Newspapers Society (including Devdas Gandhi, the son of Mahatma Gandhi, and B. Shiva Rao) suggested to the GOI that small advisory committees be set up in Delhi

---

[1] Statement by Kasturi Srinivasan of *The Hindu* during a meeting of a standing committee of the AINEC, reported in *Times of India*, 11 November 1940.

and other provinces consisting of representatives of the press, which would then assist the CPA on matters relating to the press.[2]

The essence of the 'Press Advisory' system was this: newspapers would, at their editors' discretion, refer statements or reports to the PA for advice. In case the provincial government or the GOI took exception to publication, the matter would be referred (except in cases of grave emergency) to the Central or Provincial PAC, which would then decide on the matter of publication. The idea was that powers of suspension, suppression, and pre-censorship that were given to the GOI under the DIR would still remain, but that they would not be exercised on a knee-jerk basis, and not used without justification and consultation. To be 'press-advised' is a term commonly used in newspaper reports of the time.

At the same time, the formation of the AINEC in November 1940 was an important step in the creation of an organized lobby of journalists. It came into existence to protest against restrictions placed by the GOI on the Indian press after the outbreak of war. When it was founded, the AINEC was a body representing all interests and ideologies. As every important newspaper was represented, and there was unanimity of opinion, the GOI reached an agreement with the press: the press agreed not to impede the war effort and not to encourage lawlessness for political reasons, and the GOI agreed to the setting up of an advisory system.

The Press Advisory system functioned reasonable efficiently all through 1940. The CPA, Desmond Young, told PAs that while they were to use their influence with the press wherever possible to induce editors to 'refrain from publishing matter which might be considered objectionable, whether or not it was strictly actionable'.[3] Censorship by persuasion rather than by punishment was being recommended here. Although Bombay and Bengal planned to engage another PA, the consensus was that staff was adequate. Twenty-four-hour press advisory service was maintained at Bombay and Calcutta.[4] PAs could pass three kinds of remarks on matter submitted to them: 'Passed for Publication', 'Not Passed for Publication', and 'Responsibility for Publications rests with the Editor'. The CPA did not want the last category to be used since

---

[2] *Times of India*, 2 and 11 November 1940. This society was set up in 1939 to safeguard common interests of the newspaper industry.

[3] Summary of Proceedings of PAs' conference on 18 December 1940, GOI Home Political (I), f. 33/32, 1941, NAI.

[4] Appendix II and note (regarding adequacy of staff) by CPA Desmond Young dated 19 March 1941, GOI Home Political (I), f. 33/32, 1941, NAI.

it constituted, in his opinion, passing the buck to editors who had taken the trouble to consult the PA.[5] Some problems were experienced in coordinating provincial and central censorship of press telegrams. For instance, news of hunger strikes by political prisoners in jails was banned by the Bengal government but allowed to be published in the rest of India. The CPA ruled that such messages would continue to be published in other provinces once they were approved by the GOI. As for coordination between PAs and censors at ports (processing incoming press telegrams), this worked smoothly except in Bengal, where it was felt that even when censors sought advice of the PAs regarding inward telegrams, they ignored it, and a message passed by the PA was often stopped by a censor. The CPA ruled that the 'ultimate responsibility' lay with the censor, who was within his rights to disregard advice by the PA. The Chief Censor also agreed with this view.[6] In other words, military censors could override the advice of civilian press advisers.

Opinion on the efficacy of the Press Advisory system was divided. While Madras and Bombay thought the system had obtained good results, Bengal and UP were 'sceptical of good results being achieved so long as the attitude of the Press remained what it was'. On the whole, however, the GOI was able to conclude, in December 1940, that the PA system was working 'satisfactorily', by which they meant that it '... does enable the authorities to exercise a measure of what appears in the Press without causing undue friction, without alienating newspapers, and without need for recourse to the drastic method of pre-censorship'.[7]

However, the government was reluctant to lay down precise rules for the conduct of Provincial PACs because of different conditions in different provinces. Instead, they preferred to leave it to the discretion of PAs and SPAs 'who, subject to general instructions from the Central Government, must adopt their own means of promoting friendly relations with the press without jeopardizing the efficient conduct of the War or the ends of good Government'.[8] Vague, rather than rigid, rules were preferred as they afforded maximum flexibility to the state personnel implementing them.

---

[5] These three possible decisions were as per the 'Regulations for Press Censorship in War, 1938'. Summary of Proceedings of PAs' conference on 18 December 1940, GOI Home Political (I), f. 33/32, 1941, NAI.

[6] Ibid.

[7] Ibid.

[8] Summary of Proceedings of PAs' conference on 18 December 1940, and note by CPA Young, 28 February 1941, GOI Home Political (I), f. 33/32, 1941, NAI.

The Press Advisory System Falters

The arrangement worked satisfactorily until January 1941, when the GOI—without reference to these committees—banned two statements by Gandhi. The GOI's dilemma was this: some, though not all, slogans raised by *satyagrahis* were anti-war, but not all of Gandhi's statements could be said to impede the war effort. Newspapers that demanded the freedom to be allowed to report the *satyagraha* (non-violent mass resistance) campaign, and at the same time committed not to impede the war effort, were treading a very thin line indeed.[9]

In February 1941, the AINEC passed a resolution requesting the GOI not to ban statements made by Gandhi—or to at least consult the Central PAC before doing so. This was done keeping in mind both Gandhi's position in public life and the interest with which his statements were received by the Indian public. As the resolution put it, the Indian press aimed

> ... to strive for the freedom of the country without fear or favour and consequently to give legitimate publicity to news about the political movement in the country.... The Indian Press is wholly opposed to the totalitarian doctrines of Nazism and Fascism and has no intention of hindering Britain's war efforts against her enemies.[10]

The AINEC demanded, among other things, that the GOI issue instructions to the press only in writing; that circulars issued to the press (except those relating to defence, military and foreign affairs) be allowed to be published; that police officers not be employed (except in cases of search and arrest) in dealing with the press; and that there be uniformity in all provinces regarding enforcement of rules about the publication of *satyagraha* news.[11]

As a consequence of this resolution, restrictions placed on newspapers over coverage of the *satyagraha* campaign were removed. The GOI accepted the AINEC's suggestion that Gandhi's statements would not henceforth be banned automatically, but the GOI would consult the Central PAC before taking action. In return for this concession, the GOI suggested that Gandhi's statements be issued through regular news agencies, so that all papers would

---

[9] The problem was summarized in a *Times of India* editorial, 'Editors Confer', 8 February 1941.

[10] AINEC resolution passed on 3 February 1941, reported in *Times of India*, 4 February 1941.

[11] Ibid.

have access to them.[12] The AINEC also took up cases from the provinces where they thought newspapers had been wronged by the provincial government. In the case of *Sainik*, a Hindi newspaper from UP, protests by the AINEC over a security demand of 10,000 rupees from the paper by the UP government led to a reduction in the amount to 1,000 rupees, although this did not satisfy the AINEC.[13] On its part, the AINEC assured the government that 'the press in India had no intention of impeding India's war effort', and in fact would disapprove of a 'deliberate or systematic' attempt to do so. The AINEC had to convince the GOI that it could not suppress news about political activity in India either.

Gandhi's statements—the controversy over which had threatened to break the fragile cooperation between government and press—were divided into two categories after this. Those referring to *satyagraha* or anti-war activities were to be submitted to either the central or the local government prior to publication, while statements on other topics could be published by a newspaper at its editor's discretion. If the government took objection to a published statement, then the matter was referred to the PAC. However, in case of a difference of opinion, the government was free to take any action they saw fit. The final call on censorship thus rested with the government, although the process of banning now took a more circuitous route via the PAC. As to why statements by Gandhi were singled out, and not those by, say, Muhammad Ali Jinnah (president of the All India Muslim League), Additional Secretary Tottenham provided a candid explanation in May 1941:

> The obvious answer is that Jinnah does not attack Government or attempt activities to impede the war effort. His attacks are directed against Congress, while Gandhi's attacks are directed against the Government and often over-step the limits of the law of sedition.[14]

It was one thing for the GOI to insist that Gandhi's statements be 'advised' or censored, but how did they actually appear in newspapers? In May 1941, a statement issued by Gandhi on Hindu–Muslim riots was submitted to the Central PAC by the Associated Press of India. The statement condemned the riots, and suggested steps that Congressmen could take to prevent them,

---

[12] The *Times of India* editorial 'Press and Government', 4 March 1941, summarized these developments.

[13] *Times of India*, 4 June 1941.

[14] Note by Tottenham, 19 May 1941, GOI Home Political (I), f. 3/5-A and K.W., 1941, NAI.

including giving 'their lives to prevent mob fury'. There were two sentences in the statement that the GOI wanted omitted, and to which the Central PAC agreed. The GOI also wrote to provincial governments that they had 'reluctantly' passed this statement with the two deletions.[15]

The first was (censor's deletions indicated by a line through the text):

> At the present moment the British government is preoccupied. It is a marvel how they hold away over four hundred million people. Their amazing selfconfidence [sic] and their skill in the use of destructive weapons enable them to hold India in bondage. But they may not be expected to keep peace even to the extent they do in normal times. ~~They will ensure their control anyhow but they will allow us to kill one another and come in only when that control is in danger.~~

Another statement ran, and was censored, thus:

> In Europe two forces equally matched in destructive skill and bravery are ranged against one another. The goal before both is domination ~~inspite of all the will in the world I have found no difference in kind between the two. The difference in degree does not interest me. The British heel is bad enough for me.~~ As a man wedded to independence and nonviolence I must fight Nazism and fascism equally with the enslaving British Imperialism. But has the congress really the non-violent strength even to fight this imperialism which we know through and through.[16]

Sentences appreciating the self-confidence and skill of the British (albeit used for destructive purposes) were allowed; references to divide-and-rule and direct comparisons of British imperialism with Nazism and Fascism were eliminated. An expression of doubt about the Congress' capacity to fight imperialism was also retained, thus giving the reader the impression that Gandhi was unsure of the potential of the Congress to take on the might of the British. At the same time, enough critical statements against the British were allowed to be published so that readers would in fact believe that the

---

[15] See express letter no. 3/5-A/41-Political (I) from HD to all Chief Secretaries and Chief Commissioner Delhi, 8 May 1941, GOI Home Political (I), f. 3/5-A and K.W., 1941, NAI.

[16] Passages from API message from Sevagram, 4 May 1941, reproduced as they appear in (printed) serial no. 16, GOI Home Political (I), f. 3/5-A and K.W., 1941, NAI.

statements were indeed Gandhi's. A month later, in June 1941, the GOI complained to the AINEC that as many as 14 newspapers had published one or both sentences of the statement that they had been asked by the CPA (with the consent of the Central PAC) to omit.[17] Despite the many filters in the form of PAs and PACs put in place by the GOI, news and views that the public wanted to hear had a way of making its way into print.

By late 1941, in the wake of Allied military reversals, the GOI was even more in need of support from the Indian press. Sir Akbar Hydari, the Information and Broadcasting (I&B) Member of the Viceroy's Executive Council, met the standing committee of the AINEC and appealed to newspaper editors thus, terming them 'leaders of public opinion':

> Your influence, great in peace time, will now be magnified many times and the steadiness and soundness of Indian opinion will largely depend on your success by avoiding optimism and over-confidence on the one hand, and pessimism and defeatism on the other.

He appealed to editors to provide balanced coverage of the war, to find points of agreement rather than disagreement between communities, and to work with the GOI against the common enemy during wartime.[18] Hydari's view exemplified the GOI's near desperation to have the press on their side during the war. Despite hiccups, until mid-1942 it could be—and was—argued that the Press Advisory system functioned well. It created a precedent for consultation between the press and government on an all-India basis, and engendered a united front among newspapers of various hues.[19] The value of the system was, according to the *Times of India*, that

> ... in return for freedom from cramping official restrictions, it puts the newspapers in their honour not to embarrass India's war effort; the only alternative is the unrestricted use by Government of their powers without consultation, leading to friction and a state of open warfare between the authorities and a section of the press.[20]

---

[17] Letter no. 3/5-A Political (I) from Tottenham to K. Srinivasan, 8 June 1941, GOI Home Political (I), f. 3/5-A and K.W., 1941, NAI.

[18] Sir Hydari's address to the standing committee of the AINEC reported in the *Times of India*, 19 December 1941.

[19] *Times of India*, 'Press Advisory System', editorial, 16 January 1942.

[20] *Times of India*, 'Government and the Press', editorial, 14 May 1942.

This positive assessment, made in May 1942, was soon to be proved wrong.

Censorship during the Quit India Movement

A threat of breakdown of the Press Advisory system came loomed large even before the Quit India movement was launched in August 1942. In May 1942, on account of the increased Japanese threat to India, the GOI wrote to the AINEC that in view of the changed situation it might no longer be possible for the GOI to participate in the system.[21] The GOI's view was that in the face of what constituted an imminent threat and possible emergency, the PA system was too slow for drastic action against papers that published statements 'calculated to cause fear and alarm to the public and to undermine confidence in the Government in times of war'. The AINEC protested against this, reminding the GOI that it needed the press' support in times of emergency more than ever,[22] and the GOI dropped the idea.[23] The AINEC suggested that in cases of emergency the Delhi Agreement be supplemented by the Bombay Agreement according to which the GOI could immediately prevent the publication of objectionable reports via orders, but would reserve penal action till the PAC had been consulted. At the same time, Home Member Sir Reginald Maxwell met with a deputation of the AINEC, and impressed upon editors the need for 'greater support from newspapers in dealing with alarmist rumours, defeatism, anti-war propaganda, and the weakening of public morale'.[24] The crisis in press–government relations had been averted, but only temporarily.

With the launch of the Quit India movement and the arrest of Congress leaders, the GOI again imposed restrictions on the press, and around 80 newspapers suspended publication in the short as well as the long term.[25] To take one example, during the Quit India movement the Congress-affiliated newspaper *National Herald* closed voluntarily as it heeded Gandhi's call that

---

[21] Letter from the HD to the AINEC President, 4 May 1942, quoted in *Times of India*, 13 May 1942. For an account of the severity of the Japanese threat to India, and how it rattled the colonial state, see Indivar Kamtekar, 'The Shiver of 1942'.

[22] Letters from the AINEC President to the HD, 7 and 8 May 1941, quoted in *Times of India*, 13 May 1942.

[23] Letter from Tottenham to the AINEC President, 11 May 1942. quoted in *Times of India*, 13 May 1942.

[24] Reported in *Times of India*, 14 May 1942.

[25] Estimate was reported in the *Times of India*, 5 November 1942.

newspapers should not come out with censored versions. Later, its office premises were locked up by the UP police, and all journalists turned out so that the newspaper would not become a centre of sedition. The newspaper only resumed publication in November 1945.[26]

J.M. Shrinagesh (an Indian ICS officer who joined the service in 1928) had this to say about the control of news during the Quit India movement: 'With the means to block enemy transmissions and administrative powers to seize seditious reports, very little news other than the odd item about hooligans cutting telephone wires and dacoits threatening police constables reached the nation at large.'[27] On the other hand, historians including Paul Greenough and Jim Masselos who have studied underground literature (including broadsheets, leaflets typed or copied by hand, cyclostyled or printed, chalked on pavements or pasted as posters on walls) have emphasized the reach and influence of these. According to Masselos, the specific impact of these is 'indeterminable'. On the one hand, the Governor of Bombay, Sir Roger Lumley, dismissed this literature as carrying 'little influence'; on the other, and despite the seizure of thousands of pamphlets, several times more continued to circulate in Bombay.[28] In this case, it seems that the colonial state wanted to minimize the importance of something that it found difficult to staunch. When banning was impossible, belittling took its place.

Faced with a major internal crisis, the GOI took the view that preservation of law and order was vital, and prior consultation with the press was both impractical and inadvisable. As the Indian press had previously agreed not to publish news that might be of value to the enemy, the main point of difference with the government was over whether and how to publish news about the Quit India movement. A GOI order of 8 August 1942 imposed pre-censorship on news relating to the mass movement/disturbances. Press Notice XIX banned the publication (unless released to the press by government) of the following categories of news: reports of interruptions to road and railway

---

[26] M. Chalapathi Rau, *Journalism and Politics* (Delhi: Vikas, 1984), 163.

[27] Jayavant Mallanah Shrinagesh, *Between Two Stools: My Life in the ICS Before and After Independence*, ed. Rudolf and Shakuntala Hartog (New Delhi: Rupa, 2007), 77.

[28] Jim Masselos, 'Bombay, August 1942: Re-readings in a Nationalist Text', in *Turbulent Times: India, 1940–44*, ed. Biswamoy Pati, 67–107 (Mumbai: Popular Prakashan, 1998), 79. For an account of censorship of Congress bulletins during the Quit India movement as well as a detailed case study of a Bengali underground publication at this time, see Greenough, 'Political Mobilization and the Underground Literature'.

communications, acts of sabotage, and strikes or interruptions of work in factories chiefly engaged in producing war materials. The subject matter that could not be published varied according to the time and situation; in August 1942, according to the CPA, a special watch was kept on 'Congress propaganda disguised as a general expression of public opinion'. After the Quit India movement was launched, 'allegations against military or police were stopped, as were reports of interrupted communications or sabotage or interruptions of work in war factories', as well as what the CPA deemed exaggerated reports of the extent of the movement. After the arrest of Congress leaders in August 1942, no news about them was permitted except what was officially announced.[29] Despite the multiplicity of don'ts, press correspondents were still confused about what they could and could not report. Could they, for instance, report speeches made in the LA related to the disturbances? Yes, they could, but these speeches, allegations and the GOI's response (given as points or extracts) to allegations made on the floor of the house were subject to pre-censorship too.[30]

The AINEC was able to persuade various newspapers across the country that had suspended publication in August 1942 to reappear by the first week of September.[31] In any case, the Viceroy, Lord Linlithgow, had interpreted the suspension of publications of papers most cynically, and expressed the opinion that they were surely being funded by some subversive organization, or else they would not have been able to bear financial losses.[32] In early October 1942 the AINEC passed a unanimous resolution (in a meeting attended by about 100 editors from various provinces) taking 'strong exception' to restrictions imposed on the press by the GOI since August, and blaming the GOI for violating the Delhi Agreement.[33] The AINEC wanted newspapers to be free

---

[29] Note by CPA for Viceroy, January 1944, Appendix III in GOI Home Political (I), f. 24/3, 1944, NAI.

[30] Notes by Home Member, 5 September 1942, and by Secretary I&B, 7 September 1942. Notes by Kirchner, 8, 10 and 14 September 1942. All notes and correspondence in GOI Home Political (I), f. 3/59, 1942, NAI.

[31] *Times of India*, 'Press Agreement', editorial, 2 September 1942.

[32] Linlithgow estimated that the circulation of the *Amrita Bazar Patrika* was 45–50,000 and it must therefore be incurring a substantial loss on account on suspension of publications. Letter from Linlithgow to Amery, 17 August 1942. Nicholas Mansergh and EWR Lumby ed., *Constitutional Relations between Britain and India: The Transfer of Power, 1942–7* (London: H.M. Stationery Office, 1970-83), vol. 2, 741–743.

[33] Full text of the resolution reproduced in the *Times of India*, 6 October 1942.

to report any incident in connection with the mass movement without pre-censorship. Further, the AINEC resolution not only recorded its members' 'dismay' at the suppression and suspension of various newspapers, but also warned the government:

> The fact that newspapers find it difficult to perform their duties to the public increases unrest throughout the country, multiplies the force of rumour and is a direct aid to enemy propaganda which can point to the disappearance of newspapers as proof of an oppressive regime.[34]

Here was an argument for press freedom that spoke in terms that the GOI could understand, spelling out the advantages from a lack of pre-censorship that accrued to the government, rather than to the press. On its part, the AINEC not only set limits for editors but also recommended to the GOI that it take action—in consultation with the Provincial PACs—against those that violated these guidelines.[35]

On 1 November 1942, the GOI cancelled the notification of 8 August, which meant that provincial governments were again left free to establish their own relations with the press. However, both before and after this date provinces continued to dictate what the press could and could not report. In October 1942 (before the notification was cancelled) the NWFP government, for example, directed newspapers to submit, before publication, to the Provincial and District PACs all news (reports and pictures) pertaining to disturbances and demonstrations connected to the Quit India movement, measures taken by the government to control the movement, and judicial proceedings arising as a result of the movement.[36] A month later (after the notification was cancelled) an Orissa government notification prohibited publishing, unless officially announced, reports of interruptions in road and railway communications, reports of acts of sabotage or attempted sabotage directed at railways, military and civil aerodromes, power houses, water supply installations, telegraph and telephone lines or any other public utility, and reports of strikes in factories engaged in producing materials required for military purposes.[37]

---

[34] Ibid.
[35] The *Times of India* approved of these proposals, and hoped that it would break the deadlock. *Times of India*, 'Editors' Conference', editorial, 8 October 1942.
[36] *Times of India*, 2 October 1942.
[37] *Times of India*, 12 November 1942.

Censorship of—and by—the Press: The Bhansali Case

In the aftermath of the Quit India movement an incident occurred that proved that if the government could control what newspapers published, newspapers too could determine what the government published. This was the 'Bhansali case' and it erupted in November 1942 over the CP government's ban on publishing news of a fast by a Gandhian, Professor Bhansali, to protest against the alleged misbehaviour of white troops with Indian women. On 16 August 1942, a mob killed two magistrates, a police inspector, and a constable at Chimur in CP. Troops were sent to quell the disturbance, and on 22 September the CP government received written complaints of rape and looting by British and Indian troops. It conducted an investigation, and in a report published in October 1942 announced that the complaints were false. In November 1942, Professor Bhansali went to Delhi and began fasting over the issue, resuming his fast when he was removed to CP. The CP government, fearing that news of the fast would incite more public protests, banned publication of all news about Professor Bhansali.[38]

The AINEC was not consulted before the order was passed, and even reporting this ban was banned. The CP government requested other provincial governments to impose a similar ban, a request with which most of them complied, and orders were accordingly served to newspapers. When Provincial PACs suggested that news of the fast be allowed publication subject to the terms laid down in the Bombay Agreement (that is, objectively, and in a manner not calculated to incite public feeling) local governments did not agree to the proposal on the grounds that the fast could lead to serious disorders.[39]

On its part, the AINEC fixed dates for a *hartal* by newspapers to protest against this order, and suggested, in a resolution passed in December 1942, that the press carry out reverse censorship against the state by not publishing official news and announcements (including official circulars and the New Years' honours list), and not reporting speeches of members of the government; only decisions and announcements were published. All in all, 150 newspapers adopted and followed this instruction. As a result, pre-censorship was imposed on the *Hindustan Times*, and reporters of *The Hindu* in Madras were denied facilities. In turn, nationalist papers suspended publication on 6 January 1943.

---

[38] Events summarized on the basis of information contained in a *Times of India* editorial published after Professor Bhansali broke his fast. *Times of India*, 'A Fast Broken', 14 January 1943.

[39] Ibid.

A week later, on 13 January, the CP government withdrew the ban order and conceded the demand for an inquiry. When newspapers resumed publication, they published it all: news of the lifting of the ban, the inquiry order, and the end of Professor Bhansali's 63-day fast. [40] Censorship, at least during wartime, was no longer the prerogative of the state alone.

Not all newspapers agreed on censorship by—rather than of—the press. The *Times of India* thought this method of protest 'futile', and expressed the view that the voluntary suppression of a newspaper meant depriving the public of information to which it was entitled, and it meant punishing the public for 'what the press regards as the delinquencies of those in authority'.[41] On the other hand, *The Hindu* commented that the CP government had learnt belatedly that '... public opinion cannot be rendered powerless by being muzzled'. It termed the ban by the government as something that offended 'the first principles of democracy and freedom', in addition to being a violation of the agreement between the organized press and the GOI. The editorial acknowledged that although the public had been inconvenienced, newspapers had undertaken this measure ('a voluntary restriction on their own usefulness') because

> ... only a paramount sense of duty to the public could have sustained them in their effort to vindicate the right of the public to be kept informed, even during war and consistently with the need for respecting military secrets, of everything that might be of interest or concern to them.[42]

In any case, a ban on news of reporting fasts—whether Gandhi's more famous ones or those undertaken by his followers—was an emotive and important issue for newspapers. In early 1943, news of Gandhi's plans to fast was banned (till his correspondence with the Viceroy was released), as was speculation about his condition 'especially if alarmist'. The AINEC passed a resolution protesting against censorship of news and comments regarding Gandhi's fast, and urging the GOI to provide all relevant information about Gandhi's fast by incorporating it in bulletins released to the press by the

---

[40] An account of this is available in Jagannathan, *Independence and the Indian Press*, 125–127.

[41] *Times of India*, 1 January 1943.

[42] *The Hindu*, 'Vindication', editorial, 14 January 1943, reproduced in G. Kasturi (ed.), *The Hindu Speaks* (compilation of 100 editorials to mark 100 years of the paper) (Bombay: Interpress, 1978), 210–212.

government so that the press could publish 'adequate objective details'.[43] As for the GOI, the principle followed in banning news of fasts (both of Gandhi and of Professor Bhansali) was (according to a report prepared by the CPA for the Viceroy) that 'the fast was a publicity stunt designed politically to blackmail Government, and that it was the business of censorship to prevent undesirable publicity'.[44]

Banning Bad News: The Bengal Famine (1943)

The Bengal famine was a disaster on an epic scale: 3 million people are believed to have perished.[45] Historians have laid the blame for the famine on man-made, and specifically British-made, causes, citing the 'scorched earth' policy (burning boats and other resources which were thought to be potentially useful to the Japanese), and diversion of food grains towards Allied troops instead of the local population as causes of the famine. The famine was not the first natural disaster the news of which was sought to be suppressed by the state. Shyama Prasad Mookerjee, later to become Nehru's opponent in independent India's Parliament, was the Finance Minister of Bengal between 1941 and 1942. After a cyclone devastated Midnapore in Bengal on 16 October 1942 and claimed 30,000 lives, the news was kept from appearing in the newspapers (on the instructions of the HD) so that it would not reach the enemy. As Mookerjee put it, 'This was a preposterous argument, for within twenty-four hours of the incident the enemy radio, I was told later, was broadcasting reports of the terrible damage and the Government's apathy.'[46] Mookerjee believed that the strict operation of the DIR also prevented news of the Bengal famine from reaching provinces other than Bengal.[47] A news story that Kedar Ghosh, at the time an employee of an Indian news agency in Calcutta, had written on an arrangement between the Bengal government and Indian commercial interests to monopolize the purchase of rice from Bengal's coastal areas threatened by the Japanese was first objected to by his own agency's news editor (on the

---

[43] AINEC resolution published in the *Times of India*, 18 February 1943.

[44] Note by CPA for Viceroy, January 1944, Appendix III in GOI Home Political (I), f. 24/3, 1944, NAI.

[45] Amartya Sen, *Poverty and Famines: An Essay on Entitlement and Deprivation* (Oxford: Clarendon Press, 1981), Appendix D, 195–216. This is double the estimate made by the Famine Inquiry Commission in 1945.

[46] S.P. Mookerjee, *Leaves from a Diary* (Calcutta: Oxford University Press, 1993), 82.

[47] Ibid., 91.

grounds that its publication would infringe the DIR), and then by Bengal Home Secretary.[48]

Ultimately, it was *The Statesman*, a British owned and edited paper—and not the nationalist press—that took up the cause of the victims of the famine, with the publication of editorials, photographs and news. Ian Stephens, editor of *The Statesman*, had also served as a Director of Public Information with the GOI earlier, and was thus uniquely placed to appreciate the government's position on the Bengal famine. All the same, *The Statesman* published, in August 1943, photographs and editorials on victims of the famine; the story was picked up not only elsewhere in India but also in the United States.[49] The photographs had not been submitted for 'press advice'.[50] Writing his memoirs more than two decades after the event, Stephens recalled that being the editor of a British-owned paper, he could afford to publicize the famine whereas pro-Congress rival papers, scared of closure and official reprisal, could not.[51] Other newspapers were, indeed, not so privileged. In October 1943, under the DIR, the Bengal government imposed pre-censorship on the *Amrita Bazar Patrika*, forbidding it to report on the famine.[52]

In early 1944, the CPA claimed that as the seriousness of the Bengal famine became apparent, censorship was relaxed 'though correspondents were not allowed to indicate congestion of destitute in particular areas' (such as Howrah Station, Howrah Bridge or Sealdah). The CPA also admitted that censors were asked not to publicize attempts made by Mookerjee to 'make political capital' out of the famine. Additionally, the CPA informed the Viceroy in early 1944, 'At all times there is a stop on suggestions that there is uncontrolled currency inflation in India or, more generally, on messages calculated to undermine confidence in the Indian currency.'[53] Here, state censors were being optimistic about the efficacy of censorship: historians including Indivar Kamtekar, Srimanjari, Yasmin Khan and Srinath Raghavan have proved beyond doubt

---

[48] Kedar Ghosh, *No Apology*, 35.

[49] This story is narrated in Madhusree Mukherjee, *Churchill's Secret War: The British Empire and the Ravaging of India during World War II* (New York: Basic Books, 2010), 174–175.

[50] Stephens, Ian M., *Monsoon Morning* (London: Ernest Benn, 1966), 176.

[51] Ibid., 186.

[52] Sunit Ghosh, *Modern History of the Indian Press* (New Delhi: Cosmo Publications, 1998), 247–249.

[53] Note by CPA for Viceroy, January 1944, Appendix III in GOI Home Political (I), f. 24/3, 1944, NAI.

that the Indian public was not only aware of war setbacks, but their confidence in the colonial state was at an all-time low during the war.

Legacies of War

By 1945, the AINEC was of the opinion, and publicly stating, that the press in India was not as free as that in England and the United States because 'the regime which controls the destiny of this country is totalitarian and autocratic'.[54] The same year it passed a resolution demanding that press laws in India be aligned with those in Great Britain and the United States. The AINEC resolution demanded the Princes Protection Act and the Press (Emergency Powers) Act be immediately repealed, and the relevant provisions of the IPC and the CrPC be amended. [55] The operation of colonial difference was starkly apparent to the colonized, and more than five years of war had tested their patience. Irrespective of the AINEC's strong protestations, free speech was of secondary importance to a state engaged in war.

According to the journalist N.S. Jagannathan, the Second World War ushered in a new phase of government–press relations.[56] Not all journalists thought this was a good thing. Veteran journalist and historian of the Indian press, S.P. Thiaga Rajan, writing two decades after the end of the war, was of the opinion that during the Second World War '... the press got its tail behind [sic] its hind legs and entered into a subordinate partnership with the Government by extracting some concessions here or there'. To his mind, the AINEC was a symbol of that subordination.[57] As the various examples cited in this chapter indicate, the GOI was willing to discuss the question of censorship with representatives of the organized press, and preferred to impose censorship in collaboration with the press rather than unilaterally by statutory measures. The GOI often spoke of 'friendly relations with the press' during this time. Even official press histories, such as that of *The Tribune* (published four decades after the end of the war) admitted that 'to avoid legal action, however, it [*The Tribune*] decided, like many other journals, to exclude reports

---

[54] Statement made by the AINEC president, S.A. Brelvi, while inaugurating a series of lectures on journalism at Calcutta University. *Times of India*, 27 January 1945.

[55] *Times of India*, 30 and 31 January 1945.

[56] Jagannathan, *Independence and the Indian Press*, 105.

[57] S.P. Thiaga Rajan, *History of Indian Journalism* (Thanjavur: The Columbia House, 1966), 21.

about the progress of the national movement'.[58] No doubt due to the shuffling of priorities during wartime, the GOI had, in effect, made the following deal with the Indian press: so long as the latter did not publish material that would incite people to take part in the anti-war movement, the government would not interfere with the working of the press.[59] If, as has been argued, the significance of Gandhi's participation in the Round Table Conference lay in recognition accorded to him as a leader of the Indian people, then negotiations with the Indian press—no matter in whose favour they were ultimately decided—reveal how important a role it played in India in the 1940s.

However, even as the GOI depended on the cooperation of the Indian press to ensure that news of military importance was not published, the press was dependent on the government for newsprint, a commodity in short supply, and this factor strengthened the government's hand. The GOI passed a newsprint control order according to which, after 15 June 1941, newsprint could only be sold to a newspaper press and could not be used by the proprietor of such a press for any purpose except for printing newspapers. Dealers in newsprint as well as newspapers were to send the government returns of consumption.[60] The editor of *The Statesman*, Ian Stephens, recalled that in 1942, newspaper sizes were further reduced to six pages on account of shortages. *The Statesman* had ample supplies (as the earlier editor, Arthur Moore, had purchased them before war broke out) as did *The Pioneer* and the *Times of India* but 'almost every other paper in the country was in difficulties'.[61] *The Tribune*, for instance, reduced its size as well as its price (to one *anna*, or 1/16th of a rupee, per copy).[62] Towards the end of the war, the AINEC protested against the manner in which the order was used, and which, they alleged, had less to do with the conservation of newsprint and more to do with preventing the growth and expansion of newspapers that were not to the liking of the government.[63]

---

[58] Prakash Ananda, *A History of the Tribune* (New Delhi: The Tribune Trust, 1986), 93.

[59] *Times of India*, 4 March 1941.

[60] *Times of India*, 2 and 4 June 1941.

[61] Stephens, *Monsoon Morning*, 32. Stephens came to India in 1930, and in 1932 became the Central government's 'public relations officer'. He joined *The Statesman* in October 1937.

[62] Prakash Ananda, *A History of the Tribune*, 93.

[63] At the same time, the conference also noted that some newspapers were prone to personal and abusive writing, and suggested that these be discouraged. *Times of India*, 30 and 31 January 1945.

There is indeed some evidence that bureaucratic discretion over the allotment of newsprint allowed the GOI to patronize favourable press. Although the Principal Information Officer, A.S. Iyengar, stated forcefully in August 1946 that release of newsprint had not been used as a measure of censorship in India during the war, an Indian ICS officer's recollection was at odds with this assertion. Dharma Vira, who joined the ICS in 1931, recalled in his memoirs that during the Second World War there was great shortage of newsprint, and newspapers and magazines had to work on a quota basis. He acknowledged that 'the power of granting quotas was sometimes misused for pressurizing or punishing newspapers, for political reasons'. As Deputy Secretary in the HD in charge of assigning quotas, Vira was approached by Pandit Ravi Shankar Shukla, a leader from the CP (later the Chief Minister of Madhya Pradesh), who was at that time running Hindi papers with strong Congress views. The newsprint quota for his papers was refused for this reason, as Vira acknowledged, and Shukla told him that the death of his papers would also mean a setback to the national movement in the CP. Vira recalled that he allotted a fresh quota, as he felt that it had been wrongly withheld. Sir Francis Mudie expressed his disapproval of this decision; in his view, the quota should have been withheld given the 'subversive and seditionist writings' to which the paper was prone. In arguing his case, Vira invoked the letter of the law and the spirit of fairness: there were no official government orders to this effect with regard to the grant of newsprint quotas, and in all fairness they could not be withheld for extraneous reasons. Sir Francis took the matter to the Viceroy, Lord Wavell, who concluded that as there were no instructions to the contrary, the Deputy Secretary was justified in giving the quota.[64]

Even as events during the war helped consolidate the Indian press (the formation of the AINEC being a case in point) the war also brought some journalists closer to the state. In the spring of 1941, as many as 22 of *The Statesman*'s British employees were drawn away for war service.[65] The boundary between a career in journalism and a career in government, including the army, was not impermeable. Ivor Jehu, a senior journalist who held an editorial position in the *Times of India* at the outbreak of the war, worked as the Director of Public Relations at army headquarters during the war, and re-joined the newspaper as editor at the end of the war. Ivor Jehu in turn invited Prem Bhatia

---

[64] Dharma Vira, *Reminiscences* (New Delhi: Vikas, 1990), 21–22. Vira served as Cabinet Secretary as well as the Governor of three Indian states after Independence.

[65] Stephens, *Monsoon Morning*, 18.

to join the organization in 1942. Bhatia (who went on to become editor of *The Tribune* after Independence, in addition to holding several diplomatic positions) began his army career as Second Lieutenant, and ended it four years later as a Lieutenant Colonel, without, as he recalled, having fired a single shot. His job, as he put it, was to serve as 'a war correspondents' uniformed guide with an unused service revolver in my holster'. He was by no means the only journalist in uniform during the war. Bhatia's transition to civilian life was via another government appointment, as the Director of Public Information (ex-officio Joint Secretary in the Information Department) in the Bengal government in 1944. His senior contemporary at Government College, Lahore, today remembered as the legendary Urdu poet Faiz Ahmad Faiz, also served in the Army Public Relations Directorate. The poet, who had also worked previously as a college lecturer, wore a uniform, edited *Fauji Akhbar*, a monthly magazine for officers and men, and left the army a Lieutenant Colonel. Journalists who joined the government's information or publicity departments were, of course, not insulated from political influences. Altaf Husain, who had served as the Director of Public Information in the Government of Bengal until 1944 (and later became editor of the *Dawn* in India and then in Pakistan), regularly wrote articles in favour of the Muslim League in *The Statesman* under the pseudonym of 'Shahed'. Since the Director of Public Information was not supposed to engage in political writing, his identity was concealed by the editor of *The Statesman*, Ian Stephens.[66] As we have seen, press censors or 'advisers' were also often drawn from the ranks of journalists.

The presence of Indians on advisory committees also altered the relationship between the state and the press, not only for the duration of the war but also after it, as they could rely on networks of personal friendships to soften the operation of censorship. Durga Das, who served as the President of the UP PAC recalled that in 1941 he repeatedly 'came to the rescue' of the *National Herald* at Lucknow, by maintaining that comments by it to which the government took exception did not breach either the AINEC code or the DIR.[67] The proliferation of rules during war tends to obscure our vision of a tendency towards informalization of censorship, a tendency that was encouraged by the GOI. During the First World War too, journalists were given some special privileges: publicity boards were established, tours of battlefronts were organized for important journalists such as for Kasturi Ranga Iyenger of *The*

---

[66] See Prem Bhatia, *Of Many Pastures* (New Delhi: Allied, 1989).
[67] Das, *India from Curzon*, 199.

Hindu, and Stanley Reed of the *Times of India* (who late became the first journalist in India to be knighted) placed his services at the disposal of the GOI for publicity and propaganda purposes.[68] However, anti-colonial nationalism had not, during the First World War, reached its zenith, the context was different, and the co-option was mild as compared to the Second World War.

Gerald Barrier, in his brief survey of major press–GOI relations during the Second World War, has argued that censorship of the press continued at a low level until 1942, when the GOI 'blacked out all news on demonstrations and Congress activities', and this brought it into direct confrontation with the Indian press. He has also shown how, by early September 1942, the GOI had reached a compromise with the press and removed the ban on news of disturbances, while editors undertook to work more closely with censors.[69] In his opinion, repression in 1942 has 'clouded' the larger trend of diminishing controls over the Indian press during the war years, as 'propaganda, indirect supervision and influence received preference over reliance on open force'.[70] This is amply borne out by the account presented here; its long-term legacy in independent India will be explored in the next part of this book.

Censorship in Britain during the Second World War

Given that the national and colonial versions of the British state were fighting the same war, but were answerable to, and dependent on, a national and a colonial public, it is of some value to compare the practice of and reactions to state censorship in India and in Britain.[71] During the war, there were some similarities in the way censorship was conducted in India and in Britain: in both countries defence services were actively involved in censorship activities;

---

[68] Iyengar, *The Newspaper Press in India*, 25. The case of Stanley Reed is discussed in Pat Lovett, *Journalism in India* (Calcutta: Banna Publishing Company, 1929), 54.

[69] Barrier, *Banned*, 147–149. Barrier's discussion of censorship during the Second World War is a brief survey of trends and major decisions rather than detailed analysis.

[70] As evidence he cites the fact that between 1943 and 1945, less than three dozen Indian publications were banned (in addition to the comprehensive ban on Congress publications), while in the same period approximately 700 publications coming from outside India were detained. Barrier, *Banned*, 151.

[71] For a comparison of the British and Indian experience of the Second World War at the level of both state and people, see Indivar Kamtekar, 'A Different War Dance: State and Class in India 1939–1945', *Past & Present*, 176, no. 1 (August 2002): 187–221. The present analysis is inspired by this article.

in both, advisory committees consisting of press representatives were set up; in both, it was largely 'voluntary'; in both, there was no sustained pre-censorship of newspaper leading articles; in both, control was exercised via notes of guidance issued to the press via the censor. In India, as in Britain, editors—except during the Quit India movement—followed a policy of cooperation with the government. That is, they 'agreed to regulate the industry from within through provincial press committees in return for relaxed controls'.[72]

In Britain the Chief Censor was, for a large part of the war, a senior naval officer, Rear Admiral G.P. Thomson. The British public's annoyance at the methods of censorship (and not so much the fact of censorship, which was accepted as a necessity of war) during wartime was made quite clear in their letters to that British institution, *The Times*. Many letters referred to the attempts—sometimes draconian, occasionally absurd and often unsuccessful— of the government to prevent British publications from reaching enemy nations. A month after the outbreak of war, one letter-writer noted that although his London newspapers were confiscated before he boarded a boat to France, the same papers were being sold on the boat and in France. On his return journey he had taken the precaution of not carrying any foreign newspapers, but an ordinary English novel was confiscated, and forwarded to the Chief Censor at Liverpool, while a briefcase full of written and typewritten documents aroused no interest. Not surprisingly, he decried the 'blind and pompous folly of inflated functionaries'; he exemplified the attitude of many others: censorship could be tolerated during exceptional circumstances such as war, but only if it was effective and not arbitrary. He wrote:

> By all means let our trembling rulers forbid us the neutral and allied Press. By all means let them forbid to Allies and to neutrals the indiscreet or treasonable columns of *The Times*; but surely there must be on the booksellers' shelves some harmless trifles which might be exempted and even prescribed for those like myself who, endeavouring to serve their country, must undertake the long and slow and most uncomfortable journeys of war-time.[73]

The sheer absurdity, or perhaps impossibility, of effective censorship is illustrated by the example of a man who wrote that upon landing in England from Europe he was deprived by officials of his *Dutch Grammar*, the works of Homer and Horace, a book containing reproductions of Dutch paintings,

---

[72] Barrier, *Banned*, 147.
[73] Letter from H.N. Robertson, *The Times*, 5 October 1939.

his personal dairy and address book, two anti-fascist works (Kurt Ludecke's attack on Hitler titled *I Knew Hitler* and Sinclair Lewis's *It Can't Happen Here*) and a roll of film. What was *not* confiscated was the German edition of *Mein Kampf*.[74] Another correspondent complained that American publications were being held up by the British Ministry of Information, and that this was not only bad policy but also bad propaganda: if the British people were deprived of neutral newspapers, they would 'read more gloom into the meager news releases than the events themselves justify'.[75] The editor of an academic journal of Spanish studies complained that the two Spanish daily newspapers on which his publication so depended were no longer reaching them, despite Spanish neutrality.[76] A man who urged patience on grounds that 'war ... is an abnormal state ... it raises abnormal problems ... and such problems necessitate abnormal remedies' found himself very much in a minority in the letters column of *The Times*.[77]

In a similar vein, Edward John Thompson (father of the famous historian E.P. Thompson) noticed upon his return to England from India in November 1939 that censors 'confiscated every scrap of printed or written matter'. He recorded that an Australian farmer leaving England had to relinquish his copy of Thackeray's *Virginians* and an Australian woman lost her English classics to the censor; in fact, she was also asked to hand in her prayer book, but she 'flatly refused to surrender it'. A young engineer had to part with an expensive technical book, and everyone lost Penguin paperbacks, of which there were 'two tall piles'. Thompson reported that the Australians 'left our shores angry, saying that there was no difference between us and the other totalitarian governments'. They had, according to him, considered themselves robbed.[78] The Australian woman whose case was referred to by Thompson had written an indignant letter to *The Times* in which she complained about not even being allowed to take Noel Coward's short stories with her to Sydney. Her writing case containing newspaper clippings and review articles was confiscated, and 'even the blotting paper carefully looked at in the hopes of discovering some secret code'. Her letter gave voice to a sentiment felt by many people: they

---

[74] Letter from H.M. Threlfall, *The Times*, 9 October 1939.

[75] Letter from J.F. Bleasdale, *The Times*, 5 October 1939.

[76] Letter from E. Allison Peers, *The Times*, 5 October 1939.

[77] Letter from J. Leonard Stone, *The Times*, 9 October 1939.

[78] Thompson quoted in Mary Lago, *India's Prisoner: A Biography of Edward John Thompson, 1886–1946* (Columbia: University of Missouri Press, 2001), 279–280.

understood and accepted that wartime meant inconvenience, but wanted restrictions to be reasonable.[79]

In Britain, yet another mechanism of preventing certain items of information from being published was the centralized dissemination of war news from the Ministry of Information, from where it was issued to foreign correspondents. Rare praise for the ministry, otherwise ridiculed as 'the national Aunt Sally', came from the president of the Foreign Press Association in London. Far from resenting such a measure, he expressed his admiration for this system, and wanted it maintained as a way of sending news abroad. He also absolved the ministry of all blame for the lack of news.[80] Arrangements which would have been unacceptable to journalists in peacetime were appreciated during war.

The operation of 'cooperation' between press and government in Britain can be illustrated with an example. In 1942, a journalist of the Australian Newspaper Service sent a dispatch of 600 words to newspapers in his country to the effect that because of the difficult shipping situation Australia could not expect war supplies on a large scale from either Britain or the United States. This dispatch, rather dramatically titled 'Sacrifice Australia', invited the attention of the cable censor and was referred to the Chief Censor, after which the journalist added two more words to satisfy his censors. The title now became 'Necessary sacrifice Australia temporarily', and the dispatch was forwarded without any alterations to the content. The story, however, did not end here. The unedited version of the dispatch was later included by the Ministry of Information among other examples of offending messages that it argued necessitated stricter censorship on cables sent abroad. In his indignant letter to *The Times*, the journalist observed that although censorship had become more efficient since 1939 (which he clearly did not consider a negative development), he was against the imposition of gags on foreign correspondents that were not imposed on domestic ones.[81] From the evidence, it seems that foreign correspondents faced more problems with censorship in Britain than did the British ones. The president of the Overseas Empire Correspondents' Association, for instance, pointed to the delays and inconvenience caused when the War Office and the Admiralty, for instance, insisted on vetting articles in exchange for facility visits. Changes made to articles, he said, were frequently not on security grounds, but 'solely because they disapprove of phrasing, or

---

[79] Letter from Elsie W. Dangar, *The Times*, 16 October 1939.

[80] Letter from Stefan Litauer, *The Times*, 9 October 1939.

[81] Letter from Gordon Gilmour, *The Times*, 23 April 1942.

comment and conclusions that flow naturally from the facts the writer is permitted to ascertain'.[82] He suggested that centralization of censorship at the Ministry of Information (with the occasional assistance of defence experts) would be the best solution, and urged that there be no interference with copy except on security grounds. Political versus military reasons for censorship, so often discussed in the Indian context as we have seen, were not absent from the British context either.

By the middle of the war, as censorship mechanisms evolved through a process of trial and error, the Minister of Information, Brendan Bracken, deemed the censorship of news going abroad from Britain to have been successfully implemented. As he put it:

> When it was considered that over 11,000,000 words went out of this country every week, and had to be dealt with by about 360 censors it was amazing that the censors made so few errors and so very few enemies. Journalists of all free nations had declared that our censors were the best in the world.[83]

Bracken concluded by praising the Chief Censor, Rear Admiral G.P. Thomson, for his tireless and splendid efforts. The statements made by him may be dismissed as self-praise, but they were met by cheers in the house, so his sentiments were shared by at least a few other British parliamentarians as well.[84]

In 1942, Rear Admiral Thomson admitted that his task was not easy. The price of keeping the enemy in the dark was keeping one's own people in the dark as well, and this 'would never do'; people in Britain '... have a right to know what is going around them. They have a right to draw their own conclusions, to criticize, and demand that what appears wrong to them should be put right'. He acknowledged that the press worked in very difficult conditions in wartime, and if it made mistakes (that is, published news useful to the enemy) this was due to staff shortages or the carelessness of sub-editors. The motto of the press censor was, as he put it, 'Cooperation and not Prosecution'. He concluded that after more than two years of war, censorship in Britain had successfully met the two conflicting requirements: 'a free people who refuse to be kept in the dark and a whole nation organized to fight a total war'.[85] The head of the 'best censors in the world', however, was conscious that though

---

[82] Letter from Leonard W. Matters, *The Times*, 26 November 1943.
[83] *The Times*, 9 December 1942.
[84] Ibid.
[85] *The Times*, 6 January 1942.

it was activity tolerated during wartime, it was never entirely acceptable to the British public. In a public address in 1944 Thomson noted that although censorship was an 'ugly thing', it was also an 'unfortunate necessity'. Further, for Britain as a democratic country

> ... the very word censorship seemed to be foreign to our ideas, and to what we were fighting for—the right to think, speak and act according to our consciences. A free press was one of the liberties to which British people were most strongly attached, for the press was largely responsible for moulding the public opinion, which was the sovereign power in a democratic State. But when war came we could not afford to tell the enemy all that we were doing, going to do and hoping to do in the fight against him.[86]

After five years of enforcing it, Thomson concluded that censorship in Britain was working reasonably well in meeting 'the conflicting requirements of a free people who refused to be kept in the dark, and of a nation organized to fight a total war'. After the war ended, Thomson was honoured at by the Newspaper Proprietors' Association. A member recalled that far from being 'public enemy No. 1 of Fleet Street', the Chief Censor had become the 'uncle of Fleet Street', as he had always trusted newspapers to be patriotic. At the same time, a representative of the provincial press urged vigilance 'until they were satisfied that the censorship virus had been destroyed', and suggested that the time had returned for the newspapers to stand on their own feet again, instead of being guided.[87]

This discussion indicates that while ordinary people in Britain were often frustrated by the operation of censorship at ports, and over the post, by and large even journalists accepted the need for thorough censorship so as to deprive Axis powers of vital information. Although foreign correspondents had problems with coordination among various agencies (the Ministry of Information, the War Department, and the Admiralty) before reports could be sent out of Britain, the domestic British press was willing to play along with the directives of the Chief Censor. In India, although the same model of government–press cooperation was instituted via the Press Advisory system, the relationship between the organized press and the colonial state was, not surprisingly, more adversarial, although there were—as described in this chapter—periods of cooperation as well. Common to both countries was the

---

[86] *The Times*, 7 November 1944.
[87] *The Times*, 29 September 1945.

state's assumption that complete censorship, even if it were possible, was not desirable as it would be counter-productive.

With regard to specific instances of publications, colonial difference manifested itself in the same book being adjudged suitable for circulation in Britain and unsuitable for circulation in India. To take one example, Tom Winteringham's *New Ways of War*, published by Penguin in Britain, which contained instructions for making a home-made hand grenade, was one such book, and the deliberations over allowing it in to India are revealing. In 1941 the IB had established that this book enjoyed wide circulation in Delhi, as all copies with two distributors had sold out. Incidentally, the book had been screened by the IB in November 1940, but the four pages that carried these instructions had not been noticed at the time. The IB was reluctant to ban the book for two reasons: the harm had already been done, and banning the book would gain it publicity. The DIB, Sir Denys Pilditch, recommended 'quiet negotiations' with the English publishers to stop further export of the book into India as the best course of action,[88] while a HD official did not favour this as he thought it was too late to do so.[89]

In April 1941 the Bengal government wrote to the GOI about the book, complaining that 'terrorists here have for long had the ambition of making a really effective bomb which this information now enables them to gratify', and asking them to consider taking action against other similar books, even if it was too late to do anything about this one.[90] Without a notification, the GOI could not ask the Chief Censor to intercept copies of *New Ways of War*, but asked him to withhold other publications that gave similar information to subversive organizations.[91] In the next six months (that is, till October 1941), six copies of the book were noticed by the IB coming into India through Bombay, while two copies were available for sale in Delhi. Some passages from the book—including the grenade recipe—had appeared in British publications (including the *Daily Mirror* and *Picture Post*) that enjoyed wide circulation in India.[92] Three more copies were detained at the Madras censor station in

---

[88] Note by W. Kidd expressing the DIB's views, 26 February 1941, GOI Home Political, f. 41/7, 1941, NAI.

[89] Note by J.W. Simms, 28 February 1941, GOI Home Political, f. 41/7, 1941, NAI.

[90] D.O. no. 2578 P. from Additional Secretary Bengal, A.E. Porter, to Tottenham, 10 April, GOI Home Political, f. 41/7, 1941, NAI.

[91] Note by Simms, 22 April 1941, GOI Home Political, f. 41/7, 1941, NAI.

[92] Note by Puckle, 5 November 1941, GOI Home Political, f. 41/7, 1941, NAI.

the January 1942.[93] Although the GOI had earlier asked the India Office to ask the British Ministry of Information to warn British publishers about the dangerous use to which such books could be put in India[94], the India Office was unable to help. As they explained:

> ... at the present time articles of modern warfare such as those published in Daily Mirror and Picture Post are not merely popular here but are recognized as having definite instructional value.... While such articles are a regular feature in British Press material which you are likely to consider dangerous for example manufacture of home made bombs appear only occasionally as part of general scheme of advice for home defence organisations. Miniform [Ministry of Information] feel that any approach [to publishers to stop sending such publications to India] would court rebuff and possibly still more hostile reactions.[95]

The India Office suggested that the GOI take whatever action they thought suitable to prevent circulation in India in individual cases.[96] In other words, if a self-defence guide in Britain served as a guide for anti-government violence in India, the India Office could do little about it.[97] The GOI could and did take action, but too little and too late. Here is colonial difference, rendered visible, exemplified in one book and its attempted suppression.

---

[93] U.O. no. C19/Censors, 28 January 1942, and note on it (initials unclear), 4 February 1942, GOI Home Political, f. 41/7, 1941, NAI.

[94] Telegram R. no. 158 from Governor General to Secretary of State, 20 April 1941, GOI Home Political, f. 41/7, 1941, NAI.

[95] Telegram R. no. 5227 from Secretary of State to Governor General, 11 May 1941, GOI Home Political, f. 41/7, 1941, NAI.

[96] Ibid.

[97] In 1943, the IB once again sought information (regarding circulation and possible danger) about this book from its various branches, proposing to re-examine the book from 'a security point of view'. It acknowledged that the work was of 'undoubted value' in the Britain, but would be dangerous in India in the hands of terrorists and saboteurs. IB Circular Memo no. 11/Int/43, 3 September 1943, GOI Home Political, f. 41/7, 1941, NAI.

PART IV

The Censored Turn Censors
Freedom and Free Speech

A historian of political censorship in 19th-century Europe has called censorship a 'combination of Rorschach test and barometer'. As a Rorschach test, the censorship conducted by a state allows us to see the 'type and degree of fears' harboured by its political elite; as barometer, it gauges the political atmosphere.[1] In other words, what is not allowed to appear in print or expressed in public tells us more about the nature of a state than what is allowed to be freely expressed. In the context of the 20th century as well, the degree of censorship exercised over the media by a state is often taken as an index of the freedom that state allows its citizens. For example, the presence and application of censorship laws in colonial India is often taken as confirmation of the authoritarian character of the colonial state. But what do the censorship practices of the early post-colonial Indian state tell us about that state? This is a question that existing academic literature has not addressed in a sustained manner, and one which is at the heart of this book.

In the years leading to Independence and during Partition, the Indian state's experience of trying—and failing—to control publication of communal and inflammatory news and views had important ramifications for the future of free speech in independent India. After the easing in of Indian leaders into positions

---

[1] Goldstein, *Political Censorship of the Arts and the Press*.

of power in the year before Independence, their ideological commitment to the idea of free speech was severely tested when faced with communal violence. The manifesto of the Indian National Congress for the central and provincial elections of 1945–1946 listed—as the very first fundamental right—the right of 'free expression of opinion'.[2] As the Congress assumed state power in the midst of communal carnage, several qualifications and restrictions hemmed in this right, and several experiments (with their roots in the Second World War period) in organizing state–press relations were carried out, with varying degrees of success. The 'long' 1950s (from Independence in 1947 up to the Indo-China war in 1962) has been conceptualized by a recent chronicler, Gyanesh Kudaisya, as a period both 'transformative' and 'definitive' for India, and for our understanding of India's contemporary history.[3] The three chapters in this part illustrate and discuss the experiments with free speech legislation and lived experience of this decade, and their legacy for India today.

---

[2] Extracts from the Manifesto published as Appendix I in G. M. Nandurkar, ed., *Sardar's Letters—Mostly Unknown: Post-Centenary* (Ahmedabad: Sardar Vallabhbhai Patel Smarak Bhavan, 1977, hereafter *SLMU*), vol. 4, 312.

[3] Gyanesh Kudaisya, *A Republic in the Making: India in the 1950s* (New Delhi: Oxford University Press, 2017), vii and 172. Kudaisya does not discuss free speech issues, or the First Amendment to the Indian Constitution.

7

Free Speech or Hate Speech?
Partition and Censorship

The colonial state believed that hate literature with communal overtones caused communal riots. The GOI estimated that between 1923 and 1930 approximately 450 people had been killed and 5,000 injured in communal riots in India.[1] In an official memorandum submitted to the Indian Statutory Commission in 1930 (better known as the Simon Commission), the GOI noted that the Kohat riots in NWFP in September 1924, in which 36 people died, were caused by the circulation of a 'violent anti-Islamic poem'.[2] It observed that during the Calcutta riots in 1926 inflammatory printed leaflets were circulated by Hindus as well as Muslims, and hooligans were hired; the Bengal government believed that 'money was being spent to keep the fight going'. The GOI thus held 'partisan writing in the press' responsible for fanning communal feeling.[3] In the province of Punjab as well, the GOI noted in 1930:

> ... communal writing of an extremely provocative type has assumed serious proportions and has been greatly responsible for exacerbating communal feeling. Not a few papers are said to owe their circulation almost entirely to the virulence of their attacks on the rival community.[4]

---

[1] The number of casualties included those killed by the rioters as well as those killed by 'forces of law and order, whether police or military'. *Memoranda Submitted to the Indian Statutory Commission by the Government of India*, vol. 1 (Calcutta: GOI Central Publication Branch, 1930, hereafter *Memoranda*), 106.

[2] Ibid., 109.

[3] Ibid., 5.

[4] Ibid., 105–106.

Having made this causal connection even before 1930, the GOI took legal steps to curb hate literature (that is, to facilitate punitive action against it). In August 1926 the GOI amended the CrPC to enable authorities to confiscate publications that promoted enmity or hatred among its subjects; a year later, in August 1927, it amended the IPC, making it a specific offence 'deliberately and maliciously to insult the religion or the religious beliefs of any class of His Majesty's subjects'. This second legislation was prompted when the Punjab High Court took a decision acquitting the publisher of the notorious pamphlet *Rangila Rasul*.[5]

In the eyes of state personnel, this causal connection (between what people read about another religious community and how they later behaved towards members of that community) was one that was reinforced during events leading up to and accompanying the Partition of India and the attendant communal riots. Eyewitness accounts of the Partition confirm this view. The writer Krishna Sobti blamed religious revivalist movements (such as the Arya Samaj) and the vernacular press in the Punjab for exacerbating tensions. In her words, 'The entire vernacular press, including the *Zamindar* and the *Paisa Akhbar*, was full of stories that helped sharpen the identities of Hindus and Muslims—to ensure that the differences between them were absolutely clear.'[6] Referring to East Punjab in the month after Partition, Justice G.D. Khosla too blamed the press thus: 'The vernacular Press added fuel to the fire of frenzy by giving highly coloured and unilateral accounts of the unfortunate happenings on both sides of the border.'[7] Less distinguished but perhaps more representative Indians—newspaper readers—made this connection. In 1947 a reader wrote to *The Tribune* pleading that schools not be allowed to subscribe to sectional newspapers and literature as it sowed hatred in young minds.[8] Foreign visitors

---

[5] Ibid., 106. For a detailed analysis of this case, see Nair, 'Beyond the "Communal" 1920s', 317–340.

[6] Alok Bhalla (ed.), *Partition Dialogues: Memories of a Lost Home* (New Delhi: OUP, 2006), chapter titled 'Memory and History: In Conversation with Krishna Sobti', 145.

[7] G.D. Khosla, *Stern Reckoning: A Survey of the Events Leading upto and Following the Partition of India* (Delhi: Oxford University Press, 1989 [1949]), 280.

[8] Raghuvendra Tanwar cites a letter written on 13 January 1947 to *The Tribune* by R.K. Tuli. Raghuvendra Tanwar, *Reporting the Partition of Punjab: Press, Public and Other Opinions* (New Delhi: Manohar, 2006), 139n230. Tanwar writes that there were other letters by ordinary people pleading for harmony. His study is based on eighteen newspapers in four languages (English, Hindi, Urdu and Punjabi) published in 1947.

agreed: in his eyewitness account of the Calcutta riots of 1946, young American Phillips Talbot noted: 'On all sides one observes inflammatory speeches and writings tossed off without regard for consequences....'[9] So did the new, Indian, leaders of India. Nehru's first major press conference after Independence was held at Delhi on 28 August 1947, in which he appealed to the press to show restraint as a great deal depended on how and what the press said. *The Statesman* reported that Nehru's face flushed with anger as he spoke of the undue emphasis on accounts of killings in East Punjab given in the Pakistani press.[10] In December 1947, while inaugurating a public library in Mehrauli, Home Minister Vallabhbhai Patel said: 'In your Library, you must be careful in the selection of books and newspapers, as poisonous reading material is liable to bring about mental ill-health....'[11] During a visit to Alwar in February 1948 (at a time when the government suspected that the state administration was complicit in the assassination of Gandhi on 30 January 1948), Patel asked his audience the question: 'Why were the people of Alwar sleeping when a person in the garb of a sadhu was distributing leaflets which asked for Gandhiji's death in a most brutal and criminal fashion?'[12] These attitudes towards free speech (of certain hues, at any rate) were to have repercussions on policymaking as well as lived experience of Indians just before, and even after Independence from colonial rule.

The Press Advisory System and the Delhi Code

In October 1946, the president of the AINEC, Tushar Kanti Ghosh, commented: 'We are on the threshold of a great transition—from suppression to liberty, from frustration to fulfilment.' The Interim Government comprised members from the newly elected Constituent Assembly, and included the British Viceroy and Commander-in-Chief, as well as Nehru (as Vice-President) and Vallabhbhai Patel (the Home Member and the Member for Information

---

[9] Phillips Talbot, *An American Witness to India's Partition* (New Delhi: Sage, 2007), 193.

[10] *Hindustan Times* and *The Statesman*, 29 August 1947, cited in Tanwar, *Reporting the Partition*, 349 and 351.

[11] Speech at Mehrauli, Delhi, 29 December 1947, in *Sardar Patel: Indian Problems (Selected Speeches)* (Bombay: Director Publications Division, Ministry of Information and Broadcasting, GOI, Times of India Press, 1948), 56.

[12] Speech at a public meeting in Alwar, 25 February 1948, *Sardar Patel: Indian Problems*, 35.

and Broadcasting in the Interim Government; later to become independent India's first Home Minister and Deputy Prime Minister). Even at this point, Patel sounded a note of caution with regard to (fully) free speech:

> The Press must have unfettered freedom in the presentation of news and expression of views, but it also has the obligation to preserve the integrity of the State and support the legitimate activities of a popular Government. It must, when occasion demands, help the Government in defeating the forces of disruption.... When feelings run high and tempers are frayed, it is the duty of every responsible person to desist from saying or doing things which are likely to inflame passions. Incitements to violence will, of course, not be tolerated. But there are other forms of writings, containing veiled incitement, which do great harm. I do hope and trust you will avoid both.

After reminding the Indian press of its rights *and* duties, Patel assured the assembly of editors that the phrase of suppression was in the past as foreign rule was about to end.[13] That the press was to 'educate' Indians was reiterated frequently by both Patel and Nehru on various occasions; a clear link was established between education and the exercise of citizen's duties. Addressing journalists in Trivandrum in May 1950, Patel linked the educative role of the press with the training of people to exercise their franchise responsibly.[14]

Ground reality was different. Newspapers—in Punjab in 1947, for instance, as Raghuvendra Tanwar's well-documented study indicates—carried reports based on oral accounts, and therefore were 'often a readable mixture of fact and rumour'; editors took sides, and were driven less by idealism and more by the sales and the imperative to boost circulation.[15] As an example of misreporting, Tanwar cites the case of the anti-Muslim League press in Punjab using, in March 1947, a photograph of a large group of people on a dusty road as evidence of returning looters and murderers. Two weeks later, the official organ of the Muslim League, *Dawn*, proved that the photograph was of people, including Hindus, returning from the *urs* (death anniversary commemoration) ceremony of a Sufi saint. In April 1947, the Fire Department of Lahore made a public appeal to newspaper reporters and the public to verify facts; on

---

[13] *Bombay Chronicle*, 14 October 1946, in *The Collected Works of Sardar Vallabhbhai Patel*, ed. P.N. Chopra (Delhi: Konark, 1997, hereafter *CWSP*), vol. 10, 269–70 and 267–269, respectively.

[14] *Hindustan Times*, 13 May 1950, *CWSP*, vol. 15, 137–138.

[15] Tanwar, *Reporting the Partition*, 99.

one day in April 1947 when the fire brigade was called out seven times, six of those were genuine accidents, not arson, but the newspaper and rumour mills built up stories around them.[16] Beginning in late 1946, Patel regularly corresponded with two successive British Viceroys, Lord Wavell (till February 1948) and Lord Mountbatten, expressing concern about the role of the press in stoking communal tension. He stressed the 'desirability of taking action in respect of the continuous outpouring of communal venom and hatred which is being indulged in by a section of the Press *and is largely responsible for the recent unfortunate happenings'*.[17] To Patel, it was clear that the press was not merely reporting riots, but *causing* them to happen.

Provincial governments took their own measures, which were often contested by the press. PACs set up during the Second World War had continued to function after the war ended. In politically charged and chaotic times, however, this mechanism did not always function smoothly. For instance, on 29 September 1946, the Bengal government passed an order banning provocative news and comment on communal riots, after which Calcutta's Hindu-owned press decided to suspend publication. The government-imposed ban applied to news and comments on communal disturbances if they contained the following: information about locality in a town or subdivision, manner of death or injury, name and community of the assailant or the assailed, and/or description of desecration of place or object of worship. Also banned was any photograph, drawing or cartoon of a communal incident, or of the dead or injured. Prior to passing the order, H.S. Suhrawardy, the Premier of Bengal, had invited journalists to a conference explaining the government's decision to them. The AINEC, which opposed the ban, proposed an alternative plan: the press would itself organize a daily evening meeting of seven representatives to whom all news and rumours would be submitted. This committee would pool together all reports into one summary report, which would then be submitted to all newspapers. Nothing would appear in the papers that had not been already passed by this committee. However, the Premier rejected this proposal, although he assured the press that material already passed by the Bengal PAC would not be affected by the order.[18]

---

[16] According to Tanwar, Punjab officials pleaded with people not to believe rumours but the trend continued; as he puts it, 'More commonly, the smaller newspapers were the culprits.' Both examples cited in Tanwar, *Reporting the Partition*, 142.

[17] Letter from Patel to Wavell, 7 November 1946, *CWSP*, vol. 10, 279, emphasis added.

[18] AINEC plan communicated in a letter to the Premier. *Times of India*, 1 October

The press, which had offered to join hands with the government in what may be termed 'collaborative censorship', was not satisfied. To protest against the order, Congress papers not only gave large banner headlines to the news about the 'gag order', but one paper even carried a blank column under the heading 'Disturbances in Bengal.' After the Bengal papers resumed publication, they did set up an ad hoc committee for the preparation of a common report, and the system worked successfully for the most part, barring certain exceptions.[19] To take one example, in December 1946, the British editor of *The Statesman*, Ian Stephens, and its printer-publisher were summoned by the Chief Presidency Magistrate of Calcutta (under the Bengal Special Powers Ordinance No. VI of 1946) because of news items published in issues in October that year titled 'Nose Chopped Off' and '22 Killed in the City Yesterday' and for the publication of photographs showing arson in the city.[20] These examples indicate the complexity of the situation as well as the concerted attempts made by the press to function in the situation, meeting with both success and failure.

In New Delhi, all through the period of the Interim Government, the Viceroy, Lord Wavell, periodically asked Patel to take action against the *Dawn* (a newspaper affiliated with the Muslim League) as well as the *Hindustan Times* for publishing inflammatory accounts regarding disturbances in Punjab, and suggested that central government restrictions be 'applied impartially to all newspapers'.[21] Patel also admitted to having spoken informally to the managing editor of the *Hindustan Times*.[22] Part of the problem was that in those troubled times, even responsible and respected newspapers like *The Statesman* were given to carrying inflammatory accounts that were later picked up and reproduced by other newspapers.[23] Lord Wavell—mindful no doubt of the experiment

1946.

[19] *Times of India*, 15 October 1946.

[20] *Times of India*, 5 December 1946.

[21] Letters from Wavell to Patel, 28 November 1946 and 16 March 1947, in *Sardar Patel, Select Correspondence, 1945–50*, ed. V. Shankar (Ahmedabad: Navajivan Publishing House, 1977, 2 vols, hereafter *SPSC*), vol. 1, 426 and 428. To the directive of acting impartially, Patel responded by saying that HD hardly needed any reminder that the law was to be implemented impartially. Letter from Patel to Wavell, 29 November 1946, *SPSC*, vol. 1, 427–428.

[22] Letter from Patel to Wavell, 19 March 1947, *SPSC*, vol. 1, 428–429.

[23] For instance, the report on the Punjab in the *Hindustan Times* in March 1947 to which Wavell had objected took its lead from *The Statesman*. Letter from Patel to Wavell, 19 March 1947, *SPSC*, vol. 1, 428–429.

during the Second World War—suggested that a 'gentleman's agreement' with the press of all parties would be the best way to prevent intensification of communal ill-feeling. This would be an alternative to a punitive regime of press censorship. Patel was, however, pessimistic about the likely success of voluntary or self-censorship, as in his opinion the

> ... attitude of the *Dawn* and other papers of that type has been progressively deteriorating rather than improving even under the stimulus provided by recurrent tragedies. Its latest activity is a cleverly disguised and mischievously conceived incitement to violence to the Muslims of the Punjab in retaliation for what has happened in Bihar. I doubt whether the approach of this section of the Press would at all be helpful.[24]

Here is an instance of a British viceroy urging 'collaborative censorship' or censorship by consensus, and an Indian nationalist politician expressing faith in punitive measures! Patel's lack of trust in the self-regulatory capacities of the press was also apparent in his admission to Gopichand Bhargava, a Congress leader in the Punjab (and Punjab Premier between 1947 and 1951). Patel confessed that his policy was 'to watch for the time being, but to act swiftly if the arrangement appears inadequate or defective'.[25]

In November 1946, the Central PAC along with a group of leading editors (designated an ad hoc PAC) formulated a new code, termed the 'Delhi code', for reporting news of communal disturbances. A veritable who's who of Indian journalism at the time were involved in its framing: B.J. Kirchner (*The Statesman*), Devdas Gandhi (*Hindustan Times*), Altaf Husain (*Dawn*), J.N. Sahni (*National Call*), Desabandhu Gupta (*Tej*) and Sardar Ali Sabri (*Anjam*) were its members.[26] This committee addressed an appeal to all editors of newspapers and news agencies, referring to the 'grave emergency' when the lives of countless innocents were at stake, and appealed to the press to accept 'this temporary curtailment of their liberties'. If they failed to do so, not only would this aggravate tension but also force the government to resort to statutory restrictions.[27]

---

[24] Letters from Wavell to Patel and Patel to Wavell, 7 November 1946. Both letters in *SPSC*, vol. 1, 418.

[25] Letter from Patel to Bhargava, 14 November 1946, *SPSC*, vol. 1, 419–420.

[26] I&B Department press communique, 14 November 1946, GOI Home Political, f. 33/31, 1946, NAI.

[27] Appeal addressed to editors of newspapers and news agencies by the PAC, 14 November 1946, GOI Home Political, f. 33/31, 1946, NAI.

What were the terms of the Delhi code? News of riots was received from three main sources: newspaper correspondents, news agencies and government sources. Editors were asked to ensure that news was 'factual and objective', that the community of the victim/assailant was 'not indicated either directly or indirectly' and that casualty figures were not mentioned in headlines or prominently displayed. These could, however, be mentioned in the text, along with the source. If official figures for casualties were not available, the term 'not officially confirmed' was to be used. 'In no circumstances' were photographs of dead bodies of victims of violence to be published. The statements of ministers and of members of the Interim Government could be published, but those of other individuals and organizations bearing on the communal situation were subject to pre-censorship: that is, they were not to be published unless passed for publication by the ad hoc PAC instituted by the GOI. The one thing that newspapers were free to do was to express their views on the 'political aspects of the communal situation', provided they did not encourage lawlessness and violence. Insulting and abusive language was to be avoided, and all the above restrictions applied to cartoons as well.[28]

Following Wavell's suggestion, and despite Patel's reservations, 'Press advice' thus began on 15 November 1946, and two officers of the Press Information Bureau were placed on duty for the purpose. How did the Press Advisory system work? The infrastructure was provided by the Press Information Bureau, and messages about which editors had doubts had to be sent to the committee in triplicate, marked 'Immediate'. The Bureau would then immediately contact members of the CPAC and obtain their advice, which would then be conveyed 'by the quickest means available'.[29] However, the GOI was, as they say, hoping for the best and preparing for the worst. It instructed provincial governments that the advisory system was not to affect any punitive action that they wanted to take; they were merely required to check whether the matter deemed objectionable had first been subjected to press advise or not.[30]

Assessment of the success of the code at the provincial level was mixed. In mid-November 1946, the GOI asked provincial governments to report if the

---

[28] *Bombay Chronicle*, 13 November 1946, *CWSP*, vol. 10, 281–283.

[29] Press Information Bureau circular issued to editors of newspapers and news agencies, 15 November 1946. I&B Department press communique, 14 November 1946, GOI Home Political, f. 33/31, 1946, NAI.

[30] Express letter no. 225/2/46-I.P. from Secretary, I&B Department, G.S. Bozman, to all Chief Secretaries and Chief Commissioners, 15 November 1946, GOI Home Political, f. 33/31, 1946, NAI.

press in their province was observing the Delhi code. Bengal reported that the press there was breaking the code to 'suit its convenience', and in Bombay the Delhi code was being followed with minor modifications.[31] The Punjab government reported that the Punjab press had followed the Delhi code in the sense that they had avoided mentioning the communities of assailants or victims as well as the number of casualties, and had not published photographs of the dead or of scenes of arson. However, there had been no improvement in editorial comments on communal strife, since they referred to incidents of rape, carnage and forced conversion and marriage. Additionally, there was 'no unreserved condemnation of communal violence'. According to the Punjab government, newspapers in that province were divided along communal lines:

> Hindu papers have continued to emphasise Muslim oppression in Noakhali; the Muslim papers doing the same in the case of Bihar though in a comparatively milder tone. In other words, the technique of both consists in enlarging upon the rival community's aggressiveness and minimizing its own community's excesses.[32]

In Punjab, as is clear from this assessment, it was the letter of the code that was being followed, but not the spirit. Vernacular papers in Punjab often took leads from the English papers and reproduced their stories. The press in that province was, evidently, divided not along the English/vernacular line, but along the lines of community.[33] The UP government noted that although many papers were encouraging communal amity, some papers were still carrying false and exaggerated news. For instance, on 13 November 1946 *Alsadiq* (Urdu) asserted that 100,000 Muslims had been killed in riots in Bihar; a week later *Sanmarg* (Hindi) stated that there was air-bombing at Telihara in Bihar at the behest of Nehru, and the victims were Hindus who had been lured to the spot by being told they were attending a peace meeting. This paper asserted that more Hindus than Muslims had died in the Bihar riots.[34]

---

[31] These replies were received in response to a letter sent by the I&B Department on 15 November 1946, GOI Home Political, f. 33/31, 1946, NAI.

[32] 'A Brief Report to the Extent to Which the Punjab Press Observed Principles of the Code Drawn Up by the Delhi Ad Hoc Committee of Editors', date unclear, GOI Home Political, f. 33/31, 1946, NAI.

[33] Tanwar, *Reporting the Partition*, 12.

[34] Press note from the UP Information Department, 27 November 1946, GOI Home Political, f. 33/31, 1946, NAI.

A fortnight after it was put into practice, B.J. Kirchner wrote to Patel that the mere existence of the advisory system had 'a salutary effect', and that there had been some improvement in the tone of the press.[35] Between 16 and 30 November 1946, 44 messages were submitted for scrutiny to the Central PAC, of which 20 were passed without alteration, 18 were modified, and 6 not passed at all. Except for one message submitted by a newspaper, all the rest were submitted by news agencies. Of the six messages that were not passed, four related to the situation in East Bengal, one to an incident at a Patna station and one was a 'vehement exhortation'.[36] In its next meeting on 11 December, the PAC decided, in response to a query by the Home Secretary, that letters to the editor came within the definition of 'comment'.[37] Even though Kirchner was optimistic about the success of the advisory system, the number of messages submitted compared to the number published in hundreds of newspapers across the country was a mere drop in the ocean. In any case, even Kirchner admitted, in January 1947, that whereas there had been an improvement in the tone of the leading English language newspapers in Delhi, the staff of some Urdu papers seemed unaware of the existence of the Delhi code. News agencies had occasionally followed the code only in the letter and not in spirit. Speeches which were provocative (even though they only indirectly pertained to communal disturbances) were often released without press advice. The committee also felt that provocative statements by members of the government placed a strain on the code. Despite these factors, the PAC chose to believe that restraints imposed on the press had eased communal tension. As Kirchner put it in January 1947:

> Whether the improvement in the communal situation and the lessening of tension, are due to the greater sobriety of the Press, or whether the latter is merely a reflection of the general easing of the situation, must be a matter of opinion. In the absence of conclusive evidence to the contrary, however, the Committee believe that the restraint observed by the Press has been an important contributory factor to this improvement.[38]

---

[35] Letter from Kirchner to Patel, 30 November 1946, GOI Home Political, f. 33/31, 1946.

[36] Minutes of Meeting of the PAC held on 29 November 1946, held in the presence of four editors, B. Kirchner, D. Gandhi, A. Husain and J. Sahni, GOI Home Political, f. 33/31, 1946, NAI.

[37] Minutes of Meeting of the PAC held on 11 December 1946, GOI Home Political, f. 33/31, 1946, NAI.

[38] Report submitted to the HD by Kirchner on 11 January 1947, GOI Home Political f. 33/31, 1946, NAI.

The creators of the code were willing to amend it in light of changing requirements. In March 1947, Kirchner wrote to the Home Secretary mentioning strong representations made to the AINEC by journalists against the embargo on the mentioning of communities involved in communal incidents. The PAC also felt that some modification of the code was required, as press communiques issued by provincial governments had not disguised the identity of the communities involved in violent incidents.[39] The PAC maintained that the identity of communities should not be published in headlines or in giving casualty figures, but that in reports where the identity could be deduced from events leading up to incidents or from the context, there it should be allowed. The PAC felt:

> The practice which has come into force of referring to the 'majority or 'minority' community, is, in the Committee's view, not strictly in accordance with the 'code' and is a clumsy and undesirable expedient which should not be encouraged.[40]

The code was amended accordingly, and all Chief Secretaries and Chief Commissioners were informed that 'ordinarily' communities of assailants or victims in communal incidents were not to be indicated, except when they were easily deducible. 'In no circumstances' were communities to be mentioned in headlines; referring to 'majority' and 'minority' communities was to be avoided.[41] This amendment was also publicized through a press communiqué.[42]

Despite its flexibility, the advisory system unravelled in the next few months, with complaints being made it was enforced too rigorously in some areas and was too lax in others. By May 1947, the PIO, A.S. Iyengar, was of the opinion that newspapers preferred to edit their copy themselves, and did not seek press advice. In some places, the Delhi code was being enforced all too rigorously: the ban on photographs of dead bodies or victims of violence as included in the Delhi code was being taken so seriously by the Bengal government that they

---

[39] Letter from Kirchner to Porter, 15 March 1947, GOI Home Political, f. 33/31, 1946.

[40] Minutes of a meeting of the Ad Hoc PAC held on 13 March 1947, GOI Home Political, f. 33/31, 1946, NAI.

[41] D.O. no. 225/2/46-I.P. from Joint Secretary I&B Department, M.A. Husain, to All Chief Secretarys and Chief Commissioners, 17 May 1947, GOI Home Political, f. 33/31, 1946, NAI.

[42] Press communique issued by the HD, 21 May 1947, GOI Home Political, f. 33/31, 1946, NAI.

even objected to 'photographs taken on the occasion of the Bihar Governor's visits to the hospitals in his province consoling the victims of riots'. Iyengar suggested that photographs in which heads of government 'show personal sympathy for the victims [of riots] may be published'. Another problem was that the code exempted statements made by members of the Interim Government or ministers of provincial governments (from pre-censorship by the PAC), and when these were provocative the press could not be expected to observe self-restraint. Iyengar nevertheless suggested that the press was not to publish such inflammatory statements.[43] The HD agreed with both suggestions, although it emphasized that both the code and the exceptions to it were 'voluntary'.[44] By June 1947, the PIO commented that no messages had been tendered since the last fortnight, and the average for the previous month was 'hardly four a week'.[45] The British government's announcement of 3 June (accepting the principle of Partition) had, according to the PIO, brought the system of press advising to a standstill, and consequently the amendments to the code were also put in abeyance.[46] Voluntary censorship, 'collaborative censorship', censorship by consensus, self-censorship, and censorship by persuasion all had limitations that became starkly apparent by early 1947. By February of that year, Press Ordinances were in force in Bengal, UP, Punjab and Bihar, and one was promulgated in Delhi as well, given the communal tension in the area.[47]

Interestingly, state actors who believed in the power of certain kinds of writings to instigate riots also credited other kinds with the ability to promote peace. In April 1947, for example, Patel sent a message to the AINEC appealing to editors to help the government at a difficult time, and later issued a statement to all newspapers (as papers supporting the Muslim League were not represented in the AINEC by this time) asking them to print the Gandhi–Jinnah appeal (for communal amity) at a prominent place. In a similar vein, the All India Radio was also instructed to use the Gandhi–Jinnah appeal frequently, and especially in rural areas where newspapers may not be read.

---

[43] Note by PIO, A.S. Iyengar, 14 May 1947, GOI Home Political, f. 33/31, 1946, NAI.

[44] Note by Home Secretary, R.N. Banerjee, 21 June 1947, GOI Home Political, f. 33/31, 1946, NAI.

[45] Note by Iyengar, 9 June 1947, GOI Home Political, f. 33/31, 1946, NAI.

[46] Note by Iyengar, 27 June 1947, GOI Home Political, f. 33/31, 1946, NAI.

[47] Patel said in the Assembly: 'It is not possible for a small province like Delhi to be a pocket for disseminating objectionable materials and to frustrate the good efforts that are being made in other provinces to prevent communal disorders.' Report in *Bombay Chronicle*, 4 February 1947, *CWSP*, vol. 12, 10.

Film exhibitors' associations were asked to use the appeal on a slide during intervals.[48] In his statement to all newspapers Patel reminded them that 'a moment's reflection on the message and significance of the [Gandhi–Jinnah] appeal may prevent a hasty word or deed from doing incalculable harm to life and property'.[49]

Partition Riots and the Press

In mid-August 1947, the Lahore-based *Civil and Military Gazette* carried headlines screaming 'LAHORE SITUATION AGAIN WORSENS: 48 Stabbings, 14 Deaths and Seven Fires on Monday', 'KILLINGS CONTINUE IN LAHORE: 33 Dead and 25 Injured on Tuesday. 33 Fires blaze all day long' and 'MURDER AND ARSON REACH NEW PEAK: 111 KILLED AND 116 INJURED IN LAHORE ON WEDNESDAY'.[50] Even good news was accompanied by bad, as in: 'IMPROVEMENT IN LAHORE ON FRIDAY – OFFICIAL. 10 Persons killed in Firing by Troops'.[51] When real-life events were so horrific, even sober newspapers with any degree of commitment to keeping the public informed were bound to publish news that could be considered inflammatory.[52] Because the state was no longer dealing with a small section of the press bent on inflaming communal tension but with the press as a whole doing its job of reporting horrific events, its task of censoring what people read in newspapers was rendered impossible. Some newspapers too realized that although it was ironical that the Indian press was facing more severe restrictions from an Indian government than from an

---

[48] Letter from Patel to Mountbatten, 20 April 1947, *SPSC*, vol. 1, 437–440. Mountbatten (1900–1979) served as Supreme Allied Commander in South East Asia between 1943 and 1946 and as Viceroy/Governor General of India between February 1947 and June 1948.

[49] Message from Sardar Patel to newspapers, enclosed with letter to Mountbatten, 20 April 1947, *SPSC*, vol. 1, 437–440.

[50] *Civil and Military Gazette*, 14 August 1947, G.D. Khosla Private papers, f. 17, NMML.

[51] Headlines reproduced from *Civil and Military Gazette*, 12, 13, 14 and 17 August 1947, respectively, G.D. Khosla Private papers, f. 17, NMML.

[52] In Lahore, at least, the reading public had plenty of choice in terms of newspapers. In 1947, 23 newspapers were published from Lahore: 1 Gurmukhi, 2 Hindi, 5 English and 15 Urdu. The city had four major libraries: Punjab Library run by the government, and Dayal Singh, Sir Ganga Ram and Dwarka Dass libraries managed by non-Muslims. Tanwar, *Reporting the Partition*, 64.

alien bureaucracy, this state of affairs could be attributed to the presence of communal tension in the country.[53]

Even before Partition, newspapers could be quite casual in reporting riots. A correspondent of the *Madras Mail* once sent a long telegram reporting a Hindu–Muslim riot in the town in which he was stationed, and this story appeared as a main story on the front page, creating a sensation. The Madras government, which had no information, asked the police to confirm the news, and it turned out that the *Mail* correspondent was '... misled by his cook who had reported that he heard in the bazaar that a Hindu–Muslim riot had broken out....' The *Mail* duly published an apology and sacked the correspondent, but he escaped prosecution because the authorities 'had a soft corner for him'.[54] At the same time, censorship exerted on unverified news reports by the state's men on the ground had the power to save countless lives. J.M. Shrinagesh (who, in August 1947, was the Commissioner of the Jalandhar division in Punjab as well as the Additional Commissioner, Lahore) was on his way to Ludhiana when he met Ian Stephens, the British editor of *The Statesman*, who had just returned from Ludhiana. He told Shrinagesh that Ludhiana was in flames, and described horrible rioting and scenes of Hindus hacking Muslims to pieces. Unconvinced, Shrinagesh asked the editor to accompany him back to Ludhiana, which was completely quiet. The editor took the plea that he had heard the news from a very reliable source. Since he had not cabled this 'news' to Lahore, Shrinagesh then insisted that he telephone the Governor of West Punjab in Lahore and inform him about the correct situation. In his memoirs Shrinagesh speculates—and he was certainly qualified to do so—that 'if this journalist's story had reached the people of Pakistan, another town, the equal size of Ludhiana, but on the other side of Lahore, would have been in flames the next day.'[55] Although the news was incorrect, and suppressed informally, censorship (in the sense of its prevention from publication) imposed on it prevented another riot.

With regard to the censorship of publication in the context of riots, the state's dilemma was this: banning news reports—whether based on fact or deliberately inflammatory—could save lives, but was difficult to enforce with any degree of success. In May 1947, when the Punjab government ordered newspapers

---

[53] *Times of India*, 'Press Restraint', editorial, 29 April 1947.

[54] Parthasarathy, *Memoirs*, 61–62. Parthasarathy does not mention the year, but he served (beginning as apprentice sub-editor) the paper between 1936 and 1944, and this incident is likely to have happened during that time.

[55] Shrinagesh, *Between Two Stools*, 96–97.

not to publish any photo or statement regarding communal disorders until the information was officially stated or released, the *Civil and Military Gazette* questioned the logic of this order, taking the view that the prevention of publication of factual information would actually fuel more rumours.[56] In any case, migrants from across the border too were—uncensorable—carriers of news. Kamla Patel, famous social worker Mridula Sarabhai's associate in the task of recovering abducted women during Partition, recalled that despite attempts made to keep the news of the massacre of refugees on a train coming from the Frontier province spreading in East Punjab, the moment her car crossed the Wagah border she was surrounded by a crowd who asked her for confirmation of the news. They wanted to know how many people had been killed, and how many wounded; although she did not divulge the number, the mob threatened to kill twice that number.[57]

After analysing political cartoons and editorials in English-language newspapers published in north India in 1946–1947, Sukeshi Kamra concludes that whereas these newspapers accepted the government's 'gag order' regarding reporting of communal tension (having recognized as legitimate the goal of reducing tension), editorials and cartoons continued to 'speak' frankly.[58] In any case, any kind of news vacuum would only fuel more rumours. And rumours, as historian Yasmin Khan puts it, 'were not necessarily the innocent by-product of violence but played a part in creating it in the first place'. In her opinion, journalists and propagandists had a role to play in the riots as 'bureaucratic killers in words if not in deed'.[59]

The most comprehensive account of censorship in 20th-century India, Gerald Barrier's *Banned*, does not discuss censorship during the Partition of India, except to say in one paragraph:

> The initiative and power that remained in British hands was directed, not towards the press, but towards the communal rioting, which spread like bushfire. The suspicions and tension between adherents to the various religions

---

[56] *Civil and Military Gazette*, 20 May 1947, cited in Tanwar, *Reporting the Partition*, 171.

[57] Kamla Patel, *Torn from the Roots: A Partition Memoir*, trans. Uma Randeria (New Delhi: Kali, 2006; original in Gujarati published in 1977), 64.

[58] Sukeshi Kamra, *Bearing Witness: Partition, Independence, End of the Raj* (New Delhi: Lotus, Roli Books, 2002), 8.

[59] Yasmin Khan, *The Great Partition: The Making of India and Pakistan* (New Delhi: Penguin, 2013 [2007]), 138.

were at least partially suppressed by war-time restrictions; they now resurfaced and took their toll. In the year before independence, central and provincial authorities desperately tried to contain communalism through stringent public order ordinances, but to no avail.... The task of maintaining order and the difficult choice between dismantling or using the accumulated apparatus for controlling controversial writings, now passed to the British government's successors in India and Pakistan.[60]

Using several examples, this chapter has demonstrated that decision makers at the highest levels, both Indian and British, were keeping a close watch on the content of publications, and discussing at great length among themselves possible measures to tackle communal publications, and even the censorship of realistic news reports that could nevertheless have an inflammatory effect. The communally charged atmosphere of the months leading up to Independence and Partition manifested itself in disunity in the press as well, with representatives of 16 Muslim-owned newspapers, including *Dawn* and *Anjam* of Delhi, characterizing the AINEC as 'an organisation of Hindu capitalist newspapers', and stating that Muslim papers would not be bound by any convention agreed to, or any decision taken by, the AINEC. They termed the AINEC an organization that was brought into existence by the GOI in order to serve its own purposes.[61] Newspapers like the *Dawn* benefitted from this culture of consultative—as opposed to centralized, instant, authoritarian censorship—as various branches of the state (the HD, the Legislative Department, the Advocate General, the PAC, and so on) could not agree among themselves on one course of action. In the tense and violent atmosphere, censorship of the press, always a political act, was rendered even more difficult and political at the very moment that it was considered most necessary. It is widely acknowledged that the Partition of the subcontinent cast a long shadow on its subsequent history; it also tested the boundaries of free speech in a context where it degenerated into hate speech.

Anxiety over Free Speech: Policy Makers' Opinions Immediately after Independence

In the immediate aftermath of Partition and in the midst of communal violence, inflammatory writings in the press caused much concern to those

---

[60] Barrier, *Banned*, 154.
[61] *Times of India* and *Dawn*, 16 October 1946.

at the highest levels of the state. States justify censorship by citing examples of an irresponsible press, and of this there was plenty of evidence in the days following Independence. Ralph Izzard, the correspondent of the British paper *Daily Mail*, saw some British soldiers at Connaught Place in Delhi three weeks after Independence, and on the basis of this evidence filed a despatch to the effect that the Indian government was cracking up, and Mountbatten had called back British soldiers to help save the country. In reality, these soldiers were part of a unit on its way from Meerut to Bombay, who were merely window shopping in Delhi.[62] The extraordinary dislocation caused by the conjunction of three major events—a World War, Independence from colonial rule and Partition—had created a situation where anything could be reported, and everything believed.

In the months immediately after Independence, Nehru complained to Patel about newspapers 'of a very low class' started immediately after Independence that were 'poisoning the atmosphere of Delhi and lowering our standards.' Nehru was incensed that in Delhi local authorities were not taking strong enough action to quell communal disturbances. Not only was preventive action not being taken in terms of arresting 'suspicious people', but '… in other matters also, such as the suppression of highly undesirable periodicals and leaflets, nothing was done for weeks.…'[63] Nehru advocated 'strong and swift' action against these papers.[64] Patel replied that there was 'no doubt' that one publication in question, the *Hindu Outlook* (the official organ of the Hindu Mahasabha, a right-wing political organization), 'did not deserve to exist as a newspaper', that a pre-censorship order had been passed against the paper, and that he hoped that 'either its contents would improve or it will come into further trouble and will eventually have to stop publication.'[65] Some of the items published in the *Hindu Outlook* that so irked Nehru included charges that Asaf Ali (who had served as India's first ambassador to the United States in 1947) was an agent of Pakistan, that Vijayalakshmi Pandit (Nehru's sister) had purchased expensive furniture for the Indian embassy in Stockholm, and that the UP government had presented her with 'six hundred silk sarees and silver articles worth rupees twenty thousand'. The *Hindu Outlook* was

---

[62] D.R. Mankekar, interviewed by Dr Aparna Basu, 3 November 1968, 16, NMML OHP.
[63] Letter from Nehru to Patel, 30 September 1947, in *Nehru–Patel*, ed. N. Singh, 81.
[64] Letter from Nehru to Patel, 30 September 1947, in *Nehru–Patel*, ed. N. Singh, 245.
[65] Letter from Patel to Nehru, 11 October 1947, in *Nehru–Patel*, ed. N. Singh, 246.

banned in early November 1947 by the Delhi administration.[66] Earlier, on 9 October, the District Magistrate of Delhi had imposed pre-censorship on eight newspapers published from Delhi, and asked for security deposits in the range of 500–1,000 rupees.[67] One option available to the GOI in countering news items it deemed undesirable was to issue contradictions. However, Nehru rejected this as a viable option on the grounds that it merely gave publicity to the paper. Even the AINEC was sufficiently concerned about the tone of newspapers at this time to advocate a general code of conduct for newspapers. At this stage at least, the GOI and a section of prominent newspaper editors were very much collaborators in drawing up a code of conduct for the press.

A few months into Independence and Nehru was already despairing of being able to control the press. As he put it:

> I do not know how one can deal with this matter. Press regulations and laws go some way, demands for security may help a little, but there is so much in these newspapers which is tendentious and objectionable and yet which perhaps does not offend against any specific provision that it is difficult to do much in the matter.[68]

Here, free speech was not being defended on philosophical grounds but out of sheer pragmatism: it was difficult to stop newspapers from publishing what they wanted. On the other hand, Patel refuted G.B. Pant's suggestion that AIR broadcasts were having an 'exciting effect' on disturbed conditions. This could not be, he suggested, because the AIR only broadcast matter received from official sources or reliable news agencies, and very rarely news of individual newspaper correspondents. Patel also mentioned that as he was a regular listener, and had instructed AIR that 'news regarding disturbances must be given in subdued terms', he had no reason to believe that this instruction was not being followed. 'If anything,' Patel continued, 'AIR errs on the side of too much suppression.'[69] Indeed, in the 1950s, journalists would accuse AIR of being a government monopoly and level precisely this charge of 'too much suppression' against it.

---

[66] *Nehru–Patel*, ed. N. Singh, 32n2.

[67] Ibid., 31n1.

[68] Letter from Nehru to Patel regarding newspapers aggravating communal tension, 27 October 1947, in *Nehru–Patel*, ed. N. Singh, 30–31.

[69] *Nehru–Patel*, ed. N. Singh, 91–92. See also letter from Patel to Nehru, 11 October 1947, *SPSC*, vol. 1, 506–507.

In November 1947, Patel laid the Press (Special Powers) Bill before the Constituent Assembly (Legislative).[70] In his prefatory speech he stressed that he was conscious of the value of the 'sacred privilege of the liberty of Press' but circumstances had forced him to present a bill of this nature. He informed the house that as the Interim Government had taken over at a time of serious communal conflict, all provincial governments (beginning with Bengal) had been forced to pass ordinances to restrict press liberty. When no ordinance was passed in Delhi, the Interim Government was accused of allowing violent propaganda to inflame communal hatred. According to Patel, it was the failure of the Delhi code that had necessitated the ordinance in Delhi, and now he was seeking the approval of the house to renew the terms of the ordinance by making it an act. He termed it an 'emergency legislation to meet with an emergency the like of which India has not seen in the past', and stated the reasons why it became necessary. There were many papers that not only attacked members of the government but also pamphlets and newspapers published by people who

> ... are full of anger because of the sufferings that they have gone through in the part of the country from which they come. These are not the people in whose hands a pen can safely be given. They are not in a fit state to handle a pen.[71]

Patel said that although he was in sympathy with people who wanted to vent their anger, as a representative of a popular government he had no choice but to have the legislation in place. While there were provisions in existing legislation, Patel felt that they gave more publicity to offenders once they took recourse to courts. The purpose of the legislation that he wanted in place for Delhi and Ajmer–Merwara was to prevent 'improper distribution of news which is undesirable; improper circulation of news and comments; exaggerated and false news which tend to create disturbance and violence'. It is important to remember that Patel's recourse to legal measures followed his several appeals.

Provincial leaders had their own notions about the role of the press in independent India. In April 1948, the Home Minister of Bombay, Morarji Desai, justified restrictions on the press (without consultation with the Provincial PAC) under the Bombay Public Security Measures Act by stating

---

[70] The editor of Patel's *Collected Works* found the length of Patel's prefatory speech on this occasion evidence of 'his inner disinclination for even a temporary measure of this kind that circumstances forced him to move....' See editorial note in *CWSP*, vol. 12, 238.

[71] Patel's speech on 19 November 1947, *CWSP*, vol. 12, 238–240.

that these had been necessitated by a section of the press refusing to carry out 'certain minimum obligations towards the state'. He attributed disturbances in the province to inflammatory writings, and stated that the government would not tolerate the preaching of communal or class hatred. Desai expressed the view that the Provincial PAC had failed in its task of restraining newspapers by persuasion.[72] A few months later, B. G. Kher, the Premier of Bombay, told the AINEC that unless there was 'complete cooperation' between the press and government, the country would neither progress nor prosper. In a somewhat unfortunate analogy, he asked the press to 'die' for the country, if necessary. As he put it, 'As a soldier dies for the country, a doctor for the patient, so the press should be ready to die for noble traditions and for the good of society and the country.'[73]

Nehru and Patel were also conscious that by using punitive powers against the press or against organizations such as the Rashtriya Swayamsevak Sangh (RSS), they were open to the charge of being enemies of civil liberties. In May 1948, Patel wrote to Nehru complaining that High Courts in UP and in Bombay had been acquitting men arrested in connection with RSS activities. 'If we take extra powers to deal with such a situation,' he wrote, 'we are charged with attacking civil liberties.'[74] This ambivalence—recognizing the need to control the press, especially when it published material inciting communal violence, yet an acute consciousness that the 'national' state was to appear markedly different from the colonial one—marked Nehru's attitude and therefore also his instructions to officials. In his letters to Chief Ministers in the year following Independence, he railed against a section of the press that spread 'hatred, communal bitterness and the cult of violence'. On some occasions he urged urgent action, writing in February 1948, for instance, that 'some of our processes to deal with such papers are slow. They have to be speeded up'.[75] Yet on other occasions Nehru instructed Chief Ministers about the need to suppress violent activities without closing all options for peaceful

---

[72] Statements made by Desai while addressing the Bombay Union of Journalists, *Times of India*, 6 April 1948.

[73] Statement made by B.G. Kher in a meeting with newspaper editors at Bombay, *Times of India*, 24 July 1948.

[74] Letter from Patel to Nehru, 4 May 1948, in *Nehru–Patel*, ed. N. Singh, 37.

[75] *Nehru: Letters to Chief Ministers, 1947–1964* (hereafter *LCM*), ed. G. Parthasarathi, 5 vols (New Delhi: Oxford University Press, 1985–1989), vol. 1, 60, 5 February 1948. A few days after this letter, a number of daily newspapers in Delhi were banned on 9 February 1948. *LCM*, editorial footnote 60n8 refers to this.

protest. Even as states, notably Madras and West Bengal, passed Public Safety Acts and ordinances so as to keep the courts out of reviewing arrests made by the police, Nehru was aware of the damage this caused to India's reputation. In a letter to Chief Ministers, he wrote, 'I am sorry to say that all the reputation that we acquired in the past as defenders of civil liberty and freedom is fading away. Our stock in the world had been high. It is not so high now.'[76] He expressed disquiet at the growing trend of legislation via ordinance in many states, and reminded their executive heads that 'to us, who preach civil liberty at a thousand occasions, any suppression is painful', although even he conceded that it had to be undertaken on occasions when the 'vital needs of the state' so demanded.[77] Even as the Madhya Bharat Public Safety Bill was passed in January 1949, Nehru wrote to Chief Ministers that India's reputation was being sullied for relying excessively on 'the repressive arm of the state', and that the government was thought to ban and arrest readily without paying any attention to the cause of protests against it.[78] In another letter, Nehru reminded them that although repression of civil liberties was to be considered in the context of the 'safety and security of the State and the great majority of our people', such 'repressive legislation' had a 'bad odour' about it. The solution he proposed in July 1949 was to deal with emergencies as and when they arose, *without* having temporary or permanent legislation on the statute book.[79]

Nehru's argument against repression, apart from it alienating the public from the government, was that it '… has never crushed an idea or solved a problem. It is a temporary expedient for special occasions'.[80] This should, in his opinion, have been clear to Congressmen from their own experience. After all, as he put it, 'We have thrived on repression.'[81] Another argument that Nehru made against repression was that it lost its value if used too often.[82] The yardstick for state governments when deciding on whether or not to repress was, according to Nehru, the presence or absence of violence.[83]

---

[76] *LCM*, vol. 1, 123–124, 5 May 1948.

[77] Ibid., 213, 4 October 1948.

[78] This bill gave the state government wide powers for detention in case unlawful activity was suspected. *LCM*, vol. 1, 270–271, 24 January 1949.

[79] Ibid., 412–413, 20 July 1949.

[80] Ibid., 283, 3 February 1949.

[81] Ibid., 351, 14 May 1949.

[82] Ibid., 398, 1 July 1949.

[83] 'In other words, while we should proceed firmly with every attempt at violence, in regard to other matters we should refrain, as far as possible, from repressive action.' Ibid., 398, 1 July 1949.

If this ambivalence translated into confused policy, it also led to the use of informal, invisible methods of proscribing what appeared in the press. Close to Independence, Patel felt free to dictate to the nationalist press what they ought not to publish, as his correspondence with the *Bombay Chronicle* in 1947 and 1948 (regarding that newspaper's assertion that Patel would become India's 'first premier') amply indicates.[84] When the press in Bengal expressed its deep scepticism of the Indo–Pakistan Nehru–Liaquat agreement in 1950 (signed by the two Prime Ministers to end communal riots and mass migration in East and West Bengal, and to make minorities feel secure), Patel not only organized a press conference for about 50 editors in Calcutta, appealing to them to view the agreement dispassionately and with a new and friendly approach, but also met 6 of the more prominent editors separately over an 'informal tea'. He reported to Nehru that by the end of that meeting, he had succeeded in converting even the sceptical ones to see the GOI's point of view. He reported:

> The result has been on the whole good. The Jugantar and the Amrita Bazar Patrika which had been very hostile, have now changed, although they are not enthusiastic, they are not ill-disposed either. Some venom they will put forth here and there but I do not think they will adopt an attitude which would misguide public opinion.[85]

In addition to punitive action, Patel also used tea diplomacy to win over editors, putting this legacy of the Second World War to his own uses in independent India.

Revising Press Laws after Independence

In October 1946, Home Member Patel had assured the AINEC that a Press Laws Enquiry Committee (PLEC) would be set up, and the GOI announced its formation on 15 March 1947. It consisted of eight members

---

[84] As Patel put it in his letter to the editor, such reports were '… likely to create misunderstanding amongst friends and public workers. We have enough troubles of our own at this critical juncture and if a nationalist paper were to publish such mischievous reports, it will certainly add to our trouble'. Letter from Patel to S.A. Brelvi, *CWSP*, vol. 12, 136, 17 July 1947. In January 1948, Patel wrote to S.A. Brelvi again, this time complaining about a reporter's version of his speech regarding his relationship with Gandhi. See letter from Patel to Brelvi, 20 January 1948, in *SLMU*, vol. 1, part 2, 370–371.

[85] Letter from Patel to Nehru, 18 April 1950, *SPSC*, vol. 2, 262–263.

in addition to the Chairman, Rai Bahadur Ganga Nath, who had served as a judge of the Allahabad High Court and as Chief Justice of Kashmir State. Of its members, five were from the legislature (two members of the Council of State, three of the Central Legislative Assembly) and three were representatives of the press (nominated by the AINEC and finalized by the Home Member): Kasturi Srinivasan, editor of *The Hindu*, S.A. Brelvi, editor of *Bombay Chronicle*, and Tushar Kanti Ghosh, editor of the *Amrita Bazar Patrika* (who was also at this time President of the AINEC, and had therefore nominated himself).[86]

The PLEC was given the brief to examine laws relating to the press in various countries of the world as well as recommend to the GOI reform in the press laws of India. In fact both the erstwhile colonizer and the colonized were amending their press laws close in time to each other. In Britain, the Royal Commission on the Press was appointed in 1947 and submitted its report in 1949. In India the idea was, as the GOI resolution announcing the measures in the *Gazette of India* put it, to bring press laws in India 'into line with the Press laws of other progressive countries'.[87] It first met in April 1947 and circulated a questionnaire, but the replies received till end-July were sketchy, and the GOI deemed public response far from satisfactory.[88] One reason for the lack of interest in responding to the committee was, ventured Home Secretary R.N. Banerjee, that 'in view of the constitutional changes those interested in the matter feel that the disabilities and restrictions under which the press has had to work will perhaps disappear'.[89] This was, however, to remain an unfulfilled hope. The PLEC recommended the abolition of special laws for the press, favouring instead their incorporation in ordinary laws. It did, however, recommend the retention of the Official Secrets Act, sections 124A, 153A and 505 of the IPC (relating to 'sedition', communal hatred and loyalty of the armed forces), as well as the SCA and Post and Telegraph Act. The PLEC took the view that in a democracy, peaceful agitation should be allowed for social and economic change.[90]

---

[86] GOI Home Political, f. 33/33, 1946, NAI.

[87] *Bombay Chronicle*, 16 March 1947, *CWSP*, vol. 12, 16–17.

[88] Note by G.V. Bedekar, 12 August 1947. Bedekar was appointed Secretary to the PLEC, GOI Home Political, f. 33/33, 1946, NAI.

[89] Note by R.N. Banerjee, 14 August 1947, GOI Home Political, f. 33/33, 1946, NAI.

[90] For an account of the report of this Committee, see S. Natarajan, *A History of the Press in India*, 289.

The committee also paid due attention to the law regarding 'sedition', which had been the bane of journalists' lives during the colonial period. It recommended that sedition be more narrowly defined by amending section 124A. The Indian government—populated as it was by many people who had spent large parts of their lives railing against colonial sedition laws—strangely rejected this recommendation on the grounds that in a democratic polity with fundamental rights, dangers of misuse of the law against sedition were negligible.[91] The national state, no less than a colonial one, wanted to be prepared for all exigencies.

During the Constituent Assembly Debates (1946–1949), there was a demand by a few members to list freedom of the press separately in the new Constitution, but the Chairman of the Drafting Committee, B.R. Ambedkar, held that the rights of the press were no different from the rights of citizens, and thus there was no need for mentioning press freedom separately. Press freedom was therefore made a sub-set of the freedom all citizens had of expressing their views openly. This avoided the creation of a new class of citizens (associated with the press) who would have had greater rights than others, thereby violating the basic principle of equality before the law.[92]

This chapter has illustrated how Partition, the attendant communal carnage, and the role attributed to a section of the press in fanning the flames resulted in a reconfiguration of nationalist leaders' attitude to free speech. Unqualified approbation of the merits of freedom of expression (uttered so often when opposing the colonial state) gave way to a more restrictive, much more nuanced and qualified application as nationalists became administrators. Censorship via advice, a legacy of the Second World War, continued after the war too, although with ever-diminishing success. The failure of the Delhi code led to the imposition of various provincial press ordinances in 1947. At the same time, Prime Minister Nehru urged Chief Ministers to avoid taking punitive action that would attract adverse publicity. This pattern—the informalization of censorship, censorship-through-advice supplemented by laws on the statute book—continued in the 1950s. Partition riots revealed to decision makers

---

[91] *The Statesman*, 24 May 1951. The editorial called this 'an interesting piece of irony'.

[92] B. Shiva Rao (ed.), *The Framing of India's Constitution: A Study* (New Delhi: The Indian Institute of Public Administration, 1968), vol. 5, 211. These debates have been discussed in an entire chapter, 'Munshi's Coup in the Constituent Assembly', in Chandrachud, *Republic of Rhetoric*, 55–71. Gautam Bhatia discusses the debates too, in his *Offend, Shock, or Disturb*, 88–91, as does Anushka Singh in *Sedition in Liberal Democracies* (New Delhi: Oxford University Press, 2018).

at the highest levels of the Indian state the perils of completely free speech. Once the concept of free speech itself was thus sullied, a path was cleared for the imposition of further restrictions (as through the passage of the First Amendment in 1951, discussed in the next chapter).

8

'An Education in Realism'

The First Amendment to the Indian Constitution

In discussions of press censorship in the Indian context, two periods garner the most academic and public attention: first, the colonial; second, that of the internal Emergency declared by Prime Minister Indira Gandhi for 21 months between 25 June 1975 and 21 March 1977.[1] In both periods censorship was seen as the natural accompaniment to authoritarian rule as well as its most visible, even symptomatic feature. This chapter looks at an era sandwiched between—and eclipsed by—these two. The decade after Independence and after the adoption of the Indian Constitution in 1950 was one in which the legal framework of the democratic nation state was laid down and tested. The First Amendment (FA) to the Indian Constitution in 1951 included, among other things, changes in Article 19, which dealt with the freedom of expression and the limits that the state could impose on this freedom.[2] The FA debate revolved around the content and meaning of the big questions of the age: the

---

[1] For example, in Ramachandra Guha's authoritative study of post-colonial India, all references to censorship are made in the context of the Emergency of 1975. See Ramachandra Guha, *India After Gandhi: The History of the World's Largest Democracy* (New Delhi: Picador, 2007). A recent exception is Chandrachud, *Republic of Rhetoric*, where the First Amendment (FA) gets an entire chapter: 'Prasad and Mookerjee Trigger an Amendment', 72–97. The Press Act of 1951, however, is mentioned but not discussed or described.

[2] The other two major articles that were amended dealt with the state's right to acquire land (Article 31) and the state's right to make special provisions for backward classes (Article 15). For a discussion of these three articles together, see Nivedita Menon, 'Citizenship and Passive Revolution: Interpreting the First Amendment', *Economic and Political Weekly*, 1 May 2004: 1812–1819.

circumference of freedom, the ramifications of democracy, and the rights of the individual versus state and society. For the generation of Indians living in a time of transition from colonial to self-rule, the issue of state-imposed limits on the freedom of expression was a prickly one. It is therefore not surprising that the parliamentary debate spilled over to the pages of newspapers, and journalists and readers alike participated in what was then—and is today—'... too important a matter to be left alone to the press to defend'.[3]

The First Amendment in Context

Debates over the future of free speech in India outlived the term of the Constituent Assembly (December 1946–January 1950) and intersected with debates about other kinds of liberties. The FA was preceded by the passage of a controversial legislation in February 1950, the Preventive Detention Act (PDA), which provided central and state governments the authority to detain people on grounds very similar to those listed in the FA clauses pertaining to the press. That is, prejudicing the defence and security of India, friendly relations with foreign states, the maintenance of public order, and the maintenance of supplies and services were all actions that could result in preventive detention. The act enabled the detention of saboteurs, and was valid for one year. It was an emergency measure, passed at a time when around 2,000 detenus, mostly communists, were detained for violent and subversive activities, and were due to be released on account of High Court judgments in their favour. In other words, the act came about as the reaction of the executive to judicial decisions that questioned the validity of existing Public Safety Acts. Patel had justified the PDA by terming it the 'minimum evil' necessary to safeguard democratic institutions, and had stated: 'We want to protect and defend civil liberties, but I hate criminal liberties.'[4] He also justified it by suggesting something akin to the idea of the greatest liberty for the greatest number. As he put in Parliament, 'When we think of civil liberties of an extremely small number

---

[3] The phrase was used by the British political scientist, W.H. Morris Jones, in his introduction to Soli Sorabjee's book on a later period, *The Emergency, Censorship and the Press in India: 1975–77* (New Delhi: Central News Agency, New Delhi, 1977), 9.

[4] *Hindustan Times*, 26 February 1950, *CWSP*, vol. 15, 64. After it lapsed, it was replaced by another act by the same name in February 1951, with two important changes: all detention cases had to be referred to an advisory board, the recommendations of which were binding on the government. Second, a system of parole was introduced.

of people considered, let the House think of the liberties of millions of people threatened by the activities of the individuals whose civil liberties we have sought to curtail.' He also stated that he himself was most sensitive to the state of a mind of a detainee, liable to be arrested in the middle of the night, and released temporarily to attend the funeral of a family member, as he had undergone the same experience before Independence.[5]

In his speeches in Parliament soon after Independence, Patel repeatedly identified 'threats of disorder' from organizations animated by two different ideologies from opposite ends of the political spectrum: communal and communist. In mid–February 1949, for instance, Patel told Parliament that the number of people detained for RSS–affiliated and communist activities was 1,400 and 1,611 respectively.[6] Nehru considered communalists more dangerous than communists. Writing to C. Rajagopalachari (Minister for Home Affairs since Patel's death in December 1950) in July 1951, he expressed the opinion:

I have no doubt that the Communist Party have been guilty of atrocious crimes and that we have to deal with it as such. Nevertheless, I feel that certain communal elements in India are far more dangerous to our unity and to any progress that we might hope to make, than the Communists. The Communists could never have brought about a situation which existed in Punjab or in Delhi in August-September-October 1947.[7]

Nehru's focus on curbing communal disorder is also evident in his letter to B.N. Rau (at that time India's Permanent Representative to the United Nations) in which he stated:

What we are really concerned with is not what is normally called sedition, but communal disorder or something in the nature of section 153A. This had been put an end to by legal decisions and we want to have that power as the communal situation continues to be bad.[8]

Nehru lamented that Hindu communal leaders in India delivered speeches that were 'practically incitements to murder', and suggested that if war came with Pakistan, that country would be largely responsible, but 'a considerable

---

[5] *Hindustan Times*, 26 February 1950, *CWSP*, vol. 15, 58–62.

[6] *Hindustan Times*, 18 March 1949, *CWSP*, vol. 14, 111.

[7] Letter from Nehru to Rajagopalachari, 25 July 1951, *SWJN2*, vol. 16, part 2, 466.

[8] Letter from Nehru to B.N. Rau (India's permanent representative to the United Nations), 29 May 1951, *SWJN2*, vol. 16, part 1.

share of that responsibility will rest with the communalists in India'.[9]

In 1948, Nehru wrote to states where communists were being arrested, instructing them to go slow. 'Even in England', he wrote to the Chief Minister of Bihar, 'we are now being called a police state where civil liberties have vanished.... We are now doing exactly what we have bitterly opposed in the past.'[10] To the Chief Minister of Orissa he wrote, 'I do not want any more banning of organizations. We have got a bad name for this outside.'[11] When the question arose of banning the Communist Party, the Cabinet decided in April 1949 to refrain from doing so. Nehru wrote to Chief Ministers explaining why this decision was taken: if banned, communists would pose as 'ideological martyrs instead of saboteurs and terrorists'. The GOI wanted the public to be clear that it was communist activities of sabotage that the government was against, rather than their ideology.[12] In other words, the battle was to be fought on grounds of law and order, and violence, and not on those of ideology. In contrast to the United States in the 1950s, communist ideology was far from being outlawed in India; even Loy Henderson, the American Ambassador to India, writing in 1951, noticed that bookshops were full of communist publications.[13]

In the years following Independence, both Nehru and Patel felt the competing pulls and pressures of a liberal Constitution and judiciary on the one hand, and the need for strong executive action in the face of communal and communist-inspired disturbances on the other. As Patel put it in a letter to Nehru in March 1950:

> I think figures will bear out that we have controlled the communal Press far more drastically than the Communist and our action has been circumscribed only by the provisions of the law as interpreted by our legal advisers and the High Courts. We put thousands in jail and adopted a policy of release only after we were continuously attacked on the score of maintaining civil liberties.... We are now faced with a Constitution which guarantees fundamental rights—right

---

[9] Ibid.

[10] Letter from Nehru to Sri Krishna Sinha, 8 June 1948, *SWJN2*, vol. 6, 392.

[11] Letter from Nehru to Hare Krishna Mahtab, 8 June 1948, *SWJN2*, vol. 6, 391.

[12] *LCM*, vol. 1, 339, 16 April 1949.

[13] Henderson mentioned *Crossroads* and *Blitz* as papers that attacked America 'all the time'. In fact the Ambassador expressed worry over the availability of communist propaganda and the absence of American publicity material. Note by Nehru regarding his meeting with the American Ambassador, *SWJN2*, vol. 16, part II, 629, 15 September 1951.

of association, right of free movement, free expression and personal liberty—which further circumscribe the action that we can take. That means that for every executive action there must be legal sanction and judicial justification.[14]

In May 1950, the Supreme Court reversed two decisions of state governments banning publications: it quashed the pre-censorship order on *Organiser* (an English weekly in Delhi that served as the mouthpiece of the RSS) and permitted *Crossroads* (an English weekly in Bombay, a self-declared communist publication) to enter Madras.[15] In the shadow of these decisions, Nehru termed the 'problem of dealing with the press' a 'very difficult and urgent one'.[16] His ire was not directed at political opposition via the press, but at rumours and false reports published in newspapers in Indian languages, particularly Hindi and Urdu.[17]

Newspaper canards also had the effect of creating, or at least amplifying, differences of opinion among the ruling elite. In his private correspondence, Patel had blamed a section of the press for publishing false stories about his parting of ways with Nehru,[18] and for creating misunderstanding between them.[19] Another instance of what was referred to as a 'dangerous misuse of freedom' occurred in April 1950, when an article in *Janashakti* (the mouthpiece of the Bombay Socialist Party) alleged that Patel had tried to sabotage the

---

[14] Letter from Patel to Nehru, 28 March 1950. Patel was responding to Nehru's opinion that the GOI's attitude to communal hatred had been too lenient. *Nehru–Patel*, ed. N. Singh, 307.

[15] The two 1949 cases are fairly well known and are competently summarized in Lawrence Liang, 'Reasonable Restrictions and Unreasonable Speech'. Reports in *Times of India*, 20 September 1949 and 22 April 1950. Arudra Burra has examined the content of *Crossroads* and concludes that, evaluated in legal terms, the judgment exonerating it was flawed. Arudra Burra, 'Freedom of Speech and Constitutional Nostalgia', *Seminar*, 697, 2017.

[16] *LCM*, vol. 2, 113, 30 May 1950.

[17] Statement by Nehru in Parliament, *SWJN2*, vol. 16, part 1, 219.

[18] Letter from Patel to Gosibehn Captain (Dadabhai Naoroji's daughter) blamed the *Blitz* for falsely claiming that he and Nehru had differences, *SLMU*, vol. 5, 301, 25 September 1948.

[19] In October 1950, in a long letter to Nehru, Patel expressed distress over reports in newspapers alleging massive expenditure by him during his trip to Hyderabad. He assured Nehru that the expenditure was not more than 12,000 rupees, and that the news had appeared in two or three papers 'of no importance'. The expense incurred included that on police protection, travelling allowance to officers, and so on. Letter from Patel to Nehru, 13 October 1950, *SLMU*, vol. 3, 51.

Nehru–Liaquat pact, had protested against it, and had wanted to arrest Khan and to sign another pact with Pakistan but '… because of weak policy of Nehru he could not act'.[20] A similar story, alleging that Patel had wanted to arrest Liaquat Ali Khan, was published in the weekly *Janata* (closely associated with the Socialists); it drew the ire of socialist leader Jayaprakash Narayan, Nehru and Patel himself, and the journal published a letter of apology.[21]

What else was being published in the Indian press in the 1950s that caused such anxiety? The report of the First Press Commission published in 1954 contained a clue: the commission examined 'objectionable writings' (supplied to it by the government) in great detail and in many languages, and concluded that the majority could be classified into two categories: those promoting communal hatred, and those 'offending decency by publishing obscene matter defaming individuals, ministers, wealthy individuals and particularly against cinema personalities'[22] Like many other trends in India, the Press Commission was to discover, objectionable writing too conformed to geographical–linguistic criteria. In other words, each regional language developed its own repertoire of objectionable writing. In the Tamil, Telugu and Malayalam press, for instance, it was common to find obscene matter regarding ministers and cinema stars. In West Bengal and Punjab, the press carried communal matter inciting hatred among communities. While the Sikh press incited violence for a separate Sikh state, the Marathi press idolized Gandhi's assassin, Godse, and the Gujarati and Marathi press both used 'unjournalistic language' for making a case for linguistic states. The Urdu press was denounced by the Press Commission as being 'most culpable' in inciting violence against ministers, often reproducing inflammable writing from the Pakistani press. The Hindi press specialized in personal attacks on ministers 'in articles as well as imaginary conversations'. English newspapers were not beyond reproach either: some published from

---

[20] The article was published on 18 April 1950. Patel termed it 'wicked' and 'dirty propaganda'. Letter from Patel to Kanjibhai Kapadia, the editor of the Ahmedabad-based *Swadesh*, 23 April 1950, *CWSP*, vol. 15, 121.

[21] Narayan wrote an angry letter to editor, urging that the journal's popularity was not to be bought by indulging in 'sensationalism, vulgarism, cheapness and falsehood'. In its next issue (and even before receiving Patel's letter), the journal had published an apology for report containing 'several inconsistencies and absurdities, which cannot be true'.

[22] *Report of the Press Commission*, part 1, 1954, 386. The commission was presided over by Justice Rajadhyaksha, who had started his careers as an ICS officer in 1920. It was constituted in 1952, and submitted its report in 1954.

Bombay and Calcutta indulged in a triumvirate of sins: 'vilification of persons in authority', 'ferreting out official secrets' and 'publishing spicy scandals with a political tinge'. Another problem, not strictly related to the press, was reported from West Bengal, where the government noticed that the production, import and sale of obscene and pornographic literature in the form of periodicals, pamphlets and books had 'grown in alarming degree, and become a social menace'.[23] Independence had demonstrably released more than just political energies.

Much like his colonial predecessors for whom censorship was a way of protecting the ignorant masses of India from misguided ideas, Nehru too believed that the 'morale and standard of the poor villager or townsman or anybody or our soldier' would go down after reading such publications.[24] The situation was such that even journalists were concerned about the growth of 'yellow' journalism. Swaminath Natarajan—a journalist who served as founder–editor of the *Indian Social Reformer* for more than 50 years, and a press historian—recalled that 'the Press developed in those early years of freedom the sensational side of journalism which has now become a permanent factor in Indian journalism'; he recounted the comments of an editor–proprietor in Bengal who told him that playing down riots curbed newspaper sales since 'even the newsboys refuse to touch my paper if my rivals report a larger number of deaths than I do'.[25]

Debating 'Reasonable Restrictions' Inside and Outside Parliament

Nehru's support for the FA clauses dealing with restrictions on press freedom was considered by some of his opponents inside Parliament as hypocritical for an erstwhile champion of the freedom of the press. Some journalists, including Nehru's long-term associate and personal friend M. Chalapathi Rau, found the government's motives 'suspect', as they tried to widen the scope of reasonable restrictions.[26] During the parliamentary debate on the bill, Hridaynath Kunzru called the measure 'more undemocratic than anything else that has happened in the world', said that the Constitution had finally been aligned with the PDA, and asked a rhetorical question regarding terms like 'offence': 'Is there any limit

---

[23] Ibid., 386–387.

[24] *SWJN2*, vol. 16, part 1, 219.

[25] S. Natarajan, *A History of the Indian Press*, 283–284.

[26] Rau, *Journalism and Politics*, 171. Rau also served as a member of the first Press Commission.

to the meaning of these words?'[27] Deshbandhu Gupta, a parliamentarian and president of the AINEC (which at this time had 200 members, representing 90 per cent of circulation of newspapers in India),[28] asked Nehru as to why he had 'lost his faith in the good sense of the people'. In a letter to Nehru, Gupta stated that the AINEC could not support the amendment as wide powers granted by it were 'an open invitation to parliamentary majorities to abridge the freedom of the press'.[29] H.V. Kamath, ICS officer turned politician, called the FA in totality a measure both revolutionary (the clauses related to property rights) and reactionary (the clauses regarding restrictions of the freedom of expression). He recalled that a mere 18 months ago, the Drafting Committee of the Constitution had deliberated on adding 'public order' as a clause, but rejected the suggestion.[30]

A journalist from Bombay suggested that instead of passing resolutions the AINEC should ask for the suspension of publication of all newspapers for a couple of days, followed by blackout of all news emanating from the GOI.[31] The AINEC did protest by suspending the working of all its committees acting in an advisory or associated capacity with the government at the centre and states.[32] Although it had fixed 12 July as the day of *hartal* by the press as a mark of protest, its president urged that it be postponed in view of the situation in Kashmir and the exodus of Hindu refugees of East Bengal, and referred to the necessity of the press and government closing ranks 'in order to prevent the situation being exploited by India's enemies'.[33] The post-colonial predicament of Indian journalists in the 1950s was this: opposing a colonial government was worn as a badge of pride; opposing the policies of a national government was a much more fraught exercise. The Nehruvian consensus was a difficult hegemon to tackle.

During the FA debate, MPs, journalists and readers of newspapers all compared India's press laws not only across time (the colonial and post-colonial periods) but also across place (India and the United States or United Kingdom). Syama Prasad Mookerjee—the principal spokesman of the Hindu

---

[27] *Hindustan Times*, 19 May 1951.

[28] *The India and Pakistan Year Book and Who's Who*, vol. 37, ed. Frank Moraes (Bombay: Times of India, 1951), 71.

[29] Letter from Gupta to Nehru quoted in *Times of India*, 24 May 1951.

[30] *Hindustan Times*, 18 May 1951.

[31] Letter to the editor by S.A. Sabavala, *Times of India*, 7 June 1951.

[32] *Times of India*, 26 June 1951.

[33] AINEC president's statement reported in *Times of India*, 10 July 1951.

Mahasabha and founder of the Bharatiya Jan Sangh, who had served as the Finance Minister of Bengal (1941–1942), and in the Nehru Cabinet as the Minister for Industry and Supply—was the most strident opponent of the FA.[34] He argued that although changes were made to the American Constitution within three years of its enactment, these changes had the effect of expanding rights, not curtailing them. Deshbandhu Gupta, in the unenviable position of being both a newspaperman and a parliamentarian and thus open to criticism from both camps, advocated 'self control' on behalf of the press. Emphasizing that one of the duties of the AINEC was to keep an eye on the yellow press, he ventured a comparison between the Indian and the American responsible/yellow press respectively: while responsible newspapers in India maintained 'even greater restraint, fair mindedness and objectivity than the responsible sections of the US press', the sections of the yellow press in that country had 'hardly a parallel even among the news sheets to which the Prime Minister has referred'.[35] In Gupta's opinion, the problem of scurrilous news sheets could be solved by 'moral persuasion' and 'positive codes of conduct' developed by the AINEC. Hridaynath Kunzru also invoked the example of Britain, if only to contrast the law relating to sedition between Britain and India:

> While in England sedition is treated as a minor offence, in India it is regarded as a major offence for which severe punishment can be imposed. Now that India is free it should find no place in a statute book in its existing form.[36]

By and large, however, even those who objected to Nehru's stand on this issue acknowledged his personal integrity and conceded that he himself was

---

[34] Mookerjee went on to become founder of a right-wing political party, the Bharatiya Jan Sangh, the progenitor of the Bharatiya Janata Party, or the BJP. Nivedita Menon refers to the irony that a champion of the Hindu right should have assumed the classic liberal position during the debate on the freedom of expression and state-imposed limits on it. Menon, 'Citizenship and the Passive Revolution', 1817. More recently, Arudra Burra has reconstructed the role of public figures from the Hindu Right in the 1950s in defending free speech. Arudra Burra, 'What Self-Styled Nationalists Could Learn from the Hindu Right's Own Past Record on Free Speech', Scroll.in, 27 January 2016, available at https://scroll.in/article/802327/what-self-styled-nationalists-could-learn-from-the-hindu-rights-own-past-record-on-free-speech (accessed 19 January 2019).

[35] *Hindustan Times*, 17 May 1951.

[36] *Hindustan Times*, 26 May 1951.

not opposed to freedom of expression.[37] However, the disappointment at the fact of free speech being curtailed in independent India was palpable, and intense. As Deshbandhu Gupta put it:

> During the last hundred and fifty years the press has been fighting for the repeal of various laws which sought to restrain or repress it. It was a relentless war and the contribution of the Prime Minister has not been by any means small. We were looking forward rightly to a free press after the fight was over....[38]

Outside Parliament, reactions were framed in much less parliamentary language. The Bombay State Lawyers' Conference held a meeting in April 1951, when the news of the amendment was in the air. Its president, M.R. Jayakar, compared the Constitution to a living organism and said that like a seed sown, it would require time to take root. 'Only monkeys dig up the seed to see if it had sprouted.'[39] Thus, his objection was, like many, to the way in which the FA was being 'rushed through' before the general elections scheduled less than a year later.[40] A month later, at a public meeting at Delhi's Constitution Club, a Congress politician expressed support for the measure, the journalists present opposed it, and a bureaucrat put forward an interesting justification: Shankar Prasad found it anomalous that while he could not stop a man from expressing his views on any subject, he could lock him up under the recently passed PDA. This meant that under the Constitution, while complete curtailment of liberty was possible, partial was not. Thus, he supported the amendment in the interest of law and order.[41]

---

[37] G.D. Khosla recalled that Nehru was a careful and critical reader, who had read Vladimir Nabokov's *Lolita* '... carefully because there was a proposal that the book should be banned. He said there is nothing to be banned'. G.D. Khosla, interview recorded on 9 February 1967, interviewer not mentioned, NMML OHP, 11.

[38] *Hindustan Times*, 17 May 1951.

[39] *The Statesman*, 22 April 1951. See also statement issued by Pran Nath Mehta, general secretary of the Constitution of India Society, *Times of India*, 23 May 1951.

[40] The argument was also made by some that the present Parliament had no authority to amend the Constitution as it was not an elected body, but rather the unelected Constituent Assembly by another name. Both the *Hindustan Times* and *The Statesman* took the view that the Constituent Assembly turned Parliament had every right to amend the Constitution it had created.

[41] *Hindustan Times*, 21 May 1951.

Newspaper editors, via editorials published in their papers, listed various reasons for their opposition to the FA clauses pertaining to press freedom. *The Hindu* felt there were too many restrictive qualifications on free speech.[42] The *Times of India* opposed it in strong terms, and listed potential scenarios: a communist government in the future could use the amendment to make the Indian press subservient to the Kremlin, a future dictatorial administration could use it to forbid comment on workers' right to strike, or it could also issue a blanket ban in the interests of public order.[43] 'Public order' could, by an 'unscrupulous regime', be collapsed with 'their own safety', and used to stifle all protest.[44] Hemendra Prasad Ghose, who had written for Aurobindo Ghose's famous *Bande Mataram*, in his lecture at the University of Calcutta, could clearly see the continuity before and after 1947: 'The old laws regarding the press have not been changed though they were laws enacted to suit despotism ... and already administrators are assuming the role of their British predecessors ... and taking shelter under enactments they themselves had condemned unreservedly.'[45]

Newspaper readers too pitched in with their opinions, both for and against the FA, in readers' letters columns. Readers of *The Statesman*, particularly, revealed a familiarity with the American Constitution and with thinkers like Orwell and Harold Laski that would have put many a legislator to shame. One reader pointed out that since the Indian Constitution did not recognize the doctrine of 'implied powers' of the government (that is, powers that the government had to safeguard its other more explicit powers) unlike the American one, the Parliament had no option but to intervene and list these powers clearly.[46] Another described the press as the 'People's Parliament, Always in Session', and asked it to shed its inferiority complex as it did not realize 'the tremendous power the Fourth Estate wielded in a Democracy'.[47] A professor of political science in Calcutta argued that 'even so radical a thinker as Harold Laski' had stated, 'Our rights are not independent of society.' [48] One strident critic of Nehru and admirer of S.P. Mookerjee (for his 'lone and

---

[42] *The Hindu*, 'Changing the Constitution', editorial, 14 April 1951.

[43] *Times of India*, 'Freedom of the Press', editorial, 21 May 1951.

[44] *Times of India*, 'Not Enough', editorial, 28 May 1951.

[45] Hemendra Prasad Ghose, *The Newspaper in India* (Calcutta: Calcutta University Press, 1952), 51–52.

[46] V.P. Karunakaran Nambiar, New Delhi, *The Statesman*, 26 May 1951.

[47] R.J. Venkateswaran, Calcutta, *The Statesman*, 31 May 1951.

[48] D.N. Banerjee, Calcutta, *The Statesman*, 24 April 1951.

heroic opposition to the amendment') invoked George Orwell's phrase to say, 'Like all enemies of intellectual liberty, Mr. Nehru, too, has tried to present his case as a plea for discipline versus individualism.' The writer concluded, 'Many must regret that they have lived to witness an Indian Prime Minister taking away a right which English Viceroys had conceded.'[49]

Regretfully or not, The FA was finally passed in Parliament by 228 votes to 20 amidst what one newspaper described as 'an intemperate and impassionate slanging match' between Nehru and S.P. Mookerjee. The former accused the latter of making false statements and telling lies with regard to the purpose of the bill, and Nehru was in turn accused of speaking 'the language of a dictator'. Nehru stated that India must have 'ordered liberty, because disordered liberty is not democracy', and lauded the bill for widening the scope for lawmaking, particularly with respect to 'communal discord'.[50]

Writing to Chief Ministers of states after the FA was passed, Nehru warned them that the passage of the amendment was not license to use old acts on the press. However, in his mind, there was a hierarchy of offences, of which sedition ranked low, and defamation of government servants as well as spreading communal hatred ranked very high. Accordingly, Nehru instructed Chief Ministers that

> the law of sedition, as such and as applied in the old days, should have no place in our statute book. But what must continue to have a place and be acted upon is the law dealing with the spread of racial and communal hatred. About this, we have to be careful and not prevent the atmosphere to be vitiated more than it already is.[51]

Further, Chief Ministers were told that any action they took as a result of being given more leeway by the constitutional amendment was to be referred to the centre, and that

---

[49] S.K. Ghosh, Calcutta, *The Statesman*, 9 June 1951. The reference is to Orwell's essay titled 'The Prevention of Literature' (1946). The quotation is: 'The enemies of intellectual liberty always try to present their case as a plea for discipline versus individualism. The issue truth-versus-untruth is as far as possible kept in the background.'

[50] *Times of India*, 3 June 1951.

[51] *LCM*, vol. 2, 403–405, 2 June 1951. Nehru reiterated the same point (about not using the old laws against the press) in his next letter to Chief Ministers. See *LCM*, vol. 2, 418–419, 15 June 1951.

... any interference with the freedom of the press has to be avoided, except in cases of extreme vulgarity and defamation. In such cases, it is desirable to have recourse to the criminal law. It is not proper to allow false charges to remain unanswered.... [Pre–censorship] should not be indulged in under any circumstances.[52]

The FA made possible a new Press Act in 1951. The Act, not intended to be a permanent measure, lapsed in 1956, and was repealed in 1957, which probably explains its absence in literature on censorship in India.[53] What were the provisions of this Act, and how did it compare with the 1931 Press Act?

The Press (Objectionable Matters) Act of 1951

In its report in 1948, the PLEC had stated that 'pernicious propaganda' published in newspapers was more effective than that in speeches, as it could be repeated on a daily basis. It had concluded that special press laws were required to deal with such offences, as ordinary penal laws were premised on the fixing of individual responsibility, difficult in the case of a newspaper, which was a collaborative enterprise.[54] Home Minister C. Rajagopalachari believed that separate laws were required for the press as 'the spread of the harm is wider'; to use his dramatic analogy, freedom of the individual was to freedom of the press what a stick was to a rifle.[55]

In March 1951, the AINEC had passed a resolution regretting and condemning 'the degrading tendency in a small section of the press to publish matter which is false, malicious, indecent'. Rajagopalachari used this admission to bolster his claim that even press bosses acknowledged the need for controls on the press.[56] For opponents of the Press Act, public opinion as well as self-regulation via PACs was sufficient to check abuses of press freedom, but this

---

[52] Ibid., 407, 2 June 1951. In another letter he reiterated, '... where defamatory statements are made against Ministers or officers of Government, legal action should be taken. It is not proper to ignore such allegations.' Ibid., 429, 25 June 1951.

[53] The 1951 act was originally to be in place for two years, but in its report the Press Commission recommended that it be extended for a further two years.

[54] Report of the PLEC cited in *Towards a Responsible Press: Shri C. Rajagopalachari's Speeches on the Press Bill in Parliament* (New Delhi: Publications Division, Government of India, 1952, hereafter *Rajagopalachari's Speeches*), 7 September 1951, 8. See also *Report of the Press Laws Enquiry Committee* (Delhi: Manager of Publications, 1948).

[55] *Rajagopalachari's Speeches*, 15 September 1951, 18.

[56] Ibid., 31.

was not a view with which the Home Minister agreed. Rajagopalachari's response to the suggestion of public opinion was that it was like a mother, 'fond and loving', but the press also required a father, 'who is sometimes harsh'.[57] Presumably, the new Press Act of 1951 was to fulfil the paternal role. Here was, quite literally, state paternalism.

In the aftermath of the FA, Nehru was well aware of the hostile attitude of the Indian press to the government. One way in which the GOI tried to placate opponents of any new press act was by promising repeal and replacement of the Press Act of 1931, and the introduction of a new press bill more in keeping with the provisions and spirit of a democratic constitution. The new bill that was introduced in Parliament in August 1951 explicitly stated that all previous laws that went further than the present bill or contradicted constitutional provisions stood repealed, and that no pre-censorship would be imposed on any newspaper. As the Home Minister put it, '... those who are in charge of newspapers and periodicals will be entitled to commit their offences.'[58] According to Rajagopalachari, press laws were required in independent India precisely because old tradition, or the use of force, could not be used in a democracy to ensure order.[59] That Rajagopalachari believed that the 2 million copies of various papers, each read by five or six people (making a paltry total of 12 million, even by his estimate), determined the 'action and behaviour' of the people bears testimony to the excessive—rather than lack of—respect and importance he accorded the press.[60]

The Press (Objectionable Matters) Act of 1951 (introduced in Parliament on 31 August and passed by it on 7 October 1951) was a mixed bag. There were major points of divergence from the IPA 1931: one, securities were not done away with, but would only be demanded if and after objectionable matter was published (and not before, at the time of registration itself, as in the 1931 act); two, a judicial and not an executive authority (a Sessions Judge) would decide, after an inquiry, if security was to be demanded or forfeited. Additionally, respondents could claim trial by jury composed of people with experience of journalism and public service, and could appeal to a High Court against a

---

[57] Deshbandhu Gupta offered the former opinion during the parliamentary debate. *Rajagopalachari's Speeches*, 33.

[58] Statement by C. Rajagopalachari in Parliament, 7 September 1951, *Rajagopalachari's Speeches*, 4.

[59] *Rajagopalachari's Speeches*, 15 September 1951, 15.

[60] Ibid., 16.

decision by the Sessions Judge.[61] Lastly, unlike the IPA 1931, this was not a permanent measure. The act repealed those provisions of provincial acts that provided for pre-censorship or the demand for security. Rajagopalachari was well aware of the perils of defining an offence too specifically or too widely, and suggested that in the case of objectionable writing, the 'tendency' was to be discerned, as it was hardly likely that crimes would be incited directly. As he put it, 'Nobody in the world, no editor worth his name, would write "I appeal to people to commit murder...." He chooses his language carefully.'[62]

What was considered objectionable under this new act? To use Rajagopalachari's striking turn of phrase, what were the 'the essential Don'ts for printed stuff'[63]? They were: incitement to violence, sabotage, murder or 'overthrowing or undermining' the government; interference with the administration of law and justice, law and order, or with the essential supply of goods and services; tampering with the loyalty of the armed or police forces; intimidation of public servants; spreading class enmity and hatred; criminal intimidation (by damaging reputation); and finally, matter that was 'grossly indecent or scurrilous or obscene'.[64] How did these ground compare with the colonial Press Act of 1931? Table 8.1 illustrates this.

Going by this checklist, both the colonial and the post-colonial states shared several areas of concern in common, concerns that they wanted to address with a specific legislative weapon dealing with the press. These common concerns included the fear that Indians could or would be roused to murder and/or violence by the written word, that military and police personnel could be either prevented from joining their jobs or doing their duties, and that different classes of Indians would be animated by feelings of enmity towards one another. Concerns that only the colonial state seems to have had included the worry that works of history and fiction could incite violence, that some Indians could be pressured to commit illegal offences (not paying taxes, for instance), that public servants (non-military and non-police, that is) could be made not to do, or prevented from doing, their duties, and that loyalty of

---

[61] 'No action will be taken in anticipation but only after a proved abuse of the freedom of the Press....' was mentioned explicitly in the Statement of Objects and Reasons, Press (Objectionable Matter) Bill, 1951. Ibid., 7 September 1951, 3–6.

[62] Ibid., 5.

[63] Ibid., 15 September 1951, 15.

[64] Ibid., 7 September 1951, 6–7. As for the addition of the word 'grossly' to qualify indecent, Rajagopalachari justified it by saying that since 'ordinarily indecent things have come to be permitted', a further qualification was required. Ibid, 11.

Table 8.1 Matter deemed objectionable, and punishable, under the Press Acts of 1931 and 1951, respectively

No.	Matter Deemed Objectionable	The Indian Press (Emergency Powers) Act of 1931	Press (Objectionable Matters) Act of 1951
1	Inciting or encouraging murder or violence	Yes	Yes
2	Inciting sabotage	No	Yes
3	Inciting violence or sabotage for undermining or overthrowing the government	No	Yes
4	Directly/indirectly expressing approval of offence involving murder or violence by real/fictitious/ historical persons	Yes	No
5	Seducing a member of the armed/police force from his allegiance to his duty	Yes	Yes
6	To prejudice the recruitment of persons to serve in the armed/police force or to prejudice the training, discipline and administration of any such force	Yes	Yes
7	Bringing into hatred or contempt, or exciting disaffection against the King, the GOI, the administration of justice, or any class or section of subjects	Yes	No
8	To promote feelings of enmity or hatred between different classes of subjects	Yes	Yes
9	Using fear or annoyance to induce a person to do any act he is not legally bound to do/ omit any act that he is legally entitled to do/ inducing him to deliver any property or valuable security	Yes	No
10	Encouraging or inciting a person to interfere with the administration of the law or maintenance of law and order, to commit an offence, to refuse payment of various dues etc. to the government	Yes	No
11	To induce a public servant to do or omit an act connected with his public functions, or to induce resignation	Yes	No
12	Inciting anyone to interfere with the supply of food, or essential commodities and services.	No	Yes
13	Publishing grossly indecent or obscene matter intended for blackmail	No	Yes

Source: Table compiled by author on the basis of the text of both acts.

Indians subjects to the GOI and the King could be tampered with. Taking the 1951 Press Act as a keyhole from which to view the fears of the post-colonial state, it seems that state feared sabotage and violence that could overthrow or undermine the government, economic offences such as black-marketing, and blackmail via publication of indecent matter in the press. The non-payment of dues to the goverment, and the non-cooperation of public employees was not a concern.

As in the case of the FA, the Press Bill was attacked both inside and outside Parliament as being restrictive, and compared to colonial legislation. The AINEC also opposed the Press Act because it 'seeks to penalize as objectionable the publication of material capable of being dealt with under the ordinary law of the land'.[65] It also recommended the revival of the PA system, asked the GOI to ensure that advertisements were placed 'on a non-partisan and strictly commercial basis', and requested state governments to consider refunding securities they had demanded before the promulgation of the new Constitution.[66]

On the other hand, B.V. Keskar, the Minister for Information and Broadcasting, defended the Press Act on a number of grounds, among them that the act was not an Indian innovation (and that even in the United States 'the widely sweeping term of "un-American activities" can engulf anybody and everybody') and that the number of cases instituted under the act was small and done only in exceptional cases.[67] Nehru was of the opinion that the act was different from colonial laws in two major ways: for one, the nature of the executive which it armed with punitive power had itself changed and was 'popular and responsible'; for another, he stated, unlike earlier laws, it was not the executive that could take final action, but the decision was to be arrived at by judicial process.[68] Nehru acknowledged that even a good law could lead to incorrect action, but in his view the

> ... more obvious risk [is] of our public life being poisoned by a certain section of depraved journalism. Anyone can bring out a newspaper; any monied person can use the press for his own personal advantage.[69]

---

[65] AINEC resolution passed in September 1952. *Times of India*, 18 September 1952.
[66] Ibid.
[67] Keskar's address to AINEC, quoted in *Times of India*, 18 September 1952.
[68] *LCM*, vol. 2, 503, 4 October 1951.
[69] Ibid.

Nehru's argument was that the law needed to keep pace with technological changes. He analogized the press to 'dangerous weapons of war', in fact to an 'atom bomb':

> ... the press today is something different from what it was even a generation ago. Mechanical devices have made it easy to produce newspapers and periodicals on a large scale. Only money is required. There is no other standard of capacity or moral behaviour. No one suggests that the more dangerous weapons of war should be given freely to anybody who wants them or who can even pay for them. A press which is allowed to sink below a certain standard of behaviour might be more dangerous than any weapon of war, even the atom bomb, in degrading society and indeed in pulling down the standards of even the bigger newspapers.[70]

In the matter of publications, as in the matter of people, violence was the yardstick used by the government to determine cases suitable for punitive action. In March 1952, Nehru stated at the AICC session that it was not the GOI's policy to detain people for expression of opinion, 'provided it had nothing to do with violence or instigation to violence'. He reiterated the same policy to Chief Ministers regarding detainees, particularly communist ones.[71] In journalist-turned-official press historian J. Natarajan's view (echoing Nehru's), the 'real gain to the press' was that executive action was subject to judicial decisions. He did admit, though, that the 'mere thought of prosecution acted as a deterrent against the full exercise of the freedom of the press'. On the other hand, action taken under this act, especially when compared to the Press Acts of 1910 and 1931, was low.[72] Whereas under the 1931 Press Act between 1931 and 1946 'well over a thousand newspapers were victimized',[73] under the 1951 act, over a period of 21 months (February 1952–October 1953), action was taken in 134 cases (of which securities were demanded in 86 cases, and forfeited in 48).[74]

In 1954, while inaugurating a session of the AINEC, Nehru stated that he would not prevent criticism of his government by the press, as he also

---

[70] *LCM*, vol. 2, 503–504, 4 October 1951.

[71] Ibid., 592–594, 15 April 1952.

[72] J. Natarajan, *History*, 214.

[73] Ibid., 202. The maximum demands for security were from Bombay (596) and the maximum forfeitures were from Bengal (48).

[74] Ibid., 214.

had the freedom of reply not only in Parliament but also in the market-place and in front of common people.[75] At the same session, the AINEC passed a resolution condemning the ill-treatment of journalists by district authorities: in UP a journalist was led through the streets in handcuffs by the police even though his bail had been arranged, while in Poona an editor was made to give his thumb impression to the police in the same manner as criminals. These instances were evidence, according to the AINEC, of harassment by district authorities 'whose displeasure the newsmen might have incurred by exposures, reports and statements, fully substantiated, unpalatable to the authorities'.

The Issue of 'Proprietorial Chains'

A matter widely discussed in the context of press freedom was Nehru's frequent allusion to the fact that the press in India was not really free as it functioned under the monopoly of wealthy proprietors.[76] As early as February 1946, while inaugurating the fifth session of the AINEC at Allahabad, Nehru warned of the dangers of big combines controlling the press in India.[77] During the FA debate, Nehru stated:

> So much freedom of the press we have got today. But the freedom only means suppression or lack of suppression by governmental authority. When huge press chains spring up perverting the individual freedom of the press, when practically the Press in India is controlled by three or four groups of individuals, what is that Press?[78]

The Prime Minister was exaggerating, but nevertheless pointing in the right direction. In its report published in 1954, the Press Commission concluded that of the 330 dailies produced in India at that time, five owners controlled 29 newspapers and 31.2 per cent of the circulation, while 15 others controlled 54 newspapers and 50 per cent of the circulation.[79] In other words, 20 capitalist entrepreneurs together controlled more than 80 per cent of all newspapers read in India.

---

[75] *Times of India*, 14 August 1954.

[76] This comment drew 'loud cheers' in Parliament. *Times of India*, 19 May 1951.

[77] *Times of India*, 18 February 1946.

[78] Extracts from Nehru's statement to Parliament on 18 May 1951, *SWJN2*, vol. 16, part 1, 183.

[79] *Report of the Press Commission of India*, 1954.

Addressing a press conference in June 1951, Nehru referred to a weekly that had changed its policy and tone in 10 days, being constant only, he said, in its dislike of him personally and his government.[80] The perception that newspaper proprietors manipulated the content and 'tone' of their newspapers was shared widely. The legendary cartoonist R.K. Laxman recounts in his autobiography that his one–time employer in Bombay, the *Free Press Journal*, once 'shamelessly' wrote a complimentary article about a political party only a few days after the editor had attacked the same party in the same paper.[81] K.G. Joglekar, who became a journalist in 1945, recalled that it was only after Independence that a new breed of proprietors made editors mere cogs in the wheel.[82] The reason for this was that the newspaper business was not a lucrative one before Independence, whereas both circulation and revenue from advertisements grew beyond expectations after it.[83]

J.N. Sahni, who became an editor of the *Hindustan Times* at the age of 26—and described himself as having 'a Congress background and a political outlook'[84]—nevertheless had this scathing critique to make the post-colonial context within which the press functioned:

> Although after independence the Press in India began to enjoy legal freedom, editors and journalists soon discovered that politicians and proprietors between themselves could make the exercise of that freedom almost illusory. Rich proprietors used silver chains to keep editors or those whom they designated as editors on the leash. The politicians in power employed various pressure tactics and secret devices to thwart the freedom of editors, or to prevent hostile criticism or inconvenient disclosures by them. The position in this respect became worse and worse with the passing of time.[85]

In another book Sahni made the point that after Independence limitations on the press were not so much legislated as organizational. Under the British,

---

[80] *The Statesman*, 12 June 1951.

[81] R.K. Laxman, *The Tunnel of Time: An Autobiography* (New Delhi: Viking, 1998), 90.

[82] K.G. Joglekar, *Press Freedom: The Indian Story* (New Delhi: Publications Division, Ministry of Information and Broadcasting, GOI, 2005), i–ii.

[83] Ibid., 5.

[84] J.N. Sahni, *Truth about the Indian Press* (New Delhi: Allied, 1974), 226.

[85] Ibid., 216. The average monthly salary of journalists working for Indian language and English language newspapers was 150 and 350 rupees respectively, in the mid-1950s. GOI, *India: A Reference Annual–1956* (New Delhi: Ministry of Information and Broadcasting [I&B], GOI), 284.

while the fear of 'iron chains' threatened press freedom, it also acted as a challenge to journalists. After Independence, he writes, '... silver chains made more "cowards" of many a star writer than penal restrictions'. 'Most Editors', writes Sahni, 'therefore struggled between the prudence of self interest and the abandon of self expression. The result was higher salaries and controlled opinions.'[86] His assessment of the context within which the Indian press operated is compatible with Nehru's belief (oft stated in Parliament and elsewhere) that press freedom was threatened less by laws and more by proprietorial control. Sahni believed that since most newspaper proprietors also had other business interests, this made them particularly susceptible to government pressures. According to veteran editor B.G. Verghese, proprietors of newspapers felt that their newspapers should not undo their other business interests. The government would appeal to proprietors, and what mattered was editors' sense of independence.[87]

Prem Bhatia, another veteran editor whose career spanned the colonial to post-colonial divide, blamed editors themselves—and not proprietors—for not keeping a professional distance from politicians, and for being susceptible to proprietorial control. Bhatia recalled that while *The Statesman* was owned by a British company (during the 12 years of his tenure with that paper), neither of the two British editors—Ian Stephens and G.A. Johnson—were required to 'kowtow to the owners'. Staff of the papers only dealt with the editor. Lord Cato, who owned the company, lived in Britain and did not bother with events on the ground, while the managing company, Andrew Yule, was a commercial concern, 'too amorphous' to be noticed as the proprietor's functional instrument.[88]

'The Meanest Levers': Extra Legal and Informal Modes of Censorship after Independence

The passage of the FA—which provided for greater state control over publications—and the simultaneous directive to state governments *not* to use legislative measures against the press did not eliminate the exercise of state

---

[86] J.N. Sahni, *The Lid Off: Fifty Years of Indian Politics, 1921–71* (New Delhi: Allied, 1971), 319.

[87] Personal interview, B.G. Verghese, New Delhi, 15 November 2011.

[88] Prem Bhatia, 'A Delicate Question of Status', *The Tribune*, 29 March 1986, Prem Bhatia Private Papers, f. 2. NMML.

censorship; it merely drove it underground. If state censorship of the press can be understood to include all measures taken by the government to control what did and did not appear in newspapers, then in the post–colonial period one discerns the increasing use of measures not in the rule book. Examples of some of these are discussed here.

Personal Influence

The use of personal influence with editors to prevent publication of specific matter (or to present news in a certain way) may be termed informal censorship. It leaves little trace in the historical record, although there are glimmers here and there in historical sources. During the 'police action' in Hyderabad in September 1948, for instance, Nehru was keen that the impression be stemmed in the mind of the public that the action was in any way anti-Muslim. He urged Chief Ministers to brief selected editors and journalists, and emphasized that 'off-the-record conferences will be better than normal public press conferences'. The purpose of these was that

> ... exaggerated news or the giving of publicity to vague rumours, or indeed to anything that might excite public opinion, is to do a grave disservice to India.... It is desirable that such news should be checked before it is published, not only in order to avoid the spread of rumours and unconfirmed news, but also to avoid the publication of anything which accentuates communal ill-will.[89]

With regard to migration of refugees from East Bengal too, Nehru urged Chief Ministers to 'privately' explain to journalists not to publish items that encouraged the exodus.[90] In early 1950, Nehru asked Chief Ministers to keep in touch with editors in their states on an informal basis for 'off-the-record' talks, supply them with news, and make it clear to them in 'friendly but firm language' that 'we cannot tolerate the spread of rumour and vague allegations or the deliberate fostering of communal hatred'. He also suggested that action be immediately taken against the newspapers if any of this occurred.[91]

---

[89] Nehru referred specifically to a report about the massacre of 150 people by Razakars in a village in Andhra Pradesh on 26 August 1948, of which no confirmation was available apart from the report that Nehru thought 'ghastly' and exaggerated. *LCM*, vol. 1, 203–204, 9 September 1948.

[90] Ibid., 223, 16 November 1948.

[91] *LCM*, vol. 2, 34–35, 27 February 1950.

Withdrawal of Privileges

When *Blitz* (an English weekly published from Bombay) published an inaccurate report about a revolt in Tibet in August 1949, Nehru not only decried the report as 'fantastic nonsense' at a press conference but also ensured that the Delhi correspondent was deprived of permission to work as the accredited correspondent in Delhi. Reporting—and justifying—this action to Chief Ministers, he reminded them that although the government had been tolerant of everything from 'false and malicious criticism' to 'the stream of abuse', a limit had necessarily to be imposed when false news began affecting foreign relations adversely.[92] A month later, Nehru acknowledged that although he had been criticized by the Indian press for this action, it was long overdue as the correspondent had been given repeated warnings, and the story about Tibet had been picked up by the Chinese communist press, which had begun criticizing India's interest in Tibet.[93]

Newspapers that annoyed the GOI, by leaking information, for instance, had to pay a heavy price. The journalist M.V. Kamath recalled that at the time of the Junagadh affair,[94] the *Free Press Bulletin* (the evening paper of the *Free Press Journal*) published exclusive news about movement of ships and troops to Junagadh by the Indian government, gained via sources in the navy.[95] The report was not cleared by the Defence ministry, and Patel called the proprietor of the paper, Sadanand, 'chewed him up for his paper's indiscretion', and asked him to sack the editor, S. Natarajan. In Kamath's words, Sadanand had '... withstood fiercer onslaughts on his freedom during British days—and he was not about to succumb to the Sardar's blandishments. Nothing happened'.[96] Except that something did happen. The *Free Press Bulletin* was on the verge of launching a news service with bureaus in Washington, London and New York, but the GOI refused permission and facilities for the news service to function.[97]

---

[92] *LCM*, vol. 1, 440, 15 August 1949.

[93] Ibid., 468, 16 September 1949.

[94] Junagadh was a Hindu majority state in present-day Gujarat, the Nawab of which opted to join Pakistan, leading India to send in its troops to the state.

[95] M.V. Kamath, *Behind the By-Line: A Journalist's Memoir* (New Delhi: Vision, 1985), 19.

[96] Ibid.

[97] In Kamath's words, 'The Sardar was mad at what he considered the FPJ's irresponsible journalism and cut Sadanand dead. That was the reason for his refusing Sadanand the press facilities.' Kamath, *Behind the By-Line*, 20–21.

Withdrawal of Government Advertisements

One of the 'meanest levers' to control the press was the 'use of public funds to subsidize favourable press media'.[98] This was done by awarding printing jobs (such as electoral rolls, examination results and government advertisements) to newspapers that were uncritical of government policies. The policy of using advertisements as a means to control the press was by no means a new one. It had been a great subject of debate among colonial officials, some of whom were even of the opinion that obvious government subsidizing of a newspaper would simply be rejected by readers as it would be perceived to be pro-government.[99] S. Natarajan points out: 'The declared official policy of not using its advertisements for political purposes which the British government had affirmed in 1940 was reversed [after Independence].'[100]

In March 1953, the Bombay government decided to withhold government advertisements from the *Times of India*, with Chief Minister Morarji Desai on his part defending the action on the ground that a government could not possibly support a newspaper that termed that same government foolish, and sought that very government's overthrow.[101] The *Times of India* editor Frank Moraes recalled that it was his criticism of Morarji Desai's Prohibition policy that was so rewarded. It was only because the *Times of India* was sufficiently affluent that it survived, and in time the advertisements were restored.[102] The AINEC termed the action 'a blow to the freedom of the press', and held political sensitivity to stringent criticism as the cause of the ban. Its president, A.D. Mani, held that since government advertisements were paid for by the public, only the criterion of maximum return for money spent should determine where they were placed; if such a criteria were to be applied, the *Times of India* could not be excluded on account of its large circulation.[103] Mani termed the action

---

[98] Sahni, *Truth about the Indian Press*, 241.

[99] I have discussed this is greater detail in my unpublished M. Phil dissertation submitted to Jawaharlal Nehru University in 2007. See 'To Suppress Sedition, To Obliterate Obscenity: Censorship and Information Control in Colonial India, 1900–1930'.

[100] S. Natarajan, *A History of the Press in India*, 258.

[101] Desai's speech of 21 March reported in *Times of India*, 24 March 1953.

[102] Frank Moraes, *Witness to an Era: India 1920 to the Present Day* (London: Wiedenfeld and Nicolson, 1973), 311–312. J.N. Sahni adds that the government in this case successfully 'twisted the tail of the proprietor', and advertisements were only restored when Moraes was removed from editorship. Sahni, *Truth about the Indian Press*, 217. This was confirmed by S. Natarajan, *A History of the Press in India*, 258.

[103] *Times of India*, 21 March 1953.

against the *Times of India* worse than that under the (then new) Press Act, as in the latter there was at least the possibility of judicial appeal. He urged the government to consider the negative publicity the action would get abroad.[104]

In the early years after Independence, the British press kept a watchful eye on India, and news that Desai had withheld government advertisements from the *Times of India* on account of the paper criticizing his policy of Prohibition was carried in at least four British newspapers that year.[105] In April 1953, the AINEC adopted a resolution stating that government advertisements 'should not be placed as patronage or withheld from a newspaper as a punitive measure by the Government on the ground of publication of news and comments unpalatable to it'.[106] Desai's action attracted the attention of smaller provincial newspapers as well. The Meerut Hindi journalists' association termed the decision 'Fascist in its trend'. A local weekly in Meerut, *Sandesh*, pointed out that papers getting advertisements from the Bombay government would be regarded as government bulletins. *Visalandhra*, a Telugu daily published by the Andhra Communist Party, commented that while the Congress espoused democratic principles, it was intolerant of criticism.[107]

Similarly, in 1954, when the *National Herald* criticized the functioning of the Information ministry in Uttar Pradesh, government advertisements were withheld from the paper, even though it was widely perceived to be a Congress newspaper.[108] Although the *Times of India* case outraged the press, the dependence of the Indian press on government advertisements in fact grew over the decades. In 1951, newspapers derived 45 per cent of their revenue from advertisements; of this, revenue from government advertisements (the withdrawal of which could be considered a measure of censorship) was less than 7 per cent of the total.[109] However, by the mid-1960s the situation had

---

[104] Mani's rejoinder to Desai's speech defending his government's policy published in *Times of India*, 24 March 1953.

[105] *The Times*, *The Spectator*, the *Evening Standard* and the *News Chronicle* all covered the news, and this was reported back to India by an erstwhile editor of the paper, Sir Francis Low, and carried on the front page of the *Times of India*. *Times of India*, 1 April 1953.

[106] *Times of India*, 27 April 1953.

[107] *Times of India*, 28 March 1953.

[108] Rau, *Journalism*, 130.

[109] *India: A Reference Annual–1956*, 284. The GOI claimed in 1956 that it was 'increasingly patronizing Indian language newspapers and Indian agencies and about 60% of all government advertisements are now placed with them'.

changed to such an extent that an American scholar of the Indian press, Ronald E. Wolseley, commented in 1966 that that unlike in Western nations, in India 'one of the largest advertisers, if not the largest, is the central government'. Wolseley found it noteworthy that even as the press depended heavily on the government for advertising revenue, 'large elements of it succeed in being harshly critical of that same government'.[110] To a foreign observer in 1966, it appeared that the Indian press as a whole had not allowed advertising to be used as a tool of complete control. For editors who had to face the brunt of censorship by other means, it was not all-India percentages that mattered, but their individual experience.

In their annual session in 1957, the AINEC again passed a resolution stating that the government's advertising policy was discriminatory. After his attention was drawn to this, B.V. Keskar, the Minister for Information and Broadcasting, replied that he did not agree with the resolution, as a definite policy had been laid down by the government regarding a fair distribution. The accepted policy, he said, was to give advertisements 'on the basis of circulation and standing of the paper. No discrimination is made on account of political opinions'. However, Keskar acknowledged:

> No discrimination is made on account of political opinions. Government is, however, definitely of the opinion that newspapers which follow a policy of consistent and continuous communal incitement should not be encouraged, and, therefore, does not give advertisements to such papers. Government also feel that what is generally known as the 'yellow' Press, should not be encouraged by giving advertisements.[111]

In other words, the GOI did reserve to itself the power to use—and of course define—criteria other than purely commercial ones while awarding advertisements to the press.

Availability of Newsprint

Another way in which the post-colonial state could literally stop newspapers from publication was the withdrawal—or threat of withdrawal—of newsprint

---

[110] Ronald E. Wolseley, 'The Press of India: An Overview', *International Communication Gazette* 12, no. 4 (1966): 243–258, 249 and 251.

[111] B.V. Keskar's reply to a question in Parliament by A.B. Vajpayee and M.K. Kumaran, Lok Sabha (LS) Debates, Series 2, vol. 10, 10 December 1957, col. 4398–4399.

itself. Supply constraints were used as a means of exerting control over the press. According to the Newsprint Control order of 1947, the total number of pages in issues of a daily newspaper over the course of a week could not exceed 70 (or 60, if the paper was published six days a week). The maximum price for a daily newspaper was fixed between 3 and 2 *anna*s per copy. The order was cancelled in June 1949, after remaining in force for over two years.[112] But by 1951, newsprint was in the news again, because it was scarce. The *Times of India* yearbook reported that the General Manager of the company that owned the paper had 'to go on a tour to Canada and U.S. in search of newsprint'.[113]

The GOI passed an order (to come into effect on 1 January 1951) limiting the maximum number of pages which a daily newspaper could publish (60 over seven days; or 48 over six days). Even before this order came into force, the Indian and Eastern Newspaper Society members had agreed to a voluntary cut in the number of pages since November 1950. The same society recommended to the GOI in February 1951 that a price–page schedule be adopted, and this was done in April 1951.[114] Even 10 years after independence, there was only one newsprint factory in India (the Nepa newsprint factory at Madhya Pradesh, which started production in 1947). While annual demand for newsprint in India was about 90,000 tonnes, in 1956 this factory had produced only 10,792 tonnes, and the rest was imported.[115] Newsprint was a commodity the supply of which grew only after the mid-1950s.[116]

The Statesman was a victim of discretionary newsprint denial. Its editor, Ian Stephens, adopted a very critical attitude to the Indian administration and according to his colleague in another paper, showed a bias towards Pakistan, and

---

[112] Newsprint Control (no. 2) Order 1947, Department of Industries and Supplies Notification no. N-3(1)C/47, 3 April 1947. *Manual of Control Orders: A Handbook Containing the Central Control Orders in Force on March 1 1949* (Delhi: Ministry of Industry and Supply, GOI, 1949).

[113] *The India and Pakistan Year Book*, vol. 37, 72.

[114] Ibid.

[115] Reply to question in the LS by Satish Chandra, Deputy Minister for Commerce and Industry. The capacity of the factory was 30,000 tonnes. LS Debates, Series 2, vol. 5, 21 August 1957, col. 9027–9031.

[116] Wolseley noted that between 1957 and 1964 the supply of newsprint (both produced in India and imported) increased by more than 60 per cent. In 1957–1958 the total available newsprint from all sources was 77,872 metric tonnes, and this increased to 125,598 metric tonnes by 1963–1964. While indigenous production grew by 47.7 per cent, imports grew by 66.6 per cent. Overall the supply increased by 62 per cent. Wolseley, 'The Press of India', Table II, 252.

started a Pakistani edition of the newspaper as well. The Indian government did not have any grounds for legal action, but an opportunity presented itself when the Delhi edition mistakenly carried advertisements calling for tenders for military supplies for the Pakistani government. Ironically, the Indian government was supplying newsprint on which the Pakistani edition was published, and threatened to withdraw this supply. The editor was dismissed; the Indian government had scored a victory without firing a single legal shot.[117]

Physical Violence

Though the use of advertisements and newsprint as tools for controlling newspapers was held in contempt by editors, there were some other tactics that were more reprehensible. These were employed not by the centre but by state governments. One victim of this was J. Natarajan, then editor of the Ambala-based *The Tribune*, author of a landmark history of the Indian press, son of veteran journalist S. Natarajan, and considered by a colleague to be 'one of the most responsible journalists that India had produced'. In the pages of his newspaper, Natarajan praised the Chief Minister of Punjab, Pratap Singh Kairon (who served in this position between 1956 and 1965) for certain progressive measures, but criticized him for dictatorial methods and increasing corruption. There was nothing in this to which legal exception could be taken, the trustees of the newspaper supported their editor, and what followed has been described by J.N. Sahni as a 'nerve-wrecking process of goondaism and blackmail', during which Natarajan and his wife were constantly shadowed, 'even to the club', by two large, gun-toting men, who whispered 'coarse abuses and homicidal threats', and threatened them on the phone at all hours. When complaints to the administration had no results, Natarajan evaded his stalkers and reached Delhi, never again going back to *The Tribune*.[118] Sadly, Natarajan was not the only victim of this peculiar form of intimidation-censorship. S.C. Sarkar, editor of *The Searchlight* at Patna, recounted in 'Woes of a Small Town Editor' the harassment which 'a conscientious newspaperman in provincial towns is subjected'. He recalled being summoned by a Chief Minister who

---

117 Sahni, *Truth about the Indian Press*, 218–219.
118 Ibid., 219–220. The incident involving Natarajan also finds mention in Robin Jeffrey, *India's Newspaper Revolution: Capitalism, Politics and the Indian Language Press, 1977–99* (London: C. Hurst & Co., 2000), 194, but it occurred in 1958 and not in the 1960s (as Jeffrey suggests), since Prem Bhatia replaced Natarajan in 1958, and Amolak Ram served as the acting editor in the meantime.

did not like his piece about famine in the state, and warned him in schoolyard bully fashion that if state protection were withdrawn from him, then Sarkar's office and house were both liable to be attacked. Sarkar also recounted that he was denounced as a communist, and the state intelligence department supported the charge. Clearly, India had its indigenous albeit less developed form of McCarthyism.[119]

Another journalist, Kedar Ghosh, recalled that during the first general election, when he served as Chief Reporter with *The Statesman* in Calcutta, state Congress leaders termed him and his paper anti-national for their comments on the organizational weaknesses of the party. Public meetings were held in *maidans* against the paper, and its copies burnt. Similarly, when dailies in Bengal tried to enhance circulation by reporting exaggerated accounts of events in East Pakistan, and *The Statesman* did not, the paper was accused of being pro-Muslim, pro-Pakistani, and therefore anti-national.[120] Whereas Congressmen held that *The Statesman*, and Ghosh in particular, were against the Congress, communists believed him to be anti-communists, and expressed their resentment over his criticism of their policies by writing angry letters to the editor (a couple signed in blood) and by surrounding him on his way to work with 'venomous curses'.[121]

This book does *not* make a case for the erosion of Indian democracy in the 1950s with the passage of the FA and Press Act of 1951; rather, the argument is that once the executive successfully claimed—in addition to the judiciary—the right to set limits for demarcating acceptable from objectionable writings, there could be no going back. Journalists' accounts have testified that both Nehru and Patel did not mind criticism of their policies, and only drew the line at personal attacks.[122] The same, however, cannot be said of their successors, or indeed of many of their contemporaries holding political positions, as has been indicated in this chapter.

---

[119] S.C. Sarkar, 'Woes of a Small Town Editor' in *What Ails the Indian Press: Diagnosis and Remedies*, ed. D.R. Mankekar (New Delhi: Somaiya, 1970).

[120] Ghosh, *No Apology*, 91–92.

[121] Ibid., 98–100.

[122] Rau, *The Press in India*, 77; Joglekar, *Press Freedom*, 9; Inder Malhotra, 'A Superior Person, Thorough Professional' in *The Indian Media: Illusion, Delusion and Reality—Essays in Honour of Prem Bhatia*, ed. Asha Rani Mathur (New Delhi: Rupa, 2006), 9; Harish Khare, 'Political Reporting' in *The Indian Media*, ed. Mathur, 41; Sahni, *Truth about the Indian Press*, 216; P.D. Tandon, *Yours Sincerely: A Collection of Letters written to P.D. Tandon* (New Delhi: Arnold Heinemann, 1975), 80–81.

There is no doubt that the FA laid the blueprint of the state–press relationship in independent India. However, the historiographical focus on FA and on laws in law books generally exclusively obscures another crucial, evolving process in the 1950s: the informalization of censorship. In some ways, the post-colonial state was a victim of its self-image. Acutely conscious of comparisons with its predecessor, in the sphere of press controls and any other variety of repression, senior policymakers adopted an ambivalent attitude to press control. Partition violence had revealed the many uses to which free speech could be put, but any clamps on free speech were considered politically incorrect too.

In the year before and the few immediately following Independence, Nehru and Patel attempted to harness the press to their vision of national progress, urging—without mentioning the term—self-censorship. The informalization of censorship, which began with the Second World War and was a consequence of the state recognizing the potential of the press as an ally in achieving its aims, continued in the post-colonial period as well. The post-colonial Indian state relied on informal networks, but was reluctant to forego the safety net of laws to deal with the press. This explains the FA and the Press Act of 1951, made possible by it. By pushing the passage of press control laws on the one hand, and asking Chief Ministers to be cautious when applying these laws, Nehru's ambivalence on the issue of press control in the years following Independence was communicated to other state personnel as well. Informalization of censorship had an acceptable face (chats with editors over tea, or on the phone) but also an ugly one (threats to and intimidation of journalists). Incidentally, Nehru's son-in-law and an MP, Feroze Gandhi, succeeded in 1956 in getting the 'Protection of Publication' bill passed through the Lok Sabha, which extended immunity to the press for reporting parliamentary proceedings.[123]

By the mid-1950s, the Indian government's capacity to tolerate criticism was being appreciated not only by Nehru himself but also by independent observers.[124] The *Manchester Guardian*, for instance, carried an article in 1956 by their India correspondent mentioning: 'The only body of people who can be criticized in India with absolute immunity, is the Government: call them corrupt, inefficient, dictatorial, or Communist, and they will turn the other

---

[123] See chapter 'A Guardian of Freedom of the Press' in Bertil Falk, *Feroze the Forgotten Gandhi: A Personal Narrative* (New Delhi: Roli Books, 2016), 199–201.

[124] According to veteran journalist B.G. Verghese, in the 1950s there was hero worship of Nehru and no one criticized him openly. Personal interview, B.G. Verghese, New Delhi, 15 November 2011.

cheek.'[125] On his third visit to India in 1956, Paul Appleby (a well-known American theorist of public administration) wrote another report in which he too mentioned the tendency in the Indian press and public sphere generally to make 'sweeping and extravagant' criticism of the government, and Nehru cited this report as evidence that the GOI had '… encouraged opposition and criticism and even many kinds of action which few countries would tolerate'. Nehru had been making similar statements, especially in Parliament since Independence. By 1956, however, he added a qualifying statement to it. 'But it is time', wrote Nehru, 'that people realized that politics and economics or any kind of progress or democracy in India are not served by violence, indecency and vulgarity.'[126] If, as Partha Chatterjee argues, the tension between citizens with rights and populations in need of regulation is a feature of contemporary democracies,[127] India in the 1950s provides a clear example of this. Citizens of a democratic republic who had been awarded universal adult franchise were nevertheless considered to be in need of 'protection' from certain kinds of publications and films.[128]

However, the GOI—or Nehru—was not complicit in every act of censorship that took place in its name. In an atmosphere of hero-worship that prevailed with regard to Nehru in the decade after Independence, often the Prime Minister's word was law, and statements uttered casually regarded as instructions to act, or to censor. A puzzled Prime Minister wrote to the top official at the Ministry of Finance in 1958 about income tax raids on an individual called Baburao Patel, who published India's first film trade magazine called *Filmindia*, and in a book titled *Burning Words: A Critical History of Nine Years of Nehru's Rule from 1947 to 1956* (published in 1956) had called Nehru a 'hard-driving power politician' in one place, and a 'prize schizophrenic' and a 'power-crazy Moghul of Delhi' in other places. A compilation of Patel's

---

[125] Nehru cited this quotation in his letter to Chief Ministers. *LCM*, vol. 4, 437–438, 20 September 1956.

[126] Ibid., 439, 20 September 1956.

[127] Partha Chattejee, *Politics of the Governed: Reflections on Popular Politics in Most of the World* (New York: Columbia University Press, 2004), 38.

[128] In the context of film censorship, Tejaswini Ghante argues: 'While film censorship was instituted by the British to uphold the legitimacy of colonial rule, the independent Indian state characterized the continuance of the practice in paternalist terms, befitting its role as the main agent of development and modernization.' Tejaswini Ganti, 'The Limits of Decency and the Decency of Limits: Censorship and the Bombay Film Industry', in *Censorship in South Asia*, ed. Kaur and Mazzarella, 92.

articles, the book suggested that India's freedom was the by-product of the Second World War, and had nothing to do with the Congress, and that not one promise made on Independence Day had been fulfilled. In fact, all the articles included in the volume were a tirade against Nehru, Gandhi, Pakistan and Islam.[129] Baburao Patel had written to Nehru complaining about harassment, and Nehru recalled that he himself had expressed a negative opinion about the magazine, which he thought to be 'exceedingly vulgar and objectionable'. Nehru did not, however, remember sanctioning any prosecutions—including income tax ones—against the man, and the puzzled tone of his note suggested that he suspected that his statements against the magazine had been taken as sanction, by overzealous tax officials, for prosecution against the publisher.[130]

The paradox of censorship in this decade immediately after Independence is this: the GOI amended the Constitution but asked state governments not to use the new provisions. The latter were conscious that legal action would beg comparisons with the colonial period, and thus refrained from using legal provisions to counter unwanted publications, preferring instead threats of bodily harm to editors and journalists. Independence had complicated the life of journalists in ways they could never have imagined. It appears that colonial censorship—with its plethora of acts, wartime codes and lists of things not to be published—left relatively less scope for discretion. Post-colonial censorship may not have been so rule bound, and this exercise of discretion at various levels accounts for its invisibility.

The legacy of Nehru's oft-repeated assertions regarding the necessity for a free press had a longer life than his assertions in favour of certain kinds of censorship. Just before he was jailed for two months during the Emergency, journalist Kuldip Nayar wrote to the then Prime Minister, Indira Gandhi, urging her to let the press operate freely, and quoting Nehru's statement to the AINEC in 1950 to the effect that a free press was preferable to a suppressed one, even if the government considered a free press dangerous.[131] According

---

[129] Sushila Rani Patel (ed.), *Burning Words* (Bombay: Sumati Publications, 1956). Not only was the book not banned in India, a second edition appeared in 1957.

[130] Nehru's note to A.K. Roy, Secretary (Revenue), Ministry of Finance, 8 March 1958, *SWJN2*, vol. 41, 1, 439.

[131] Nehru had addressed the AINEC on 3 December 1950. Nayar wrote the letter to Indira Gandhi on 16 July 1975, and was arrested on 24 July 1975. Indira Gandhi's Director of Publicity, H.Y. Sharada Prasad, replied: 'Freedom of the press is part of the personal freedoms which in any country are temporarily abridged in times of national emergency.' Letter (and reply) quoted in Kuldip Nayar, *In Jail* (New Delhi:

to Barbara and Thomas Metcalf in their survey of modern Indian history, immediately after Independence, 'All were agreed that the new India must be a democratic land, with universal suffrage and freedom of press and speech.'[132] This chapter has shown that while the foundational promise of universal suffrage was fulfilled, that of freedom of press and speech was a much more contested terrain. The next chapter discusses the case of a controversial book in 1956, when both visible (through public pronouncements, well-publicized acts) and invisible (through persuasion and back-channel discussions) censorship was mobilized by the Indian state to tackle a book, protests against which were causing loss of human lives.

Vikas, 1978), 4–6. Discussing press freedom during the Emergency is outside the scope of this book, but comparing colonial censorship to that in the Emergency, veteran M. Chalapathi Rau felt that the latter was more harsh; the British had allowed the *National Herald* to quote a restrictive order, stop publishing editorial articles, and to leave a blank space as a mark of protest. During the Emergency, even leaving blank spaces was not allowed. Rau, *Journalism and Politics*, 31–32.

[132] Barbara D. Metcalf and Thomas R. Metcalf, *A Concise History of Modern India* (Cambridge: Cambridge University Press, 2006, 2nd ed.), 232.

9

The *Living Biographies of Religious Leaders* Controversy (1956)

This chapter is a case study of a specific book which aroused controversy in both India and Pakistan. An investigation into the circumstances surrounding the publication as well as banning of this long forgotten book[1] has much to tell us about the roots of present-day censorship debates and demands in India.

The Book

In September 1956, the reprinting of a book first published in the United States in 1942, titled *Living Biographies of Religious Leaders*, written by Henry and Dana Lee Thomas, led to agitation and communal violence in Uttar Pradesh, Madhya Pradesh (then Vindhya Pradesh) and West Bengal. The book, comprising short biographies of Moses, Luke, Joseph, Buddha, Prophet Muhammad and Gandhi, was not noticed in India in the years after the

---

[1] The riots are discussed in one paragraph (as part of his discussion of the imposition of constraints by Nehru on communal activities) in Christophe Jaffrelot, *The Hindu Nationalist Movement and Indian Politics, 1925 to the 1990s: Strategies of Identity Building, Implantation and Mobilization (with special reference to Central India)* (London: Hurst and Company, 1996; first published in French in 1993), 107. Jaffrelot estimates that six people died in Bareilly, and five in Jabalpur. He refers in passing to the 'vigorous' action taken by Nehru against the book and the violence that followed its publication. Paul R. Brass has discussed the riots in the context of Muslim and Hindu militant mobilization in Aligarh in his *The Problem of Hindu–Muslim Violence in Contemporary India* (Seattle: University of Washington Press, 2003), 76–80. However, his concern is with analysing the riots at Aligarh, not so much with the book itself or with measures taken to stop its circulation.

publication of its American edition. It was noticed only when printed in India as part of a collaboration agreement in 1955 between the original publisher and the Bombay-based Bhartiya Vidya Bhawan (BVB) specializing in low-price editions. The book carried a foreword by K.M. Munshi, then the Governor of Uttar Pradesh. The agitation over the book, followed by riots that erupted when rumour spread that the *Gita* had been burnt and torn in Aligarh, led to the death of 15 (Nehru's estimate)[2]/23 people (*Time* magazine's estimate),[3] as hundreds more were arrested and curfew imposed in Aligarh and Jabalpur.[4] When K.M. Munshi (who also happened to be the founder of BVB as well as a general editor of the series) was due to visit Bhopal in early September 1956, 5,000 people demonstrated against him, and he cancelled his visit.[5] This was despite the fact that BVB had already announced that it was stopping the sale of the book, and that passages that had offended people would be removed in subsequent editions. Actively and most visibly involved in the agitation were students of Aligarh Muslim University, the Vice-Chancellor of which, Zakir Husain (later to serve as India's first Muslim president), had regretted the involvement of students of his university, reminding them that '… your action should have caused pain to the soul of the Prophet'.[6]

What was found to be offensive in the book? The *Siyasat Jadid* (an Urdu newspaper from Kanpur edited, printed and published by K.G. Zaidi, also known as Ishaq Ilmi), reproduced, under the screaming headline 'Take Up the Challenge! PROPHET INSULTED IN GOVERNOR MUNSHI'S PUBLICATION', several passages from the book in several issues published

---

[2] Figure cited by Nehru at a public meeting in Ramlila Maidan, Delhi, on 23 September 1956, AIR Tapes, NMML, transcribed, translated into English (from original Hindi), *SWJN2*, vol. 35 (1 September–30 November 1956), 8 (hereafter cited as 'Nehru's speech in Delhi, 23 September 1956').

[3] *Time*, 1 October 1956. *Time* magazine also estimated that 500 people had been arrested, and called the riots India's 'bitterest' since 1947.

[4] There were demonstrations against the book at Aligarh on 31 August and 1 September, followed by riots on September 14 after demonstrations by students of the university. A curfew was imposed and 200 people arrested. 500 were arrested at Jabalpur. Nehru also sought to squash the rumour then current that a copy of the *Gita* had been torn and burnt in Aligarh by Muslims. Nehru's speech in Delhi, 23 September 1956, *SWJN2*, vol. 35, 8.

[5] *Hindustan Times*, 6 September 1956.

[6] Zakir Husain's comments on 18 September 1956, cited in *LCM*, vol. 4, 436n8, 20 September 1956.

between 28 August and 16 September 1956.[7] These included a narrative to the effect that after seeing visions, and while attempting to ascertain their divine or satanic character, the Prophet sat in his wife Khadija's lap as she put him to an 'infallible test' by disrobing herself. Although the 16-page chapter contained many complimentary references to the Prophet, and to Islam, the book also printed his portrait, and repeated many of the charges of promiscuity and violence that were, as we have seen in Chapter 4 of this book, standard tropes in biographies of the Prophet written by Westerners in the 20th century. *Time* magazine, reporting the riots, commented: 'This story jibes essentially with the earliest and standard account of Mohammed's life (by Ibn Ishaq—8th century), but the tone of the book's 16-page biography might well give offense to devout Moslems.'[8]

Damage Control

Nehru's own opinion of the book, and one that he shared with other Indians at a public speech in Delhi delivered in end-September, after the riots, was that it was

> ... not of a very high standard. It is a very ordinary book, neither well written nor good, a mere journalistic hotchpotch. Well, there must be people who read these things. Also, when I read it carefully, there is no doubt that some wrong facts and often absurd things have been written in the chapter on Hazrat Muhammad. It was wrong, there was no doubt about it. A Muslim would not have tolerated it, for even I could not tolerate it.[9]

So much for the review. Nehru then suggested what ought to be done about it; or to be more accurate, what ought *not* to be done about it:

---

[7] Ilmi had been arrested several times between 1950 and 1954, in 1951 for publishing rumours to the effect that Hindu refugees in Kanpur were killing Muslim children and selling their cooked flesh in hotels owned by them. Details of charges in 1956 and in earlier cases against Ilmi in AIR 1957 All 782, 1957 CriLJ 1361 (Mohd. Ishaq Ilmi vs The U.P. State And Ors. on 21 June, 1957).

[8] Henry Thomas and Dana Lee Thomas, *Living Biographies of Religious Leaders* (New York: Blue Ribbon Books, 1946), 103–121. Headline and offending passage also reproduced in *Time*, 1 October 1956.

[9] Nehru's speech in Delhi, 23 September 1956, *SWJN2*, vol. 35, 6–7.

Anyhow, that does not mean that just because someone has written a useless book or said some wrong things we should fight among ourselves. Let us take whatever action we can regarding the book and try to have it banned or change the text or something. This is the sensible way of going about things instead of creating an uproar.[10]

Compared to communal rioting, it was banning, or removing the book from circulation by any other means, that was a far more preferable option. By the time he made this speech, Nehru had already taken action against the book and conducted damage control on a number of fronts: he had written to K.M. Munshi more or less ordering him to withdraw the book, as it was 'second–rate', was causing him (Nehru) to be inundated with telegrams asking that the book be banned, and because it had raised a big issue not only in India but also in Pakistan. Nehru's reprimand was unequivocal: 'I think you should withdraw this book immediately and announce this fact. Presumably, you had not read the book, although you are a General Editor of the series.'[11] He also instructed Munshi to issue a press communiqué as he felt that a public statement on the matter was necessary.[12] Nehru then communicated to the Chief Minister of Bombay, Morarji Desai, Maulana Azad's suggestion that the publishers hand over remaining copies to the Bombay government.[13] Seven thousand copies had been printed in all, of which 3,000 had already been sold.[14] Even prior to this communication, BVB had already announced that they were stopping the sale of the book, and this announcement was released by the Director of Information of the Uttar Pradesh government, thereby reaching a larger audience.[15] This did not, however, as we have seen earlier, stop riots in Aligarh and elsewhere in mid-September.

Nehru also corresponded with several petitioners and complainants: He wrote to the president of the Muslim League in India (and Rajya Sabha member), M. Muhammad Ismail, agreeing that some passages were 'very objectionable', and that Munshi himself had been 'greatly distressed' when

---

[10] Ibid., 7.

[11] Letter from Nehru to Munshi, 2 September 1956, *SWJN2*, vol. 35, 255.

[12] Letter from Nehru to Munshi, 4 September 1956, *SWJN2*, vol. 35, 253.

[13] Nehru wrote to Morarji Desai, the Chief Minister of Bombay, that the book was written in 'the usual American style which, I think, is wholly inappropriate for such a subject'. Letter from Nehru to Desai, 6 September 1956. *SWJN2*, vol. 35, 255–256.

[14] *Hindustan Times*, 11 September 1956.

[15] *Times of India*, 4 September 1956.

he had seen them, after the book's publication.[16] To students from Aligarh University who wanted to meet him regarding the book, Nehru wrote that he too considered certain passages 'very objectionable', regretted its publication, had raised the matter with the publishers, and issued instructions that the sale of the book be stopped and offending passages be removed.[17] A similar reply was sent to two Muslim Lok Sabha members who had asked for the book to be banned. Nehru replied that there was no need for the book to be banned as booksellers had been asked to return copies, and all existing copies had been taken over by the Bombay government. Additionally, he assured them that Munshi had not read the book prior to its publication.[18] Finally, he made sure that he told the public about the steps taken by his government.[19] On his part, Munshi said that since the book was a reprint, it had not been scrutinized carefully, and that he himself had often spoken about the Prophet and celebrated his birthday.[20]

In the first week of September, after protest meetings were held at several places in Bihar (Bhagalpur, Arrah, Buxar and Gaya), and 6,000 Muslims participated in a procession at Patna, the Chief Minister, Dr Sri Krishna Sinha, ordered the contents of the book to be examined by law officers of his state government.[21] Eventually, Bihar and West Bengal banned the book,[22] although the Uttar Pradesh government refused to ban it, the Chief Minister, Sampurnanand, being unsure of the legality of such an action. Sampurnanand also publicly expressed the opinion that 'penal action will have to be decided by law, not by the desire of any individual'.[23] In his opinion, legal action could be based on proof of 'malicious intent' alone, and this would be difficult to prove. He did not contest that religious feelings had been hurt, but since the book

---

[16] *Hindustan Times*, 7 September 1956.

[17] Note from Nehru to his Personal Secretary, 3 September 1956, *SWJN2*, vol. 35, 254.

[18] Note from Nehru to B.N. Kaul (Principal Private Secretary to the PM) contained a draft of the letter to be sent to Maulana Hifzur Rahman and S.K. Razmi, MPs from Moradabad and Sehore, respectively. *SWJN2*, vol. 35, 258–259.

[19] Nehru's speech in Delhi, 23 September 1956, *SWJN2*, vol. 35, 7.

[20] *Hindustan Times*, 7 September 1956.

[21] *Hindustan Times*, 7 and 8 September 1956.

[22] See Nehru's speech in Delhi, 23 September 1956, *SWJN2*, vol. 35, editorial footnote 7n4. Nehru was only aware of one state having banned the book.

[23] Sampurnanand to the Times of India News Service. *Times of India*, 10 September 1956. He also stated in the Uttar Pradesh Vidhan Sabha on 8 September that banning would be contrary to the legal advice received by the government.

had been withdrawn he thought legal action impossible.[24] Nehru responded to a letter by the Uttar Pradesh Chief Minister about the issue by agreeing that although the agitation over the book had begun some 'dangerous trends', slogan shouting per se could not be penalized as it was difficult to identify the culprit in a crowd.[25] To the Chief Minister of (then) Vindhya Pradesh, Nehru also reiterated his view that it was the attitude of district officials that determined the intensity of a riot.[26] Nehru asked the Chief Minister to make sure that the impression was not created that the government was partial (to Hindus) in communal matters.[27]

A section of the press in India was aware, even before the dust had settled over the controversy, that publications inciting communal hatred not only caused riots but also jeopardized the freedom of the press as a whole. The Uttar Pradesh Press Committee, for example, passed a resolution on 18 September 1956 urging that inflammatory writings of the kind carried in the *Siyasat Jadid* cease immediately, in the interest of peace, freedom of the press and even solidarity of the nation.[28] Nehru considered the material in *Siyasat Jadid* an act of incitement. When Ishaq Ilmi, the founder–editor of the newspaper, was arrested on 16 September (and detained under PDA), Nehru wished 'it had been done earlier'.[29] For Nehru, the argument that the editor had acted under provocation held no water, and he considered his crime of incitement 'a much more serious offence than any normal crime'.[30]

In fact, Nehru kept all options open except for that of banning the book, which he considered to be 'of very doubtful legality', although he added that he was not much concerned about the law. He also did not consider the demand for banning a bona fide one, considering that the book had been withdrawn by other means.[31] Nehru repeatedly emphasized (in public meetings as well

---

[24] *Hindustan Times*, 8 September 1956.

[25] Letter from Nehru to Sampurnanand, 15 September 1956, *SWJN2*, vol. 35, 256–257.

[26] Letter from Nehru to Sampurnanand, 22 September 1956, *SWJN2*, vol. 35, 264–265.

[27] Nehru had received reports that Muslims were badly affected, and that the local administration had been shielding Hindu communal elements. Letter to Shambhunath Shukla, 9 October 1956, *SWJN2*, vol. 35, 266–267.

[28] *Times of India*, 20 September 1956.

[29] Nehru's speech in Delhi, 23 September 1956, *SWJN2*, vol. 35, 6–7.

[30] Letter from Nehru to Shibban Lal Saxena (MP from Gorakhpur), 23 October 1956, *SWJN2*, vol. 35, 267–68.

[31] Letter from Nehru to U.N. Dhebar, 21 September 1956, *SWJN2*, vol. 35, 263.

as in letters to Chief Ministers) that the agitation was manufactured by vested interests:

> I can understand people objecting to some passages in that book and drawing attention to them. But, there was something much deeper, and it was obvious that mischief was afoot and had been deliberately organized. The offending passages were broadcast in cyclostyled papers by the very persons who objected to them.[32]

He found it extraordinary that '... these passages which were so objectionable should have been given so much publicity by the very people who objected to them', and concluded that publicity was given solely in order to create trouble.[33] As we have seen in Part II of this book, in several cases where bans were demanded by members of the public, publicity of offensive material was most often done by the offended themselves, if only to prove that their sentiments were justified and not without merit.

Nehru's faith in the freedom of the press—the communal organs of which he blamed for inciting the public by spreading 'communal poison'—was shaken after this episode. Although he conceded the right of people to take offence, he found it worrying that during demonstrations against the book, some Muslims had raised slogans (such as 'Pakistan Zindabad' [Long Live Pakistan]) that were 'not only anti-national but also treasonable'. Nehru lamented that right-wing organizations such as the Jan Sangh and the Jamaat-e-Islami took advantage of situations such as these, and that 'the freedom of the Press and of speech and our democratic Constitution spread out their wide umbrella to cover all this evil brood'.[34] He considered this issue so important that in addition to his fortnightly letters to Chief Ministers, he wrote a special letter to them explaining how demonstrations against a book had turned into a situation where looting of shops, stabbing and police firing took place. He listed inflammatory writing in the press in addition to processions as two things that fanned communal trouble, and suggested that processions be checked by district authorities whenever there was a likelihood of disturbance. The course

---

[32] *LCM*, vol. 4, 436, 20 September 1956.

[33] Note from Nehru to B.N. Kaul, *SWJN2*, vol. 35, 259.

[34] *LCM*, vol. 4, 437, 20 September 1956. The Jamaat-e-Islami was established in 1941 and was an organization that concerned itself with religious education, and organized a campaign against the civil code.

of action to be taken against newspapers, was, as Nehru put it, 'peculiarly difficult'. As he put it:

> I have personally come to the conclusion that we must have fresh legislation to deal with the spread of communal hatred by newspapers, etc. I would confine this to offensive communal writings, and not extend it at all in the political or other fields. This matter is one of high importance and I feel sure that we shall have the approval of the general public if we take stronger measures than we have done thus far in dealing with communal incitement and violence.[35]

Nehru also proposed a solution:

> I have an idea that most of our Governments have become much too legal-minded. When a newspaper or an individual misbehaves, we dare not take action lest the law court might acquit the person concerned.... So we spend a long time in taking legal advice and meanwhile the situation changes.... We should act much more promptly. If we are convinced that a newspaper editor or any other individual has spread communal hatred and incited people to communal violence, we should arrest him and either proceed against him in a court of law or keep him under preventive detention.... A crisis has to be met by immediate and effective action and usually arrests of official offenders is the best preventive.... It does not matter much if he is acquitted. Government will have discharged its function and the general public will realize that we are going to stand no nonsense in regard to communal troubles. *In fact such acquittals in obviously bad cases would strengthen the hands of Government to bring legislation to deal with such matters.*[36]

In other words, the executive would end up looking much better than the judiciary in the eyes of the peace-loving public. In public, Nehru emphasized his commitment to free speech even in the aftermath of the riots over the book, but confessed that he had come to the conclusion that newspapers that spread communal violence had to be controlled by law. This was in a context when the Press Act of 1951 had lapsed and not been extended, and Nehru solicited the public's help in censoring certain kinds of newspapers. He said:

> I called the newspaper-men and asked why they did such things [spread communal violence through the press] and circulated false rumours. They said that they did it to increase their circulation. Now, you can see that it is

---

[35] Ibid., 446–448, 20 September 1956.
[36] Ibid., emphasis added.

not a joking matter. You must understand this and prevent the circulation from going up.[37]

The agitation over the book spanned not only India but also other countries, including Pakistan. During his visit to Saudi Arabia in late September 1956, Nehru was asked by King Saud about the conditions of Muslims in India, and told that he (the King) had received many telegrams about the publication of the book *Living Biographies of Religious Leaders*. Nehru informed the King about the withdrawal of the book, and also told him that the Indian law was being amended to prevent 'scurrilous writing'.[38]

Developments in Pakistan

In fact, there were strikes in Karachi against the publication of the book, in which (according to *Time* magazine) as many as 15,000 students participated, and during the course of which a portrait of Nehru was garlanded with shoes.[39] The general secretary of the Jamaat-e-Islami Pakistan called for a 'protest day' to be observed on 14 September all through the country.[40] There was a *hartal* in Dacca, the capital of East Pakistan, and the government there banned the import, sale and publication of *Living Biographies*.[41] Twenty-first September was observed by the Muslim League as a 'protest day' all through Pakistan.[42] A 2-mile long procession was taken out, described as 'the biggest meeting Karachi has ever seen'. *Dawn* reported that crowds had shouted 'blood for blood', and urged their government to 'declare war on Bharat'.[43] *Dawn*—the masthead of which declared that its 'circulation exceeds the combined circulations of all other English language dailies in West Pakistan'—gave the matter coverage on its front page and in several editorials all through September, reporting that

---

[37] Nehru's speech in Delhi, 23 September 1956, *SWJN2*, vol. 35, 23.
[38] Record of a talk between Nehru and King Saud on 25 September 1956 at Riyadh, *SWJN2*, vol. 35, 491.
[39] *Time*, 1 October 1956.
[40] *Dawn*, 14 September 1956.
[41] *Dawn*, 15 September 1956.
[42] Sisir Gupta, *India's Relations with Pakistan, 1954–57* (New Delhi: Indian Council of World Affairs, 1958), 49.
[43] *Dawn*, 22 September 1956.

three people had been killed in Moradabad[44] and riots in Orai,[45] Bareilly,[46] Jabalpur,[47] and so on. An editorial titled 'Inadequate Regrets' criticized the 'traditionally flippant manner' in which 'authority in that country' dismissed blasphemy against Muslims. It noted that the publishing house was 'owned and looked after' by the Governor of Uttar Pradesh himself, and concluded: 'If the secular claims and professions of Bharat have any meaning, Government's deterrent action in a test case such as the present can have a wholesome restraining influence....'[48] After the book was banned by the governments of Bihar and Bengal, the *Dawn* took this as proof that 'Muslims were right to agitate'. In an editorial titled 'The brute amok', it termed India 'that jungle of fraud called secular Bharat' and exhorted Pakistan to inform the rest of the world 'of what is going on in the jungle land of the communal brutes, masquerading as a modern peace-loving and secular state'.[49] This was not an issue, the *Dawn* opined, of freedom of expression since 'it was the duty of every civilized government to prevent the publication of slanderous attacks against the founders of great religions'.[50] The day after the protest day the top headline on the front page of the *Dawn* was: 'Nation Protests Against Bharati Genocide'.[51] Even Fatima Jinnah, sister of Muhammad Ali Jinnah, in an address to college students in end-September, referred to the 'deep anxiety and sympathy' she felt for the 'helpless Muslim minority of Bharat ... subjected to oppression and atrocities'.[52] Ironically, Nehru was, at this time, being accorded a warm welcome in Saudi Arabia, against which too the *Dawn* protested.[53]

Nehru was certain that Pakistan was involved in fomenting riots. In Agra, authorities scrutinized visas of Pakistani citizens there as they suspected that 'anti-national elements' were involved.[54] The *Hindustan Times*, which had criticized the Indian government's handling of the matter (stating that India had constitutional provisions to deal with such literature, and protestors could not take the law in their own hands), alleged a conspiracy behind the protests

---

[44] *Dawn*, 8 September 1956.
[45] *Dawn*, 9 September 1956.
[46] *Dawn*, 10 September 1956.
[47] *Dawn*, 14 September 1956.
[48] *Dawn*, 8 September 1956.
[49] *Dawn*, 19 September 1956.
[50] *Dawn*, 21 September 1956, editorial 'Today's Protest'.
[51] *Dawn*, 22 September 1956.
[52] *Dawn*, 25 September 1956.
[53] *Dawn*, 28 September 1956.
[54] *Hindustan Times*, 8 September 1956.

and the attendant violence in India. It claimed that telegrams with directions had been sent to many towns in Uttar Pradesh, that communal organizations had joined hands, and that the issue was raised in the Uttar Pradesh Legislative Assembly by a Congress member who was president of the Uttar Pradesh Jamiat-ul-Ulema. It observed that the proximity of the general elections increased the 'bellicosity of Muslim leadership in UP'.[55] In a public speech in Delhi, Nehru declared that the controversy over the book had continued in Pakistan long after it was over in India, that the Muslim League was behind the agitation in Pakistan and that communal organizations in India were fanning trouble here. He appealed to his audience not to fall prey to incitement.[56]

The Pakistani Prime Minister, H.S. Suhrawardy, wrote to Nehru expressing worry about the riots, and stating that public opinion in his country was agitated about the matter. Nehru explained the measures taken by India to curb the publication of the book, and launched a counter-offensive. He found it 'surprising', he wrote:

> ... that all this animus should have been directed against India when the book is really an American book which has been before the public for fifteen years. It is possible that the book might have been sold in Pakistan also during these years without any objection being taken. Indeed, there are other books which contain rather objectionable remarks about the Prophet Muhammad. I think, H.G. Well's Outline of History is one of them. Then there is another book by H.A. Davies which I am told was actually prescribed as a text book by the Pakistan Board of Education till last year. Evidently, this was due to an oversight and the book was subsequently withdrawn.[57]

Nehru also made it clear to his Pakistani counterpart that he believed that the trouble in India occurred not so much on account of the book per se, but on account of reproduction of its extracts in the *Siyasat*, the newspaper from Kanpur. He suggested that some Pakistanis had also been involved in the disturbances in India.[58] In the Indian Parliament, the Ministry of External

---

[55] *Hindustan Times*, 8 and 11 September 1956.

[56] Nehru's speech in Delhi, 23 September 1956, *SWJN2*, vol. 35, 8–10.

[57] Letter from Nehru to Suhrawardy, 23 October 1956, *SWJN2*, vol. 35, 269–270.

[58] *SWJN2*, vol. 35, 270. A few years previously, a banned Pakistani newspaper had led the Indian police to arrest a man in Amreli suspected of being a Pakistani spy. Postal officials who intercepted copies of the banned Gujarati daily *Milap*, published from Karachi, in the post alerted the police, who searched the house of the addressee, and found copies of the same newspaper. *Times of India*, 4 August 1953.

affairs stated that a protest had been lodged with the Pakistan government regarding the mobbing of the Indian High Commissioner's residence there. The Government of Pakistan had denied any insult to the Indian national flag, claimed that students who tried to enter the premises were dispersed, and action was taken against the 'misguided and irresponsible urchins' who had participated in the protest. They also expressed regret for the inconvenience caused to the High Commission.[59] The Karachi administration banned the book in the last week of September 1956.[60]

The Legacy

Although no specific law was passed against communal publications by the Central government, in September 1956 the Punjab Vidhan Sabha (Legislative Assembly) unanimously passed the Punjab Special Powers (Press) Bill, citing the contribution of the press in that state to fanning inter-communal strife. The new law gave the state executive the power to impose pre-censorship on publications.[61] In May 1959, Nehru asked all Chief Ministers to instruct district officials that they were not to permit 'any type of communal propaganda in speech or news-sheets and nip this in the bud'.[62] The GOI under Nehru's direction did exercise censorship over *Living Biographies*, but not via banning. Instead, the book was removed from circulation by ordering the publishers to do so, and this measure was amply publicized. Legal action was taken, however, against the newspaper editor who had published inflammatory articles.

The *Living Biographies* case provides a good illustration of the enormous complexity surrounding censorship issues. Irrespective of the truth claims of India and Pakistan (the former alleging that Pakistani agents were involved in creating the controversy over a book long in circulation, the latter alleging that Nehru's India was not a secular state) agitation over the book was costing human lives and disruption of normal life at various places in India. Nehru

---

[59] LS Debates, series 2, vol. 1 (10–22 May 1957), 22 May 1957, col. 1357–1358.

[60] *Times of India*, 24 September 1956. The Karachi administration also banned H.G. Wells' *A Short History of the World* and H.A. Davies' *An Outline of the History of the World* for being 'outrageous to Islam'.

[61] In an editorial titled 'Pre-Censorship', the *Times of India* commented that these powers were likely to be misused, and that since abetment to crime was in any case an offence in the ordinary law, no special provision for the press was required. *Times of India*, 8 September 1956.

[62] *LCM*, vol. 5, 244, 18 May 1959.

clearly distinguished between state censorship of political criticism and of what he called 'offensive communal writings', and advocated only the latter. As with examples of offensive/offending publications discussed elsewhere in this book, protests against *Living Biographies* and demands for it to be banned resulted in enormous publicity being given to the offending material, something that Nehru commented upon. By exhorting the public to boycott newspapers given to publishing communally inflammatory matter, Nehru advocated censorship by public boycott. At any rate, at this point, with human lives at stake, there was no questioning of, or railing against, some or the other variety of censorship for some or the other reason. According to the journalist Vir Sanghvi, the precedent was established during the tenure of Indira Gandhi and Rajiv Gandhi as Prime Ministers that 'if a book, or even a painting, could provoke riots, then it was better to ban it than to risk loss of life'. Writing in 1998, Sanghvi argued that while upper-middle classes in India were growing increasingly liberal, politicians and special interest groups were 'opening the floodgates of mass agitation'. As this chapter has shown, the floodgates were never closed in the first place.

Conclusion

This book has examined formal as well as informal measures of censorship in colonial and post-colonial India. The latter included friendly chats with editors, threats of prosecution and a system of voluntary censorship, or 'press advice', during and after the Second World War. Censorship did not always involve an intolerant censor with a red pencil; it could be achieved equally successfully over a cup of tea. What are the insights generated by this historical survey of three crucial decades?

'Liberal Imperialism', Public Opinion and Anxiety

After a detailed and careful study of the operation of the 1908 Newspapers Act in colonial India, historian Robert Darnton concludes that the colonial state in India censored via elaborate trials rather than more drastic methods in order to demonstrate the justice of their rule to the ruled, and to themselves. In his words, 'Liberal imperialism was the greatest contradiction of them all; so the agents of the Raj summoned up as much ceremony as they could, in order to prevent themselves from seeing it.'[1] The 'legal ritual' was, in his opinion, 'to demonstrate the justice of their rule to the "natives", and even more important, to themselves'.[2] As this book has shown, at every step the colonial state attempted to make its censorship measures legally unassailable. The legal ritual manifested itself when the state tackled mass movements too.[3]

---

[1] Darnton, 'Literary Surveillance in the British Raj', 167–168.

[2] Ibid.

[3] Sucheta Mahajan, *Independence and Partition: The Erosion of Colonial Power in India* (New Delhi: Sage, 2000), 119. Mahajan contends that the colonial state tried to avoid 'a naked show of force' at all times, and 'even mass movements were sought to be dealt with constitutionally'.

This oxymoron—'Liberal Imperialism'—has been explained by historian Peter Robb thus: 'Repression was thus represented as liberal in a higher sense, because it sought to prevent the perversion of public opinion, and because it protected a great work in which no fundamental change was needed.'[4] In this sense, censorship was a measure of protection for the Indian public (to prevent them from going astray). Censorship is dependent on surveillance and complementary to propaganda. Richard Popplewell, in his book on intelligence gathering in colonial India between 1904 and 1924, comments on the self-image of the GOI as that of a 'fair-playing' state; one which used intelligence gathering minimally and only in exceptional circumstances.[5] Like intelligence-gathering activities, censorship too conflicted with the self-image of a liberal colonial state.[6]

But one also gets a sense of a government desperate for support from the Indian population. The overwhelming interest of the colonial state in keeping tabs on the Indian press is explained by the press' pivotal role as the purveyor of public opinion. Whereas democratic states rely on periodical elections to gauge popular feelings, non-democratic ones (insofar as they do not suppress the press in totality) must necessarily rely on the press for this purpose. The various measures of information control via censorship (and also propaganda) indicate the importance attached to that vague, intangible thing called 'public opinion'. Where one would intuitively expect a colonial state to ride roughshod over public opinion (since it was not dependent on the people in terms of soliciting their votes to retain power), in reality one gets a sense of a state constantly monitoring and seeking to evaluate and influence public opinion, denying statements in the press that showed it in a bad light, and rallying moderate opinion at every opportunity. One is tempted to conclude that the stones of empire rested on the shifting foundations of 'public opinion'. Surely that is a telling comment on official perception of the nature—and stability—of the colonial state in India at the turn of the century.

---

[4] Robb makes this comment in the course of his analysis of the 1910 Press Act. Robb, *The Evolution of British Policy*, 302.

[5] In Popplewell's words, 'A strong aversion to the use of spies was one of the alien traditions of government which the British brought to India'. Richard J. Popplewell, *Intelligence and Imperial Defence: British Intelligence and the Defence of the Indian Empire 1904–1924* (London: Frank Cass, 1995), 10 and 33–36.

[6] As Ranajit Guha puts it, 'What made it [the Raj] worse and difficult to forge was the absurdity of Britain's claim to have fitted the roundedness of colonial autocracy to the squareness of metropolitan liberalism.' Ranajit Guha, 'Not at Home in Empire' in *Postcolonial Passages: Contemporary History Writing on India*, ed. Saurabh Dube, 38–46 (New Delhi: Oxford University Press, 2004), 40.

The overwhelming concern of the colonial state with public opinion meant that censorship was carried out not only to proscribe or ban publications but also as a means of exercising surveillance over what was being written and debated in the public sphere. This study suggests that non-democratic states can be acutely conscious of criticism and more vigilant about public opinion than democratic ones, since they are less sure of their standing and legitimacy. A colonial state displaying great concern for public opinion: *this* is the paradox of the British colonial state in India. Soli Sorabjee has argued that those in power want censorship regulations as '... it is the fear about the stability of the current regime, its security, which is often equated with security of the State, which impels intolerance and consequent imposition of censorship to effectuate the popularity and ensure continuance of the regime'. [7] In other words, censorship emanates not from a position of strength, but one of weakness. A study of colonial and post-colonial censorship in India is necessarily a study of anxiety. [8] This book has indicated how censorship gives us insights into the weaknesses and anxieties—as opposed to the strengths and certainties—of the state in India.

The colonial state had a self-image of itself that is most visible in colonial discourse. In their official correspondence and decisions, British colonial officials constantly tried to reconcile their personal ideas about the freedom of the press as an abstract principle with the necessities of colonial rule, which demanded that the press be gagged. To justify this, they invoked the idea of 'public interest', wherein the state claimed to guard the vast majority of uneducated Indians against dangerous ideas that might mislead them. While measures taken to control the press and subsequent prosecution proceedings show that the government was keen to stem violent opposition to its existence, there is also a sense one gets of a government desperate for support from the majority of the Indian population, who they thought liable to be 'misguided' by what they read in print. In independent India, paternalistic views about Indians continued to flourish among state personnel.

---

[7] Sorabjee, 'Intolerance, Censorship and Freedom of the Press', 50.

[8] Ranajit Guha has made a forceful case for the study of anxiety in the context of empire; he urges a questioning of the conventional image of empire 'as a sort of a machine operated by a crew who know only how to decide but not to doubt, who know only action but no circumspection, and, in the event of a breakdown, only fear and no anxiety'. Ranajit Guha, 'Not at Home in Empire', 42. Yasmin Khan among others has pointed to 'authoritarian violence' as a 'product of a government in a position of weakness' rather than of strength in the last days of the Raj. Khan, *The Great Partition*, 29.

Another remarkable argument put forth by colonial officials was that the 'tyranny' of the press actually hampered the free expression of many shades of opinion, by giving vent overwhelmingly to anti-government views. In any case, by the 1920s, as this book has shown, the colonial state was not the only entity dictating what newspapers could and could not publish (or indeed, what books Indians could or could not read). The fact that the most prominent nationalist leaders such as Nehru and Gandhi were writing for or running newspapers meant that they enjoyed a crucial power over public opinion, including when they were imprisoned. Even when he was in prison, Nehru wrote notes to the editor of the English daily *National Herald*, M. Chalapathi Rau, on editorial matters. The *National Herald* was run by a company called Associated Journals, of which Nehru was the chairman. The notes, written between 1938 and 1942, included various suggestions: while giving publicity to the *satyagraha* movement the newspaper was to emphasize Congress ideology and objectives, the newspaper was to leave no reader in doubt that the 'one and only issue is Indian independence', it was 'not necessary to refer often to these so-called peace efforts and needless publicity should not be given to them in the way of display', captions such as 'Vote for Gandhi' were to be avoided as his name was not to be exploited for election or in any other way, and so on.[9]

Censorship in a Time of War

Much like a juggler, the GOI during the Second World War had to keep an eye on three objects simultaneously: keeping civilian and military morale high, suppressing rumour, and keeping 'bad news' away from Japanese and German propaganda agencies. As this book has shown, suppression of news could lead to alarmist rumours, its non-suppression to panic and loss of morale among the civilian population. Complete censorship was not in the interest of the colonial state either, as it would leave the field free for rumour in India and for publication of exaggerated stories abroad, in the American press, for example. Cooperation with the press was supplemented by a safety net of laws, ordinances and regulations, to which resort was taken when cooperation had reached its limits.

---

[9] These notes are recounted in Rau, *Journalism*, 50–55. After 1947 Nehru never wrote anything for the *National Herald* in consideration of propriety. The newspaper only published his Independence Day messages, which were given to the entire press. Rau, *Journalism*, 103 and 144.

The tolerance of the press and public both in India and Britain for state censorship increased considerably during times of war. This is as true today as it was 70 years ago.[10] In the words of war correspondent Margaret Bourke-White, 'No correspondent objects if censors stick to the rules. Censorship is intended to serve the very important purpose of military security.'[11] Although the press and public opinion were more likely to accept censorship on military rather than political grounds, as the war drew on it became impossible to separate the military from the political. This was especially true of India, where political 'bad news' (from the colonial state's perspective) could either be used by Axis powers for propaganda, or divert and distract the state's resources towards quelling internal disturbances. Censorship in India during the war years was political *and* military.

Gerald Barrier suggests that although censorship measures used by the state in India during the Second World War were similar to those used during the First World War, censorship became even more elaborate due to the presence of the Japanese threat. He suggests that the colonial state, with its new, urgent priorities tried to reduce conflict with its political opponents in India.[12] This is borne out by the evidence, and the organized press (which was well aware of the role it could play in mobilizing support for or against the state) was able to negotiate terms of control with the state in a way that had never before been possible. The narrative of press–government relations in the 1940s is, contrary to the conventional image, not one of state repression alone. Although journalists served as MLAs even in the 1930s, their co-option into the state as censors or press advisers grew stronger during the war years. This was a double-edged sword with regard to freedom of expression. That wartime censorship could have a lasting impact on press–government relations even after the war ended was suspected not only in India but also in Britain, where the British Institute of Journalists submitted a memorandum to the Royal Commission on the Press in 1947 stating that the system of Public Relations Officers in government departments had established the danger of press censorship.[13]

---

[10] An Indian journalist who covered the Kargil war in 1999 recalled that he was asked by an Indian army officer not to report a story of a severed head (probably that of a Pakistani officer) hanging from a tree in Drass. 'It was war; no one did, though a newsmagazine did carry something, a sanitized story of a body hanging from a tree.' Srinjoy Chowdhury, *Despatches from Kargil* (New Delhi: Penguin, 2000), 191–192.

[11] Bourke-White, *Portrait of Myself*, 252.

[12] Barrier, *Banned*, 144–145.

[13] *Times of India*, 18 September 1947.

In India, we have seen examples of provincial governments being asked by the GOI to 'sound' editors about not publishing this or the other news items (reports of Vinoba Bhave's anti-war speeches, for example). After the war was over, the *Times of India* lauded the consultative machinery as a positive legacy and urged its continuation, stating that direct contact with the local press would be more effective in countering irresponsible newspapers than direct censorship.[14] The Press Advisory system, a legacy of the Second World War, continued functioning well into the late 1940s, and even after Independence.[15] Even some years after the war ended, Provincial PACs, when shown samples of writings deemed objectionable by the state government, called upon editors to explain their actions, and then recommended measures to the government.[16] During the war years, even as the Indian press consolidated itself and, for the most part, presented a united front to the GOI in the form of the AINEC, the co-option of journalists in PACs made 'voluntary censorship' a reality, and marked an important step in the process of informalization of censorship, a tendency that was exacerbated, as this book has demonstrated, after Independence.

Censorship in a Time of Transition

In interviews given to foreign correspondent Taya Zinkin in the 1950s, Nehru alluded to the changed priorities in independent India, as well as to the question of continuity with the colonial regime. In 1950 he candidly expressed his opinion thus:

> ... you must realize that in the backward countries, individual liberty matters much less than mass welfare. The free world's first emphasis should be therefore on mass welfare rather than on liberty.... To the Indian peasant all this talk about freedom is meaningless noise; the only things he is interested in are food, clothes and housing.[17]

---

[14] *Times of India*, 'Censorship', editorial, 12 September 1945.

[15] Although a Press Consultative Committee had been set up by the Congress government of UP in 1938, it was only during the Second World War that the idea of censorship by collaboration between the state and the press was enforced on a large scale. For an account of the functioning of the UP Press Consultative Committee, see Mazumdar, *Indian Press and Freedom Struggle*, 59–64.

[16] In April 1949 the CP PAC was shown, by the Chief Secretary, samples of objectionable writing in a meeting presided over by the Chief Minister. *Times of India*, 16 April 1949.

[17] Taya Zinkin, *Reporting India* (London: Chatto and Windus, 1962), 205–206. This interview was conducted on 30 June 1950.

In another interview to her in November 1954, on his return from China and comparing India's experience with the Chinese one, Nehru said:

> We got our independence far too easily. How I envy Mao, the Long March! What a test for men it was. We did not have the Long March, we had it easy. I cannot blame the British for this ... but I must recognize that what we have gained in continuity we have lost in spring cleaning.... We still have the same administration; it still works in the same way; progress is slowed down because we have not had a revolution, only evolution. But then ... we are the product of our history; we cannot change our heritage.[18]

If the operation of colonial censorship is a window in to the functioning of the colonial state, then post-colonial censorship policies provide no less an insight into the post-colonial Indian nation state. Academics have long debated the nature of the Nehruvian post-colonial Indian state: some have argued that it displays marked continuity with its colonial predecessor, while others have argued that it was a new creature. Judith Brown has described the period after Independence as one where Nehru's generation had to either 'work with or transform existing modes of governance'.[19] She has posited that since the Indian Constitution drew 'very heavily' on the Act of 1935, 'it was no surprise that the way government was structured and functioned bore such a family likeness to the imperial regime which has preceded it, despite its proclamation of new national goals and principles'.[20] She adds that inheriting the Raj without a social or political revolution was good for stability, but in the longer term brought its own dilemmas.[21] David Washbrook exemplifies the

---

[18] Zinkin, *Reporting India*, 209.

[19] Judith M. Brown, *Nehru: A Political Life* (New Haven: Yale University Press, 2003), 3.

[20] Ibid., 204.

[21] These dilemmas were not over free speech alone, but included the problem of trying to control tendencies that its stewards (anti-colonial nationalists) had actively encouraged when they were the opposition to the colonial state. Concern about students joining political groups and avoiding the politicization of the defence forces are obvious examples. It was not that post-colonial leaders were not warned about the possibility of facing opposition once they assumed power. For example, in an interview in 1967, Mountbatten recalled that he had dissuaded Nehru from laying a wreath at the Indian National Army memorial in Singapore (during the latter's visit there in March 1946) by convincing him that they were not devoted patriots but people who could not withstand Japanese captivity, and who had tortured other Indians. Mountbatten

'continuity argument' (with regard to the colonial to post-colonial transition) by suggesting that conservative approaches to democracy and development 'became embedded in institutional practices and professional ideologies taken over wholesale by the newly independent state' and exercised 'subtle, often unseen, restraints on the imagined freedoms which India's politicians thought they had won'.[22] Partha Chatterjee too has argued that the post-colonial state only expanded the institutions it inherited from the colonial one.[23] On the other hand, Benjamin Zachariah urges that the continuity argument needs to be more nuanced than has hitherto been the case. In his words, 'The similarities ... between late imperial and early national state in India, however evocative, may well be overdrawn. The structural similarities are obvious; and yet these structures are put to various different projects.' [24] Sugata Bose and Ayesha Jalal—referring not to the state but to attitudes of Indian nationalists in the colonial and post-colonial periods—express the opinion that 'official nationalism as articulated and practiced by the post-colonial state became increasingly far removed from the ideals propagated in the anti–colonial period'. In the realm of press censorship this certainly seems to have been the case.[25]

---

recalled telling Nehru: 'When you get your independence and have your own army, the people you want are those who remain loyal to their oath, and who will stay with you, and not the people who just change according to political opportunism. Otherwise you will find that if you become unpopular in your own country one day, the opposition party will call on the army to turn you out.' Nehru took his advice and cancelled his visit. Mountbatten, interviewed by B.R. Nanda, 26 July 1967, 4–5, NMML OHP.

[22] David Washbrook, 'The Rhetoric of Democracy and Development in Late Colonial India', in Nationalism, Democracy and Development: State and Politics in India, ed. Sugata Bose and Ayesha Jalal, 36–49 (New Delhi: Oxford University Press, 1997), 37.

[23] For example, Partha Chatterjee asserts that 'the postcolonial state in India has after all only expanded and not transformed the basic institutional arrangements of colonial law and administration, of the courts, the bureaucracy, the police, the army, and the various technical services of government'. Chatterjee, The Nation and Its Fragments, 15.

[24] Benjamin Zachariah, 'The Creativity of Destruction: Wartime Imaginings of Development and Social Policy, c. 1942–46', in The World in World Wars: Experience, Perceptions and Perspectives from Africa and Asia, ed. Heike Liebau, Katrin Bromber, Katharina Lange, Dyala Hamzah and Ravi Ahuja (Leiden: Brill, 2010), 578.

[25] Sugata Bose and Ayesha Jalal, 'Nationalism, Democracy and Development', in Nationalism, Democracy and Development, ed. Bose and Jalal, 1–9, 2.

The change-or-continuity question between the colonial and the post-colonial states in India is one that cannot be answered definitively on the basis of a study of only one kind of state activity but it is nevertheless possible to chart certain trends.[26] This book, by placing its object of study in a chronological parenthesis that spans the divide from unfree to free India, has argued that while the continuities are obvious, the changes are more significant, the most crucial one being what has been termed here the 'informalization of censorship'. While colonial policies and practices pertaining to censorship were retained in early post-colonial India (weighing the balance in favour of the continuity argument) there were very important changes, in 1950s India, in the way the press was perceived by the state. Nehru rather astutely turned the concept of press freedom on its head by arguing that it consisted not only of the freedom to criticize the government of the day but also that of being free from 'proprietorial chains'.[27] He also emphasized that he was not going back on his ideals—that although he stood by every word he had said in the past in favour of the freedom of expression, 'I stand for a little more than that—for the freedom of India....'[28] By thus positing the untrammeled exercise of freedom of expression against the freedom of India, and referring often and in vague terms to 'the great dangers facing the world', Nehru successfully pushed the FA through. The colonial state claimed to protect Indians from the irresponsible ideas of nationalist leaders; the national state claimed to protect Indians from the manipulation to which they were subject by other, richer Indians.

The 'Informalization' of Censorship

There were changes in the press–government relationship too which aided the informalization of censorship. The 'Nehruvian consensus' (defined as

---

[26] In his study of cinema censorship, and focusing on the report of the Indian Cinematograph Committee 1927–28, M. Madhava Prasad has discussed how censorship guidelines formulated during the colonial period reflected conservative concerns, and commented that the post-colonial Indian state 'would continue with the same censorship rules informed by the same colonial logic', as 'nationalists, with power in their own hands, began to find comfort in the conservative opinion they had so firmly opposed'. M. Madhava Prasad, 'The Natives Are Looking: Cinema and Censorship in Colonial India' in *Narratives of Indian Cinema*, ed. Manju Jain (Delhi: Primus Books, 2009).

[27] Nehru made similar statements on many occasions, but was greeted with 'wild cheers' in Parliament on 18 May 1951 when he said this. *Hindustan Times*, 18 May 1951.

[28] *Hindustan Times*, 30 May 1951.

one 'based on a loose acceptance of four principles—socialism, democracy, secularism and non-alignment')[29] had implications for this process. On the one hand, support of the general population (including journalists) was guaranteed to the national state in the 1950s in ways in which it was denied to an alien colonial state until 1947. At the same time, there is consensus among journalists whose careers spanned the colonial–post-colonial divide that the Indian press lost a sense of mission with the coming of Independence.[30] One termed it 'a shift from evangelism to professionalism', that is, from single minded pursuit of a shared goal to a diversification of interests.[31] Another change after Independence was that as the social and racial distance between politicians and journalists blurred, their relationship became more intimate, or—to put it more cynically—more amenable to subtle pressures. Some editors of the mainstream press have also pointed to an obligation they felt, at least in the first few years after Independence, to support the fledgling government.[32] Thus, while Nehru thought, in the 1950s, that the press was controlled by proprietors (amounting to market censorship), several prominent journalists living and working at the time have recalled in their memoirs that the censorship on them was of the self-imposed variety, as a way for them to participate in the project of nation-building. However, there is an alternate viewpoint. The relationship of the ruling Congress with the press in the 1950s was also complicated. The press historian S. Natarajan, writing about this phase, has quipped that the Indian press 'felt it was able to support the Congress in adversity much more than endure it in prosperity'.[33]

---

[29] Achin Vanaik, *The Furies of Indian Communalism: Religion, Modernity, and Secularization* (London: Verso, 1997), 301.

[30] Personal interview, B.G. Verghese, New Delhi, 15 November 2011. According to Verghese, in the colonial period the press had a sense of mission, and there was internal discipline: 'Everyone was on the same side.' He described the change in the Indian press from before Independence to the present in the following phrase: 'From mission to commerce is how I would describe it.' This sentiment is also expressed by K.G. Joglekar, N.S. Jagannathan, K. Rama Rao and many other journalists. See also B.G. Verghese, *First Draft: Witness to the Making of Modern India* (New Delhi: Tranquebar, 2010).

[31] Jagannathan, *Independence and the Indian Press*, 134.

[32] Frank Moraes, editor of the *Times of India* and biographer of Nehru, refers to the trend of journalists throwing their weight behind Parliament immediately after Independence, and even the *Times of India* acting as 'an unofficial opposition outside Parliament' only after the first general election in 1952. Moraes, *Witness to an Era*, 314.

[33] S. Natarajan, *A History of the Press in India*, 235.

A notable aspect of the FA relating to Article 19 is the substitution of 'incitement to offence' for the clause used in colonial acts, 'incitement to violence'. The mere substitution of one term by another reveals something fundamental about the nature of the post-colonial state in India, and its divergence from its predecessor. Both the colonial and the post-colonial states claimed a monopoly over violence. But the colonial state had a narrower concern with violence directed against *itself*; the post-colonial state, on the other hand, had to take cognizance of many more social and economic offences, including but not limited to violent ones. According to Rajnarayan Chandavarkar, the colonial state used repressive laws to stem violent opposition to itself, because it lacked cultural hegemony. On the other hand, states Chandavarkar, the post-colonial state could maintain order using a network of social and cultural ties.[34] This explains the reliance of the post-colonial state to informal measures of censorship.

If a generalization can be made across these periods, it is this: it is much easier for a state to champion free speech as an abstract ideal in public than it is to accept or defend the consequences of every instance of its use. Writing in 1937, the secretary of the Indian Civil Liberties Union, K.B. Menon, argued that a free press in a colonial context was nothing but an 'idle expectation', where the state was not established by the will of the people.[35] He still found merit in fighting for a free press on the grounds that it alone guaranteed the safety of the individual against the state. In the post-colonial period, when the state was established by the will of the people, the fight for a free press had to be fought nevertheless, as the debate over the FA indicates.

Informalization of censorship was driven by the reluctance of the post-colonial state to invite comparisons with its colonial predecessor. Even as Nehru regularly reminded Chief Ministers not to censor political criticism using laws, the Punjab government, as we have seen, used intimidation of journalists as a means of preventing the publication of critical matter in the press, while the Bombay government withdrew patronage (withdrawal of government advertisements) to achieve the same result. Writing about the post-colonial trend in India of amending and continuing to use colonial laws, Robin Jeffrey writes that '… in India in the first thirty years after independence, the small donkey of the erstwhile colonial state was laden with a load it was not created to

---

[34] Chandavarkar, *Imperial Power and Popular Politics*, 178.
[35] K.B. Menon, *The Press Laws of India* (Bombay: Indian Civil Liberties Union, 1937), 50.

bear'.[36] In the present case, the analogy is somewhat different: the post-colonial Indian state was reluctant to use the donkey, and did not know how else to carry the load. This ambivalence translated into ever-increasing informalization of censorship, which not only makes its history more difficult to trace but also its operation more pernicious on account of being more discretionary.

The evidence, as gathered from a survey of official debates over banning books, supports Francis Hutchins' contention that British attitudes were 'never monolithic orthodoxy', but characterized by dialogue and dissent.[37] On the other hand, the colonial state, as well as the post-colonial one, both legitimized censorship by creating a monolithic image of the Indian public in need of protection from various influences—communal, communist and others. For both periods the evidence suggests that the state did not function as a monolith speaking in one voice everywhere, but was beset with tensions and contradictions. The ideological foundations justifying the need for state censorship continued (characterized primarily by a distrust of the press) from colonial to post-colonial India, strengthened further by the Partition experience, even though the precise administration of censorship changed from time to time. If one accepts that censorship is a nod, albeit surreptitious, to the power of ideas and the words that express them, then this was a presumption shared by both states.

The Banning Impulse

This book has established that the political context in which publications appeared was *the* decisive factor when it came to the censorship of publications in India. Studies of censorship in contexts other than India have established that the 'projected size and nature of a publication's readership can form a decisive factor in the censor's decision to ban and that the censor himself posits a certain kind of reader when he evaluates a work'.[38] Though these and other factors, termed and discussed in this book as the 'Ban Formula',

---

[36] Robin Jeffrey, 'Monitoring Newspapers and Understanding the Indian State', *Asian Survey* 34, no. 8 (August 1994): 748–763. He makes this statement in the context of the Press and Registration of Books Act, 1867, which was amended after the recommendations of the First Press Commission.

[37] Francis Hutchins, *The Illusion of Permanence: British Imperialism in India* (Princeton: Princeton University Press, 1967), xii.

[38] Margreet De Lange, *The Muzzled Muse: Literature and Censorship in South Africa* (Amsterdam; Philadelphia: John Benjamins Publishing Company, 1997), 2.

were important in deciding the fate of publications, context was crucial. The relationship between banning and increase in sales was always on the mind of colonial censors. Persecution of a newspaper could enlist considerable public sympathy—and financial support—for it.[39] Debates between colonial officials over the success or otherwise of instituting a prosecution against an author—and the repercussions of a failed prosecution—lay bare to us an anxious colonial state, not an authoritarian one. For anti-colonial nationalists in India, books banned by the colonial state acquired a virtuous halo, a fact which was known to the colonial state, and which also explains its reluctance to ban certain books. Indeed, the causal relationship between banning, on the one hand, and publicity and increased sales (or, in contemporary times, instant availability on the internet), on the other, is not only a universal one, but one which exercises some measure of restraint on censors as well. As we have seen in all the case studies in Part II of this book, for all their faults, colonial officials engaged seriously with books that were asked to be banned. Very many different state personnel at the very top of the hierarchy—the Home Secretary, the Home Member, the Law Member, the Directors of the Intelligence Bureau and of Public Information, and on occasion even the Viceroy—read the book in question, and debated the merits of banning it extensively before taking a decision on the matter.

Neeti Nair and Arudra Burra have complicated and called into question the common understanding of the meaning of the term 'colonial' in the phrases 'colonial laws' and 'colonial continuity', respectively. Nair has shown how, by the mid-1920s, colonial laws were crafted with the participation of Indian lawmakers (both elected and nominated) in LAs[40] and thus were not 'colonial' insofar as that term is used as a synonym for the British. Burra has argued that the colonial origins of many Indian laws (including those governing freedom of expression) is not enough, in and of itself, to condemn them.[41] In the case of publications deemed obscene, scholars including Deana Heath and Charu Gupta have suggested that Indian legislators, more than colonial officials, took the lead in urging that these be banned in India.[42] In many of the cases

---

[39] When a security amount of 12,000 rupees was demanded from the *National Herald* in May 1942, and the directors (Congress leaders) were despairing of arranging for this huge sum of money, Nehru wrote an editorial about this, and the reading public contributed the sum required in two days, and 80,000 rupees in all within a few days of the appeal. Rau, *Journalism*, 67.

[40] Nair, 'Beyond the "Communal"', 329–330.

[41] Arudra Burra, 'The Cobwebs of Imperial Rule', *Seminar* 615 (2010): 79–83.

[42] As Gupta puts it, 'The fact is that the upper castes and the middle classes, and

discussed in this book, demands for bans of other categories of publications too were raised by Indians, although the final decision was for the colonial state to make. In other words, the state was very much a co-author of a ban, and not its sole creator. A figure like the Congress MLA S. Satyamurti—who wrote to the GOI in 1938 urging them to un-ban many banned books of a political nature, on the grounds that Indians had matured enough politically to read them—had written to the GOI one year earlier asking for two books on India by non-Indians to be banned.[43]

The drive to censor, or to bring about censorship, is a powerful one. In contemporary newspaper articles in the Indian press lamenting or railing against bans from the colonial period that were not lifted by the post-colonial state, the names of certain books appear with regularity. Ironically, most of these books were banned by the colonial state not because they were critical of colonial rule, but because they were critical of Indian society, and the demand for the original ban was in fact made vociferously by Indian nationalists themselves. Censorship in colonial India was not entirely colonial. In other words, there was nothing peculiarly colonial about the desire to censor publications. The censored of one generation are often the censors of the next. This was as true of 16th-century Germany,[44] 17th-century England[45] and

---

sometimes others, adopted an ambiguous position, often complicit with British attitudes, even when they challenged imperial power.' Gupta, *Sexuality, Obscenity, Community*, 111. See also Charu Gupta, '"Dirty" Hindi Literature: Contests About Obscenity in Late Colonial North India', *South Asia Research* 20, no. 2 (2000): 89–118. Deana Heath has shown that Indian members of the Imperial legislature were keener than British officials of the GOI to stop the circulation of obscene publications in India by signing the Obscene Publications Convention of 1923. The reason for this, Heath suggests, was that Indian members viewed this as a way to stem what they considered corrupt influences from the West. Heath, 'Purity, Obscenity and the Making of an Imperial Censorship System', 166.

[43] Cited in Barrier, *Banned*, 135.

[44] Even though religious reformer Martin Luther's works were banned, he himself 'endorsed censorship and acknowledged the power of the written word when he urged his immediate temporal lord, the Elector of Saxony, to prohibit the writings of Andreas Bodenstein von Karlstadt, a follower who had gone further and faster than Luther in breaking from Catholicism'. Paul F. Grendler, 'The Advent of Printing' in *Censorship: 500 Years of Conflict* (New York: Oxford University Press, 1984), 29.

[45] The first list of that may not be sold, printed or brought in to England was issued by Henry VIII in 1529, and this list included 'heretical and blasphemous' books of and related to Luther. According to Robert Birley, in the subsequent century, '... it can hardly be said that those who fought for it were defenders of the liberty of the

19th-century Egypt.[46] Present-day state interference with the publication of views in India—online or in traditional media—may dismay us, but it should not surprise us. The myth of Indian exceptionalism is just that: a myth.

Writing of contemporary India, Mini Chandran comments on the indifference of the state to literary creations unless they are deemed 'seditious' or 'blasphemous'; in the latter scenario, she posits, pressure groups and mobs have taken on the onus of banning-by-intimidation. This, in her words, is the 'democratization of censorship'; as Chandran puts it (referring to mob censorship): 'In that sense, India seems to be functioning like a true democracy at least in the matter of literary censorship where the will *of* the people is being executed *for* the people *by* the elected representatives of the people.'[47] Though this is true, in the sense that Chandran uses the term, this book has established that the democratization of censorship in India began during, and not after, colonial rule.

Censorship and Creativity

Censorship of news reports as 'control of publicity' and censors as 'press adviser': these were some of the euphemisms used for censorship in India. The penchant of censorship authorities to use euphemisms is universal: Beate Muller notes that since the French Revolution (after which freedom of speech became a desirable, and politically significant, value in the modern consciousness) ruling elites have used euphemisms to justify their censorial practices. In the German Democratic Republic (East Germany), for instance, the licensing branch of the Ministry of Culture was known as 'Central Administration of Publishing Houses and Book Trade'. The process of pre-publication censorship was not called thus, but known as 'procedure to obtain permission to print'.[48]

It is important to remember that repression—whether of words or acts—

Press. If they were successful in gaining power themselves, so that the boot was on the other leg, they were just as anxious to suppress as heretical the works of their opponents'. Robert Birley, *Printing and Democracy* (London: Monotype Corp. Ltd., 1964), 8–9.

[46] In his study of the censorship of European-run and local Arabic newspapers in Egypt from the 1860s to the 1880s, Juan R.I. Cole concludes that following, and in the few years before, the British occupation of Egypt in 1882, 'persons who might otherwise have upheld press freedom were transformed by their colonial role into censors'. Cole, 'Colonialism and Censorship', 59.

[47] Chandran, *The Writer*, 150.

[48] Muller, 'Censorship and Cultural Regulation', 13n40.

could also act as a stimulant, and its absence could occasionally take the edge off protest.[49] Colonial jails could, among other things, be conducive to the production of books. Journalist D.R. Mankekar, who accompanied Nehru on his visit to the United States in 1949, recalled a young girl coming up to the Prime Minister and saying, 'Mr. Nehru, No jail, no books.' [50] Nehru had, after all, written his three most famous books while a guest of colonial jails.[51] Censorship can occasionally spur action and protests that serves the cause of authors. In the Indian context, Shabana Mahmud identifies a causal connection between the banning, in 1933, of the Urdu book *Angaray*, the angry demand for the creation of a 'League of Progressive Authors' made by the four authors who were thus banned, and the formation of the Progressive Writers' Association in 1936.[52] According to Carmen Tisnado, the 'beguiling paradox' of censorship is that 'it is precisely repression and censorship that move people to this enormous courage and creativity'.[53] If there is any consolation to the censored, then this may be it.

Robert Darnton believes that although modern technology in the age of digital communication has furthered the imbalance between state power and citizen's rights, this imbalance has precedents in the past too, in the age of printed texts, which we would be wise to study.[54] The methods by which ideas are disseminated have changed, as have means to regulate and prevent their transmission. The core issues and debates, and certainly the censoring impulse, however, remain the same.

---

[49] D.R. Mankekar recalled that in Karachi in 1931, District Collector Hood refused to arrest or repress the Salt Satyagraha movement, and this worried Congress leaders, 'because without repression the movement could not flourish....' The result was that within a few days the Salt Satyagraha 'just frittered away'. When Hood went on leave and *lathi* (baton) charges began, 'the whole thing flared up like a fire'. Mankekar, interviewed by Dr Aparna Basu, 3 November 1936, 4, NMML OHP.

[50] Mankekar added, 'Now that he was not going to jail there would be no books from him.' Mankekar, interviewed by Dr Aparna Basu, 3 November 1936, 24, NMML OHP.

[51] These are: *Glimpses of World History* (1934), *An Autobiography* (1936) and *The Discovery of India* (1946).

[52] Shabana Mahmud, 'Angarey and the Founding of the Progressive Writers' Association', *Modern Asian Studies* 30, no. 2 (1996): 447–467, 450–451.

[53] Carmen Tisnado, 'Performing the Unspeakable: Defeating Censorship in Two Stories by Mario Benedetti', in *Censorship and Cultural Regulation*, ed. Muller, 169–187, 180.

[54] Robert Darnton, *Censors at Work: How States Shaped Literature* (London: The British Library, 2014), 13.

Epilogue

What does an account of censorship in India over the course of three decades tell us about free speech in India today? Free speech debates in India are no longer the domain of academics alone, as writers and readers weigh in with their views on the debate; apart from reams of articles in newspapers and magazines and TV debates galore, several anthologies have been published in the last couple of years alone, geared towards the general reading public and active citizenry in India.[1] Free speech is interpreted in its broadest sense, including the freedom to eat what one likes, to dress as one pleases, to speak in a language of one's choice, and to believe (or criticize, as the case may be) in ideologies that appeal to or resonate with one (or, indeed, disgust one). In the public discourse around issues of free speech, the argument is very often made that restricting it is against Indian tradition. In this sense, the argument is that free speech should be allowed to exist today because it was allowed to exist in India for millennia.

While it is possible, fortunately, to find many examples to bolster this assertion, it is also unfortunately true that India has had an equally strong tradition of arguments with, and action against, free speech. Delving into a small slice of its rich and diverse history, a blip in time as it were, this book has highlighted the battle in India between free speech and restraint on expression. The story has taken many unexpected turns: Indians have revelled in reading banned books, and they have facilitated, indeed demanded, the banning of them; Indians have died for the power to express their views, but they have also killed for such a privilege. Indians who were powerless, once

---

[1] K. Satchidanandan ed., *Words Matter: Writings against Silence* (Gurgaon: Penguin Viking, 2016) and Ashok Vajpeyi ed., *India Dissents: 3,000 years of Difference, Doubt and Argument* (New Delhi: Speaking Tiger, 2017) are two examples.

they assumed power (in 1937, and after 1946) have demonstrated a volte face on issues of free speech. Other Indians have called them out then, as they do now. What is clear is this: desirable an ideal though free speech is, to make a case for it in India today, we have to return to first-principle arguments, and not to arguments of tradition and history.

Bibliography

Primary Sources

Government of India (GOI) Records
National Archives of India, New Delhi—NAI

Home Political (1900–1947)
Home Public (1900–1947)
Home Judicial (1900–1947)
Central Board of Revenue: Customs Duties (1930–1932)

Debates

Legislative Assembly Debates (1900–1931)
Constituent Assembly Debates (1946–1950)
Parliamentary Debates (Provisional Parliament and House of the People – 1950–1954)
Lok Sabha Debates (1956–1958)

Newspapers (selected years between 1925 and 1960)

Dawn
Hindustan Times
Times of India
Times Literary Supplement (London)
The Statesman
The Times (London)
The Tribune

Interview/Oral History Transcripts
Nehru Memorial Museum and Library, New Delhi—NMML

Das, Durga
Gujral, I.K.

Khanna, D.D.
Khosla, G.D.
Kripalani, J.B.
Mankekar, D.R.
Mountbatten, Lord Louis
Munshi, K.M.
Patwardhan, Achyut
Tandon, P.K.
Verghese B.G. (personal interview)
Yashpal
Zaheer, Sajjad

Private Papers (NMML)

Bhatia, Prem
Keskar, B.V.
Rao, B. Shiva

Government Publications/Selected Works/Correspondence/ Reference Works

Annual Report of the Registrar of Newspapers for India, July 1 to December 31, 1956. New Delhi: Ministry of Information and Broadcasting, Government of India, 1957.

Annual Report of the Registrar of Newspapers for India 1960, Part I. New Delhi: Ministry of Information and Broadcasting, Government of India, 1960.

Census of India 1931. Delhi: Manager of Publications, 1933.

Constitution of India, 1950.

Constitutional Relations between Britain and India. The Transfer of Power, 1942–7, ed. Nicholas Mansergh and E. W. R. Lumby. London: H. M. Stationery Office, 1970–83, vol. 2.

India: A Reference Annual 1953 (first issue)/1954/1956. New Delhi: Ministry of Information and Broadcasting, Government of India.

Manual of Control Orders: A Handbook Containing the Central Control Orders in Force on March 1 1949. New Delhi: Ministry of Industry and Supply, Government of India, 1949.

Moral and Material Progress and Condition of India during the Year 1910–11 /1929–30/1930– 31/1931–32. London: India Office, various years.

Nehru: Letters to Chief Ministers, 1947–1964, ed. G. Parthasarathi, 5 vols. New Delhi: Oxford University Press, 1985–1989.

Nehru–Patel: Agreement Within Differences, Select Documents and Correspondences, 1933– 1950, ed. Neerja Singh. New Delhi: National Book Trust, 2010.

Report of the Committee appointed by the GOI to examine the Press and Registration of Books Act, 1867, the Indian Press Act, 1910, and the Newspaper (Incitement to Offences) Act, 1908. London: 1921.

Report of the Indian Statutory Commission, vol. 1: *Survey, 1930*. London: His Majesty's Stationery Office, 1930.

Report of the Press Commission of India, part 1. Delhi: Manager of Publications, 1954.

Report of the Press Laws Enquiry Committee. Delhi: Manager of Publications, 1948.

Sardar's Letters—Mostly Unknown (Post-Centenary), ed. G.M. Nandurkar. Ahmedabad: Sardar Vallabhbhai Patel Smarak Bhawan, 1977.

Sardar Patel: Collected Works, ed. P.N. Chopra. New Delhi: Konark, 1997.

Sardar Patel's Correspondence: 1945–50, Durga Das, 4 vols. Ahmedabad: Navajivan Publishing House, 1972.

Sardar Patel: Indian Problems (Selected Speeches). Bombay: Director Publications Division, Ministry of Information and Broadcasting, Government of India, Times of India Press, 1948.

Sardar Patel: Select Correspondence, 1945–1950, ed. V. Shankar, 2 vols. Ahmedabad: Navajivan Publishing House, 1977.

Selected Works of Jawaharlal Nehru, Series 1 and 2, ed. S. Gopal. New Delhi: Jawaharlal Nehru Memorial Fund.

Speeches by the Marquess of Linlithgow, vol. 1, 17 April 1936 to 23 April 1938. Simla: Government of India Press, 1940.

The Coronation Number and Who's Who in India, Burma and Ceylon, ed. Thos. Peters. Poona: The Sun Publishing House, 1936.

The India and Pakistan Year Book and Who's Who, vol. XXXVI (1950) and vol. XXXVII (1951). Bombay: *Times of India*.

The Framing of India's Constitution: A Study, ed. B. Shiva Rao. New Delhi: The Indian Institute of Public Administration, 1968.

Towards a Responsible Press: Shri C. Rajagopalachari's Speeches on the Press Bill in Parliament. New Delhi: Publications Division, Government of India, 1952.

Towards Freedom 1937–47, vol. I: *Experiment with Provincial Autonomy 1 January–31 December 1937*), ed. P. N. Chopra. New Delhi: Indian Council for Historical Research, 1985.

Towards Freedom: Documents on the Movement for Independence in India 1938, part I, ed. Basudev Chatterji. New Delhi: Indian Council for Historical Research/ Oxford University Press, 1999.

India Office Records, British Library, London

IOR: MSS EUR F243: Publications Proscribed by the government of India: 1910–47

IOR: MSS EUR F242: Proscription Notifications, United Provinces: 1910–30

National Archives and Records Administration, College Park, USA

Office of Censorship, Record Group 216

Collection of proscribed literature (India Office Library, University of Goettingen Library, Staatsbibliothek Berlin and German Inter-Library Loan System)

Bolitho, William. *Twelve Against the Gods.* London: Penguin, 1939 [1929].

Dibble, R. F. *Mohammed.* New York: The Viking Press, 1929.

Mayo, Katherine. *Slaves of the Gods.* London: Jonathan Cape, 1929.

———. *Volume Two.* New York: The Viking Press, 1926.

Miles, Arthur. *Land of the Lingam.* London: Hurst and Blackett, 1933.

Minney, R.J. *Shiva, or the Future of India.* London: Kegan Paul, 1929.

———. *India Marches Past.* London: Jarrolds Publishers, 1933, 2nd impression.

Murray, Gilbert. *The Cult of Violence.* London: Lovat Dickson Ltd, 1934.

Southgate, D. H. *As a Man's Hand.* London: Methuen & Company, 1937.

Wells, H.G. *The Outline of History: Being a Plain History of Life and Mankind.* New York: Garden City Publishing, 1920.

Memoirs

Aziz, Inam. *Stop Press: A Life in Journalism* (translated from Urdu by Khalid Hasan). Karachi: Oxford University Press, 2008.

Bhatia, Prem. *All My Yesterdays.* New Delhi: Vikas, 1972.

———. *Of Many Pastures.* New Delhi: Allied, 1989.

Bourke-White, Margaret. *Portrait of Myself.* New York: Simon and Schuster, 1963.

Carritt, Michael. *A Mole in the Crown: Memoirs of a British Official in India Who Worked with the Communist Underground in the 1930s.* Calcutta: Rupa, 1986.

Das, Durga. *India from Curzon to Nehru and After.* London: Collins, 1969.

Dwarkadas, Kanji. *India's Fight for Freedom, 1913–37: An Eyewitness Story.* Bombay: Bombay Popular Prakashan, 1966.

Gandhi, M.K. *An Autobiography or My Experiments with Truth,* trans. Mahadev Desai. Ahmedabad: Navajivan Publishing House, 1927; repr. 1969.

Ghosh, Kedar. *No Apology.* New Delhi: Orient Longman, 1971.

Gundevia, Y.D. *In the Districts of the Raj.* Bombay: Disha Books, 1992.

Jung, Sher. *Prison Days: Recollections and Reflections.* New Delhi: BR Publishing Corporation, 1991.

Kamath, M.V. *Behind the By-Line: A Journalist's Memoir.* New Delhi: Vision Books, 1985.

———. *A Journalist at Large.* Mumbai: Jaico, 2006.

Laxman, R.K. *The Tunnel of Time: An Autobiography.* New Delhi: Viking, 1998.

Mankekar, D.R. *Leaves from a War Reporter's Dairy.* New Delhi: Vikas, 1977.

Mehta, Chandralekha. *Freedom's Child: Growing Up during Satyagraha.* New Delhi: Puffin Books, 2008.

Mookerjee, S.P. *Leaves from a Diary.* Calcutta: Oxford University Press, 1993.

Moraes, Frank. *Witness to an Era: India 1920 to the Present Day.* London: Wiedenfeld and Nicolson, 1973.

Nehru, Jawaharlal. *An Autobiography.* New Delhi: J. N. Memorial Fund/Oxford University Press, 1989 [London: John Lane, 1936].

Parthasarathy, Rangaswami. *Memoirs of a News Editor: 30 Years with The Hindu.* Calcutta: Naya Prakash, 1980.

Patel, Kamla. *Torn from the Roots: A Partition Memoir, trans. Uma Randeria.* New Delhi: Kali, 2006; original in Gujarati published in 1977.

Rao, K. Rama. *The Pen as My Sword: Memoirs of a Journalist.* Bombay: Bhartiya Vidya Bhawan, 1965.

Rau, M. Chalapathi. *Journalism and Politics.* New Delhi: Vikas, 1984.

Russell, Wilfrid. *Indian Summer.* Bombay: Thacker and Company, 1951.

Sahgal, Nayantara. *Prison and Chocolate Cake.* New Delhi: Harper Perennial, 2007 [1954].

Sahni, J.N. *Lid Off: Fifty Years of Indian Politics, 1921–71.* New Delhi: Allied, 1971.

———. *Truth about the Indian Press.* New Delhi: Allied, 1974.

Shrinagesh, Jayavant Mallnah. *Between Two Stools: My Life in the ICS Before and After Independence,* ed. Rudolf and Shakuntala Hartog. New Delhi: Rupa, 2007.

Shroff, Hiro. *Down Memory Lane.* Bombay: Eeshwar, 1998.

Stephens, Ian M. *Monsoon Morning.* London: Ernest Benn, 1966.

Talbot, Phillips. *An American Witness to India's Partition.* New Delhi: Sage, 2007.

Tandon, P.D. *Flames from the Ashes: Memoirs of a Lone Traveller.* Allahabad: St. Paul's Society, 1981.

Trumbull, Robert. *As I See India.* New York: William Sloane, 1956.

Verghese, B.G. *First Draft: Witness to the Making of Modern India.* New Delhi: Tranquebar, 2010.

Vijayan, O. V. *A Cartoonist Remembers.* New Delhi: Rupa, 2002.

Vira, Dharma. *Reminiscences.* New Delhi: Vikas, 1990.

Secondary Sources

Books

Anand, Mulk Raj (ed.). *The Historic Trial of Mahatma Gandhi.* New Delhi: National Council of Educational Research and Training, 1987.

Ananda, Prakash. *A History of the Tribune.* New Delhi: The Tribune Trust, 1986.

Anderson, A.J. *Problems in Intellectual Freedom and Censorship.* New York: R. R. Bowker Company, 1974.

Anderson, Benedict. *Imagined Communities: Reflections on the Origins and Spread of Nationalism.* London: Verso Books, 1983.

Bagchi, A.K., Dipankar Sinha and Barnita Bagchi (eds). *Webs of History: Information, Communication and Technology from Early to Post-Colonial India.* New Delhi: Indian History Congress, 2005.

Barns, Margarita. *The Indian Press: A History of the Growth of Public Opinion in India.* London: George Allen & Unwin, 1940.

Barrier, N. Gerald. *Banned: Controversial Literature and Political Control in British India 1907–1947* Columbia: University of Missouri Press, 1974.

———. *American Publishing on India, 1930–85.* New Delhi: Manohar/American Institute of Indian Studies, 1986.

Basu, Durga Das. *Law of the Press in India.* Nagpur: Wadhwa and Company, 2002, 4th ed. [1980].

Bhalla, Alok (ed.). *Partition Dialogues: Memories of a Lost Home.* New Delhi: Oxford University Press, 2006.

Bhargava, G.S. *The Press in India: An Overview.* New Delhi: National Book Trust, 2005.

Bhatia, Gautam. *Offend, Shock, or Disturb: Free Speech under the Indian Constitution.* New Delhi: Oxford University Press, 2016.

Bhattacharya, Sanjoy. *Propaganda and Information in Eastern India 1939–45: A Necessary Weapon of War.* Richmond: Curzon, 2001.

Birley, Robert. *Printing and Democracy.* London: Monotype Corp. Ltd., 1964.

Bose, Brinda (ed.). *Gender and Censorship.* New Delhi: Women Unlimited, 2006.

Bose, Mihir. *The Lost Hero: A Biography of Subhas Bose.* London: Quartet, 1982.

Bose, Nemai Sadhan. *Ramananda Chatterjee.* New Delhi: Publications Division, Ministry of Information and Broadcasting, Government of India, 1974.

Bose, Sugata. *His Majesty's Opponent: Subhas Chandra Bose and India's Struggle against Empire.* New Delhi: Penguin/Allen Lane, 2011.

Boyer, Paul S. *Purity in Print: Book Censorship in America from the Gilded Age to the Computer Age.* Madison: University of Wisconsin Press, 2002, 2nd ed.

Brass, Paul R. *The Production of Hindu–Muslim Violence in Contemporary India.* Seattle: University of Washington Press, 2003.

Brown, Judith M. *Nehru: A Political Life.* New Haven: Yale University Press, 2003.

Calder-Marshall, Arthur. *Lewd, Blasphemous and Obscene.* London: Hutchinson, 1972.

Chandavarkar, Rajnarayan. *Imperial Power and Popular Politics: Class, Resistance and the State in India, c. 1850–1950.* Cambridge: Cambridge University Press, 1998.

Chandra, Bipan, Mridula Mukherjee, Aditya Mukherjee, Sucheta Mahajan and K.N. Panikkar. *India's Struggle for Independence, 1857–1947.* New Delhi: Penguin, 1989 [1988].

Chandrachud, Abhinav. *Republic of Rhetoric: Free Speech and the Constitution of India.* New Delhi: Penguin Random House India, 2017.

Chandran, Mini. *The Writer, the Reader and the State: Literary Censorship in India.* New Delhi: Sage, 2017.

Chatterjee, Partha. *The Nation and Its Fragments: Colonial and Postcolonial Histories.* New Delhi: Oxford University Press, 1994.

———. *Politics of the Governed: Reflections on Popular Politics in Most of the World.* New York: Columbia University Press, 2004.

Chatterji, Probhat Chandra. *Broadcasting in India.* New Delhi: Sage, 1987.

Chibber, Vivek. *Locked in Place: State-Building and Late Industrialization in India.* Princeton: Princeton University Press, 2006 [2003].

Choudhury, Golam Wahed. *Pakistan's Relations with India 1947–1966.* London: Pall Mall Press, 1968.

Chowdhury, Srinjoy. *Despatches from Kargil.* New Delhi: Penguin, 2000.

Coetzee, J.M. *Giving Offense: Essays on Censorship.* Chicago: University of Chicago Press, 1996.

Cohen, Stephen P. *The Idea of Pakistan.* Washington D.C.: Brookings Institution Press, 2004.

Cooper, R.C. (ed.). *Without Fear or Favour: A Selection of Articles by Frank Moraes.* New Delhi: Vikas, 1974.

Daechsel, Marcus. *The Politics of Self Expression: The Urdu Middle-Class Milieu in Mid-Twentieth Century India and Pakistan.* Oxford: Routledge, 2006.

Daily, Jay E. *The Anatomy of Censorship.* New York: Marcel Dekker, 1973.

Darnton, Robert. *The Forbidden Best-Sellers of Pre-Revolutionary France.* New York: Norton, 1996.

———. *Censors at Work: How States Shaped Literature.* London: The British Library, 2014.

De Lange, Margreet. *The Muzzled Muse: Literature and Censorship in South Africa.* Amsterdam; Philadelphia: John Benjamins Publishing Company, 1997.

Dhavan, Rajeev. *Only the Good News: On the Law of the Press in India.* New Delhi: Manohar, 1987.

———. *Publish and Be Damned: Censorship and Intolerance in India.* New Delhi: Tulika, 2008.

Dube, Saurabh (ed). *Postcolonial Passages: Contemporary History-writing on India.* New Delhi: Oxford University Press, 2004.

Elias, Jamal J. *Aisha's Cushion: Religious Art, Perception, and Practice in Islam.* Cambridge, Mass: Harvard University Press, 2012.

Falk, Bertil. *Feroze the Forgotten Gandhi: A Personal Narrative.* New Delhi: Roli Books, 2016.

Ghose, H. P. *Press and Press Laws in India.* Calcutta: D. K. Mitra, 1930.

———. *The Newspaper in India.* Calcutta: University of Calcutta, 1952.

Ghosh, Durba and Dane Kennedy (eds). *Decentering Empire: Britain, India and the Transcolonial World.* New Delhi: Orient Longman, 2006.

Ghosh, Sunit. *Modern History of the Indian Press.* New Delhi: Cosmo Publications, 1998.

Goldstein, Robert Justin. *Political Censorship of the Arts and the Press in Nineteenth-Century Europe.* New York: St. Martin's Press, 1989.

Gopal, Sarvepalli. *British Policy in India 1858–1905.* Cambridge: Cambridge University Press, 1965.

Guha, Ramachandra. *India After Gandhi: The History of the World's Largest Democracy.* New Delhi: Picador, 2007.

Gupta, Charu. *Sexuality, Obscenity, Community: Women, Muslims, and the Hindu Public in Colonial India.* New Delhi: Permanent Black, 2001.

Gupta, Sisir. *India's Relations with Pakistan, 1954–57.* New Delhi: Indian Council of World Affairs, 1958.

Habib, S. Irfan. *To Make the Deaf Hear: Ideology and Programme of Bhagat Singh and His Comrades.* Gurgaon: Three Essays Collective, 2007.

Haight, Anne Lyons. *Banned Books: Informal Notes on Some Books Banned for Various Reasons at Various Times and in Various Places.* New York: R. R. Bowker Company, 1955, 2nd ed. [1935].

Heath, Deana. *Purifying Empire: Obscenity and the Politics of Moral Regulation in Britain, India and Australia.* Cambridge: Cambridge University Press, 2010.

Hodson, Harry V. *The Great Divide: Britain–India–Pakistan.* London: Hutchinson, 1969.

Hutchins, Francis G. *The Illusion of Permanence: British Imperialism in India.* Princeton: Princeton University Press, 1967.

Israel, Milton. *Communications and Power: Propaganda and the Press in the Indian Nationalist Struggle, 1920–1947.* Cambridge: Cambridge University Press, 1994.

Iyengar, A.R. *The Newspaper Press in India.* Bangalore: The Bangalore Press, 1933.

Iyer, V. R. Krishna and Vinod Sethi. *Essays on Press Freedom.* New Delhi: Capital Foundation Society, 1996.

Jackson, Holbrook. *The Fear of Books.* Urbana and Chicago: University of Illinois Press, 2001 [1932].

Jaffrelot, Christophe. *The Hindu Nationalist Movement and Indian Politics, 1925 to the 1990s: Strategies of Identity-Building, Implantation and Mobilization (with special reference to Central India).* London: C. Hurst & Co., 1996 [first published in French in 1993].

Jagannathan, N.S. *Independence and the Indian Press: Heirs to a Great Tradition.* Delhi: Konark, 1999.

Jansen, Sue Curry. *Censorship: The Knot that Binds Power and Knowledge.* New York: Oxford University Press, 1988.

Jayawardena, Kumari. *The White Woman's Other Burden: Western Women and South Asia during British Colonial Rule.* New York: Routledge, 1995.

Jeffrey, Robin. *India's Newspaper Revolution: Capitalism, Politics and the Indian-Language Press, 1977–99.* London: C. Hurst & Co., 2000.

Jha, Manoranjan. *Katherine Mayo and India.* New Delhi: People's Publishing House, 1971.

———. *Civil Disobedience and After: The American Reaction to Political Developments in India during 1930–1935.* Meerut: Meenakshi Prakashan, 1973.

Joglekar, K.G. *Press Freedom: The Indian Story.* New Delhi: Publications Division, Ministry of Information and Broadcasting, Government of India, 2005.

Jones, Derek (ed.). *Censorship: A World Encyclopedia,* 4 vols. London and Chicago: Fitzroy Dearborn, 2001.

Kamra, Sukeshi. *Bearing Witness: Partition, Independence, End of the Raj.* New Delhi: Lotus, Roli Books, 2002.

Kasturi, G. (ed.). *The Hindu Speaks* (compilation of 100 editorials to mark 100 years of the paper). Bombay: Interpress, 1978.

Kaur, Raminder and William Mazzarella (eds). *Censorship in South Asia: Cultural Regulation from Sedition to Seduction.* Bloomington: Indiana University Press, 2009.

Khan, Yasmin. *The Great Partition: The Making of India and Pakistan.* New Delhi: Penguin, 2013 [2007].

———. *The Raj at War: A People's History of India's Second World War.* Gurgaon: Random House India, 2015.

Khosla, G. D. *A Taste of India.* Bombay: Jaico, 1970.

———. *Stern Reckoning: A Survey of the Events Leading upto and Following the Partition of India.* Delhi: Oxford University Press, 1989 [1949].

————. *Pornography and Censorship in India*. New Delhi: India Book Company, 1976.

Kolsky, Elizabeth. *Colonial Justice in British India: White Violence and the Rule of Law*. Cambridge: Cambridge University Press, 2010.

Kudaisya, Gyanesh. *Region, Nation, 'Heartland': Uttar Pradesh in India's Body Politic*. New Delhi: Sage, 2006.

————. *A Republic in the Making: India in the 1950s*. New Delhi: Oxford University Press, 2017.

Kumar, Girja. *Censorship in India: With Special Reference to the Satanic Verses and Lady Chatterley's Lover*. New Delhi: Har-Anand, 1990.

————. *Censorship in India: Studies in Fundamentalism, Obscenity and Law*. New Delhi: Har-Anand, 2009.

Lago, Mary. *"India's Prisoner": A Biography of Edward John Thompson, 1886–1946*. Columbia: University of Missouri Press, 2001.

Lal, Chaman (ed.). *Bhagat Singh: The Jail Notebook and Other Writings*. New Delhi: LeftWord, 2007.

Lovett, Pat. *Journalism in India*. Calcutta: Banna Publishing Company, 1929.

Mackay, Robert. *Half the Battle: Civilian Morale in Britain during the Second World War*. Manchester: Manchester University Press, 2003.

MacKenzie, John M. *Propaganda and Empire: The Manipulation of British Public Opinion, 1880–1960*. Manchester: Manchester University Press, 1984.

Maclean, Kama. *A Revolutionary History of Interwar India: Violence, Image, Voice and Text*. New Delhi: Penguin, 2016.

Mahajan, Sucheta. *Independence and Partition: The Erosion of Colonial Power in India*. New Delhi: Sage, 2000.

Mankekar, D.R. *What Ails the Indian Press: Diagnosis and Remedies*. New Delhi: Somaiya Publications, 1970.

Mazumdar, Aurobindo. *Indian Press and Freedom Struggle, 1937–42*. New Delhi: Orient Longman, 1993.

Menon, K.B. *The Press Laws of India*. Bombay: Indian Civil Liberties Union, 1937.

Metcalf, Barbara D. and Thomas R. Metcalf. *A Concise History of Modern India*. Cambridge: Cambridge University Press, 2006, 2nd ed.

Minattur, Joseph. *Freedom of the Press in India: Constitutional Provisions and Their Application*. The Hague: Martinus Nijhoff, 1961.

Moraes, Frank. *Nehru: Sunlight and Shadow*. Bombay: Jaico, 1964.

Mukherjee, Madhusree. *Churchill's Secret War: The British Empire and the Ravaging of India during World War II*. New York: Basic Books, 2010.

Muldoon, Andrew. *Empire, Politics, and the Creation of the 1935 India Act: Last Act of the Raj*. Farnham: Ashgate, 2009.

Nakaya, Andrea C. (ed.). *Censorship: Opposing Viewpoints*. Farmington Hills, MI: Greenhaven Press, 2005.

Natarajan, J. *History of Indian Journalism (Part II of the Report of the Press Commission)*. New Delhi: Publication Division, Ministry of Information and Broadcasting, 1955.

Natarajan, S. *A History of the Press in India*. Bombay: Asia Publishing House, 1962.

Niazi, Zamir. *The Press in Chains*. New Delhi: Ajanta, 1987.
———. *The Press under Siege*. Karachi: Karachi Press Club, 1992.
———. *The Web of Censorship*. Karachi: Oxford University Press, 1994.
O'Higgins, Paul. *Censorship in Britain*. London: Nelson, 1972.
Oldenburg, Philip. *India, Pakistan, and Democracy: Solving the Puzzle of Divergent Paths*. Oxford: Routledge, 2010.
Omissi, David (ed.). *Indian Voices of the Great War: Soldiers' Letters, 1914–1918*. London: Macmillan, 1999.
Padhy, K.S. *Battle for Freedom of Press in India*. New Delhi: Academic Foundation, 1991.
Padhy, K.S. and R.N. Sahu. *The Press in India: Perspective in Development and Relevance*. New Delhi: Kanishka, 1997.
Padover, Saul K. (ed. and trans.). *Karl Marx on Freedom of the Press and Censorship*. The Karl Marx Library, vol. 4. New York: McGraw Hill, 1974.
Pandey, Gyanendra. *The Ascendancy of the Congress in Uttar Pradesh: Class, Community and Nation in Northern India, 1920–1940*. London: Anthem, 2002.
Patel, Sushila Rani (ed.). *Burning Words*. Bombay: Sumati Publications, 1956.
Paul, S.N. *Public Opinion and British Rule*. New Delhi: Metropolitan, 1979.
Petley, Julian. *Censoring the Word*. London: Seagull Press, 2007.
———. *Censorship: A Beginner's Guide*. Oxford: Oneworld, 2009.
Popplewell, Richard J. *Intelligence and Imperial Defence: British Intelligence and the Defence of the Indian Empire 1904-1924*. London: Frank Cass, 1995.
Raghavan, Srinath. *India's War: The Making of Modern South Asia, 1939–1945*. Penguin: New Delhi, 2016.
Rajan, S.P. Thiaga. *History of Indian Journalism*. Thanjavur: The Columbia House, 1966.
Rao, B. Shiva (ed.). *The Framing of India's Constitution: A Study*, vol. 5. New Delhi: The Indian Institute of Public Administration, 1968.
Rau, M. Chalapathi. *The Press in India*. New Delhi: Allied, 1968.
———. *The Press*. New Delhi: National Book Trust, 1974.
Robb, Peter. *The Evolution of British Policy towards Indian Politics, 1880–1920: Essays on Colonial Attitudes, Imperial Strategies and Bihar*. New Delhi: Manohar, 1992.
Samaddar, Ranabir. *A Biography of the Indian Nation, 1947–1997*. New Delhi: Sage, 2001.
Sarkar, Sumit. *Modern India, 1885–1947*. New Delhi: Macmillan, 1983, repr. 2001.
Satchidanandan, K. (ed.). *Words Matter: Writings against Silence*. Gurgaon: Penguin Viking, 2016.
Sen, Amartya. *Poverty and Famines: An Essay on Entitlement and Deprivation*. Oxford: Clarendon Press, 1981.
Shaw, Graham and Mary Lloyd (eds). *Publications Proscribed by the Government of India: A Catalogue of the Collections in the India Office Library and Records and the Department of Oriental Manuscripts and Printed Books*. British Library Reference Division. London: The British Library, 1985.
Sidhu, Gurdev Singh (ed.). *The Hanging of Bhagat Singh*, Vol. IV: *The Banned Literature*. Chandigarh: Unistar Books, 2007.
Singh, Anushka. *Sedition in Liberal Democracies*. New Delhi: Oxford University Press, 2018.

Singh, Ujjwal Kumar. *Political Prisoners in India*. New Delhi: Oxford University Press, 1998.

Sinha, Mrinalini. *Specters of Mother India: The Global Restructuring of an Empire*. Durham, NC: Duke University Press, 2006.

Sorabjee, Soli J. *Law of Press Censorship in India*. Bombay: N.M. Tripathi Pvt. Ltd., 1976.

———. *The Emergency, Censorship and the Press in India, 1975–77*. New Delhi: Central News Agency, 1977.

Southgate, D.H. *Root in the Rock: An Indian Saga, 1876–1936*. New York: A.A. Knopf, 1938.

Srimanjari. *Through War and Famine: Bengal 1939–45*. New Delhi: Orient BlackSwan, 2009.

St. John-Stevas, Norman. *Obscenity and the Law*. London: Secker and Warburg, 1956.

Sutherland, John. *Offensive Literature: Decensorship in Britain, 1960–82*. Totowa, New Jersey: Barnes and Noble Books, 1983.

Tanwar, Raghuvendra. *Reporting the Partition of Punjab: Press, Public and Other Opinions*. New Delhi: Manohar, 2006.

Thomas, Donald. *Freedom's Frontier: Censorship in Modern Britain*. London: John Murray, 2008 [2007].

Vajpeyi, Ashok (ed.). *India Dissents: 3,000 years of Difference, Doubt and Argument*. New Delhi: Speaking Tiger, 2017.

Vanaik, Achin. *The Furies of Indian Communalism: Religion, Modernity, and Secularization*. London: Verso, 1997.

Voigt, Johannes H. *India in the Second World War*. Michigan: Arnold Heinemann, 1988.

Warburton, Nigel. *Free Speech: A Very Short Introduction*. New York: Oxford University Press, 2009.

Williams, Francis. *Dangerous Estate: The Anatomy of Newspapers*. London: Longmans, Green and Co., 1957.

Wolseley, Ronald E. (ed.). *Journalism in Modern India*. Bombay and Calcutta, Asia Publishing House, 1953, repr. 1954.

Zinkin, Taya. *Reporting India*. London: Chatto and Windus, 1962.

Unpublished Dissertation

Chander, Sunil. 'The Congress Ministries and the British Authorities in the Working of Provincial Autonomy, 1936–39: Aspects of Conflict between the Congress and the Raj'. Unpublished M.Litt. dissertation submitted to Trinity College, Oxford, 1983 (copy in NMML, New Delhi).

Chapters in Edited Volumes

Barrier, N. Gerald. 'Punjab Politics and the Press, 1880–1910', in *Aspects of India: Essays in Honor of Edward Cameron Dimock, Jr.*, ed. Margaret Case and N. Gerald Barrier,

118–133. New Delhi: Manohar Publications for American Institute of Indian Studies, 1986.

Bayly, C.A. 'Colonial Rule and the 'Informational Order' in South Asia', in *The Transmission of Knowledge in South Asia*, ed. Nigel Crook, 280–315. New Delhi: Oxford University Press, 1996.

Bose, Sugata and Ayesha Jalal. 'Nationalism, Democracy and Development', in *Nationalism, Democracy and Development: State and Politics in India*, ed. Sugata Bose and Ayesha Jalal, 1–9. New Delhi: Oxford University Press, 1997.

Chander, Sunil. 'Congress, the Raj and Conflict in Provincial Autonomy, 1937–39', in *Oxford University Papers on India*, ed. N.J. Allen et al., vol. 1, part 2, 74–96. New Delhi: Oxford University Press, 1987.

Cole, Juan R.I. 'Colonialism and Censorship', in *The Man on the Spot: Essays on British Empire History*, ed. Roger D. Long, 45–62. Connecticut/London: Greenwood Press, 1995.

Das, Biswajit. 'Mediating Modernity: Colonial Discourse and Radio Broadcasting, c. 1924–1947', in *Communication Processes vol. 1: Media and Mediation*, ed. Bernard Bel et al, 229–255. New Delhi: Sage, 2005.

Eliot, Simon and Jonathan Rose. 'Introduction', in *A Companion to the History of the Book*, ed. Simon Eliot and Jonathan Rose, 1–6. London: Blackwell, 2007.

Ganti, Tejaswini. 'The Limits of Decency and the Decency of Limits: Censorship and the Bombay Film Industry', in *Censorship in South Asia: Cultural Regulation from Sedition to Seduction*, ed. Raminder Kaur and William Mazzarella, 87–122. Bloomington: Indiana University Press, 2009.

Gilmartin, David. 'Democracy, Nationalism and the Public: A Speculation on Colonial Muslim Politics', in *The Decolonization Reader*, ed. James D. Le Sueur, 191–203. New York: Routledge, 2003.

Grafton, Anthony. 'The Power of Ideas', in *A Concise Companion to History*, ed. Ulinka Rublack, 355–379. New York: Oxford University Press, 2011.

Grendler, Paul F. 'The Advent of Printing', in *Censorship: 500 Years of Conflict*, 24–33. New York: Oxford University Press, 1984.

Guha, Ranajit. 'Not at Home in Empire', in *Postcolonial Passages: Contemporary History Writing on India*, ed. Saurabh Dube, 38–46. New Delhi: Oxford University Press, 2004.

Heath, Deana. 'Purity, Obscenity and the Making of an Imperial Censorship System', in *Media and the British Empire*, ed. Chandrika Kaul, 160–173. Basingstoke: Palgrave Macmillan, 2006.

———. 'Obscenity, Censorship, and Modernity', in *A Companion to the History of the Book*, ed. Simon Eliot and Jonathan Rose, 508–519. London: Blackwell, 2007.

Joseph, Pothan. 'An Apology for My Life', in *Pothan Joseph—Idylls Past and Present: An Editor's Wet Copy*, selected by Jaiboy Joseph, 3–10. New Delhi: Orient Longman, 1979.

Kaul, Chandrika. 'India, the Imperial Press Conferences and the Empire Press Union: The Diplomacy of News in the Politics of Empire, 1909–1946', in *Media and the*

British Empire, ed. Chandrika Kaul, 125–144. Basingstoke: Palgrave Macmillan, 2006.

Khare, Harish. 'Political Reporting', in *The Indian Media: Illusion, Delusion and Reality, Essays in Honour of Prem Bhatia*, ed. Asha Rani Mathur, 37–48. New Delhi: Rupa, 2006.

Liang, Lawrence. 'Free Speech and Expression', in *The Oxford Handbook of the Indian Constitution*, ed. Sujit Choudhury, Madhav Khosla and Pratap Bhanu Mehta, 814–833. New Delhi: Oxford University Press, 2016.

Malhotra, Inder. 'A Superior Person, Thorough Professional', in *The Indian Media: Illusion, Delusion and Reality, Essays in Honour of Prem Bhatia*, ed. Asha Rani Mathur, 1–12. New Delhi: Rupa, 2006.

Malik, Kenan. 'Interview with Kenan Malik', in *The Content and Context of Hate Speech*, ed. Michael Herz and Peter Molnar, 81–91 (Cambridge: Cambridge University Press, 2012).

Masselos, Jim. 'Bombay, August 1942: Re-readings in a Nationalist Text', in *Turbulent Times: India, 1940–44*, ed. Biswamoy Pati, 67–107. Mumbai: Popular Prakashan, 1998.

Mazzarella, William. 'Making Sense of Cinema in Late Colonial India', in *Censorship in South Asia: Cultural Regulation from Sedition to Seduction*, ed. Raminder Kaur and William Mazzarella, 63–86. Bloomington: Indiana University Press, 2009.

Mehta, Deepak. 'Words That Wound: Archiving Hate in the Making of Hindu-Indian and Muslim-Pakistani Publics in Bombay', in *Beyond Crisis: Re-evaluating Pakistan*, ed. Naveeda Khan, 315–343. New Delhi: Routledge, 2010.

Moraes, Frank. 'India's Free Press', in *Era of Rapid Change: 1947–67*, 28–30. New Delhi: Publications Division Ministry of Information and Broadcasting, 1968.

Muller, Beate. 'Censorship and Cultural Regulation: Mapping the Territory', in *Censorship and Cultural Regulation in the Modern Age*, ed. Beate Muller, 1–31. Amsterdam: Rodopi, 2004.

Niazi, Zamir. 'What the Press Has Endured', in *Fettered Freedom*, ed. Syed Jaffar Ahmad, 35–44. Karachi: Pakistan Study Centre, University of Karachi, 2005.

Noorani, A.G. 'Freedom of the Press and the Constitution', in *Freedom of the Press in India*, ed. A.G. Noorani, 24–35. Bombay: Nachiketa Publications, 1971.

Parekh, Bhikhu. 'Is There a Case for Banning Hate Speech?' in *The Content and Context of Hate Speech: Rethinking Regulation and Responses*, ed. Michael Herz and Peter Molnar, 37–56 (Cambridge: Cambridge University Press, 2012).

Pinney, Christopher. 'Iatrogenic Religion and Politics', in *Censorship in South Asia: Cultural Regulation from Sedition to Seduction*, ed. Raminder Kaur and William Mazzarella, 29–62. Bloomington: Indiana University Press, 2009.

Prasad, M. Madhava. 'The Natives Are Looking: Cinema and Censorship in Colonial India', in *Narratives of Indian Cinema*, ed. Manju Jain, 3–18. Delhi: Primus Books, 2009.

Sarkar, Chanchal. 'The Indian Press since Independence', in *India Since 1947*, ed. Atulananda Chakrabarti. Bombay: Allied Publishers, 1967.

Schlesinger Jr., Arthur M. 'Preface', in *Censorship: 500 Years of Conflict*. New York: Oxford University Press, 1984.

Sivaraman, A.N. 'The Vernacular Language Newspapers', in *Journalism in Modern India*, ed. Roland E. Wolseley, 16–34. Bombay and Calcutta, Asia Publishing House, 1953, repr. 1954.

Sorabjee, Soli J. 'Intolerance, Censorship and Freedom of the Press', in *The Indian Media: Illusion, Delusion and Reality, Essays in Honour of Prem Bhatia*, ed. Asha Rani Mathur, 49–58. New Delhi: Rupa, 2006.

Strauss, David A. 'Freedom of Speech and the Common-Law Constitution', in *Eternally Vigilant: Free Speech in the Modern Era*, ed. Lee C. Bollinger and Geoffrey R. Stone, 33–59. Chicago: University of Chicago Press, 2002.

Tisnado, Carmen. 'Performing the Unspeakable: Defeating Censorship in Two Stories by Mario Benedetti', in *Censorship and Cultural Regulation in the Modern Age*, ed. Beate Muller, 169–187. Amsterdam: Rodopi, 2004.

Varshney, Ashutosh. 'The Idea of Pakistan', in *The Great Divide: India and Pakistan*, ed. Ira Pande, 2–21. New Delhi: India International Centre/HarperCollins, 2009.

Washbrook, David. 'The Rhetoric of Democracy and Development in Late Colonial India' in *Nationalism, Democracy and Development: State and Politics in India*, ed. Sugata Bose and Ayesha Jalal, 36–49. New Delhi: Oxford University Press, 1997.

Zachariah, Benjamin. 'The Creativity of Destruction: Wartime Imaginings of Development and Social Policy, c. 1942–46' in *The World in World Wars: Experience, Perceptions and Perspectives from Africa and Asia*, ed. Heike Liebau, Katrin Bromber, Katharina Lange, Dyala Hamzah and Ravi Ahuja, 547–578. Leiden: Brill, 2010.

Articles in Journals/Online Sources

Burra, Arudra. 'The Cobwebs of Imperial Rule'. *Seminar* 615 (2010): 79–83.

―――. 'What Self-Styled Nationalists Could Learn from the Hindu Right's Own Past Record on Free Speech'. Scroll.in, 27 January 2016, available at https://scroll.in/article/802327/what-self-styled-nationalists-could-learn-from-the-hindu-rights-own-past-record-on-free-speech (accessed 19 January 2019).

―――. 'Freedom of Speech and Constitutional Nostalgia'. *Seminar* 697 (2017): 50–55.

Darnton, Robert. 'The High Enlightenment and the Low-Life of Literature in Pre-Revolutionary France'. *Past & Present* 51 (May 1971): 81–115.

―――. 'Literary Surveillance in the British Raj: The Contradictions of Liberal Imperialism'. *Book History* 4 (2001): 133–176.

―――. 'Book Production in British India, 1850–1900'. *Book History* 5 (2002): 239–262.

Dutt, Clemens. 'The Outsider's India'. *Labour Monthly* 11, no. 5 (May 1929): 313–316. Available at Marxists Internet Archive, https://www.marxists.org/archive/dutt-clemens/1929/05/x01.htm (accessed 19 January 2019).

Elkin, Frederick. 'Censorship and Pressure Groups'. *Phylon* 21, no. 1 (1960): 71–80.

Ghosh, Tushar Kanti. 'A Tribute to Discipline' (part of 'India: Two Viewpoints'). *Index on Censorship* 5, no. 21 (1976): 21–22.

Greenhough, Paul R. 'Political Mobilization and the Underground Literature of the Quit India movement, 1942–44'. *Modern Asian Studies* 17, no. 3 (1983): 353–386.

Guha, Ramachandra. 'The Independent Journal of Opinion'. Seminar 481 (September 1999). Available at https://www.india-seminar.com/1999/481/481%20guha.htm (accessed 19 January 2019).

———. 'Silent Archivists: Historians and Newspapers'. *The Telegraph*, 28 December 2013. Available at https://www.telegraphindia.com/opinion/silent-archivists-historians-and-newspapers/cid/235603 (accessed 19 January 2019).

Gupta, Charu. '"Dirty" Hindi Literature: Contests about Obscenity in Late Colonial North India'. *South Asia Research* 20, no. 89 (2000): 89–118.

Hopkin, Deian. 'Domestic Censorship in the First World War'. *Journal of Contemporary History* 5, no. 4 (1970): 151–169.

Jeffrey, Robin. 'Monitoring Newspapers and Understanding the Indian State'. *Asian Survey* 34, no. 8 (August 1994): 748–763.

———. 'Advertising and Indian-Language Newspapers: How Capitalism Supports (Certain) Cultures and (Some) States, 1947–96'. *Pacific Affairs* 70, no. 1 (Spring 1997): 57–84.

Kamra, Sukeshi. 'The "Vox Populi," or the Infernal Propaganda Machine, and Juridical Force in Colonial India. *Cultural Critique*, 72 (Spring 2009): 164–202.

Kamtekar, Indivar. 'The Shiver of 1942'. *Studies in History* 18, no. 1 (February 2002): 81–102.

———. 'A Different War Dance: State and Class in India 1939–1945'. *Past and Present* 176, no. 1 (August 2002): 187–221.

Leary, William M. Jr. 'Books, Soldiers and Censorship during the Second World War'. *American Quarterly* 20, no. 2, part I (Summer 1968): 237–245.

Liang, Lawrence. 'Reasonable Restrictions and Unreasonable Speech'. *Sarai Reader 04: Crisis Media*, 434–440. New Delhi: Sarai/CSDS, 2004.

Mahmud, Shabana. 'Angarey and the Founding of the Progressive Writers' Association', *Modern Asian Studies* 30, no. 2 (1996): 447–467.

Menon, Nivedita. 'Citizenship and the Passive Revolution: Interpreting the First Amendment'. *Economic and Political Weekly* 39, no. 18 (May 2004): 1812–1819.

Nair, Neeti. 'Beyond the "Communal" 1920s: The Problem of Intention, Legislative Pragmatism, and the Making of Section 295A of the Indian Penal Code'. *The Indian Economic and Social History Review* 50, no. 3 (2013): 317–340.

Nandy, Ashis. 'Manufacturing Consent: How Thought Police States Are Created'. *Times of India*, 15 January 2005. Available at https://timesofindia.indiatimes.com/edit-page/THE-LEADER-ARTICLE-Manufacturing-Consent-How-Thought-Police-States-Are-Created/articleshow/990705.cms (accessed 19 January 2019).

Nauria, Anil. 'Some Did Not Seek Clemency: Pandit Parmanand of Jhansi', *Indian Express*, 1 March 2001. Available at https://www.scribd.com/doc/93896220/Pandit-Parmanand-of-Jhansi (accessed 19 January 2019).

Pandey, Gyanendra. 'Mobilization in a Mass Movement: Congress "Propaganda" in the United Provinces (India), 1930—34'. *Modern Asian Studies* 9, no. 2 (1975): 205–226.

Post, Robert C. 'Censorship and Silencing'. *Bulletin of the American Academy of Arts and Sciences* 51, no. 5 (May–June 1998): 32–35.

Rossuck, Jennifer. 'Banned Books: A Study of Censorship'. *The English Journal* 86, no. 2 (February 1997): 67–70.

Roy, Kaushik. 'Discipline and Morale of the African, British, and Indian Army Units in Burma and India during World War II: July 1943 to August 1945'. *Modern Asian Studies* 44, no. 6 (2010): 1255–1282.

Saunders, A.J. 'The Indian Central Banking Enquiry Committee, 1931'. *The Economic Journal* 42, no. 165 (March 1932): 32–41.

Wolseley, Ronald E. 'The Press of India: An Overview'. *International Communication Gazette* 12, no. 4 (1966): 243–258.

Name Index

General Index